France in the
Second World War

France in the Second World War

Collaboration, Resistance, Holocaust, Empire

Chris Millington

BLOOMSBURY ACADEMIC
LONDON • NEW YORK • OXFORD • NEW DELHI • SYDNEY

BLOOMSBURY ACADEMIC
Bloomsbury Publishing Plc
50 Bedford Square, London, WC1B 3DP, UK
1385 Broadway, New York, NY 10018, USA
29 Earlsfort Terrace, Dublin 2, Ireland

BLOOMSBURY, BLOOMSBURY ACADEMIC and the Diana logo are
trademarks of Bloomsbury Publishing Plc

First published in Great Britain 2020
Reprinted 2020, 2021

Copyright © Chris Millington, 2020

Chris Millington has asserted his right under the Copyright, Designs and
Patents Act, 1988, to be identified as Author of this work.

Cover design: Tjaša Krivec
Cover image: Mass of the peace in Chaillot palace gardens in Paris in 1945
in homage to former prisoners and victims of war with a former prisoner
interned in a concentration camp. (© Tallandier / Bridgeman Images)

All rights reserved. No part of this publication may be reproduced or transmitted
in any form or by any means, electronic or mechanical, including photocopying,
recording, or any information storage or retrieval system, without prior
permission in writing from the publishers.

Bloomsbury Publishing Plc does not have any control over, or responsibility for,
any third-party websites referred to or in this book. All internet addresses given in this
book were correct at the time of going to press. The author and publisher regret
any inconvenience caused if addresses have changed or sites have ceased to
exist, but can accept no responsibility for any such changes.

A catalogue record for this book is available from the British Library.

Library of Congress Cataloging-in-Publication Data
Names: Millington, Chris, author.
Title: France in the Second World War : Collaboration, Resistance, Holocaust,
Empire / Chris Millington.
Other titles: Collaboration, resistance, Holocaust, empire
Description: London ; New York : Bloomsbury Academic, 2020. |
Includes bibliographical references and index. |
Identifiers: LCCN 2019045175 | ISBN 9781350094963 (hardback) |
ISBN 9781350094970 (paperback) | ISBN 9781350094987 (epdf) |
ISBN 9781350094994 (epub)
Subjects: LCSH: France–History–German occupation, 1940–1945. |
World War, 1939-1945–France. | War and society–France–History–20th century. |
Holocaust, Jewish (1939-1945)–France.
Classification: LCC DC397 .M54 2020 | DDC 940.53/44--dc23
LC record available at https://lccn.loc.gov/2019045175

ISBN: HB: 978-1-3500-9496-3
PB: 978-1-3500-9497-0
ePDF: 978-1-3500-9498-7
eBook: 978-1-3500-9499-4

Typeset by Integra Software Services Pvt. Ltd.

To find out more about our authors and books visit www.bloomsbury.com
and sign up for our newsletters.

For Madeleine

CONTENTS

List of illustrations ix
Preface xi
Abbreviations xiv

1 The defeat 1
   The Battle of France 2
   The causes of the defeat 6
   A global struggle 15
   The civilian experience 20
   Conclusion 23

2 Vichy 25
   Redrawing the map of France 26
   Vichy's governments 31
   The National Revolution 37
   Remaking citizens and subjects 40
   Tracas, Famine, Patrouille: Everyday survival 46
   Conclusion 52

3 Collaboration 55
   Types of collaboration 57
   Working for Germany 60
   Sex with the Occupier 63
   Collaborationism 66
   Fighting for Hitler 71
   Conclusion 73

4 Resistance 75
   De Gaulle and the Free French 77
   The global Free French 83
   Defining resistance 87
   Movements and networks 90

The resisters 93
1943: Uniting the resistance 96
Conclusion 100

5 Persecution 103

Law and order 104
Gypsies, homosexuals and blacks 111
Vichy's anti-Semitism: Aims and origins 114
1940–1942: Exclusion 116
Anti-Semitism overseas 121
1942–1944: France and the Final Solution 122
Survival 126
Conclusion 129

6 Liberation 131

Liberations 133
Experiencing Liberation 137
The purge of collaborators 143
The local purge 144
The national purge 148
Conclusion 151

7 History and memory 153

Mythologizing the resistance: 1944–1969 155
Inconvenient truths: 1971–1995 161
Diversification and revisionism: 2000 to present 167
Conclusion 173

8 Conclusion 175

Collaboration or resistance? The eternal question 177
Persecution: Vichy's raison d'être 179
A pluralist historiography 180

Glossary 183
Notes 192
Annotated Bibliography 228
Index 240

ILLUSTRATIONS

Figures

1 The Nazi leadership at Rethondes, 22 June 1940 5
2 French soldiers in the underground tunnels of the Maginot Line 9
3 Soldiers from Indochina take part in a ceremony to mark the gift of twenty ambulances to France in January 1940 16
4 Review of Japanese troops in Indochina, 1940 19
5 French refugees take to the road in summer 1940 21
6 German troops in Marseille 27
7 The cabinet at Vichy c. 1942. Marshal Pétain sits opposite Pierre Laval 33
8 Youths of the Chantiers de la Jeunesse marching in Saint-Bonnet-Tronçais in 1941 44
9 Women queue outside a dairy shop in Paris in June 1940 48
10 Mother and children with a portrait of Pétain 50
11 The inauguration of an anti-Bolshevik exhibition at the Salle Wagram in Paris, c. March 1942 64
12 A PPF rally at the Vélodrome d'Hiver in Paris, in August 1943 70
13 Collaborationist Philippe Henriot sees off a contingent of LVF volunteers in June 1944 72
14 De Gaulle in Carthage, Tunisia, 1943 78
15 De Gaulle in Great Britain, 1941 80
16 A Free French infantryman from Chad 83
17 French 'Maquis' Guerillas in the mountains 99

18	Children held prisoner at the Rivesaltes camp, May 1941 110
19	Notice in a restaurant window banning Jews from entering, 1940 118
20	Opening of the Institute of Jewish Questions, May 1941 119
21	Jewish prisoners at the Drancy camp c. 1942 124
22	Residents of Dunkirk evacuate the town in September 1944 to escape the fighting 139
23	Execution for collaboration, Grenoble 146
24	A group of femmes tondues, one carrying her baby, in Chartres, 25 August 1944 147
25	Jean Moulin's remains in the Panthéon, 1964 160

Map

1	The geography of France, 1940–1944 xvi

Tables

1	Allied and German military forces in the campaign of 1940 7
2	Colonial forces and the French war effort 18

PREFACE

On 9 May 1940, Adolf Hitler boasted to the leaders of the German army: 'Gentlemen, you are about to witness the most famous victory in history.' The Nazi invasion of Western Europe had begun. Belgium, Luxembourg and the Netherlands fell quickly. Hitler's armies needed just six weeks to conquer France. The German invasion through the difficult terrain of the Ardennes region took Allied military leaders by surprise. Unable to adapt to the unexpected situation and with no plan B, the Western powers were routed within days. As the defeated British fled back across the Channel, the French Prime Minister, First World War hero Marshal Philippe Pétain, requested an Armistice; thus began the 'Dark Years' of the Occupation.

Hitler inflicted a humiliating peace upon France. A punitive financial settlement saw the French saddled with the costs of their own occupation. The army was reduced to a rump and the navy confined to port. Over a million prisoners of war resided in German camps as hostages. France itself was dismembered and carved into a number of zones, the largest of which were the Occupied Northern Zone and the Southern Free Zone. An internal border – the Demarcation Line – separated the North from the South. In the northeast of France, the Third Reich annexed and rapidly Germanized the region of Alsace and the department of the Moselle. In the southeast, 800 square kilometres of territory fell under Italian control. Rome seized and Italianized the town of Menton where shops now displayed the sign, 'Here we speak Italian and give the fascist salute.'

A despairing French nation turned to Pétain for comfort. Few people protested when, in July 1940, the Marshal liquidated the Third Republic, the regime that had governed France since 1870. Many French blamed the democratic Republic for the catastrophe of the defeat. Pétain subsequently founded the Etat Français (French State), otherwise known as the Vichy regime (after the southern spa town where it was based). Vichy promised to revive the country through a root-and-branch reform of political, social, economic and cultural life – the 'National Revolution' – and the vigorous persecution of France's alleged enemies, namely Jews, communists and Freemasons. At the same time, Pétain sought to win a place in Hitler's New Order through the policy of collaboration. In the space of barely two months in 1940, France had swapped democracy for authoritarianism.

The French Empire largely remained under Vichy's control, a fact that ensured that the National Revolution was a global experiment. Pétain's laws applied as much to the 25 million people in Indochina and the 16 million people in French West Africa as they did to the tiniest hamlet in rural France. Still, experiences necessarily diverged and differed. Colonial governors and their subordinates adapted directives from the mainland to local contexts while preserving their broadly exclusionary and repressive nature. Meanwhile, for many subjects of the Empire, the war was not marked by foreign invasion and occupation; in imperial territories, the *French* were the invaders and occupiers. Consequently, in the colonial memory of the war the terms to describe the period differ. For the Caribbean peoples of Guadeloupe, for example, it means little to call the Second World War the 'Dark Years' or the 'Occupation'; the period is remembered instead as 'Life in the Time of Sorin' (*la vie an tan Sorin*), named after the brutally repressive wartime governor of the island Constant Sorin.

For the French who refused to accept Pétain's leadership, General Charles de Gaulle urged resistance. De Gaulle and his France Libre (Free France) movement waged a propaganda and military campaign against the Vichy regime from London and Brazzaville (in the French Congo). The General's campaign to liberate France and its territories was of global dimensions: in 1940, colonial peoples joined the nascent Free French and de Gaulle's early power base was not located in the UK but in French Equatorial Africa. A plethora of resistance movements and networks, large and small, operated in French territory. These groups worked to turn public opinion against Vichy and obstruct the Occupier. Only during 1942 did de Gaulle make contact with resisters within France itself. The unification of the Free French and the internal resistance during 1942–1943 allowed the French to make an important contribution to the liberation of their country in summer 1944.

The painful experience of the war years has marked the decades since 1944, evoked in novels and films, history books (it is perhaps the most intensively studied period in French history) and educational curricula, commemorations and monuments. By the end of the 1980s, according to Henry Rousso, France's preoccupation with its Vichy past had become pathological; the so-called 'Vichy Syndrome' ensured that this was a 'past that does not pass'.[1] The memory of the Occupation has proved a site of contest between groups who have vied to imprint their own interpretations of the period upon the collective memory of the nation. Narratives have changed to suit the political preoccupations of the time and the past is never far away. As Pierre Laborie wrote in 2014, 'Incessant [and] at certain times oppressive [enough] to render France sick from its history, reminiscences of the troubles, of the moments of shame, and of the heartbreak of [those] dark days continue to weigh on the present.'[2]

This book is an introduction to the Dark Years. I do not pretend that it offers an exhaustive history of the subject; it is a *survey* rather than an *encyclopaedia*. The literature on France and its Empire during 1940–1944 is huge. It is the goal of *France in the Second Wold War* to pay suitable heed to this vast historiography while presenting it in a succinct and logical form. Aimed at an Anglophone audience, it comprises the aspects of the war and Occupation most important to an understanding of the subject while accounting for the French experience in all its diversity. To distil the topic of each chapter into a clear and manageable essay was tricky. I wrote each chapter with my students in mind and I therefore offer the reader a comprehensive and readable study aid suitable for university classes of all levels.

I dedicate this book to Madeleine who, despite her young age, is already aware of her dad's intermittent disappearances to a place called France. I hope that she will develop the love and appreciation of foreign cultures, histories, attitudes and languages that are so lacking in today's world.

ABBREVIATIONS

2DB	Deuxième Division Blindée
AFAT	Arme Féminine de l'Armée de Terre
BCRA	Bureau Central de Renseignement et d'Action
BEF	British Expeditionary Force
CDL	Comités Départementaux de Libération
CDLL	Ceux de la Libération
CDLR	Ceux de la Résistance
CFLN	Comité Français de Libération Nationale
CGQJ	Commissariat Général aux Questions Juives
CNR	Conseil National de la Résistance
CVF	Corps des Volontaires Françaises
FAFL	Forces Aériennes Françaises Libres
FFI	Forces Françaises de l'Intérieur
FFL	Forces Françaises Libres
FLN	Front de la Libértaion Nationale
FN	Front National
FTP	Francs-Tireurs et Partisans
GTE	Groupements de Travailleurs Étrangers
LVF	Légion des Volontaires Français contre le Bolchevisme
MbF	Militärbefehlshaber in Frankreich
MSR	Mouvement Social Révolutionnaire
MUR	Mouvements Unis de la Résistance
OCM	Organisation Civile et militaire
OVRA	Organizzazione per la Vigilanza e la Repressione dell'Antifascismo

POW   Prisoner of War
PPF   Parti Populaire Français
PSF   Parti Social Français
RNP   Rassemblement National Populaire
RPF   Rassemblement du Peuple Français
SOE   Special Operations Executive
SOL   Service d'Ordre Légionnaire
SD   Sicherheitsdienst
SS   Schutzstaffel
UGIF   Union Générale des Israélites Français

Map 1 *The geography of France, 1940–1944*

1

The defeat

Nazi Germany invaded France on 10 May 1940. On 25 June, with the French army and the British Expeditionary Force (BEF) routed, Paris and Berlin declared a ceasefire. The fighting had lasted six weeks yet, in truth, the battle was lost in a matter of days. Hitler and his army commanders had fooled the Allies into believing that the main thrust of the German advance would come from the north through Belgium. In fact, the Nazi spearhead struck further south in the relatively poorly defended Ardennes region. Britain and France realized their error too late. By 15 May, with German forces having broken through French lines, Prime Minister Paul Reynaud informed his British counterpart Winston Churchill: 'we are beaten; we have lost the battle'.[1] The Wehrmacht soon encircled Allied forces. The evacuation from Dunkirk averted catastrophe for the British but the French were not so fortunate. On 17 June, Marshal Philippe Pétain, successor to Reynaud as Prime Minister, announced that he would seek an end to hostilities with Germany. On 25 June, fighting ended. French writer Jean Guéhenno recorded the moment in his diary: 'The bells for the "Ceasefire" rang at midnight. I had not realized that I loved my country so much. I am full of pain, anger, and shame'.[2] France was beaten.

The rapidity of the Allied collapse stunned the world. Historian Nicole Jordan has described the defeat as 'one of the great military catastrophes in world history'.[3] In Washington, President Franklin Roosevelt endured sleepless nights as he pondered the seemingly inevitable invasion of Britain. In Moscow, Stalin raged at the French capitulation, sensing Hitler's gaze now upon the Soviet Union. Marc Bloch, a French medieval historian who had fought in the battle of 1940, turned his fire on society, attributing the disaster to a long-term rot present from top to bottom.[4] American journalist William Shirer likewise perceived deep causes to the so-called 'débâcle' (rout). The French had had, 'no will to fight, even when their soil was invaded'. The defeat amounted to no less than 'a complete collapse of French society and of the French soul'.[5]

Until the late 1970s, historians of the defeat tended to take their lead from such contemporaneous accounts. Jean-Baptiste Duroselle's hugely influential 1979 book on interwar French foreign relations – damningly entitled *La décadence* (in English, decline) – blamed a political class unable to mount an effective response to foreign threats.[6] The French public seemed to agree. An opinion poll in *Le Figaro Magazine* in 1980 found that more than half of respondents blamed the Third Republic for the catastrophe.[7] A second school of thought has since contested this view, preferring to focus on the immediate military factors behind the defeat rather than looking for long-term causes in French society. In his 2003 *The Fall of France*, by far the best text on the subject, Julian Jackson concluded that '[t]he defeat of France was first and foremost a military defeat – so rapid and so total that ... [long-term] factors did not have time to come into play'.[8] France lost the fight on the battlefield not in the bitter divisions of the interwar years.

This chapter investigates the defeat of France in 1940. Firstly, it examines the causes of the French collapse and debunks some of the myths regarding the country's preparedness for war. It recognizes, too, that the catastrophe of 1940 was an *Allied* defeat. While the bulk of forces engaged in the battle were French, the BEF and the RAF also fought to hold back the invader. The Allied Supreme War Council co-ordinated French and British economic and military planning for the conflict with Germany. London *and* Paris approved the strategy that would eventually undo the Allies' campaign. Secondly, the chapter explores the repercussions of the war in Europe in the territories of the French Empire. Between 1939 and the Armistice of June 1940, over 600,000 troops were recruited from French African and Asian territories.[9] The deaths of thousands of these troops and the imprisonment of many more had an impact on communities around the world. Finally, the plight of men and women far from the battlefield comes under consideration. Eight million civilians from northeast France and the Low Countries fled their home to escape the advancing German army. Life on the road during the 'Exode' (Exodus) was tough: food and water were scarce, families experienced separation, and the threat of attack from German planes was constant. The Battle of France was not only a military and political disaster but also a human one.

The Battle of France

The German invasion of Western Europe began on 9 May 1940 with attacks on Belgium, Luxembourg and the Netherlands. Supreme Allied commander General Maurice Gamelin – under whose authority lay the French military and the BEF – immediately implemented 'Plan D' to defend French territory. This so-called 'Dyle manoeuvre' entailed an eastward push into northern Belgium by the very best French and British forces. These crack troops would obstruct the German advance at the rivers Dyle and Escaut in Belgium. The

Allies planned to fight the conflict with Germany on Belgian soil, sparing France the destruction that it had experienced during the First World War.

With Allied minds concentrated on obstructing the invasion in Belgium, German eyes turned to the Ardennes, a region spread across Luxembourg, southern Belgium and northeast France. Allied commanders believed that this hilly and forested terrain presented a natural barrier to the invader. They dismissed reports of columns of German vehicles moving in this direction as alarmist.[10] In any case, the Allies estimated that it would take ten days for an army to break through the Ardennes; in fact, it took German soldiers only sixty hours.[11] The German move into northern Belgium was a feint, a 'matador's cloak'. Further south, four columns of tanks and motorized vehicles, each stretching back over 400 kilometres, advanced towards the river Meuse. With the element of surprise paramount, the Wehrmacht progressed for three days and nights without a break, their drivers dosed with the amphetamine Pervitin.[12]

The German army encountered little resistance before reaching the strategically important Meuse river. This was the weak point of French defences. The vanguard of the invasion, General Ewald von Kleist's group, comprised 134,000 troops, 1,200 tanks and 1,000 aircraft. In total, forty-five German divisions faced nine-and-a-half French, made up mainly of reservists in poor shape with inadequate equipment.[13] Strength of numbers and the massive aerial bombardment of French positions ensured that German troops were able to cross the river at Sedan, Houx and Monthermé. Only on the night of 13 May, with the Germans having crossed the Meuse, did the Allies realize that the real invasion was underway in the south.

The dispersal of French forces and the unpreparedness for an attack on the Ardennes saw the disintegration of Allied defences. During the night of 16 May, Panzer Commander Erwin Rommel's division managed to advance more than 100 kilometres into French territory. The following day, Gamelin's order to his soldiers – 'CONQUER OR DIE. WE MUST CONQUER' – came too late; Reynaud replaced him with General Maxime Weygand on 18 May.[14] Three days later, German forces reached Abbéville on the shores of the English Channel. Nearly 2 million French, British, Dutch and Belgian soldiers were caught in 'the largest encirclement in military history'.[15] Allied strategists considered a joint attack to cut the head off the German advance and break out of their encirclement (the so-called 'Weygand Plan'). However, by 25 May French and British leaders ordered a retreat to the coastal town of Dunkirk. The next day, Operation Dynamo was launched to evacuate Allied forces from the continent.

When on 3 June German bombs fell on Paris, the government of the Third Republic decided to move from the capital. A week later, the City of Light was declared 'open'; it would not be defended street-by-street as Churchill had urged. Prime Minister Reynaud, his cabinet, and President Albert Lebrun travelled south to the chateaus of the Loire valley. At a meeting on 12 June, with the Germans in Paris and France at war with

Italy since 10 June, Weygand proposed an armistice. On 13 June, Pétain threw his weight behind Weygand's proposal: 'The armistice is in my eyes the necessary condition of the durability of eternal France'.[16] Reynaud hesitated, considering the possibility of continuing the fight in exile from North Africa. A further meeting on 15 June, this time in Bordeaux, saw the armistice faction strengthened. Roosevelt had telegrammed his sympathy for the French predicament but Washington had offered no practical support. British pleas that the French continue the fight were ignored. On 16 June, with his options dwindling in the face of strengthening defeatist sentiment amongst his ministers, Reynaud resigned. Pétain took over as premier. The next day, the eighty-four-year-old Marshal spoke on the radio: 'It is with heavy heart that I say to you today that it is necessary to cease fighting'.[17]

In order to understand why the French cabinet ultimately swung behind an Armistice, leaving Reynaud with few other options but to resign, we must examine reshuffles that took place during May and June 1940. Between 17 and 19 May, Reynaud brought Weygand and Pétain into the cabinet, along with the Republican Georges Mandel. Reynaud intended to appoint Weygand head of the armed forces yet in doing so he had brought into government a reactionary man who was certainly no lover of democracy. Pétain's politics were less clear yet by 26 May the Marshal was already looking to shift the blame for the disastrous situation away from the army, telling an acquaintance, 'The real guilty party is premier Daladier'.[18] On 5 June, Reynaud dismissed Edouard Daladier from the foreign ministry in a move that was likely designed to eliminate a personal rival but in fact removed a man in favour of continuing the war effort, too. At the same time, Reynaud appointed Paul Baudoin, Yves Bouthillier and Jean Prouvost to cabinet positions on the advice of his mistress Hélène de Portes. Baudoin and Bouthillier were close to the extreme right while all three men, like de Portes, were defeatists. The deterioration of the situation on the battlefield continued to strengthen the pro-armistice faction, turning their minds not just to the negotiation of a ceasefire but also to a change of regime; 'This country needs an overhaul top to bottom', argued Pétain. Reynaud's isolation in government grew. When, on 16 June, the Marshal threatened to resign if the government did not immediately seek peace terms with Berlin, the Prime Minister threw in the towel.[19]

Armistice negotiations began on 21 June at Rethondes, in the forest of Compiègne. This location was highly symbolic: it was the exact spot where Germany had agreed to the Armistice in 1918. Hitler's dark sense of theatricality did not end there. The Fuhrer had ordered that the French sign the surrender in the very same railway carriage as the German capitulation twenty-two years ago. Filmed for posterity, it is today difficult to view the humiliated French delegation arrive to be greeted by the Nazi leadership. Shirer noted that Hitler's face was one of 'revengeful, triumphant hate'. The French representatives – General Huntziger, Air General Bergeret, Vice-Admiral Le Luc and M. Noël, French Ambassador to Poland – were 'the picture of tragic dignity'.[20]

Figure 1 *The Nazi leadership, including Hitler, Goering, Joachim Von Ribbentropp and Marshal Keitel at Rethondes, 22 June 1940. Photo by Keystone-France/Gamma-Keystone via Getty Images.*

The Armistice provided for the occupation of three-fifths of France by German troops, the delivery of all military material to the Wehrmacht, and the confinement to port of the navy.[21] It imposed a crushing financial penalty on the defeated French, who would be forced to pay the costs of their own occupation. Other significant articles included the obligation that all German nationals in France surrender to the authorities. Many of these people had fled to France to escape persecution during the 1930s. Article Twenty required that all French prisoners of war (POWs) remain captive in Germany until the conclusion of a formal peace treaty. These POWs were used as a bargaining chip throughout the Occupation. Italy agreed a separate armistice with France on 24 June. Mussolini was gifted an occupation zone of 800,000 square kilometres in the southeast.[22] At 12.35 am on the morning of 25 June 1940, hostilities on the Western Front ceased. The Armistice came into effect ninety minutes later. The Battle of France had lasted for forty-four days. In Germany, Hitler ordered church bells to ring for a week. France declared a national day of mourning.

The causes of the defeat

In the immediate aftermath of the defeat, Pétain laid the blame squarely with the democratic regime of the interwar years. The Third Republic had produced too few children, manufactured too few weapons and made too few allies. This was by no means a disinterested analysis: Pétain's concern was to shift blame away from the army and onto Republican politicians. Indeed, following the signing of the Armistice, Weygand remarked, 'Military honour is safe'.[23] Vichy accused the governments of its predecessor, especially those of the left-wing Popular Front coalition (1936–1938), of failing to rearm sufficiently. The regime organized the prosecution of several senior figures in the French political establishment at a trial in Riom in February 1942. Former Prime Ministers Léon Blum and Edouard Daladier, as well as General Gamelin, figured amongst the indicted.[24]

The best-known contemporary analysis of the causes of the defeat – Bloch's 1946 *L'Etrange défaite* (first published as *Strange Defeat* in English in 1968) – lent further credibility to the so-called 'decadence' thesis. Bloch, a historian and co-founder of the Annales school of historiography, authored the manuscript between July and September 1940. *L'Etrange défaite* examined the factors behind the catastrophe, as Bloch understood them. He posited the general crisis in French society during the 1930s as the main explanation for the French collapse. Few sections of society were spared his ire. Bloch blamed the working class for hindering the rearmament effort with industrial action: '[they] thought first and foremost about selling their labour at the highest price'.[25] He claimed that pacifists had underestimated the threat from Hitler while spreading defeatism throughout the nation: '[they] worked unconsciously to produce a race of cowards'.[26] He berated the army high command for having seized upon the defeat to save itself: '[they] were ready to find consolation in the thought that beneath the ruins of France a shameful regime might be crushed to death'.[27] As for the democratic Republic, with its 'monstrously swollen assemblies' and its 'mob' parliament, the regime had not been able to prepare an effective defence.[28] *L'Etrange Défaite* gives an indication of the feelings of many French in the aftermath of the defeat and one senses Bloch's white-hot anger and grief on every page.

It was true that rearmament had not proceeded smoothly. The widespread strikes that accompanied the victory of the Popular Front in June 1936 slowed industrial output and tank production actually fell in 1937. Military dithering over the design of new weapons meant that serious production only began in January 1939. However, Blum's first Popular Front government in 1936 had allocated 14 billion Francs for weapons production. His government commandeered the tank assembly workshops at Renault and set ambitious production targets. Following the German annexation of Austria in March 1938, Daladier injected 12 billion

TABLE 1 *Allied and German military forces in the campaign of 1940*

	France	Great Britain	The Netherlands	Belgium	Allied total	Germany
Size of land army	2,240,000	500,000	400,000	650,000	3,790,000	3,000,000
Number of divisions	104 (incl. 11 reserve divisions)	13 (of which 3 were incomplete)	10	22	151	135 (incl. 42 reserve divisions)
Artillery	10,700	1,280	656	1,338	13,975	7,378
Armoured vehicles, incl. tanks	3,254	670	40	270	4,234	2,349
Combat-ready planes/ total available	879/3,097	384/1,150	72/82	118/140	1,453/4,469	2,589

Source: Frieser, *Le mythe de la guerre-éclair*, 77–106. All figures pertain to the forces ready for combat in northeastern France and the Low Countries in May 1940.

Francs more into the armaments industry. At that time, military spending accounted for one-third of total government expenditure.[29] By 1939, France had undertaken a 'rapid and massive military build-up' and expenditure on rearmament stood at over seven-and-a-half times its 1935 level (93.7 billion Francs versus 12.3 billion Francs). France was on course to overtake German armaments production by 1941.[30] When one considers Belgium, Britain, France and the Netherlands in their totality (see Table 1), it was not true that the Third Reich had outgunned Allies in the campaign of 1940.

In some respects, French armaments were inferior to those of the German adversary. French tanks were generally less manoeuvrable than German ones and they consumed more fuel. To aim the 75-mm gun of the B tank, one had to turn the vehicle itself (rather than just the turret) and its gun sights were of poor quality. Most significantly, the majority of French tanks were not equipped with a radio, making communication on the battlefield difficult. The deployment of French military equipment posed problems, too. Anti-tank weaponry relied on tractors to move across country while its ammunition was transported separately on the road network. French artillery was still largely horse-drawn and the army lacked the motorized machinery of the Germans.[31] Nevertheless, Germany did not occupy a position of technological superiority. The best 'all-round' armoured vehicle on the battlefield was the French Somua S35 while the French 'B' tank was 'possibly the best of any nation in 1940'. The B's armour was so thick as to render anti-tank guns ineffective against it.[32] Like the French forces, the Nazi war 'machine' relied in great part on horsepower. As Adam Tooze notes, '[t]he vast majority of German troops invaded France, Belgium and the Netherlands on foot, with their supplies moved forward from the railheads in the classic nineteenth-century manner, by horse and cart'.[33] Each German infantry division required between 4,000 and 6,000 horses to transport its equipment. Consequently, despite its advantages over the French in some areas, the Wehrmacht was 'far from being a carefully honed weapon of modern armoured warfare'.[34]

The 'Maginot Line' – a system of fortified regions guarding two main avenues of invasion in Alsace and Lorraine – has come to symbolize the failure of French interwar military planning. The Line protected the border south of the Ardennes, running 140 kilometres from Longwy on the border with Luxemburg to Basle on the Swiss frontier. The Line did not extend further north because of the natural defences of the Ardennes region and the boggy land that led to the Channel coastline. In any case, the French hoped that the Line would deter an attack in the south and thus funnel invading forces north.[35] Built at a cost of 7,000,000,000 Francs, the system's static defensive lines seemed to epitomize the outdated thinking of French army leaders. Yet the Line was part of a plan that *integrated* attack and defence with the forts intended to free up troops for offensive action elsewhere. Huge military installations comprised anti-tank obstacles, ditches, barbed wire, antitank and machine guns, and grenade launchers. The forts – a 'technical marvel' according to historian Ernest May – were equipped with ammunition dumps, food stores and clean air filters and could house up to 1,200 men for three months. The larger forts were divided into two sections, connected by deep bombproof tunnels through which electric railways ran.[36] When the moment of truth came, the Line performed well during the Battle of France. Only one fort, La Ferté, fell on 19 May; the others held out until the end.[37]

With hindsight, the Ardennes offensive appears to be an example of Blitzkrieg par excellence. In the aftermath of the defeat, both the French and German governments cited the tactical innovation of the Wehrmacht to explain the rapidity of the Allied collapse. German tactical genius, however, does not explain alone the defeat of France. The Wehrmacht had originally planned to cross the border elsewhere. The invasion plan (Fall Gelb or Plan Yellow) changed twice before May 1940. In January, bad weather halted a proposed thrust north to the Channel coastline. In February 1940, the plans fell into Allied hands, forcing a rethink in Berlin. General Erich von Manstein, Chief of Staff of Army Group A, subsequently developed the Ardennes attack.[38] Manstein's plan – to concentrate as much force as possible in a strategically weak area – was risky and it meant that no Panzers could remain in reserve to thwart an Allied counter-attack.[39]

The speed with which the invasion force passed through the Ardennes masked the difficulty of the crossing. On the third day after the German

Figure 2 *French soldiers in the underground tunnels of the Maginot Line. Photo by Hulton Archive/Getty Images.*

invasion, a huge traffic jam of 41,000 vehicles stretched eastward for nearly 250 kilometres. As Karl-Heinze Frieser points out, the German forces were sitting ducks for Allied air attack – if only the Allies had known about them.[40] Meanwhile, the charge of the German tanks to the English Channel, which began on 14 May, was an action largely improvised by Heinz Guderian. Such was the rapidity of the German incursion that the command to halt the invasion force on 17 May at the Vervins-Montcornet-Dizy-le-Gros line reached the advancing forces only after they had driven nearly 30 kilometres beyond this point.[41] Guderian understood that such a break would allow the Allies time to pull their forces back from the north and he thus took the initiative to continue the attack. Only when German forces neared Dunkirk was Hitler able to halt them. The Blitzkrieg of 1940 was thus largely 'improvised' and Wehrmacht leaders were surprised at its success. Hitler himself described the breakthrough at Sedan as a 'miracle'.[42]

If the defeat of France did not arise from German military superiority, was the quality of French soldiery to blame? On 18 May 1940, Gamelin wrote a report on the progress of the Allied campaign in which he bemoaned the attitude of his nation's soldiers:

> The French soldier... [does] not believe in the war .... Today's serviceman did not receive the moral and patriotic education during the years between the wars which would have prepared him for the drama in which the nation's destiny will be played out.... Too many failures to do [his] duty in battle have occurred, permitting the enemy to exploit local successes... The rupture of our dispositions has too often been the result of an every-man-for-himself attitude at key points, local first, then quasi-general'.[43]

Gamelin's condemnation of his troops – on the day he lost his job – was utterly self-serving. Yet the perception that French soldiers and civilians did not have the necessary heart was common. In *The Last Days of Paris* (1940), *Manchester Guardian* journalist Alexander Werth noted a mood of dejection amongst the French: 'How readily they were assuming their defeat'.[44] Soldiers he encountered on his journey were 'ragged, tired, demoralised-looking, many of them drunk, all of them without rifles... [they were a] routed army'.[45]

Belief in the poor quality of French soldiery spoke to deeper anxieties about the seemingly fatal divisions of the interwar years. As France collapsed in the summer of 1940, it was easy to point to the deep political crisis of the 1930s as one of the principal causes of the defeat. During January and February 1934 extreme right-wing groups known as leagues rioted in Paris against the alleged corruption of the democratic government. On 6 February, thousands of leaguers almost brought down the regime in a night of violence that saw police kill over a dozen protesters. This violence prompted a polarization of politics between the extreme right, especially

Colonel François de La Rocque's Croix de Feu movement, and the left, represented by the antifascist Popular Front alliance of the Communist, Socialist and Radical parties. Governments resorted increasingly to decree powers as parliament sank into paralysis while violent fighting between political rivals in the street intensified.[46]

The victory of the Popular Front in the elections of June 1936 solidified the division of politics. The decree of 18 June dissolved the leagues yet the extreme right emerged invigorated. La Rocque transformed the Croix de Feu into the Parti Social Français (PSF). The PSF's programme for an authoritarian revision of the Republic proved popular and the party had over one million members by 1939. Meanwhile, former communist Jacques Doriot founded the Parti Populaire Français (PPF) as a proletarian but anticommunist formation that sought to carve out a niche for itself as a third force alternative to the extremes of left and right. Adopting a uniform and salute and espousing a virulent anti-Semitism, the party came to resemble foreign fascist groups, even if Doriot continued to argue that he was a Republican.[47]

The presence of the Communist Party in the governing coalition unleashed a wave of anticommunism from the centre to the extreme right. The Popular Front's opponents framed the alliance as an anti-French gang under the orders of Stalin in Moscow and hell-bent on unleashing revolution and involving the country in the war in Spain. The right's attacks drew heavily on anti-Semitism, informed both by the alleged historical association between Marxism and Jews and the Jewishness of the coalition's first Prime Minister, the socialist Blum. Such attitudes engendered a new sympathy for Nazi Germany amongst conservatives and extremists on the right.[48] Hungarian-Jewish writer Arthur Koestler, writing of his experience in France in 1939, suspected that such sympathies had undermined the war effort. During a conversation about the unfinished state of French defences, an unnamed army lieutenant told Koestler that there was not one officer above the grade of colonel, 'whose heart was not with the Croix de Feu'. Worse still, the lieutenant mused, '[s]uppose some of the gentlemen in the General Staff preferred Hitler to Blum?'[49] Some conservatives favoured peace with Hitler in order to give him a free hand to destroy the Soviet Union in the east.[50]

Despite the concerns of Koestler's army acquaintance, France was not defeated 'from within'. A sense of political crisis does not guarantee defeat on the battlefield. In any case, a modicum of stability returned to government after April 1938 when Daladier became Prime Minister. Although a Radical, Daladier oversaw the dismantling of the Popular Front; the coalition finally fell apart on 30 November 1938 when the government repressed an attempted communist-led general strike. With the left severely weakened and the Radical Party on a rightward course, Daladier governed by decree, little concerned with winning the support of parliament. His clampdown on foreigners and (largely Jewish) refugees, his rhetorical celebration of the French Empire and his conservative family policy pleased the right. Conservatives largely embraced once again their intransigent Germanophobia as the threat from communist revolution at home paled in comparison to the Nazi menace abroad.[51] Even the vocal pacifist movement that had spearheaded a campaign to avoid conflict with Germany spoke only for a minority of the public. Few in France wanted to go to war yet they were unwilling to accept peace at any price.[52]

The resistance of French soldiers failed through the exhaustion of ammunition supplies and fuel stocks but not morale.[53] It is certain that some French soldiers did crack in the face of the invader. The fierce bombardment of French positions at Sedan on 13 May – the most concentrated air attack undertaken by the Luftwaffe during the entire war – wrought huge psychological damage on French defences.[54] However, Hitler himself paid tribute to the robustness of French fighting and the Wehrmacht endured 'a hard-pounding slog in the teeth of Franco-British resistance which was quite at odds with the strategically hopeless situation'.[55] The Germans' quick advance and the lack of Allied planning for an attack through the Ardennes had forced the French into hasty improvisations and uncoordinated counter-attacks that stretched their forces thinly. As Martin Alexander argues, 'France's soldiers did not let their generals down: rather the reverse'.[56]

The stout resistance of the French army in the Alps offers a counterpoint to the desperate situation in the northeast of France. The French commanding officer in this region, General Olry, was relatively distant from the High Command and this left him a good deal of latitude in engagements with German units advancing south and Italian units crossing the border. It is true that difficult geographical and meteorological conditions, as well as poor planning, hampered the Italian invasion of 20 June but French troops fought bravely and ignored Pétain's order to cease hostilities. At the cost of 37 dead and 62 wounded, the French inflicted losses of 542 dead and 2,631 wounded on the enemy. Unaffected by the chaos on the Western Front, the defence of the Alps demonstrated the tenacity of the French soldiery.[57]

We must bear in mind that France did not stand alone in 1940. London and Paris had co-operated closely since the declaration of war in September 1939. The joint Supreme War Council met nine times during the Phoney War and in November 1939 French *and* British commanders approved Plan D.[58] Relations at this time between Western Europe's largest democracies were not always easy. The French desired to take the initiative in the war, notably with an expedition to Finland. The British government was more reluctant to act. When Germany landed in Norway in April 1940, tensions rose: both governments had procrastinated about mining the waters off Narvik and now it was too late. Angry recriminations followed between the two allies.[59]

The British reluctance to commit significant military forces further frustrated French leaders. By the end of 1939, only five British divisions had arrived on French soil. This was a considerable achievement considering that when the War Office started planning for the operation, it did not even possess an up-to-date map of France. Five more divisions landed the following year, supplemented by eight poorly equipped territorial units.[60] Britain committed two more armoured divisions to the continent but these were not ready in time to fight.[61] Jackson suggests that General Lord Gort, commander of the BEF, was prepared to defer to Gamelin precisely because he recognized the inadequacy of Britain's military contribution to the campaign.[62] On the ground, mistrust between French soldiers and their better-paid British counterparts developed. British General Louis Spears proposed that the British Army set up 'foyers des soldats' (soldiers' clubs) at which British and French troops could get to know each other better. Behind the lines, Werth encountered Anglophobia. A French acquaintance told him: 'We've lost the war [and] it's the fault of that disastrous man, Winston Churchill'.[63]

In the air, Churchill refused to engage twenty-five RAF fighter squadrons in the defence of France, fearing that they would later be necessary to defend the British Isles. This decision infuriated the French and in 1944 Daladier remarked that the RAF had been absent from the Battle of France. This was not true. The BEF included four fighter squadrons, five cooperation squadrons and four bomber squadrons. Yet these planes primarily protected British infantry and the French had to beg for help from them.[64] The RAF lost 931 planes during the Battle of France, more indeed than the number lost in the later Battle of Britain. In comparison, Alistair Horne estimates that 650 French planes were destroyed, 235 of which were wrecked on their airstrips.[65] However, RAF planes – like the bulk of the Allied military force – were not deployed in the correct areas. Worse still, ten further bomber squadrons sent to France flew under the authority of the British Bomber Command and did not co-ordinate their action with land forces. By 14 May, Allied airpower could do little to halt the Germans forces pouring across the Meuse.[66]

The Dunkirk evacuation soured relations between Britain and France further. During Operation Dynamo, the Royal Navy, in combination with a number of civilian vessels, succeeded in transporting approximately 247,000 British and 123,000 French troops across the Channel to safety. Approximately 80,000 French remained to be captured. For some French, Dunkirk smacked of betrayal. The fact that the British ordered the evacuation to commence on 27 May, three days before the French, appeared to amount to abandonment. Pétain remarked that the British had been prepared to fight to the last drop of French blood. Thus while the British constructed the myth of Dunkirk as 'one of the great triumphs of the island race', the French considered it an act of desertion.[67]

A final attempt to rescue the alliance was made on 16 June 1940 when the British government presented Reynaud with proposals for an 'Anglo-French Union'. The plan, formulated in London with the input of the head of the Anglo-French Committee Jean Monnet and economist René Pleven, envisaged no less than the total fusion of both countries and the pooling of resources. Citizens of each country would automatically gain citizenship in that of their ally. A single war cabinet would direct the effort against Germany. If from the present the Anglo-French Union seems a fantastical idea, in 1940 it was a measure of the desperation of the situation facing the Allies. Pétain, Weygand and the defeatist faction in the French cabinet blocked the proposal. Why should France 'fuse with a corpse?', Pétain asked. The refusal prompted Reynaud's resignation.[68]

The catastrophe of 1940 stemmed from the strategic errors of the Allied commanders. Two aspects of the plan to defend Western Europe proved fatal. Firstly, the Ardennes region – 'the best antitank obstacle that exists in Europe' according to Gamelin – was not the impenetrable barrier that commanders believed. Dissenting voices in the French army *had* questioned the wisdom of leaving this area of the border under-defended: as late as June 1938, General André Prételat devised a scenario in which the Germans could reach the Meuse in sixty hours yet Gamelin dismissed his report as too pessimistic.[69] Plan D had committed the French First Army, the mechanized cavalry corps, the XVIth Corps and the BEF to a forward defence along the Antwerp-Dyle-Namur line. The Wehrmacht deployed twenty-nine divisions north into Belgium where they faced fifty-seven of the Allies' best divisions. Nineteen German divisions, mostly composed of second-rate troops, were thrown at the Maginot Line. As for the Ardennes, forty-five crack German divisions bore down on eighteen poorly trained and poorly equipped French divisions.[70] At this weak point in the Allied lines, Germany gained a temporary advantage of three-to-one in terms of men; the odds were even better when it came to tanks.[71]

Secondly, the French strategy of the 'continuous front' hobbled attempts at an effective counterattack. This plan 'vainly sought to retake every point of German breakthrough rather than regrouping for in-depth defence on French soil'.[72] It left the territory behind the lines dangerously exposed once the Germans had breached the line because Gamelin had moved the French strategic reserve (under General Henri Giraud) north to Breda in the Netherlands. Giraud's highly mobile tank divisions could respond quickly to unexpected developments in the field yet they were deployed too far north of the real German attack to be effective. When the Wehrmacht smashed French defences in the south, Churchill asked Gamelin, 'Where is your strategic reserve?' Gamelin replied, 'There is none'; it was in the Netherlands.[73] All of this was part of Gamelin's plan to fight, in Jordan's words, a 'cut price war on the peripheries' in which French territory would be spared the destruction of the conflict.[74]

The unexpected location of the German attack and the speed of the German advance left Allied military commanders unable to respond in time. French soldiers fought bravely. As many as 124,000 soldiers died for France; German losses stood at approximately 27,000.[75] French troops did not desert their posts yet morale ran low as fuel supplies dried up and units were moved across great distances in a desperate attempt to plug the hole in the lines. The fact that the Germans had not acted as expected left Allied military leaders bewildered and paralysed. In the field, command disintegrated. Ultimately, while the Allies matched the Germans in terms of important material resources as well as the number of divisions at their disposal (151 versus 135), '[w]hat mattered was the strategic use to which the equipment was put. The French were unprepared for the Germans' concentrated use of armour, in close coordination with tactical air power, at a weak point on their front'.[76]

A global struggle

Upon the declaration of war in September 1939, France ruled an empire of 110 million people, a figure that amounted to approximately 5 per cent of the world's population. The country's territorial possessions covered 12 million square kilometres of land. For the campaign of 1940, France mobilized 600,000 colonial troops and shipped 150,000 workers to the mainland to work in armaments factories.[77] Yet the contribution of the French Empire to the campaign of 1940 is virtually absent from the principal English language works on the subject. In the 700 pages of Horne's *To Lose a Battle*, the reader learns only that ten colonial divisions accounted for 9 per cent of the total defence force in France in 1940. A footnote states that 'it was frequently the French North African and colonial units which put up the best resistance in 1940'.[78] None of the authors in Joel Blatt's 1998 collection *The French Defeat of 1940: Reassessments* addressed the place of the empire in the French war effort. Ernest May's *Strange Victory* (2000) failed to explore the empire's contribution to the battle of France and Jackson's *The Fall of France* (2003) did not acknowledge the colonial contribution. Philip Nord's *France 1940* (2015) likewise neglected to recognize the military and industrial contribution of French colonial subjects. Where French overseas territories merit a mention in the historiography of the defeat, it is only in so far as they provided a potential base from which a French government-in-exile could wage war. Consequently, Myron Echenberg rightly called the participation of French colonial troops in the French war effort a 'surprisingly obscure episode'.[79]

During the First World War, the French had extracted food, raw materials and labour from colonial lands.[80] Paris was slow to recognize the potential fighting contribution of the empire in wartime: only in summer 1916 did the first African soldiers arrive on the Western Front as high casualty rates prompted recruiters to look abroad.[81] The contribution of colonial citizens and subjects troops to the war effort, which a recent estimate put at 818,000 troops and 187,000 workers, prompted a reconsideration of the value of the empire in the French government.[82] Joseph Chailley-Bert, who was secretary general of the pro-imperialist Union Colonial, stated in 1917, '[The war] has taught France that it has colonies. It was completely unaware of it [beforehand]'.[83]

Racial stereotypes conditioned French ideas of colonial troops. The military leadership considered troops from Indochina, Madagascar and French Equatorial Africa to be poor fighters. On the other hand, Moroccans and the subjects of French West Africa were widely regarded as brave and fearless warriors (the most decorated French army unit during the First World War did in fact hail from Morocco).[84] Black Africans, especially those of the Tirailleurs Sénégalais (Senegalese Rifles), were the most famous of France's colonial soldiers. Founded in 1857 as a Senegalese formation, by the turn of the century the units comprised men from Dahomey, Côte d'Ivoire and French Sudan, too.[85] The Tirailleurs acquired mythical status thanks to French General Charles Mangin. Mangin was an advocate of the establishment of a French African Army or a 'force noire' (black force). In 1911, he reported that '[black] Africans were used to heavy work and their nervous system was less developed, making them less sensitive to pain'. Subsequent colonial propaganda posters portrayed the Tirailleurs as 'men that "do not reason, do not retreat, do not forgive"'.[86] Up to 200,000 Africans fought for France during the First World War, accounting for 3 per cent of the French forces; 30,000 of these soldiers were killed.[87] In November 1922, the War Ministry designated imperial military forces 'a supplementary reserve for European war'.[88]

Figure 3 *Soldiers from Indochina take part in a ceremony to mark the gift of twenty ambulances to France. Catholic priest, Monsignor Hunsac, blesses the troops in January 1940. Photo by New York Times Co./Getty Images.*

In the late 1930s, Minister of Colonies Georges Mandel boasted that the empire could provide 2 million men and 500,000 workers if necessary.[89] With war looming, in November 1938, Daladier portrayed mainland France and its Empire as a huge 'security zone' to be defended at all costs.[90] In early January 1939, he ended a whistle-stop tour of Corsica, Tunis and Algiers with a warning: 'I would not yield one acre of the lands of this Empire... any attempt against this Empire, whether direct or indirect, whether by force or cunning, will be opposed by a determination and will that nothing will conquer'.[91] Daladier's speech came in response to the growing threat of foreign incursion into French colonial territory. Since the invasion of Abyssinia in 1936, Mussolini had made claims on Tunisia, as well as on French Somaliland and Chad. To the west of France's North African possessions, Franco's Spain looked enviously at Morocco and Western Algeria. Meanwhile, the Sino-Japanese war in Asia threatened Indochina.

In 1940, the Tirailleurs Sénégalais took up positions on the Western Front. They fought tenaciously perhaps because of the fate that awaited them if caught: German troops treated African soldiers with particular disdain and they spread rumours about black troops raping and murdering French civilians.[92] Vichy prefect Jean Moulin – who would later join de Gaulle's Free French – slit his own throat rather than sign a document that falsely attested to the murder and mutilation of French women by black Africans.[93] German hostility to black soldiers stemmed from both Nazi racial theory and the memory of the so-called 'Black Shame' (Die Schwarze Schande) of the years after the First World War when, in a deliberate act to humiliate the defeated Germans, the French army had deployed black occupation troops in the Rhineland. In 1940, German troops committed atrocities against captured African soldiers.[94] During the night of 9–10 June, soldiers hunted down and shot as many as 600 black African soldiers near Erquinvillers. On 19 and 20 June, 200 French African prisoners were massacred at Montluzin near Lyon. The Nazis executed as many as 3,000 black POWs during the invasion of France. Raffael Scheck argues that these crimes amounted to a German race war against black colonial troops in 1940.[95]

It is difficult to determine the precise number of colonial soldiers who fought for France in 1940. Table 2 offers an estimate of the numbers of soldiers recruited, deployed, killed and taken prisoner, as indicated in a number of different sources.

The Vichy regime determined in February 1942 that during the campaign 4,439 colonial soldiers died, with an additional 11,505 recorded as missing.[96] German forces took over 120,000 colonial soldiers as prisoners.[97] These men languished in prisons within France known as Frontstalags. In November 1940, all white French prisoners left for incarceration in Germany, leaving approximately 150,000 men in the Frontstalags, two-thirds of whom were colonial troops.[98] By April 1941, following a number of releases and escapes, there were 69,000 men from overseas lands in the

Table 2 *Colonial forces and the French war effort*

Territory	Total recruited, 1939–June 1940	Number present in France in May 1940	Deaths	POWs
North Africa (Algeria,* Morocco, Tunisia)	300,000[a]	340,000[c]	5,400[b]	65,000[b]
Indochina	116,000[a]	10,000[c] – 15,000[b]	–	10,000[b]
Madagascar	34,000[g]	10,500[c] – 14,000[b] – 34,000[g]	100s[b]	–
French West Africa	100,000[c] – 197,300[a]	63,300[b,e] – 68,500[c] – 80,000[f]	5,000[b] – 10,000[d,e]	15,000[d] – 30,000[b]
French Equatorial Africa	–	15,000[f]	–	–

Sources: *The numbers for Algeria are included here, though the territory comprised three departments of France; [a]Thomas, *The French Empire between the Wars*; [b]Deroo and Champeaux, 'Panorama des troupes coloniales françaises; [c]Mabon, Solidarité nationale et captivité coloniale; [d]Echenberg, '"Morts pour la France"'; [e]Scheck, *Hitler's African Victims*; [f]Headrick, 'African Soldiers in World War II'; [g]Lupo-Raveloarimanana, 'Soldats et travailleurs malgaches'.

twenty-two Frontstalags: 44,000 North Africans, 15,800 Senegalese, 3,900 Madagascans, 2,300 Indochinese, 400 Martiniquais, and 2,700 of an undetermined origin.⁹⁹ The Wehrmacht employed colonial prisoners in forced labour units. Some black Africans suffered experimental medical treatments for tropical diseases. Others were the subjects of Nazi anthropological studies. Black Africans featured, too, in German colonial propaganda films, exposed to live fire for the benefit of the cameras.¹⁰⁰

Fighting in some imperial territories continued beyond the Armistice of 25 June 1940. On 22 September 1940, Japan moved to occupy Tonkin (the northernmost territory of French Indochina) in order to cut a supply route to China. The territory was also rich in natural resources like tin, coal and rubber and it offered a strategic location for future attacks on Burma and Malaya. Recognizing the isolation of the distant colony and failing to secure American military help, French Governor-General Admiral Jean Decoux negotiated an agreement with Tokyo according to which Japan would respect French sovereignty in return for the stationing of occupation troops in Tonkin. However, Japanese General Nishishara was impatient with the slow pace of negotiations and took the initiative to attack a

Figure 4 *Review of Japanese troops in Indochina. Rokuro Suzuki, Japanese Consul Genereal in Hanoi, and Jun Matsumiya, Special Envoy of Japan, followed by French officers, review a guard of honour in Haiphong, Vietnam, on November 18, 1940. Photo by Keystone-France/Gamma-Rapho/Getty Images.*

French border outpost at Lang Son during the night of 22–23 September.[101] The 150 French soldiers who died at Lang Son were the last victims of foreign aggression in a year of tragedy and humiliation for France.

The civilian experience

The threat to civilian life during the invasion of France was high. Air raids – both German and Allied – did not distinguish between soldiers and civilians. During 1940, 210 aerial bombings caused the deaths of 3,543 civilians; Allied raids accounted for 292 of these casualties. In northern towns such as Abbeville and Amiens, raids destroyed up to 80 per cent of buildings.[102] The advance of the German army posed a further menace to the safety of civilians. Between 10 May and 25 June 1940, German troops summarily executed at least 420 civilians. Soldiers often perpetrated killings in reprisal for acts of local resistance. Such was the case at Pont-du-Gy on 21 May when twenty-three civilians, including an elderly woman in a wheelchair and an eight-month-old baby, were murdered.[103] French civilians who aided their own soldiers against the attackers were executed: French writer Léon Werth recounted a story of eight civilians summarily shot for helping French soldiers in Ladon.[104]

As the Allied war effort collapsed, a humanitarian disaster rapidly unfolded. An estimated 8 million people – 6.2 million French (including 2 million Parisians) and 1.8 million residents of the Low Countries fled the path of the invading forces. This huge movement of refugees is known as the Exode or 'Exodus'.[105] Terrifying rumours prompted departures from areas not yet touched by violence. Art historian and resident of the capital Agnès Humbert described Parisians looking into an empty sky convinced that they could see parachutists falling from the heavens. 'My eyes are pretty sharp', she recorded in her diary, 'and all I could see were swallows'.[106] Shirer reported that many Parisians fled their city because rumours of rapes and killings had panicked the population into leaving.[107]

Civilians packed up their belongings as best they could for the long journey south. Wealthier families piled high their cars with necessities and heirlooms, often placing a mattress on the roof in the hope of protection from aerial attack. Railway stations witnessed scenes of chaos as thousands of people unable to afford their own transport crammed into overcrowded carriages. One's destination depended on material wealth. Upper-class French made for their regular summer retreat, usually a holiday home in the south. Workers set out on foot with little idea of where they were going and in complete ignorance of the geography of France.[108] The reality of life on the road did not distinguish between social classes. Like pedlars and vagabonds, millions tramped southward.[109] Léon Werth described a pathetic scene of a nation on the move:

The caravan of cars is overtaken by cyclists, male and female, and by limping pedestrians. Their heads seem pulled toward their feet. Some carry a travel bag; others have one or two suitcases in hand. Imagine how exhausting this walk is with a valise at the end of your arm. Others push baby carriages – loaded with children, bundles or their most important possessions – or the strangest vehicles cobbled together by handymen out of wooden planks and old bicycle wheels. A woman is seated on the lid of a three-wheeled delivery cart, which a man pedals. An old man on a bicycle is leading his dog on a leash.[110]

Life on the road was hard. Families became separated. Humbert remembered the desperation of a woman who had lost her children – 'a

Figure 5 *French refugees take to the road in summer 1940. Photo by LAPI/Roger Viollet/Getty Images.*

woman who had gone out of her mind…shrieking for them everywhere'.[111] One mother sewed small bells to her child's clothes to avoid losing him in the tumult. Another tied her children together with scarves and led them along the road in a chain.[112] Ninety-thousand children lost contact with their parents and it often took months to reunite them.[113] Hunger, thirst and petty criminality led to theft and looting, from both other refugees and abandoned dwellings along the route.[114] Generally, locals greeted civilians with kindness as they arrived in towns and villages but this was not always the case. Dominique Veillon tells of a peasant in the Beauce who, stood by his stand pipe, called out to refugees, 'Come on, get your money out! Ten pence a glass, two Francs a bottle'.[115] Restaurant owners charged high prices for their meals in the knowledge that food was scarce and the refugees were starving. Some men, both civilians and soldiers, demanded sexual favours from women in return for aid. Journalist Alexander Werth witnessed a hostile reception to the refugees, notably in Tours where a hotel owner refused to give a room to a woman and her baby who had travelled three days from Paris.[116] In Poitiers, new arrivals were directed away from the town centre to better move them on as quickly as possible.[117]

The refugees could not escape the violence of the war. German Stuka dive-bombers fell on the long columns of defenceless refugees, their terrifying sirens wailing as they bombed the crowds. The recollections of Vietnamese Nguyễn Khắc Viện (whose account reminds us that the Exodus was a multi-ethnic experience) tell of the terror of an attack: 'A scene of total panic, no organization! Occasionally German planes flew by, which prompted no response, but cries that the German army was approaching caused crowds to scatter in panic. Not a shot was fired from the ground into the air'.[118] Illness and injury were common. Moulin described a scene from the cathedral in Chartres: 'a mass of bruised humanity lay on mattresses and stretchers. On every face, chiselled by candlelight, could be read the signs of lack of sleep, fever, fear. Old people who couldn't keep up, the sick and the injured who found no room at the hospital, all the ones who couldn't get into the air-raid shelters fast enough were brought here, to this place with no air, no light, lacking the most basic facilities'.[119] Overall, 30,000 civilians lost their lives during the Battle of France.[120]

The civilian experience of the fall of France and the Exodus was largely feminine.[121] With men enlisted to fight, women made up a significant proportion of the non-combatant population, along with the young, the elderly, the infirm and men exempted from service. Women were not, however, surplus to the requirements of the war effort. Women moved into industry to replace men called to the front. By February 1940, 570,000 female workers were working for the war effort. The hours were long (at least sixty hours per week) yet war employment was a necessity for many women with families to support.[122] A small group of women took part in the Battle of France. The law of 11 July 1938 (the so-called 'Paul Boncour law') allowed the entry of women into the armed forces as nurses and healthcare workers in the army and airforce, ambulance drivers and auxiliaries in the administrative arm of the army. Over 6,500 women served their country in this way.[123] On 17 June 1940, the government authorized the recruitment of female auxiliary pilots to fly light aircraft. One woman, Claire Ronan, enrolled as a sub-lieutenant before fighting ceased.[124] Whether working in the fields and factories or serving in the armed forces, women were not simply victims of the invasion.

Conclusion

The Battle of France was not lost in advance. Militarily, France was not in a position of weakness. The country had undertaken an astonishing effort to rearm and, despite some technological weaknesses, the French – and Allied – armies were a formidable force. On the front line, some troops may have cracked under pressure but they did not go into battle ready to lay down their arms. The myth of the might and genius of the Blitzkrieg attack served the Allied and German causes after the fact when, in reality, the invasion was a gamble that paid off.[125] The principal causes of the defeat lay in the planning of the Allied military commanders. Fatally, Gamelin believed that the 'enemy would play out the strategic scenario he had written for it'.[126] The decision to put the Dyle strategy into action and move the strategic reserve to Breda allowed the Germans to steal a march on the Allies. Taken by surprise and with little flexibility built into their tactics, the Allied military leadership was out of ideas: their armies were in the wrong place and there was no back-up plan. The rapidly unfolding humanitarian disaster south of the battle zone added to the mounting pressure on London and Paris. Bloch's tirade against French decadence in *L'Etrange défaite* is therefore less useful in explaining the causes of the defeat than in helping us to understand why so many French turned to Pétain in June 1940. The Marshal's offer of leadership and protection seemed irresistible, to both the soldiers who had surrendered to the invader and the civilians who had experienced the terror and desperation of the Exode.

Colonial communities around the world felt the repercussions of the defeat. The Armistice caused confusion in a number of colonial territories where not everyone was prepared to accept the surrender. In Chad, mutiny broke out in garrison towns such as Fort-Lamy and Fort Archambeault when soldiers refused to demobilize.[127] In Madagascar, a group of French and British settlers addressed their protests at the Armistice to France and London.[128] In Guadeloupe, Governor Constant Sorin reassured the Minister for Colonies Henri Lémery that the islanders desired only victory or death. Sorin sent the message on 18 June, *after* Pétain had requested negotiations with Berlin.[129] As for indigenous peoples, they had sent their fathers, brothers and sons to fight the Nazis in eastern France. Families mourned the loved ones who died far from home. Others endured a long wait to welcome the soldiers home. A lack of ships, resources and the French and German exploitation of POW labour meant that men remained trapped in France for months, and even years, before returning. The defeat taught colonial peoples that the once invincible imperialists could be defeated and nationalists drew succour from the French disaster.[130]

2

Vichy

On 25 June 1940, Marshal Philippe Pétain informed the French people of the terms the Armistice. In urging the nation to accept Germany's demands, he invoked the themes of sacrifice, order, morality and renewal. These qualities became mainstays of Vichy's propaganda.[1] In late June 1940, Pétain was still Prime Minister of the Third Republic. Regime change was not a requirement of the Armistice; Hitler did not wish to install a fascist government in Paris that could obstruct his plan to subjugate the country.[2] Nevertheless, the first step in Pétain's proposed resurrection of France was the destruction of French democracy. On 9 July, deputies and senators met at the casino in Vichy to vote upon a bill to permit the revision of the constitution. The bill passed by 624 votes to four. The following day, parliamentarians granted Pétain the power to rewrite constitutional law, by 569 votes to eighty, with seventeen abstentions.[3]

The Marshal wasted no time in consolidating his power. On 11 July, he decreed himself both Head of the French State (Chef de l'Etat Français) and Prime Minister (président du Conseil). He assumed the powers to appoint and dismiss ministers and to issue laws and decrees without the approval of parliament (the two houses of the Republican parliament, the Senate and the Chamber of Deputies, were suspended indefinitely).[4] Pétain thus concentrated power in his hands alone and his regime functioned like a royal court in which ministers vied for admittance to the Marshal's inner circle. However, Vichy was neither a personal dictatorship nor a puppet government of the Nazis. Initiative for legislation came from a cabinet of ministers and men in Pétain's entourage, rather than from the Marshal himself. Moreover, the regime enjoyed the latitude to design and implement its own policies. Still, German intervention in French affairs was a persistent threat and to displease the Occupier could have serious consequences.[5]

This chapter examines the content and complexion of the Vichy regime. Vichy's authority extended to the entirety of France and its loyalist colonies yet in the occupied region of northern and western France, Germany installed its own military and police authorities with which the French had to contend. At Vichy, the team of ministers that Pétain appointed in July 1940 was not the same that led France in the months before the Liberation in 1944. The makeup of the French administration underwent multiple changes as personal rivalries, German intervention, shifts in policy, and external developments in the war all came to bear on the government. Pétain alone remained in his post for the lifetime of the regime. Yet even the Marshal saw his authority reduced in April 1942 when Pierre Laval – a former Republican Prime Minister who had helped to engineer the dissolution of democracy in July 1940 – assumed the mantle of Head of Government and many executive powers with it.

Vichy's attempt to remake France and its Empire according to the precepts of its 'National Revolution' is the subject of the second part of this chapter. Epitomized in the regime's motto, 'Travail, Famille, Patrie' (Work, Family, Motherland), this multifaceted reform programme drew on a number of ideological sources in its effort to undo what it perceived to be the damaging effects of decades of democratic rule. It is difficult to identify a single ideological impulse behind the National Revolution. Given the multiplicity of political traditions present at Vichy and without a clearly defined mission, the National Revolution bore the imprint of various men in government who tried to turn the programme to their own ends. The success of the project depended greatly on the enthusiasm of ministers and administrators. Laval was particularly uninterested in the agenda and consequently reform efforts stalled at the mid-point of the Occupation. In loyal colonial possessions, governments implemented the National Revolution according to the peculiarities of local cultures. The distance from the mainland allowed some governors to enforce reform to a greater extent than was possible in France where ministerial turnover and the demands of the Occupation obstructed progress. As for the citizens and subjects of France and its Empire, food and fuel shortages rendered all matters, including the National Revolution, secondary to the struggle to survive; their daily misery is the focus of the final part of the chapter.

Redrawing the map of France

Article Two of the Armistice provided for the German Occupation of northern France and the Atlantic coastline. The headquarters of the Etat Français were in Vichy in the southern Free Zone. This state of affairs persisted until November 1942 when Germany, prompted by the Allied invasion of North Africa (Operation Torch), occupied the whole of the country. An internal border called the Demarcation Line separated the two zones. This 1,200-kilometre frontier ran in a northeasterly direction from the coast near Bordeaux, following the approximate route of the railway line to Tours, before changing direction eastward to roughly follow the course of the Cher River to the Swiss border. In drawing the line, the German authorities followed topographical markers rather than administrative boundaries. The Line cut several French departments in two and severed many small settlements from their administrative centres. Crossings of the Line were permitted only in four places: Moulins, Chalons-sur-Saône, Vierzon and Langon. A pass or Ausweis was required and few French, including Vichy's ministers, were able to move easily between the zones.[6]

Germany made further territorial changes in addition to those outlined in the Armistice. Firstly, on the shores of the English Channel, the departments of the Nord and the Pas-de-Calais came under the authority of the German military command in Belgium. This arrangement better served Berlin's plans for the invasion of Great Britain and the defence of mainland Europe. Secondly, a huge swathe of territory stretching from the Somme in the north to the Jura on the Swiss border – comprising the totality of six departments and portions of four more – was designated a 'Forbidden Zone'. Residents who had fled from their homes in this area during summer 1940 could return only in 1943. Thirdly, within this Forbidden Zone a 'reserved zone' was intended as an area for future German colonization. Fourthly, the long-disputed border regions of Alsace and the department of the Moselle were incorporated into the Third Reich and Germanized. Finally, Germany assented to the Italian Occupation of 800 square kilometres of land in the southeast, including the town of Menton.[7]

Figure 6 *German troops on the main street of Marseille during the Occupation of Vichy-France. Photo by ullstein bild/Getty Images.*

The division of France left Germany in a plum position to exploit the country's resources. Herman Goering stated famously in August 1942 that the French should 'hand over all they can until they can give no more'.[8] As early as August 1940, all stockpiled French military equipment was shipped east. On 26 August, the French government agreed to pay 400,000,000 Francs *per day* for the cost of the Occupation; this amounted to half of French government revenue.[9] While Vichy confronted the problems of hunger and the associated rising mortality rates, Germany exported French foodstuffs including 21 per cent of meat, 30 per cent of fish and 56 per cent of champagne.[10] German war factories gobbled up three-quarters of French mineral ores and aluminium, and over half of French steel.[11] The best industrial plants in the country were in the north and east and Germany asserted its right to enlist them in the war effort. For their part, French industrialists readily accepted contracts to produce materials and goods for the Third Reich: German orders accounted for 68 per cent of vehicles produced in France while 78 per cent of orders to French shipyards came from Germany.[12] The Occupier looked to exploit French labour, too. Initial efforts to recruit volunteers to work in Germany proved insufficient as the war effort ramped up during 1942. In February 1943, the Service du Travail Obligatoire (Forced Labour Service, STO) rendered all men aged between twenty and twenty-two years liable for two years' labour service in the Reich. By 1944, 660,000 French men and women were working in Germany.[13] Berlin's policy towards French economic resources mirrored that elsewhere in German-controlled Western Europe: 72 per cent of Belgian exports went to Germany in 1941 alone.[14]

French civilians felt the effects of the geographical division of France in their daily lives. The Demarcation Line split families: in 1940, when the French sought news of loved ones following the catastrophe of defeat, only 300 letters a day were permitted to cross the 'border'.[15] In the Occupied Zone, Germany imposed many restrictions that did not exist in the South, from nightly curfews to bans on American films. In the annexed region of Alsace and the Moselle, a process of 'Germanization' got underway. School pupils now took all their lessons in German; French inscriptions on public monuments and street signs were erased and rewritten in the language of the Reich; to speak French in public bought one a ticket to a concentration camp. Expulsions of French deemed unwilling or unable to assimilate saw 100,000 people deported to the Northern Zone in November 1940, including 10,000 Jews.[16]

In the southeast of France, the Italian Occupation of French territory was particularly humiliating for Vichy: had not French troops held out against the Italian invaders? Italy presided over approximately 20,000 citizens in its zone. In addition, 60,000 French lived in a demilitarized area that stretched from the frontier to the Rhone valley. Following the Allied invasion of North Africa in November 1942, the Italian zone was extended to the majority of France's southeastern departments, encompassing 4 million people.[17]

A process of Italianization was introduced in Menton in what amounted to a 'surreptitious annexation', according to Jean-Louis Panicacci. Italian law came into effect and ultimate legal authority lay with the Turin court of appeal. The lira became legal tender and preferential exchange rates were fixed. French signage was translated into Italian and the use of Italian was required in schools. A huge public works programme sought to make Menton into the 'shop window for fascist imperialism'. Postal correspondence arriving in France from the settlement bore the stamp, 'Greetings from Italian Menton'.[18]

Vichy's authority extended to all zones that remained part of France. Nonetheless, Germany reserved the right to veto legislation in the Occupied Zone; for example, Vichy's youth group, the Chantiers de la Jeunesse (literally the 'Construction Yards of Youth'), were prohibited north of the Demarcation Line. On the other hand, German directives did not necessarily apply in the Free Zone. Vichy refused, for example, to make the wearing of the yellow star mandatory for Jewish citizens as it was in the North from June 1942.[19] In the Occupied Zone, French officials had to contend further with a number of German authorities. The German Military administration (Militärbefehlshaber in Frankreich, MbF) was the top level of Nazi bureaucracy in the North. It included military and civilian wings and was largely responsible for the maintenance of order. Himmler's Sicherheitsdienst (SD) operated in France but on a smaller scale than the MbF. The German Embassy remained open in Paris, illustrating the apparent continued existence of France and Germany as separate powers. Each of the German authorities competed with the French powers for jurisdiction.

The Etat Français exercised its power around the globe in the territories of the French Empire. Vichy liaised with its colonial possessions through the State Secretariat for the Colonies, under the control successively of Henri Leméry, René Charles Platon, Jules Brévié and Henri Bléhaut. In a speech on 25 June 1940, Pétain called upon the colonies to remain loyal to France and its government. The Marshal recognized that the empire was a symbol – perhaps the *only* symbol – of French power, at a time when three-fifths of French territory was under foreign occupation. According to historian Ruth Ginio, '[n]ever before had the Empire been more central in the political discourse of the French government'.[20] Vichy's propaganda films – shown in cinemas before the main feature – celebrated the links between France and its colonial subjects. Productions such as *Le Ramadan en Tunisie* (1940) and *Français voici votre empire* (1941) highlighted the benevolence of the settler-conqueror and the gratitude of the subjugated indigenous peoples.[21] In July 1941, 'Overseas France Week' saw religious and military ceremonies, public conferences and meetings, film festivals, sporting competitions and exhibitions promote the imperial project at home and abroad.[22] Yet public opinion remained indifferent. To a certain extent, this indifference was historical: in 1939, an opinion poll asked, 'Do you think it would be just as painful to cede a piece of the colonial empire as a piece of French territory?' Barely half of respondents responded yes.[23] Apathy grew during the Occupation as the public recognized that the fate of France depended on military developments in Europe. On 29 September 1942, Léon Werth recorded in his diary that the British seizure of Madagascar had provoked little reaction: 'If I go down to the town nobody talks to me about Madagascar. They say [instead], "The Russians are hanging on".'[24]

The majority of France's overseas territories declared their loyalty to Pétain. In North Africa, Algeria (administratively a region of France) and the Moroccan and Tunisian protectorates remained faithful to the Marshal as did the French Caribbean colonies (the islands of Guadeloupe and Martinique – known as the French Antilles – and Guyane), French West Africa (Mauritania, Senegal, Guinea, Ivory Coast, French Sudan,[25] Upper Volta,[26] Togo, Dahomey and Niger), and the islands of Madagascar and La Réunion. The mandated territories of the French Levant (Syria and Lebanon) also fell into line with Vichy. In Indochina (Laos, Cambodia, Tonkin, Annam and Cochin-China[27]), Vichy loyalist Admiral Decoux governed under duress from Japanese forces. Having agreed to the presence of foreign troops in the colony, Decoux could do little more than stand aside as Tokyo exported valuable rice, corn, coal and rubber resources. Indigenous peoples suffered repression and great hardship as the French put down nationalist rebellion and the Japanese stripped foodstuffs from the territory. By 1945, as many as 2 million people had starved to death in the northern region of Tonkin. In March that year, Japan overthrew the French administration in the wake of Decoux's contact with de Gaulle's Free French.[28] Tokyo subsequently governed the territory.

Colonial governments consulted neither the European settler populations nor indigenous peoples about the decision to follow Vichy. Governors simply switched allegiance from the Republic to the Marshal. For some, this decision owed something to their shared backgrounds and professional networks in colonial administration and the military; when Governor-General Pierre Boisson in French West Africa threw in his lot with Pétain, his former colleague (and governor of La Réunion), Pierre-Emile Aubert, decided to follow him.[29] The largest section of the empire to refuse the Marshal's call was French Equatorial Africa (Chad, the French Congo[30] and Ubangi-Shari[31]; Gabon fell into Free French hands in November 1940) and the neighbouring Cameroonian mandate. A scattering of smaller imperial outposts from India to the Pacific likewise rejected Pétain's authority.[32]

In total, Jackson counts nine different sectors of French authority during the Occupation: the Occupied and Free Zones; the Annexed and Italian Zones; the Belgian-governed and Forbidden Zones; Algeria; a second Forbidden Zone created in April 1941 between Dunkirk and Hendaye; and the 1.5 million French POWs incarcerated on German territory.[33] The French Empire constituted a tenth sector of French authority, an 'Imperial Zone'. As Eric Jennings writes: 'the oath to Marshall Pétain rang out on the isle of Réunion as in the Bouches-du-Rhône. The masonic lodges were dissolved, and exclusionary measures towards Jews were applied in Algeria as in the Languedoc. The law of women's work was adopted in the Antilles as in the Haute Garonne'.[34] Vichy's authority was global.

Vichy's governments

Pétain was head of the Etat Français from 11 July 1940 until 20 August 1944. He was born in 1856 and he was aged eighty-four years when he became the last Prime Minister of the Third Republic in June 1940. Pétain acceded to the rank of Marshal of France in December 1918, thanks to his part in the victory over the German army at Verdun in 1916 as well as his handling of a series of mutinies in the ranks of the infantry the following year. Pétain remained uninvolved in interwar politics in the sense that he did not run for political office. When he took up the post of Minister for War in Gaston Doumergue's conservative 'national union' government (8 February 1934– 9 November 1934) it was as an unelected expert. The Marshal enjoyed the reputation of a man above the partisan quarrels of politicians and he was popular with the public. In January 1935, newspaper *Le Petit Journal* declared him the winner of its poll to find the most likely French dictator. Nearly 200,000 readers voted. The Marshal won comfortably, 7,000 votes ahead of Laval in second place.[35]

Pétain's popularity provided the basis for a cult of personality that developed during the war years. Postcards bearing the Marshal's image asked, 'Are you more French than him?' Posters reassured the French that they were 'neither sold out, betrayed, nor abandoned', and urged confidence in the grandfatherly figure at the head of the regime. Vichy's anthem – *Maréchal nous voilà!* ('*At your service, Marshal!*') – portrayed Pétain as a providential leader, delivered to the French in their darkest hour: 'Before you, the saviour of France, your boys swear to serve and follow in your footsteps'. In classrooms, pupils were encouraged to form 'loyalty leagues' to the Marshal. Letters attested to children having pictures of him on their bedroom wall, 'so that you're the first thing I see when I wake up', as one child wrote.[36] Early resisters recognized Pétain's popularity and it became a factor in the style of their resistance: in late 1940 Agnès Humbert feared 'damaging our own cause if we force [anti-Pétainism] down [the public's] throats'.[37] If Pétain's image lost some of its shine as resistance grew after 1942, the Marshal was never the subject of an assassination attempt and he drew large crowds to his public appearances even late into the war. For many French, he was 'above Vichy, a picture postcard in colors, an image of piety, an icon in a niche'.[38]

The most fervent of Pétain's cheerleaders were in the ranks of the Légion Française des Combattants. The Légion was established on 29 August 1940 when all existing First World War veterans' associations were fused into a single organization. The veterans had long held the 'Victor of Verdun', in high regard and they now helped to spread the message of the National Revolution. The function of the Légion depended greatly on local circumstances. In some regions of France, the group concerned itself solely with propaganda. Elsewhere, legionaries pursued a radical political agenda: in December 1941, Joseph Darnand, a veteran of interwar extremist politics, set up the Service d'Ordre Légionnaire (SOL) in Nice, a paramilitary offshoot of its parent association concerned with defeating the enemies of the regime.[39] In France's imperial lands, Colonial Secretary of State Platon intended the Légion to encourage support for the Marshal in the settler and indigenous populations.[40] As in the metropole, diversity of action was the order of the day. In Martinique, the group's 3,000 members acted as partisans of 'moral order', combating establishments of ill repute.[41] In French West Africa – a territory threatened by Gaullist dissidence – the Légion Française des Combattants de l'Afrique Noire sought to repress dissent. In fact, Boisson declared that he considered any veteran, black or white, who did not wish to join the Légion an enemy.[42] Ultimately, while some contemporaries perceived the organization to be a Dad's Army where the 'basest idiocy' (Guéhenno's words) carried the day, the Légion helped to establish the regime in local communities through a combination of persuasion, intimidation and the denunciation of 'antinational behaviour'.[43] By the end of 1941 (the year in which non-veterans and women were allowed to join the group), the Légion had as many as 1.5 million members.[44]

During July 1940 to April 1942, Vichy's second-in-command was called the vice-président du Conseil or deputy Prime Minister. This post held a good deal of power and the men who occupied it – Laval (11 July 1940–13 December 1940) and Admiral François Darlan (9 February 1941– 18 April 1942) – were as much leaders of the regime as Pétain. Laval was a veteran of Third Republican politics, serving four times as Prime Minister during the 1930s (though given the short-lived nature of Republican cabinets, his time in the post amounted to only eighteen months). His politicking in the corridors of the casino at Vichy in July 1940 helped to pave the way for Pétain's seizure of power. The Marshal subsequently named Laval his designated successor.

Laval was for a long time depicted as the dark force behind the Vichy regime in opposition to the benevolent Marshal. This interpretation owed much to the 1950s work of Robert Aron and André Siegfried who each perceived a benevolent 'Vichy de Pétain' and a malicious 'Vichy de Laval'.[45] Contemporaries likewise considered a difference between each man's ambitions. In the aftermath of Pétain and Laval's first meeting with Hitler in October 1940, Léon Werth noted: 'In the village, they're saying Laval sold out to Germany. But the marshal supposedly doesn't want to follow him. And they say several ministers – and perhaps the marshal himself – are in favor of playing a double game: signing on with Germany and, if England wins, welcoming de Gaulle and uniting with him'.[46] Relations between the Marshal and Laval *were* strained – but the cause was rarely matters of politics. Laval was a cliché of the Third Republican political class, 'a climber, a shady fixer...a manoeuvrer who believed that money, flattery and intrigue ruled the world and [he] made abundant use of all three'.[47] Pétain further disliked the politician's scruffiness and addiction to cigarettes. Laval's contacts with Germany, however, remained useful and he was the dominant political figure at Vichy in the first five months of the regime.

A cabinet reshuffle on 6 September 1940 removed all former parliamentarians – save for Laval – from government. General Weygand, who had wielded much influence at Vichy since the Armistice, had long complained that there were too many parliamentarians in government.[48] A number of officers now took up ministerial positions. General Charles Huntziger took over from General Colson as Minister of War; General Bergeret replaced General Pujo as Air Minister; Admiral Platon became Secretary of State for the Colonies. The presence of men from the upper ranks of the army and navy in government represented a strand of continuity through several Vichy administrations, not least in the colonies where a number of Governors were officers.

Laval's close relationship with the Occupation authorities – he was frequently in Paris – and the capital's press irked his rivals at Vichy. They sensed an opportunity to remove the deputy Prime Minister when Hitler offered to return the remains of Napoleon's son, the Duke of Reichstadt,

Figure 7 *The cabinet at Vichy c. 1942. Marshal Petain sits opposite Pierre Laval.* Photo by Keystone-France/Gamma-Keystone/Getty Images.

from Austria to Paris in late 1940. Pétain was initially receptive to the idea, especially when Laval invited him to attend a special ceremony. Yet plotters in the cabinet warned the Marshal that the invitation was a trap and that he would be arrested as soon as he crossed the Demarcation Line. Laval would then take Pétain's place at the head of the regime. On 13 December 1940, the Marshal removed his deputy and placed him under house arrest, much to the anger of the Germans who closed the border between the North and the South and broke off negotiations.[49]

With Vichy scrambling to re-establish relations with Germany, its second government (14 December 1940–9 February 1941) is best considered an interim administration. The majority of the previous cabinet remained in place. Three men took charge: Pierre-Etienne Flandin (another former Republican Prime Minister) assumed the deputy premiership and took charge of the foreign ministry; General Huntziger commanded the armed forces; Admiral Darlan continued to serve as Naval Minister. Flandin ultimately failed to reopen meaningful channels with the Occupier and he stepped aside in February 1941. Pétain subsequently named Darlan deputy Prime Minister and heir apparent. Darlan had enjoyed a long career in the upper echelons of the French navy, notably overseeing an expansion of the fleet during the interwar years and serving as Naval Minister in the last government of the Third Republic. He was a military man, 'cold, gruff, suspicious, authoritarian, totally lacking in charisma, vain, and extremely vulgar with an embarrassing taste for luxury'.[50] However, the Germans' favourable attitude to Darlan ensured that he remained in post for over twelve months.

Darlan assumed a large amount of power for himself in the new government. He occupied not only the post of deputy Prime Minister but also those of Foreign Minister, Minister of the Interior, Minister of Defence and Minister of Information. His government included experts or 'technocrats' to develop and implement policies in social and economic affairs: the industrialist Pierre Pucheu took over as Minister of the Interior in July 1941; Jérôme Carcapinio, a specialist in classics, became Minister of Education; Joseph Barthélemy, a legal expert, was appointed Minister of Justice. Darlan and his technocrats looked to make France fit for a future in the Nazi New Order. They proposed collaboration in various economic and technological projects: Secretary of State for Transport Jean Berthelot oversaw a European project to construct infrastructure; economist Jacques Barnaud negotiated a joint enterprise with Germany for aluminium production. Meanwhile, a project for a trans-Saharan railway that would link Algeria with French West Africa was initiated.[51]

Darlan's fall from power came in spring 1942. The Admiral's attempts to alleviate the hardships of the Occupation had stalled and he seemed as incapable as his predecessors of making a success of collaboration. Increasing resistance activity added further to his woes. Darlan grew suspicious that Pétain intended to bring Laval back into government when he learned of a secret meeting between the two men. In the vain hope that Berlin would obstruct this move, the Admiral protested to the Germans that the United States would oppose Laval's resumption of power. It was a poor strategy: the Occupier could not be seen to bend to the will of Washington. With Laval's return inevitable, Darlan resigned on 17 April. He remained head of the armed forces until his assassination in Algeria on 24 December 1942.[52]

Laval's resumption of power marked a turning point for the regime. On 18 April, the Eleventh Constitutional Act of the Etat Français created the post of Head of Government (Chef du Gouvernement). Laval immediately invested himself in the role; he would later assume the powers to make laws and decrees that no one other than Pétain possessed. Pétain became evermore a figurehead, required to rubber stamp his one-time deputy's choices for government with the power to do little to oppose him. Hitler remarked to Italian Foreign Minister Count Ciano in December 1942 that the Marshal was now 'like a sort of ghost, reflated from time to time by Laval when he looks like he's sagging'.[53] Laval's favourable relationship with the Germans rendered his position virtually unassailable.

Laval brought with him into government advocates of radical collaboration. These appointments included Abel Bonnard as Education Minister – described by Laval as 'more German than the Germans'[54] – and avid Germanophile Fernand de Brinon. Laval's goal was not to 'Nazify' France; he desired a close relationship with Germany in order to improve French standing in the future Europe. Still, he believed that the victory of Nazism would bring about the destruction of communism and to this end he was prepared to endorse Hitler's war effort. On 22 June 1942, Laval declared: 'I desire the victory of Germany, for without it, Bolshevism would tomorrow take hold everywhere'. This statement was widely reported in the press; it assumed a central role in the case against Laval during the trials of collaborators at the Liberation.[55]

In November 1942, German troops moved across the Demarcation Line to occupy the whole of France. The move came in the wake of the Allied landings in North Africa. Vichy's claim to be protecting French sovereignty evaporated overnight. During the following year, with the Allies' mounting success abroad and resistance growing in France, Vichy was subject to a process of radicalization, even a 'fascistization'.[56] In January 1943, the regime's paramilitary police force, the Milice Française, began to operate. Under the command of Darnand, miliciens waged a bloody civil conflict against the resistance and other enemies of the regime. In February 1943, Laval established the deeply unpopular STO, a scheme to recruit forced labour for German factories. The STO further undermined the legitimacy of the Etat Français in public opinion and dissidence grew. In June 1943, legal repression was reinforced. The remit of the so-called 'special sections' of French appeals courts – established in August 1941 to repress communism and anarchism – expanded to include the crime of 'terrorism' and sentences toughened.

By the beginning of 1944, Vichy was estranged from the French public. It clung to power thanks to the will of the Occupier and its own violent desire to crush its enemies.[57] New appointments to government confirmed this situation. Laval appointed Darnand Secretary-General for the Maintenance of Order. Ultra-collaborationists Philippe Henriot and Marcel Déat took over the regime's propaganda activities and labour policy, respectively. In August 1944, with the Allies advancing on Paris, the Germans transferred the Vichy leadership to the castle at Sigmaringen, on the banks of the Danube. De Brinon was selected as head of the French governmental delegation when both Pétain and Laval refused to fulfil their duties. Holed up at Sigmaringen, the men of the Etat Français awaited the end of the war in a pathetic limbo, simultaneously trying to govern a country they no longer controlled and preparing their defence for the coming retribution.

Ostensibly, Vichy operated in a state of flux.[58] Ministers and their policies fell in and out of favour as the circumstances of the war and the Occupation came to bear on the regime. Yet the turnover of administrations obscured areas of continuity in personnel. Marcel Peyrouton served as Minister of the Interior from September 1940 until February 1941; Yves Bouthillier acted as Minister of Finance from July 1940 until April 1942; Pierre Caziot was Minister for Agriculture from December 1940 until April 1942. A number of civil servants worked for the regime in the long term. René Bousquet took up a post as prefect in September 1940; he subsequently served as Secretary General in charge of the police and was instrumental in the roundup of Jews during 1942. Men close to Pétain also enjoyed long tenures at the heart of power: Pétain's physician, Dr Bernard Ménétrel, had the ear of the Marshal throughout the war and accompanied him into exile at Sigmaringen in 1944.[59]

With regard to the French Empire, Admiral Platon survived three changes of government as Secretary of State for the Colonies between September 1940 and April 1942. Pétain's representatives abroad likewise had extended stints in power. In French West Africa, Governor-General Pierre Boisson served Vichy from the Armistice until December 1942 when he severed ties with Pétain under pressure from the United States. Admiral Georges Robert served as High Commissioner for the West Atlantic possessions until 1943.[60] In Guadeloupe, the period of the war was so connected with the governorship of Robert's underling Constant Sorin (April 1940–July 1943) that locals referred to the period as 'an tan Sorin' – 'in the time of Sorin'. Governors General Léon Cayla and Armand Annet ruled Madagascar, during August 1940–April 1941 and April 1941–November 1942, respectively. Governor Aubert administered La Réunion until the fall of the island to the British in September 1942. Finally, in Indochina Decoux served as Governor-General from June 1940 until March 1945. Continuity rather than change marked Vichy's colonial governance.

The relative success and failure of relations with Germany weighed heavily on all of Vichy's governments. Pétain's priority was to secure a permanent treaty between Vichy and Berlin. The extent to which the Marshal considered his junior partners able to achieve this goal largely determined their fate. Laval, Flandin, Darlan: all fell from grace thanks to the fruitless quest for concessions in return for collaboration. Developments in the wider war affected Vichy's room for manoeuvre. The Allied invasion of North Africa undermined the regime's persistent attempts to remain autonomous and claw back sovereignty over its own affairs. With French minds focused on the future of Europe, loyalist French colonies enjoyed a comparative degree of stability at the upper echelons of their respective administrations. Governors had some latitude to pursue policies adapted to local circumstance and were troubled only when the Allied and Axis powers considered their location to be of strategic importance to the wider war effort.[61]

The National Revolution

The National Revolution was Vichy's programme for the fundamental transformation of society, at home and abroad. It was a uniquely French initiative; the Armistice mentioned nothing of such matters and the policy of collaboration did not require an overhaul of the French social order. Hitler in fact showed little interest in French affairs beyond maintaining the loyalty of Vichy through coercion, blackmail and the threat of force.[62] However, for the men in charge at Vichy, the revival of French civilization required the thoroughgoing moral and physical renovation of citizens and subjects. In a speech on 20 June 1941, the Marshal himself spoke of a coming 'moral and intellectual recovery', and his plans for a 'cultural revolution', defined simultaneously as 'national, authoritarian, hierarchical and social'.[63] Vichy pursued its National Revolution through persuasion, coercion, exclusion and persecution. The regime's servants applied its agenda most vigorously during 1940–2. Laval's return to power in April 1942 undermined the project for the new Head of Government had long been uninterested in the venture; Pétain last uttered the phrase 'National Revolution' on 5 January 1943.[64]

Vichy diagnosed a number of ills in the French nation: democracy and equality, secularism, individualism, egoism, to name but a few and all of which were attributed to the degenerate influence of Republicanism. All were linked to notions of moral and cultural decline summed up in the idea of decadence.[65] Opponents of the Third Republic had long blamed the democratic regime for a perceived decadence in society, epitomized in what they believed to be a single-minded pursuit of pleasure, sex and the high life among young French (and particularly young French *women*) at the expense of one's duty to raise a family. When Vichy claimed to be fighting decadence, it meant the waging of a moral crusade to return wholesome values to a misbehaving nation. On 29 December 1940, Guéhenno recorded in his diary his reaction to the regime's discourse as he listened to it on the radio: 'The same soppy nonsense on the family, the crafts, folklore ... flowing interminably on like a dribble of dirty water. It seems that for the past 150 years we had been living in the darkness of sin. This dirty water, like a new baptism, is supposed to regenerate us'.[66] Guéhenno was right: the National Revolution comprised a raft of laws, decrees and initiatives intended to remake the political, economic, social and cultural essence of the French. Reforms touched many areas of public and private life. The Peasant Charter of 2 December 1940 provided for the corporatist organization of agriculture; it spoke, too, to the regime's celebration of the folkloric peasant as the embodiment of moral virtue and good, honest hard work. The General Secretariat for Youth took charge of policies on youth, overseeing the Chantiers de la Jeunesses youth camps and its Compagnons de France (Friends of France) sister association. From August 1940, economic organization committees worked to facilitate state intervention in the economy while the Labour Charter of October 1941 established the framework for economic corporatism. Repressive laws targeted 'undesirables' in society: the notorious 'Jewish Statutes' of October 1940 and June 1941 withdrew the political, civil and working rights of French and foreign Jews. At the same time, Vichy waged war on 'unhealthy' influences on French minds: in April 1941, civil servants compiled lists of books to be withdrawn from public libraries on political and moral grounds.[67] The examples here represent only a handful of the provisions of the National Revolution and it is impossible to reduce the programme to a single set of policies.

The National Revolution comprised an eclectic mix of political tendencies that drew on both French political heritage and foreign examples. Firstly, the regime's emphasis on patriotism, discipline, hierarchy and clean living derived from the 'martial moralism' of the barracks, a fact hardly surprising given the presence of officers in the upper echelons of power. Righteous moralizing in propaganda offered a lesson in clean living while the Chantiers de la Jeunesse sought to reshape the character of young men through military-style regimentation. Secondly, Vichy looked to implement a spiritual renovation of the nation akin to that of the so-called 'non-conformists' of the 1930s. These radical young intellectuals had defined far-reaching solutions to the perceived crisis in French society. They scorned the established order (or 'disorder', as they termed it) and proposed a wholesale rejection of contemporary values in favour of a redefinition of human civilization.[68] Thirdly, technicians and experts – so-called 'modernizers' – were particularly influential under Darlan's administration. Favouring efficiency and innovation, they clashed with traditionalists at Vichy, in particular those who encouraged a 'return to the land' in search of a simpler, folkloric past. Fourthly, the ideas of Charles Maurras, extreme right-wing ideologue and racist, influenced much of Vichy's ideology. Since the 1890s, Maurras (leader of the monarchist league the Action Française) had systematized right-wing thought on a variety of subjects. His opposition to democracy, his Catholic-influenced authoritarianism and his conception of France's mortal enemies – the so-called 'Anti-France' of Jews, Freemasons and Socialists – guided a generation of men who found themselves in positions of power after 1940.[69]

To these home-grown tendencies, we may add a smattering of fascist-style components. Pierre Milza, for example, has identified fascist *tendencies* within the regime's preference for class collaboration on a corporatist model and its technocratic drive for economic modernization. On the other hand, Bertram M. Gordon describes Vichy as becoming a 'thoroughgoing fascist state' in its later stages. Yet most historians agree that Vichy was not a fascist state; Jackson, for example, prefers to label the regime a 'police state' rather than a fascist one.[70] Much depends upon one's definition of fascism and how far the content of the National Revolution is deemed to fulfil the 'essential' requirements of fascist ideology and practice. Milza argues that Vichy was not fascist because its political programme did not seek to create a new fascist man as did that of Germany and Italy. However, the regime did strive to remake and virilize French masculinity in ways that stand comparison with foreign totalitarian regimes.[71] The Etat Français lacked a single-party organization common to fascist governments, though the Légion functioned as a moral and political support in a similar way to those of single parties elsewhere in Europe.[72]

Few historians would deny that Vichy could at least claim 'kinship' with foreign authoritarian regimes.[73] While Pétain was reticent about Vichy's ideological debt to fascism, he openly admired the Portuguese regime of António de Oliveira Salazar. Salazar's vision of an authoritarian and Catholic ultra-conservative society based on organicism, nationalism and corporatism chimed with Vichy's plan for the moral renewal of France.[74] Yet there were significant differences, too, between the French and Portuguese dictatorships not least the absence of anti-Semitic policies in the programme of the latter. It is thus difficult to erect strict boundaries around fascist and non-fascist reactionary regimes. Vichy borrowed some features of fascism and rejected others; all regimes were subject to processes of mutual influence and adaptation. Given that historians have not yet arrived at a definition of fascism that pleases all parties; this very lack of agreement leaves open the question of Vichy's fascism.

The reach of the National Revolution was global. Vichy made appeals to French communities living abroad as well as foreign populations within France. The German authorities permitted the regime to export National Revolution propaganda to French POWs on German soil the better to ensure their political allegiance upon their return to France.[75] French cultural associations provided a further conduit through which to reach expatriates. From Indonesia to the United States, Pétainists in the Alliance Française[76] promoted the regime's agenda to French émigrés and local peoples.[77] Foreign communities on the French mainland were not spared the regime's propaganda. Vichy hoped to convert immigrant communities to its cause in a bid to reinforce indigenous loyalty within its colonies. To this end, Vichy employed Vietnamese ultra-nationalist Hoàng Văn Cơ to spread the ideals of the National Revolution among Indochinese immigrants in France. As Head of the Colonial Section in the Ministry of Information, Cơ targeted the immigrant worker and student community via radio broadcasts and the publication *Công bình*. He was careful to tailor his messages to his audience, linking Vietnamese tradition with Vichy's political programme.[78]

Vichy regarded the empire as an integral part of its project for national renewal and a 'privileged site of experimentation' in the moral renovation of French civilization.[79] French laws thus applied overseas. On the island of La Réunion – the colony that lay farthest from France – thirty-three civil servants lost their jobs when the metropolitan regime introduced new laws on naturalized foreigners in July 1940.[80] The commitment of Vichy loyalists abroad combined with distance from the metropole ensured that projects aimed at satisfying the goals of the National Revolution developed with relative autonomy compared to the situation on the mainland.[81] Colonial governors found that they had free rein to implement their own measures. In Guadeloupe, governor Sorin operated a veritable police state (Sorin was so fervent a Pétainist that he requested a parcel of earth touched by Pétain be sent from France).[82] In Madagascar, the government resorted to virtual slavery in order to provide a cheap workforce for European bosses.[83] The National Revolution thus had serious ramifications for indigenous peoples across the globe.

Remaking citizens and subjects

Notions of gender were central to the National Revolution. Its vision of 'men as producers, [and] women as reproducers' suffused Vichy's political programme.[84] The regime considered depopulation the greatest risk to France.[85] Such a concern was not new. Following the defeat to Prussia in 1870, the fear of a declining birth-rate and the eventual disappearance of France emerged as issues of national importance. The pronatalist lobby – those groups that advocated government intervention to encourage procreation – grew in strength in the aftermath of the First World War. The perceived blurring of gender boundaries that had seen women move from the (feminine) private sphere of the home into the (masculine) public sphere of work prompted fears that France was fast becoming a 'civilization without sexes'.[86] The breakdown in traditional gender roles was depicted as both symptom and cause of a deeper societal crisis epitomized in the falling birth-rate. Pronatalists argued that citizens valued their rights more than they honoured their duties; their taste for pleasure took precedence over the need for sacrifice. Right-wing extremists laid the blame for depopulation at the doors of the Republic yet pronatalism was not confined to the margins of politics. Parties across the political spectrum espoused pronatalist policies. By 1936, even the Communist Party, which had previously championed equality of the sexes in the name of revolution, had begun to promote a hierarchical vision of gender relations.

As war loomed, the apparent connection between population size and national strength worried some French. In 1937, Reynaud warned parliament, 'There is a single factor that dominates everything: the demographic factor. Forty-one million French face sixty-seven million Germans and thirty-three million Italians. As far as numbers are concerned, we are beaten'.[87] Enthusiasm for pronatalism culminated in the 1939 Family Code (Code de la Famille). The product of the High Committee for the Population (founded in February 1939), the Code sought both to encourage and to coerce. It extended the provision of family allowances, provided financial support for stay-at-home mothers and granted bonuses to large families. The Code simultaneously reinforced legal sanctions against abortion and contraception.[88]

Vichy ascribed the defeat of France in 1940 to a Republican moral disorder born of feminized men, androgynous women and a declining birth rate. The regime's solution was to revive and strengthen the French family – the 'essential cell' of society according to Pétain. Propaganda for the National Revolution was replete with gendered imagery of women as fertile child bearers and men as virile heads of family.[89] Children featured as 'chubby' and 'smiling' symbols of innocence and the key to national regeneration.[90] Meanwhile, pronatalists acceded to posts in the General Secretariat for Family and Health. In September 1941, Pétain established the General Commissariat for the Family, a body that possessed its own budget and whose task was to promote Vichy's highly politicized vision of the family.[91] Furthermore, the Fédération des Familles Françaises, founded on 29 December 1942, promulgated a quasi-official 'Family Charter' that recognized families as legal entities. It aimed to establish in each commune an association upon which the heads of local families (the father or, in his absence, the mother) would sit to defend the interests of the family in local and national affairs.[92]

Gendered thinking ran throughout Vichy's policies. The regime's campaign for the French to return to the countryside and work the land constructed a vision of rural France as a healthy environment that encouraged hard work, moral probity and child-rearing, far from the unwholesome temptations of the city. Meanwhile, understandings of gender roles informed food policy. Mothers of large families received special 'priority cards' that entitled them to extra rations and shorter queueing times; fathers were granted these cards only in exceptional circumstances.[93] The concern for the moral and physical regeneration of the family did not extend to a eugenicist programme. The 'only clearly eugenicist decree law' was that of 16 December 1942, requiring a premarital medical examination for men and women. Vichy spoke a language of renovation, renewal, and recovery rather than regeneration.[94]

The control of women's public and private lives was paramount to Vichy's gender policy. The French government hailed motherhood as a virtue without equal: public ceremonies celebrated Mother's Day and the Marshal awarded medals to women with large families. Conversely, propaganda denigrated women without children: 'The childless coquette has no role in society. She is useless'.[95] The regime mixed persuasion with coercion. On 11 October 1940, married women were forbidden from working in the public sector (exemptions applied to families who relied solely on a female wage earner). On 2 April 1941, legislation prohibited divorce within the first three years of marriage and rendered legal separation more difficult. Further measures discouraged adultery with special penalties reserved for the wives of French POWs.[96]

The culmination of Vichy's campaign against depopulation came in February 1942 when the regime passed the so-called 'Three Hundred Law' (the regime's 300th article of legislation). Described by historian Miranda Pollard as 'one of the most repressive antiabortion laws in contemporary European history', the Three Hundred Law rendered abortion a crime against society, the state and the race.[97] While the civil courts continued to prosecute the majority of cases, repeat offenders were now subject to trial in the special sections of appeals courts usually reserved for the prosecution of terrorists. Two French were executed – Marie-Louise Girard, on 30 July 1942, and Désiré P., on 22 October 1943 – while fourteen more were sentenced to life imprisonment. Many more French received heavy fines, prison terms and hard labour. The law failed to reduce the number of offences and there were as many as one million illegal abortions in 1942 alone.[98]

Concern for the future of the French race took unexpected directions in the colonies. The isolation of Indochina from France and the small European settler population prompted Decoux to employ indigenous peoples in his administration to make up for the shortfall in European bureaucrats. While this policy ensured the continued operation of the colonial administration in wartime, it threatened to undermine long-term French dominance. Consequently, during 1943, the government drew up plans to seize the children of French fathers and indigenous mothers in cases where the father had abandoned the family (children were classed as 'abandoned' even if they lived still with their native mother). Government-run orphanages were empowered to take these children – preferably those with lighter skin – from their mothers. These children would subsequently be educated to 'serve as a new, visible white presence' in the colony.[99]

Vichy's attempt to reshape and control French womanhood operated alongside its project to virilize French men. The humiliation of the defeat and the daily experience of the Occupation underscored French subservience to German manhood. The regime thus strove to revive national virility. It imbued its propaganda with a lexicon of masculine terms, posing the 'male' values of honour, discipline, selflessness, courage and will against the 'feminized' Republican vices of decadence and moral weakness. Men appeared in Vichy propaganda as fathers, heads of the household and civic warriors, their masculine features – square jaws, broad shoulders, muscular torsos – on display.[100] Young men would develop virile qualities through hard work and athleticism. Vichy did not establish a single youth movement in the style of the Hitler Youth. Rather, the regime opted to license independent youth movements. It was quite liberal in disbursing its accreditation: even the Jewish scouting movement received official recognition in June 1941. This did not mean that no one at Vichy was interested in such matters. Paul Marion, General Secretary for Information and Propaganda, tried to influence youth policy to take a more political direction and he founded the Jeunes de France et d'Outre-Mer to this end. However, the strength of existing youth movements – especially those under the control of the churches – saw Vichy opt for pluralism.

The regime founded two youth movements for boys and young men, the Compagnons de France and the Chantiers de la Jeunesse. Henri Dhavernas established the Compagnons de France as a voluntary organization for youths aged between fifteen and twenty years old. Full-time members lived in camps. Their activities – outdoor labour and social work – were heavily infused with the propaganda of the National Revolution. Yet the Compagnons' emphasis on comradeship, duty and discipline rendered it more akin to the scouts than a fascist youth movement. The movement suffered in competition with more established Catholic and Scouting groups and only 29,000 young French joined during the Occupation. The majority of members were part-time.[101]

For Vichy, the Chantiers de la Jeunesse youth camps offered a crucible in which to forge French men. Established on 31 July 1940 under the leadership of General Joseph de la Porte du Theil, these camps initially offered a measure of expediency to avoid the sudden and potentially disastrous demobilization of tens of thousands of young men in 1940.[102] The Chantiers subsequently came to resemble a form of compulsory national service for all young men aged twenty-one. They reflected Pétain's belief that 'the military was the school of the nation'.[103] Recruits spent eight months in the camps, receiving lessons in morality, the new social order, the cult of the leader and elitism, all as part of a curriculum to combat moral decadence.[104] In addition to their education in the classroom, the young men of the Chantiers undertook strenuous outdoor work according to Vichy's 'healthy body, healthy mind' philosophy. Few members enjoyed the experience; poor housing facilities, lack of food and boredom afflicted many.[105]

The Chantiers encountered mixed fortunes in overseas lands. In North Africa, Colonel Alphonse van Hecke oversaw seven regiments of the youth association. The majority of members were European settlers; indigenous Muslims were admitted only after October 1942 when 1,350 men were enrolled at Rouina. A further Muslim group operated at Sbeitla in Tunisia. The colonial mystique of the empire suffused the Maghrebin Chantiers. Companies within each regiment adopted as their mascot figures or historical episodes of historical imperial significance such as General Christophe

Figure 8 *Youths of the Chantiers de la Jeunesse marching in Saint-Bonnet-Tronçais in 1941. The sign above them reads, 'France is eternal. Let's follow the Marshal'. Photo by Keystone-France/Gamma-Rapho/Getty Images.*

Lamoricière, a hero of the conquest of Algeria, or the Battle of Isly of 1844 when General Thomas Robert Bugeaud defeated the Moroccan allies of rebel Abd-El-Kader.[106] Helped by its compulsory membership requirement, the Chantiers grew to become the largest youth group in North Africa. However, in Algeria it existed in the shadow of the Jeunesse de France et d'Outre-Mer, which had the support of extreme right-wingers in the Légion and local fascist parties.[107]

Local circumstances weighed heavily on the Chantiers elsewhere in the French Empire. On the island of La Réunion, Governor-General Aubert introduced the youth camps in January 1941. The project soon encountered difficulties due to a paucity of adequate accommodation, the relative lack of idle youths on the island, and the popularity of existing youth groups such as the scouts.[108] In Madagascar Governor-General Cayla established a Chantiers-style scheme in December 1940. Separate camps housed the children of European settlers and those of the indigenous population. These camps catered to the supposed requirements of their residents. In the largest camp at Tannarive, Europeans received indoctrination in the values of the National Revolution. Racial prejudices informed the programme for Malagasy members: physical education and training in manual labour would combat the islanders' 'inherent' laziness. For Cayla, the education of indigenous youth mattered only in so far as it would prepare them for service in settler-owned farms and factories.[109]

Sport provided a link between Vichy's concern to improve the physical and moral quality of both men and women. Under Secretary of State for Youth Georges Lamirand and General Commissioner for Education and Sport Jean Borotra (a champion tennis player), the regime invested 1.9 billion Francs in sporting infrastructure and facilities while increasing the number of hours devoted to sport in schools.[110] Men and women were encouraged into different sports. Football, rugby, boxing, racket sports and shooting were reserved for boys and young men. Borotra believed that such activities would cultivate physical and mental hardiness and virility in men. Women were channelled into gymnastics, basketball and swimming, all sports considered suitable for feminine physical fragility.[111] Thanks to the regime's initiatives, participation in athletics more than doubled during 1940 and 1941.[112] Women benefitted in particular from the expansion in sports provision. During 1941, over 26,000 women gained the national sports certificate. Female sports instructors trained at a national centre in Antibes and at Vichy's leadership training school at Uriage.[113] However, scarcity of existing sports facilities throughout France, citizens' lack of appropriate clothing and footwear, and undernourishment hindered Lamirand and Borotra's plans to train a generation of athletes.[114]

In the colonies, Vichy believed that sport would serve two purposes. Firstly, in line with its programme on the mainland, sport would improve the moral and physical health of citizens and subjects. Borotra's delegate in Algeria, Lieutenant-Colonel Barbe claimed that a young man should know 'the joys of a healthy fatigue' and in doing so, 'his spirit will be perfect because his body will be healthy'.[115] In Indochina, Decoux and his Minister for Sport and Youth Maurice Ducoroy argued that sporting practice would 'virilize' young men, especially the naturally lazy youths of Cambodia.[116] The second purpose of Vichy's colonial sports policy was to secure the loyalty of all the races of 'Greater France' through integration. To this end, Decoux hoped that membership in French sporting associations would better capture the loyalty of a youth threatened by the anti-French attitudes of the Japanese occupier.[117] In Madagascar, European and Malagasy youth competed in an interschool athletics competition in June 1941. That same year, Annet staged football championships for European and indigenous teams. The two competitions remained separate from each other because, for all Vichy's emphasis on integration, its hierarchical understanding of race could not tolerate a French club losing to a team of 'natives'.[118]

The National Revolution was a multifarious political project. Vichy's reform programme was 'open to an almost infinite variety of interpretations' at home and abroad. The domestic, colonial and international context of the war all came to bear upon the aims of the project and the relative success of its implementation. Richard Vinen therefore concludes that the National Revolution was a model of eclecticism.[119] Laval concurred. At his post-war trial, he stated, 'I never knew what the National Revolution was, it was never defined and it was an expression that personally I never used... Everyone put his own desire, ideal and the regime that he saw into these words, but the national revolution was never defined in any form at any time'.[120]

All political programmes, however, are subject to the attitudes, agendas, interpretations and aims of those who implement them. There *were* sites of convergence between Vichy's multiple ideological influences, from a rejection of individualism and egalitarianism to a xenophobic and anti-Semitic nationalism. The desire to remake men and women inspired a number of policies from anti-abortion legislation to investment in sports facilities. Vichy's appeals to fertile womanhood and a virile masculinity were part of everyday life in wartime France. We must therefore be careful about erecting barriers between factions of different ideological conviction within Vichy's global enterprise. According to Kevin Passmore: 'Vichy was a complex patchwork of shifting interests and ideologies... Categorization [therefore] obscures the diverse reasons for which people embraced Vichy, their different degrees of commitment, their various appreciations of what if stood for, not to mention their understandings and misunderstandings of foreign ideologies... Vichy was never a pure expression of any ideology, and it changed over time.'[121]

Tracas, Famine, Patrouille: Everyday survival

Vichy's 'Travail, Famille, Patrie' motto summed up the National Revolution. Its parody, 'Tracas, Famine, Patrouille' ('Worry, Famine, Patrol'), spoke to the primary concerns of millions of French citizens and subjects. In the face of hardship, loss, shortages and repression, the mere act of surviving the war preoccupied the nation. Vichy's repression is the subject of a later chapter. Here, the focus rests on the daily miseries of wartime. The story of the struggle to survive brings more than just colourful anecdotes to the history of the Second World War in France and its Empire. Deprivation and hunger trumped most other issues, including the National Revolution, which took second place to the battle to put food on one's table and clothes on one's back.[122] In the second half of October 1941, Vichy's surveillance of the postal service officials found that 18,346 letters mentioned shortages, while 2,908 referred to the Marshal and only 779 contained an allusion to collaboration.[123] Of course, hunger was a pressing concern for millions of people in Nazi Europe.[124] Yet in France, the pitiful level of basic rations imposed by the Occupier in 1940, combined with government mismanagement of the food supply and a huge fall in agricultural production, brought the country to the point of starvation. After the war, the experience of hunger dominated the memories of French citizens and subjects, at home and abroad, and it featured in some of the most celebrated novels of the Occupation.[125]

On 17 September 1940, Vichy introduced the rationing of food, fuel, clothes and shoes. Pétain framed the measure in the regime's rhetoric of sacrifice and abstention to explain that rationing was a 'painful necessity' that would guarantee equality of access to supplies for rich and poor alike.[126] The rationing system divided the nation into categories. Manual and agricultural labourers received more rations than those whose jobs did not require heavy work. Special provisions existed for pregnant or breastfeeding women and families with more than five children under twenty-one years old. Vichy denied women a tobacco ration for its moralizing discourse disapproved of female smokers.[127] The largest proportion of the population – adults aged between twenty-one and seventy – received Category A rations: 350 grams of bread (daily allowance), 250 grams of pasta (monthly), 50 grams of cheese (weekly), 200 grams of fat per month (monthly), 200 grams of margarine (monthly), 300 grams of meat (weekly), 500 grams of sugar (monthly) and 50 grams of rice (monthly). In theory, Category A rations supplied a grown adult with 1,327 calories per day. The allowance for each food type of food ration (except for sugar) declined as the war progressed.[128]

Racial discrimination in the colonies ensured that indigenous peoples consumed less food than their settler counterparts did. In French West Africa, Africans received a monthly allowance of 300 grams of sugar and 2 kilograms of bread; Europeans received 5 kilograms and 10 kilograms of these foodstuffs, respectively. Only whites had access to butter and milk.[129] In Morocco, Vichy requisitioned foodstuffs and agricultural products much to the detriment of the health of indigenous peoples. Requisitions continued after the protectorate's liberation inlate 1942. Indeed, the Gaullist administration's plunder of the countryside combined with a drought to cause a famine in 1945.[130]

The face of the French high street changed as businesses adapted to the new system. Restaurants served food in return for ration tokens and offered a choice of menu according to the maximum price of their meals: category D restaurants charged eighteen Francs per meal while establishments in category E charged seventy-five Francs.[131] Bakers frequently closed their doors due to a lack of fuel to fire their ovens. Even when bread was available, it was stale: the government outlawed the sale of fresh bread in the belief that people would consume less if their baguette was hard.[132] Long queues for shops and markets were an everyday occurrence. The average female Parisian industrial worker spent twelve hours per day, six days a week, working and queueing.[133] One concierge rented out the cellar of his building for two Francs per night for those French who wanted to be at the head of the queue for the nearby butcher's shop the next day.[134] For seven Francs an hour, one could hire a 'queutière' or queuer to hold one's place in a line.[135] The Communist Party appealed to women in queues to protest, so as to 'complement underground partisan activities' and the 'battle for bread' assumed a central position in propaganda aimed at wives and mothers.[136] Food protests sometimes turned into violent clashes with the police, such as the demonstration of Parisian women on the rue de Buci on 31 May 1942 during which two policemen died.[137] Vichy redoubled police patrols to protect sellers, suppliers and shopkeepers from angry, hungry mobs.[138]

Shortages compounded the misery of French on meagre rations. It was often impossible to obtain the full amount of one's rations: only in December 1941 and January 1942, for example, did citizens of the Seine-et-Oise department receive their allotted ration of meat. Much depended on regional supplies of foodstuffs and one's location could determine one's diet: in the wine-growing Hérault, there were severe shortages of cereals and fresh vegetables.[139] Scarcities resulted from a number of factors. Firstly, French governments before 1940 had failed to plan for rationing. Pre-war planning had envisaged a war fought beyond the borders of France, with the nation supplied by its empire, the British and the Americans. In this context, rationing, the stockpiling of food and fuel, and a reduced dependence on imported products seemed unnecessary. The subsequent rationing system under Vichy was, according to Kenneth Mouré, 'disorganized, badly staffed and predominantly reactive in nature'.[140] Secondly, overall agricultural production fell dramatically after 1940. With nearly half a million peasant farmers languishing in

Figure 9 *Women queue outside a dairy shop in Paris in June 1940. Photo by The Print Collector/Alamy Stock Photo.*

German POW camps, an absence of men to work the fields and collect the harvest had a significant impact on output. The yield of grain declined by over 2 million tonnes between 1939 and 1940 while potato production halved by 1941.[141] Total agricultural production fell by 40 per cent and by mid-1944, output stood at a quarter of its level in 1939.[142] Finally, the German requisition of agricultural supplies (19 per cent of hay), produce (21 per cent of meat) and fuel further had an impact upon resources. From early 1942, a shortage of food in Germany saw France and the Ukraine make up the shortfall.[143] German troops contributed to shortages of goods, emptying shops of food, clothes and souvenirs sent home to their families as they took advantage of the favourable exchange rate imposed on France.[144]

Huge price increases compounded shortages as the cost of living in France rose by 270 per cent. Many French scavenged for food wherever they could and 'making-do' (called 'le système D', from the verb 'se débrouiller' or 'to manage') became a way of life.[145] Fuel shortages saw cars disappear from the streets, replaced with makeshift 'vélo-taxis' (a bicycle-pulled cart), and the 'gazogènes', petrol cars converted to run off wood burning boilers.[146] The French concocted recipes for products that were either no longer available or sold at exorbitant prices: 'coffee' could be brewed from ground and roasted chestnuts and acorns, wild-rose petals and liquorice sticks. In the absence of fats, paraffin and motor oil found their way into the kitchen. Parisians farmed chickens and rabbits on their balconies. For the desperately hungry, cats provided a source of meat.[147] A culture of penury emerged comprising jokes, songs and a lexicon of terms derived from the food shortage.[148] New practices of gift-giving developed: invitees to weddings were asked to bring bread ration tickets for the newlyweds.[149] Colonial subjects likewise lived hand-to-mouth. In Madagascar, locals used rice to make bread and milk from zebu cattle to make dairy products.[150] A Caribbean version of the système D developed to replace wheat, usually imported from France. Roots, leaves and indigenous tropical fruits supplemented diets.[151]

Declining standards of living threatened the health of the nation. The daily calorific value of French rations was the lowest in Western Europe and in both 1942 and 1944 French rations were roughly equivalent to those of Poland.[152] General Casnoue, Vichy's principal negotiator in the domain of food supply, suspected a deliberate German plan to starve and weaken the French race.[153] In January 1942 the government recognized the prevalence of malnutrition in the population.[154] Malnourishment led to disease and death: the infant mortality rate climbed from 63 deaths per thousand in 1939 to 109 deaths per thousand in 1945.[155] The regime's aid organization, the Secours National, distributed vitamin tablets to school children up to the age of fifteen.[156] The organization provided 60,000 meals per day in soup kitchens and canteens in the Southern Zone.[157]

In the colonies, Governors attempted to combat shortages with campaigns to render their territories self-sufficient. To a great extent autarky chimed

Figure 10 *Mother and children with an image of Marshal Pétain. Photo in the public domain (Wikimedia Commons).*

with the National Revolution's focus on a 'return to the soil'. In practice, the struggle to grow more was tough: islanders on Guadeloupe narrowly escaped famine during 1940–1943.[158] The indigenous peoples of Indochina were not so fortunate: 1 million Vietnamese starved to death in 1945.[159] Autarky entailed an increased reliance on forced labour in territories under the control of both Vichy and the Free French. In Free French Africa, the demands of the war effort saw labourers – many of whom were forced to work illegally in the private sector – and their families coerced into growing foodstuffs.[160] Despite such hardship, propaganda encouraged colonial subjects to donate to funds intended to alleviate misery in *France*: 'Is your child cold?', one newspaper asked the Caribbean islanders before urging them to donate to the Secours National.[161] Vichy enjoined Madagascans to contribute to the Secours National in aid of impoverished French on the mainland with the sum of one's contribution read as a measure of loyalty.[162] In their African lands, Gaullists likewise encouraged poverty-stricken subjects in even the remotest of villages to contribute to the purchase of Spitfire planes for Free French pilots. In this context, too, donations served as indicators of fidelity.[163]

The illegal trade in goods on the black market offered a way to supplement one's food supply. Yet the price of goods on the black market made their purchase beyond reach. Food sold for as high as five times the legal price; clothes cost as high as ten times the price in shops.[164] Prices varied according to geography: goods were more expensive in towns than in the countryside where agricultural products were easier to procure. On the other hand, cities with large agricultural environs fared better than southern urban centres such as Toulouse. The time of year caused fluctuations in prices. When in the last days of summer the slaughtering of beef cattle saw meat return to the shops, black market prices declined.[165] Social networks mattered greatly. A friend who was a farmer or shopkeeper could supply goods at a price that, though higher than advertised in shops, could be lower than the going rate on the black market.[166] French in the countryside sent food parcels to their city-dwelling relatives. As much as 350,000 tonnes of food entered Paris by this means in 1943 alone.[167] Schoolchildren operated a roaring trade, gifted as they were with a captive market in the playground as well as the appearance of youthful innocence in the street. A fourteen-year-old black marketeer in Marseilles was discovered with 10,000 Francs on him (the average monthly salary of a Parisian factory worker was 1,500 Francs).[168]

Vichy exercised a severe repression against black marketeering. Courts had the power to punish the guilty with up to two years' imprisonment and a 200,000 Francs fine.[169] The law of 28 June 1941 permitted the internment of black marketeers in the regime's network of camps for so-called undesirables. The decision to intern lay with the prefect and not magistrates. People accused of the most significant offences appeared before the Tribunal d'Etat, a special body instituted on 7 September 1941, to try Gaullists, communists and those who profited from the misery of the country. A life sentence of forced labour awaited most convicts.[170] German participation in the black market hindered Vichy's attempts to stamp out under-the-counter trading. Occupation troops fuelled demand despite Berlin's official disapproval of illegal commerce. Furthermore, German authorities in France made huge purchases: the navy bought 60 million Francs' worth of fabric from French suppliers in March 1941 alone.[171] By 1942, German soldiers and bureaucrats were spending 8 million Reichmarks *per day* on the French black market.[172]

The inability of many French to access goods on the black market, combined with food and clothes shortages in the shops, caused much anger. Rumours spread of a 'hidden abundance' of products, denied to ordinary people but accessible to privileged social groups such as peasant farmers, shopkeepers, the rich and Jews. Accusations of black market trading featured in many letters of denunciation sent to the French authorities.[173] The regime itself was the target of great public rancour. The prefect of the Loire reported in March 1942 that '[t]he unique anxiety over finding food for their families leads the public to judge the Government's policies solely on the basis of their greater or lesser ability to find produce necessary for their families'.[174] The regime's enemies based many of their attacks on shortages and rationing.[175] Yet hunger could likewise nurture opposition to de Gaulle. In French Equatorial Africa, the purchase of basic foodstuffs such as dried fish became impossible; poverty and penury threatened to undermine support for the Free French amongst indigenous and settler populations.[176]

Hunger and shortages made daily life miserable for millions. Rationing was disorganized and ineffective, subject to abuse from French and German bureaucrats.[177] Drastic reductions in the volume of agricultural produce pushed France and its colonies towards the point of starvation. Shortages ensured the unavailability of goods to fulfil or supplement one's allotted rations. The black market, despite its high prices, accounted for a significant amount of trade – by 1943, illegal trading accounted for 50 per cent of overall sales of chickens in the country – and probably saved many from death.[178] At the same time, it produced a new sociability as people negotiated new relationships in order to secure valuable resources and objects and products took on new value.[179] The French muddled through as best they could, as did their colonial counterparts; the système D was not unique to the mainland. For many French, the National Revolution mattered only as far as it could alleviate their hunger, put clothes on their backs and heat their homes.

Conclusion

To understand the Vichy regime, we must grasp its diversity in space, time and composition.[180] Within France, Vichy was able to impose its will fully only in the southern Free Zone. The occupation or amputation of swathes of French territory hobbled the regime's authority in large parts of the country. The total occupation of France in November 1942 constrained Vichy's autonomy even further. Beyond the borders of France, far off colonies saw Vichy loyalists implement the regime's policies as they saw fit, relatively insulated from the changes of leadership on the mainland and the wider development of the war in Europe. Overseas territories could therefore put into action their own idiosyncratic National Revolutions with greater vigour than in France.

The regime's personnel and political priorities changed over time. The vigour with which Vichy's administrations pursued its political agenda fluctuated as new appointees made their own impression on the National Revolution. There were of course elements of continuity. Firstly, Pétain remained at the summit of French government throughout the Occupation. Yet even the Marshal saw his power diminished when Laval became Head of Government in April 1942. Secondly, the quest for a permanent treaty with Germany obsessed all Vichy leaders. The inclusion of ardent Germanophiles and fascists in the last government before the Liberation was the ultimate outcome of this obsession. Finally, from its very first weeks of existence, the

Etat Français was concerned above all with excluding and persecuting its enemies. The 'final' Vichy of the Milice was the culmination of this repressive tendency. To some extent, we may argue that instability characterized Vichy only if we ignore the case of the colonies. French colonial governments were remarkably stable and this stability allowed governors to enact reform to a greater extent than was possible in France where political intrigue, German intervention, French desperation and the policy of collaboration prompted changes in leadership.

The National Revolution sought to remake French civilization by undoing the damage wrought during decades of Republican rule. It touched both public and private life in France through a diverse array of policy areas. The reshaping of men and women according to Vichy's gendered ideology ran throughout the programme. Intervention to encourage certain behaviours accompanied repressive legislation to remove perceived obstacles to the success of a future France. In the colonies, the National Revolution was applied vigorously, if idiosyncratically. The empire was a high priority in Vichy's strategy for the renovation of France's citizens and subjects. The Secretariat of State for the Colonies thus became a 'machine for reproducing the National Revolution'.[181]

Vichy's success in implementing its ambitious reform agenda was partial. There were contradictions in the project: the modernization of agriculture frequently ran contrary to the Etat Français's celebration of the artisanal simplicity of peasant life. The demands of the Occupation undid some aspects of reform: the number of hours devoted to physical education in schools was reduced due to fatigue and hunger amongst the student body.[182] The law that forbade women's employment in public sector posts was soon suspended due to a shortage of workers.[183] Furthermore, the regime failed to convince the public of the importance of the National Revolution. Rationing, shortages and the daily struggle to survive preoccupied most people. In October 1941, Vichy's intelligence services reported that the French had turned away from the government without necessarily joining the ranks of its opponents. Rather, citizens had 'turned inward', and 'retreated back into their shell'.[184] By spring 1942, few French concerned themselves with the National Revolution.

3

Collaboration

On 30 October 1940, Pétain announced that France was 'entering onto the path of collaboration' with the Third Reich. The Marshal reassured the French that the policy would win the country a seat at Hitler's table in the New European Order. The previous week, Pétain and deputy Prime Minister Laval had met Hitler at Montoire in the Occupied Zone. The meeting resolved little more than France's continued governance of its Empire. Hitler was not willing to discuss a permanent peace treaty. Yet the diplomatic significance of Montoire was as nothing compared to its impact on public understandings of the new Franco-German relationship. A photograph of Pétain shaking the hand of the Fuhrer 'stupefied' the French.[1] With the defeat of Great Britain seemingly inevitable, Vichy's leaders believed that co-operation with Germany was the only way to ensure the survival of France. 'Do you think that in 1940 any intelligent man could imagine anything [else]?' Laval asked the court at his trial in August 1945, though he was evidently trying to save his skin.[2]

Vichy's policy of collaboration was founded on the mistaken belief that goodwill in relations with the Occupier would win concessions in return. From the German point of view, collaboration and concessions were separate issues. According to Fabian Lemmes: 'The German occupation policy in France was led by three main interests: to weaken France militarily and politically in a durable manner; to maintain calm and order with as few personnel as possible; and to exploit French economic resources maximally for their own war effort'.[3] As Goebbels told colleagues at the Reich propaganda ministry on 12 July 1940: 'everything which serves to encourage a political or economic revival of France will be destroyed'.[4] The disjunction between French expectations and German intentions characterized the relationship between the two nations throughout the Occupation. As some French believed in 1940, it was a collaboration between a farmer and his pig.[5]

Collaboration took a number of forms. Stanley Hoffmann termed the collaboration between the Vichy regime and the Occupier 'state collaboration' or 'collaboration d'Etat'. Historians have identified other forms of collaboration, from ideological imitation (termed 'collaborationism') to economic, military, sexual and emotional collaboration. The term 'collaboration' itself is therefore problematic. The word is a blunt instrument and a label whose association with co-operation between the Axis powers and indigenous populations during the Second World War has rendered it 'synonymous with treason'.[6] Such an understanding both obscures the many motivations behind the behaviour and implies a value judgement based on its opposition to the virtue of 'resistance'. Vesna Drapac and Gareth Pritchard have argued that '[t]he historiography of World War II has never escaped from this need to identify resisters to celebrate and collaborators to castigate'.[7] Consequently, in the case of France, Philippe Burrin casts doubt on the validity of the term 'collaboration' in contexts other than the political, seeing in it a tool used to denounce, blacken and tarnish. Burrin contends that some form of co-operation between French and Germans was inevitable because a whole nation cannot resist. He prefers the word 'accommodation', defined as, 'a regular phenomenon in almost any occupation, where certain points or interfaces of contact are inevitably created and some adjustment to the new situation has to be made', to better describe Franco-German relations during the Second World War.[8] Burrin in turn defined different forms of accommodation. Structural accommodation allowed the country to continue to function; it encompassed, for example, the continued delivery of public services such as the mail. Deliberate accommodation looked to assist the policy of the Occupier, whether directly or indirectly. This type of accommodation could be 'opportunist' (taking advantage of the conditions of the Occupation to advance one's own agenda or for one's own gain) or 'political' (implying sympathy for the Occupier's politics).

This chapter concerns the various types of behaviour described as collaboration in wartime France. The practical implications of collaboration between Vichy and Berlin are explored through the example of the French who worked for Germany – those who volunteered and those who were forced into labour service through the STO. The second part of the chapter examines public attitudes to collaboration. The public understood collaboration in complex ways and much depended on the nature of relationships between French and German. The example of sexual relations is explored here. Women who took German lovers were the targets of much hatred and their example reveals the psycho-sexual terrain upon which collaboration could be situated. Finally, the chapter considers ideological collaborationism with a focus on the parties who supported the establishment of a Nazi-style regime in France. Collaborationists disdained what they perceived to be the conservative regime at Vichy and they sought to radicalize the National Revolution. The Occupier did not wish to see a fascist government in charge of France. Nevertheless, Germany supported collaborationist parties both morally and financially for they proved useful when the time came to bring pressure to bear on the Etat Français.

Types of collaboration

Hoffmann's seminal 1968 article on the subject of collaboration described several variants. Firstly, Hoffman outlined 'collaboration for reasons of state' (collaboration d'Etat), defined as collaboration 'to safeguard French interests in interstate relations'.[9] Collaboration d'Etat stemmed in part from an appreciation of the political realities of 1940. The very existence of a French state necessitated relations with Berlin. In other parts of Europe, where Germany simply dismantled existing institutions, state collaboration was moot. Vichy's desire to defend what remained of its sovereignty is paramount to understanding the motives behind its collaboration. The preservation and expansion of French independence was an obsession of the Etat Français. It often led to the French doing the Germans' dirty work in the name of autonomy. When in August 1941 the Nazis began to execute hostages in reprisal for resistance attacks, Vichy hurriedly established its own extraordinary courts to try and execute those men and women alleged to be guilty; in Paxton's words, '[b]etter execute the innocent yourself than let the Germans [do it]'.[10] The French government's 'involuntary collaboration' therefore frequently turned into 'voluntary collaboration' as Vichy looked to anticipate and satisfy Berlin's demands in the hope of maintaining sovereignty while easing the tough political and economic sanctions imposed by the Armistice. In any case, Vichy believed that obstructionism would increase the threat of obliteration – termed 'Polonization' following the Nazi break up of Poland – that hung over its head.[11]

Collaboration between France and Germany reached a high point in May 1941 when deputy Prime Minister Darlan negotiated the Protocols of Paris. Allied action in the Middle East had at last brought Berlin to the negotiating table. During 27–28 May, Vichy formally agreed to allow German and Italian use of airfields in Syria, and to supply and train Iraqi soldiers to fight the British. This agreement essentially formalized the status quo: Darlan had already submitted to similar German demands earlier that month in exchange for negotiations on the cost of the Occupation, a relaxation of restrictions at the Demarcation Line and the return of a proportion of POWs.[12] In addition, France agreed to supply material and military goods to German forces in North Africa and permit the Axis powers to use the seaport at Bizerta in Tunisia, the Bizerta-Gabès railway and the port of Dakar in Senegal.[13] A further protocol, concluded with the German ambassador to France Otto Abetz (but not with Berlin), promised a form of political collaboration in the event of a war between France and the Allies.[14] While Germany viewed the agreements from a solely military perspective, Darlan looked to extract political concessions in return: on 14 July, he transmitted his demands to the German embassy in Paris via his Secretary General Jacques Benoist-Méchin: sovereignty over all French territory, the removal of the Occupation costs, the return of POWs and economic aid. He made it clear that French military co-operation depended on political concessions.[15] However, the Protocols ultimately amounted to little. As the situation in the Middle East evolved and Hitler turned his attention to the invasion of the Soviet Union, negotiations with France fell by the wayside. Opposition to the Protocols from within the French camp, not least from Weygand, contributed to the scuppering of the plan. It is even possible – according to Darlan's biographers – that the Admiral, in presenting the 14 July list of concessions that he knew had little chance of success, was committing an act of self-sabotage. Whatever the case, France had come within a whisker of military collaboration with the Third Reich.[16]

Secondly, Hoffman identified 'collaborationism', described as 'openly desired co-operation with and...imitation of the German regime'.[17] Collaborationism took two forms: 'servile' collaborationism entailed satisfying German demands for one's own personal gain; 'ideological' collaborationism appealed to those men and women who desired to transform France in line with Nazism. Supporters of the latter – termed 'collaborationists' – included self-interested journalists, fascist intellectuals and writers, extreme right-wing activists, pacifists and anti-Communist left-wingers. All considered the future of France and Europe to lie in a close partnership with Germany. The collaborationists and their organizations were largely based in Paris where they believed they could better win the ear of the Occupier. Collaborationists were lukewarm in their support for Vichy. They perceived the regime to be a disappointing coterie of old men and reactionaries whose programme was insufficiently radical. However, they maintained links to Pétain's regime and even sought posts in the Marshal's government, the better to radicalize policy.[18]

It is tempting to perceive irreconcilable differences between Vichy's collaborators and Paris's collaborationists, as Bertram M. Gordon does.[19] This was certainly how protagonists desired things. Collaborationists bemoaned Vichy's National Revolution, as '[amounting] to no more than a backward-looking restoration of past values', in comparison with their own more far-reaching plans for a French fascist state.[20] In turn, Vichy's leadership made much of public hostility to the collaborationists, using it to deflect criticism of the regime. We should not exaggerate the differences between the two French positions. Hoffmann identified entanglements between the two principal forms of collaboration. If collaboration d'Etat did not imply sympathy with Nazi goals, it did provide the backdrop against which more radical forms of co-operation developed.[21] Former parliamentarian Marcel Déat (who coined the term 'collaborationist' in November 1940) embodied the connection between both collaborations. Déat spent the summer of 1940 in Vichy, canvassing support for the foundation of a fascist-style single party. When Pétain and Laval rejected the project, Déat left for Paris where he developed a close relationship with Abetz. He bemoaned the conservatism of Vichy while posing his Rassemblement National Populaire (RNP) group as a single party-in-waiting. As German demands intensified and Vichy turned to drastic measures to cling on to power, entanglements between collaboration and collaborationism grew. In March 1944, Déat took up Vichy's ministerial portfolio for Labour and National Solidarity during Laval's second tenure in power. The line between collaboration as a form of accommodation and ideological collaborationism was always blurred.[22] Proponents of both saw close co-operation with Berlin as a means to transform France.

Collaboration with Italy followed economic and military lines. On 22 November 1941, France agreed to the Protocols of Rome, according to which Italy would renounce its claim on French military resources in exchange for a payment of 2.6 billion Francs. The French followed up the agreement – which they interpreted as a 'gesture of goodwill' on their behalf – with further negotiations. Darlan agreed to allow Italian supplies to pass through Bizerta; Italian forces subsequently used these supplies in the campaign against the British in Libya. Vichy kept this agreement a secret from the Germans (in fact, Germany had asked for similar arrangements earlier in the year). Collaboration with Italy thus served a political purpose for France that was absent from it collaboration with Germany: it presented the possibility of driving a wedge between the Axis powers. The supply deal with Italy lasted until March 1942 when Mussolini and Hitler agreed to deny France any further concessions.[23]

In Indochina, Vichy was initially furious that Admiral Decoux had acceded to the Japanese ultimatum in September 1940. Far from France and faced with invasion, Decoux had seen little option other than to grant Japan the use of three air fields and the stationing of 6,000 troops in Tonkin. He also permitted up to 25,000 Japanese troops to pass through the province to reinforce the front into China.[24] Following the Japanese occupation of the whole territory in July 1941, the Darlan-Kato agreement provided for the French defence of the north and the Japanese defence of the south. French authorities were required to protect and resupply Japanese forces and hand over downed Allied aircrew. In return for this form of military collaboration, Japanese authorities were prepared to respect a high degree of French sovereignty. Decoux implemented virtual state control of the economy in order to prevent the wholesale incorporation of Indochina's economy into the Japanese sphere of influence. Japanese pressure meant that he was not altogether successful to this end. On 16 May 1941, the colonial government granted Tokyo preferential status with regard to mining, agricultural and hydraulic products. Further concessions followed: on 12 April 1942, the Occupier requisitioned all French merchant ships stationed in Indochinese waters. This incorporation of the French-Indochinese economy into Japanese designs aided the war effort against the Allied.[25]

In the unoccupied territories of the colonial empire, governors justified the collaboration of the Vichy government in terms familiar to the French mainland: in May 1941, *Servir*, the La Réunion newspaper, claimed that 'unapologetic collaboration' was the only 'path to peace'.[26] However, in territories unthreatened with occupation, Vichy's programme was generally devoid of its collaborationist aspect.[27] Furthermore, Ruth Ginio reminds us that if collaboration was a French response to German colonization, subject populations in the French Empire had long lived under colonial rule. Consequently, 'African responses to Vichy policy should be examined as responses to any other colonial regime would be, without the connotations usually evoked when we hear the words *resistance* and *collaboration* in the context of World War II'.[28] In French West Africa, for example, Vichy allowed the king of the Abron tribe to remain on his throne. The king's son worked with the authorities in the hope that the colonial administration would permit him to succeed his father (tribal tradition prevented this). When French officials denied his wish, the king, likely under the influence of his son, defected to the British Gold Coast.[29] In such territories, the political decision to 'collaborate' with, or 'resist', Vichy rule was informed by local cultures, politics and history that cannot be understood with regard to Euro-centric ideas of resistance and collaboration.[30]

Behaviour described as collaboration thus took a number of forms. French and Germans (and Italians and Japanese) engaged with each other in a variety of circumstances and their interactions ranged from the simplest forms of working relationships to full-blown ideological sympathy. In Europe, Vichy acted in the hope that it could gain something from such a policy and Germany and Italy took advantage of this self-delusion. French leaders' fear of a deterioration in relations further pushed Vichy towards co-operation. In southeast Asia, French policy in Indochina was not entirely disconnected from Vichy's collaboration in Europe. In 1941, for example, Germany bought 20,000 tonnes of Indochinese plantation rubber from Vichy.[31] Decoux also adapted Vichy's rhetoric on collaboration with Germany – that it was a policy necessary to preserve French sovereignty – to his relationship with the Japanese. Yet his primary concern was to preserve the territory from annexation and he did not seek the establishment of a durable collaboration with Tokyo as Vichy did with Berlin.[32] Collaboration in the colonial context was important only in so far as it was dictated by mainland politics. Raw materials extracted from French imperial territories may have found their way into Axis hands yet Vichy's concern was to make the empire work for the National Revolution rather than to supply the Axis war machine.

Working for Germany

From the beginning of the Occupation, Germany appealed for French volunteer labour. With one million French unemployed in October 1940, Nazi propaganda framed work in the Third Reich as a means for men to provide for their family: one poster promised, 'The bad old days are over!' because, 'Daddy is earning money in Germany!' Posters linked war work in the Reich to the male duty to defend France: 'Every hour of work in Germany is a stone delivered to the rampart that protects France'. Women volunteers were eligible to work in Germany, too. Some volunteered in order to earn money for their families; some left to be close to their POW husbands; others were compelled to leave to escape abusive relationships or the shame of unmarried pregnancy. In total, 80,000 French women worked in Germany factories during the Second World War. Overall, by mid-1942, 150,000 French volunteers had left the country to work abroad. Most fulfilled short-term contracts meaning that there were never more than 75,000 French volunteer workers simultaneously on German soil. They worked alongside 250,000 French POWs who had opted to become civilian workers in German factories.[33]

Hundreds of thousands of French worked for Germany in France. The German Todt organization offered paid employment in Wehrmacht-commissioned civil and military engineering projects such as the construction of Atlantic defences on the north and west coasts of France. Todt worked with Vichy's Organization Committee for Building and Public Works to arrange for French construction companies to fill German orders. Todt works were particularly profitable for French business: between 1941 and 1944, building firms raked in 40 billion Francs from Todt contracts.[34] Todt workers received above-average salaries but their living and working conditions were poor. Tantamount to civilian prisoners, they performed back-breaking tasks for twelve hours a day. Desperation prompted some men and women to join up while immigrant workers housed in camps in southern France joined the Todt because the German organization offered better rations than the French authorities. As the war dragged on and the glut of labour turned to a shortage, French police rounded up the unemployed and shipped them to the nearest Todt site. Foreigners and even Jews were pressganged into such work.[35] By the Liberation, the Todt organization employed approximately 250,000 workers in France.[36]

In summer 1942, German labour requirements intensified as the Reich's economy moved to a total war footing. Hitler's Commissar-General for Labour, Fritz Sauckel, oversaw the exploitation of labour in Nazi-occupied territories as the Third Reich ramped up its domestic production. 'German soldiers are shedding their blood, the others must give their labour', Sauckel preached.[37] On 7 May 1942, Sauckel issued a directive to mobilize foreign labour into German factories, by force if necessary.[38] The following month, Berlin demanded 250,000 French workers for the war effort in Germany. In response, Laval – who had returned to Vichy as Head of Government the previous month – negotiated a deal with the Germans: for every three skilled French volunteer workers sent to Germany, one French prisoner of war would be returned home. This scheme was called the 'Relève'. Laval hoped to send 400,000 men to work in German factories, of whom 150,000 would be skilled workers. The response to the Relève was disappointing and only 35,000 workers had volunteered to leave France by autumn 1942.[39]

Fearing the forcible requisition of workers, and ever keen to maintain control of French affairs, Laval promulgated the law of 4 September 1942 that rendered all men aged between eighteen and fifty eligible for work wherever the state directed them. This was not the first time that Vichy had forced men and women into work. Internees in Vichy's camps had long served as forced labour while colonial POWs in the Frontstalags worked in armaments factories in violation of the Geneva Convention.[40] Yet the law of September 1942 for the first time targeted ordinary citizens. Still, France could not keep up with German demands especially when Sauckel demanded a further 250,000 labourers, half of whom would have to depart France by April 1943. Consequently, on 16 February 1943, Vichy introduced the STO, a programme that amounted to the forced labour of French in Germany. All men aged between twenty and twenty-two were enlisted in the STO. The age range was later broadened to sixteen to sixty years of age for men; women aged twenty-one to thirty-five were recruited after August 1943. Labour service was for a period of two years.

The STO was deeply unpopular with the public and train stations saw protests as workers departed. Many French refused to comply with the scheme. Réfractaires (objectors) could escape service in a number of ways. Some presented false exemption papers or were passed unfit for work by complicit doctors. University leaders declined to hand over student lists. Resistance groups stole and destroyed registration papers. Employers who were themselves short of labour protected workers from deportation to Germany. In total, as many as 45 per cent of all men eligible were réfractaires and evasion rates were as high as 99 per cent in some departments. Such large-scale opposition ensured that Vichy could not fulfil German labour quotas. Between April 1943 and October 1943, only 180,000 workers left for Germany, while 60,000 remained to work for the war effort in France. In September 1943, Laval even suggested the use of French Jewish labour to meet Nazi targets.[41] On 15 January 1944, Sauckel demanded another one million workers; by April, the STO had recruited only 20,000 more French and the scheme was suspended two months later.[42] By the end of the war, there were approximately 660,000 French workers in Germany. This figure fell far short of the some 2 million that Germany had required through successive quotas. A further 723,000 French worked in France in factories reserved for German production (the so-called S-Betriebe).[43] Thanks to years of poor rations, these men and women were often in an unfit state to perform the heavy labour required of them: 75 per cent of twenty-year-olds who fulfilled their STO were found to be underweight.[44]

Politics, money, hardship and desperation motivated the French who volunteered to work for Germany. Vichy's policy of collaboration saw it use the forced labour of its own citizens as a bargaining chip in negotiations with

Germany while French business made huge profits from the sweat of virtual slave labour. Of course, the Third Reich enrolled labour, both voluntary and involuntary, in all regions of Occupied Europe. The greatest proportion of workers came from the conquered territories of Eastern Europe: the Soviet Union and Poland provided 3.35 million workers, amounting to 51.1 per cent of all foreign civilian workers in the Third Reich. In the West, France supplied 1.05 million men and women or 12.5 per cent of the total number of German wartime foreign workers.[45] Vichy was not the only semi-independent government in Western Europe to supply labour to German industry. A total of 100,000 Danes volunteered to work in Germany while a similar number worked on sea defences on the west coast of Jutland. This represented a significant segment of the 4-million strong Danish population.[46] Nevertheless the result of Vichy's policy to French labour in addition to German demands meant that France provided the Third Reich with the largest pool of skilled workers in Europe.[47]

Sex with the Occupier

In the early months of the Occupation, the public attitude to the Germans was ambiguous. Jean Texcier's celebrated resistance pamphlet *Advice for an Occupied Population*, produced in summer 1940, suggested that the French did not yet know how to respond to the Occupier: 'Street hawkers offer [German soldiers] maps of Paris and phrasebooks; coaches unload them in waves in front of Notre Dame and the Panthéon; there isn't one without a camera to his eye. However, be under no illusion: THEY ARE NOT TOURISTS'. Yet cohabitation was unavoidable. In some cases, this cohabitation was literal: German troops were billeted with French families in the North. Relations with the Germans required a careful balancing act. To refuse to engage with the Occupier could put one's livelihood, not to mention one's life, at risk. To fraternize with soldiers was likewise risky for it drew allegations of treachery. Faced with the dangers and deprivations of the Occupation, many French simply decided to 'muddle through' until the war was over.

The Marshal's speech on collaboration in the wake of Montoire in October 1940 inspired both hope and anxiety. Few French were immediately repelled at the prospect of collaboration yet we should not mistake this stance for positive support. Burrin estimates that during the highpoint of collaboration (July 1940 and November 1942), only 20 per cent of all French were well disposed to the policy. Most people viewed collaboration as an expedient measure, a means by which France could survive at a time when an Allied victory was far from assured. As one prefect summarized in November 1941: 'On the whole, public opinion finds this policy repugnant; it will submit to it if forced to, considering it as a strictly provisional solution designed to play for time, to alleviate the weight of the occupation and to obtain a number of immediate advantages... but it will continue to hope for an Anglo-American victory.'[48] Whether we understand this decision as indifference, apathy or stoic defiance, to judge it as 'collaboration' is harsh indeed. On the subject of billeting, Burrin writes that '[i]n general, both sides coped by making mutual adjustments, being anxious to cohabit with as little tension as possible'; we might extend this description to the behaviour of the French population at large.[49]

Public disapproval of collaboration was rarely stronger than in the case of so-called 'horizontal collaboration', that is, sexual relations between French women and German soldiers. For the French, the sight of local women consorting with German troops spoke to underlying feelings of humiliation and sexual impotence.[50] In fact, Franco-German relations were often depicted using sexualized rhetoric.[51] Such understandings could be literal: the Kreiskommandant of Chinon informed a French official, 'We are the victors! You have been beaten! The women, even the children, of your country are no longer yours! Our soldiers have the right to have fun, and if you do anything to slight the honour of the German army you will be arrested'.[52] Berlin read local attitudes to fraternization between women and its soldiers as an indicator of attitudes to the Occupation more generally. Such matters were discussed at the highest political level in occupied territories.[53] As for the French, a deeper sexual symbolism was read into the relationships

Figure 11 *The inauguration of an anti-Bolshevik exhibition at the Salle Wagram in Paris, c. March 1942. Photo by Roger Viollet Collection/Getty Images.*

between French women and German soldiers, with the female body itself understood as a 'combat zone' in which the honour of France was at stake. For a Frenchwoman to have sex with a German represented a challenge to the French male's 'ownership' of female sexuality. Vichy attempted to curb such relations, for example, introducing special penalties for the wives of POWs who slept with Germans for love or money.[54]

It is difficult to determine the number of French women who engaged in sexual relations with Occupation troops. The problem was that French women encountered Germans in a variety of contexts. They worked for German employers as cleaners, hotel maids and housekeepers and they served German troops in cafes, shops, restaurants and bars. In some cases, love affairs developed and it is unlikely that many women perceived any ideological content to their trysts. Burrin suggests a figure in the 'several tens of thousands' as a minimum.[55] Richard Vinen claims that as many as 200,000 children in France had German fathers.[56] French women were not alone in bearing children to Occupation troops. In the Netherlands, Germans fathered up to 16,000 babies; in Norway, up to 12,000; and in Denmark, approximately 7,500. Only in the territories of Eastern Europe and the Soviet Union did the Occupier forbid its troops from fraternizing with local women (though many soldiers ignored this ban).[57] As Vichy fell from power in summer 1944, angry mobs attacked 'horizontal collaborators', shearing the hair from their heads and parading them semi-naked through the street in a symbolic re-establishment of French male power.[58] This punishment, however, was not unique to the period of the Liberation. During August and September 1941, the Vichy authorities in North Africa shaved the heads of women who enjoyed close relations with German soldiers.[59] A father in Chambéry shaved half the head of his sixteen-year-old daughter for consorting with Germans. Deported for his action, he later died in Mauthausen.[60] Sex with German soldiers did not threaten the security of France. However, at a time when people considered the fidelity of Frenchwomen as intimately connected to the integrity of the nation, 'horizontal collaboration' took on a symbolic meaning that far outweighed its actual significance.[61]

Despite its moralizing discourse on the sex lives of French women, the Etat Français tolerated prostitution. On the one hand, this toleration stemmed from the recognition that, with thousands of German soldiers on French soil, the resort to prostitutes was unavoidable. Vichy thus strove to monitor and regulate sex work: on 24 December 1940, a decree gave official recognition to brothels while introducing more frequent sexual health checks for the prostitutes who worked within them. Vichy did not regard female sex workers as 'real' women. The regime focused its attention on homemakers and mothers; it considered sex workers to be neither.[62] Ordinary citizens were likewise generally indifferent to sex between soldiers and prostitutes.

The Occupier was very concerned with French prostitution. The military authorities feared the spread of sexually transmitted disease and infections amongst troops. As a result, the Germans requisitioned twenty-nine brothels in Paris for the exclusive use of the Wehrmacht. Strict rules within these establishments prohibited the employment of Jewish women or women of colour. Soldiers were required to wear condoms and prostitutes submitted to regular medical checks. In spite of German efforts to regulate the sexual activity of its soldiers, unauthorized prostitution continued and as many as 100,000 'streetwalkers' operated in the capital. It is doubtful that an ideological commitment to collaboration motivated these women. Financial misery and the attraction of soldiers who possessed overvalued currency prompted women to take up sex work.[63]

The sex lives of French males received considerably less attention. In Germany, French POWs who conducted affairs with local women were liable to several years' imprisonment under German law; they were not subject to legal sanction from the French authorities.[64] Returning male POWs who had had relationships with German women were not victimized as were the women who had sex with German soldiers in France.[65] Homosexual sex between French and German men was not understood in the same way as heterosexual relations. Some contemporaries claimed that there was a preponderance of homosexuals amongst those French who supported collaboration. The centrality of virility to resistance propaganda helped to cement the association between collaboration and femininity.[66] While it is true that a number of homosexual writers and intellectuals favoured co-operation with Germany, there is nothing to suggest that their sexuality predisposed them to such politics.[67] In any case, neither Vichy nor the public at large considered homosexual sex to be an act of collaboration.

Collaborationism

Advocates of collaborationism – the collaborationists – desired to go beyond Vichy's working relationship with Germany and establish a Nazi-style regime in France. They perceived Vichy to be a bastion of conservatism that was unwilling to buy into Hitler's ideological project for the new Europe. The Occupier exploited this apparent conflict, brandishing the Paris collaborationists as a 'government-in-waiting' when it needed to bring pressure to bear on the French State.[68] Roger Bourderon has called this 'intervention by the roundabout way' in French affairs.[69] However, Berlin did not truly wish to see a fascist government installed in power because such a regime could pose a nationalist challenge to the German authorities. In August 1940, Abetz made it clear to his subordinates that France was to be 'kept in a condition of internal weakness... [and] estranged from foreign powers hostile to the Reich... Everything must be done on the German side to promote the weakness and internal disunity of France... only those forces likely to create discord should be supported; sometimes these will be elements of the Left, sometimes of the Right.'[70] Ostensible German support for the collaborationists thus masked an agenda to divide and rule the French fascists.

In reality, the worlds of Vichy and collaborationism were not entirely estranged. Denis Peschanksi believes it is wrong to reserve the collaborationist label solely for the Parisian extremists.[71] Common enemies, especially Jews and communists, united the men of Vichy and Paris and advocates of collaborationism held important posts in several governments. Marion, who took charge of Vichy's propaganda from August 1941 until the demise of the regime was a 'convinced collaborationist'.[72] In November 1941, he and Pierre Pucheu – at the time Vichy's Interior Minister – opened the ranks of the Légion to non-veterans in order to move the organization in a more radical direction.[73] Furthermore, collaborationists ostensibly held Pétain in high regard and they refrained from attacking the Marshal publicly. They celebrated the National Revolution as the means by which to transform France (though they urged Pétain to go further with his reforms). Rather, collaborationists reserved their ire for the Marshal's ministers and advisors whom they believed responsible for the slow pace of Vichy's revolution. Déat blamed the 'anonymous clique' and 'intriguers without mandate', around Pétain while Jacques Doriot, leader of the collaborationist Parti Populaire Français (PPF), condemned the 'gangsters' and 'pimps' in government.[74]

The political origins of the collaborationists were diverse. Men such as Eugène Deloncle (leader of the Mouvement Social Révolutionnaire, MSR) were veterans of the interwar extreme right. Likewise Marcel Bucard revived his fascist Francistes league of the 1930s. The team at collaborationist newspaper *Je suis partout* firmly identified with fascism. The editorial board, amongst whom where intellectuals Robert Brasillach and Lucien Rebatet, claimed to be fascists 'of the first hour' and not alleged opportunistic converts like their rivals. After 1943, the newspaper committed fully to Nazism, with Rebatet declaring, 'Death to Jews! Long live the National-Socialist Revolution! Long live France!'[75] Conversely, formerly intransigent right-wing enemies of French democracy rejected collaborationism. Charles Maurras, whose integral nationalism influenced a generation of thinkers on the French right, did not stray into explicit sympathy for Nazism even if Samuel Osgood places him 'on the side of the German hangmen and their French flunkeys'.[76] Likewise, Colonel de La Rocque, leader of the Parti Social Français (PSF, France's largest extreme right-wing party during the 1930s) lent his support to Vichy but not the Occupier. The Colonel eventually established a resistance network.[77]

Collaborationism emerged from some seemingly unlikely sources. A number of left-wingers threw their lot in with the Occupier in groups such as Marcel Gitton's Parti Ouvrier et Paysan Français and in the publishing teams behind newspapers *La France socialiste* and *Le Rouge et le Bleu*.[78] Most famously, Déat was a former socialist whose pacifism ultimately led him to oppose war with Hitler. Meanwhile, some anti-colonial nationalists saw in Nazism not only a means to win independence from France but also a model for a future independent state. Vietnamese nationalists Đỗ Đức Ho and Nguyễn Thượng Khóa nurtured political relations with Germany and Japan to further their own fight against French colonialism. Đỗ Đức Ho founded the Maison Amicale Interasiatique in Paris to foster good relations between France's Japanese and Vietnamese communities, notably through the work of the Tokyo-sponsored Société des Amis de Japon. Vietnamese collaborationism subsequently led to the formation of a Vietnamese Wehrmacht battalion in June 1944, based at Enghien-les-Bains, north of Paris.[79]

Henri Michel called the collaborationists, 'strange, swarming, often corrupt...always rageful and swaggering. They were few [yet] they spoke, they wrote, they acted as if they were the whole of Paris'.[80] As many as 250,000 French belonged to a collaborationist movement during the Occupation.[81] Sympathy for collaborationism reached beyond the confines of the parties and leagues: up to 300,000 French read the fervently collaborationist *Je suis partout*.[82] Unity proved elusive for the collaborationist movement. The only tangible agreement between like-minded groups was a pact between Doriot and Pierre Constantini's Ligue Française d'Épuration, d'Entraide Social et de Collaboration Européenne agreed on 2 September 1941.[83] Divisions between collaborationist groups stemmed from political and personal rivalries. Yet, common to these men and their followers was the idea that only a 'fascist' single party could link the fascist state with the people. Each strove to position their own formation as the only party capable of remaking France in the National Socialist mould.

The two most significant collaborationist parties were Déat's RNP and Doriot's PPF. During the interwar years, Déat had risen to the upper echelons of the Socialist Party. He broke with the party in 1933 and founded the 'neo-socialist' Parti socialiste de France-Union Jean Jaurès; its programme proposed the establishment of a technocratic and authoritarian state within a new European economic order.[84] Déat was at the forefront of the left-wing pacifist movement and when Hitler threatened Poland in spring 1939 he famously argued that the French should not 'die for Danzig'.[85] In the early months of the Occupation, Déat devoted his time to a project to establish a single party in the style of foreign fascist regimes. Pétain, long suspicious of political parties, ultimately rejected the idea in favour of the Légion. A furious Déat left Vichy for Paris where in November 1940 he declared himself a 'collaborationist'. This was a deliberate attempt to distinguish himself from what he perceived to be the Etat Français's rather tepid collaboration.[86] He did not leave behind completely the idea of a single party at Vichy, writing thirty articles on the subject between 18 July 1942 and 4 September 1942 alone.[87]

In February 1941, Déat founded the RNP. He intended to use the party both to pressure Vichy into appointing him a minister and to prove to the Occupier that political collaboration with France was possible. RNP propaganda portrayed Hitler as a socialist with whom a corporatist and authoritarian France could construct a new European political and economic order.[88] The RNP benefitted significantly from the support of Abetz who perceived in left-wing collaborationism a means to mobilize mass support behind co-operation with Germany.[89] The party was, however, a broad church and it united several different tendencies within the collaborationist milieu from fascists to left-wing pacifists.[90] The diverse composition of the party reflected Déat's desire to unite left- and right-wing strands of collaborationism into a single group. The RNP likewise reached out to diverse sectors of French society, establishing affiliated groups such as a labour section for the working class and a paramilitary wing, the Légion National Populaire.[91] At its zenith in mid-1941, the RNP had approximately 20,000 members across its various sections and affiliates. It struggled to grow thereafter, failing to increase its membership substantially even after Laval's authorization of the party in the South in April 1942.[92]

Like Déat, Doriot began his political career on the left. During the 1920s, he was a leading light of the French Communist Party, both an accomplished public speaker – 'unbeatable on the stage' with a 'powerful and consummate oratorical style' – and a fearless street fighter. These qualities saw Doriot rise to the leadership of the communist youth wing during the 1920s.[93] However, in 1934 he was expelled from the Communist Party for advocating co-operation with the socialists to halt the rise of fascism in France. This stance conflicted with that of Moscow (though Stalin would later adopt this 'Popular Front' strategy). Doriot founded the PPF in 1936 as a working-class alternative to the Communist Party. Political setbacks for the PPF, combined with a fierce hatred of his former comrades, saw Doriot turn to fascism and anti-Semitism after 1937.[94]

Doriot was initially close to Vichy. Pétain granted the PPF licence to operate in the Southern Zone. Doriot hoped to use the favour he enjoyed with the Marshal to impose his own politics onto the regime and position the PPF as a single party. He encountered greater difficulties in the Occupied Zone. Abetz preferred to work with Déat and it was only in April 1941 that the PPF was authorized to operate in the North. Such complications prompted Doriot to shift further towards collaborationism in an attempt to win favour with Germany and circumvent Abetz. The PPF subsequently worked closely with German intelligence (the Abwehr) and the Nazi Propaganda Abteilung while the SD reportedly funded the party to the order of 250,000 Francs per month. In return, party activists hunted down Jews, resisters and STO réfractaires.[95] In contrast to the RNP, the PPF was able to take advantage of its networks, established in the late 1930s, to pursue its politics in both zones. In January 1941, German sources estimated that 30,000 French belonged to the party. In August 1941, the French police revised down these estimates: the PPF had 4,000 members in the Occupied Zone and 6,000 members in the Unoccupied Zone. However,

Figure 12 *A PPF rally at the Vélodrome d'Hiver in Paris, in August 1943. Photo by LAPI/Roger Viollett/Getty Images.*

estimates of the party's membership provide only a partial picture. By 1944, the PPF's newspaper, the *Cri du Peuple*, enjoyed a circulation of over 100,000 readers.[96]

Doriot believed that a German victory was the key to future French prosperity and the defeat of international communism. On 25 May 1941, the PPF congress in the Northern Zone saw the party's leader urge France to give its adhesion to the Nazi New Order.[97] The following month, the German attack on the Soviet Union gave Doriot the opportunity to prove his commitment to Hitler's cause and he left France to fight with the Wehrmacht.[98] However, from the German point of view Doriot's loyalty to Germany mattered less than the disorder and disadvantages that bringing him to power would bring.[99] The party's pretensions to power worried the government at Vichy, too. Pucheu subsequently banned the movement in the South and Doriot cut his ties with the Etat Français.[100] With his options increasingly limited at home, Doriot did several tours of duty on the Eastern Front.

Déat and Doriot's competition to win favour with Germany pushed each man towards collaborationism. Déat's position as Abetz's preferred contact in the collaborationist milieu reinforced the Frenchman's commitment to Germany. In January 1942, he spoke for the first time of a 'totalitarian' regime for a future France. In spring 1943, the RNP was transformed into a fascist-style party; Déat was, according to Burrin, well on his way 'Nazification' by the end of the year.[101] Doriot's frustrations in the North saw him establish links with several Nazi authorities and voice publicly his commitment to the New Order. He wanted the tools to eliminate communism and establish an authoritarian government. With the fight against communists and Jews to the fore of its politics, the PPF was a natural pole for collaborationists of the extreme right.[102] There *were* differences between the RNP and the PPF's attitude to collaborationism. Déat was an uncomfortable leader who was willing to accept France as a junior partner in Hitler's Europe. Doriot wanted to lead France and was prepared to use his troops in street violence when necessary. Nevertheless, Nazism represented the means for both men to achieve their goals.[103]

Fighting for Hitler

A handful of French expressed their commitment to Germany through armed service. Firstly, the Wehrmacht and the Waffen-SS accepted French recruits. In July 1943, the Sturmbrigade Frankreich was founded as a unit of the Waffen-SS; within six months it had recruited 2,480 fighters.[104] Jean Loustau, member of the Action Française and journalist at *Je suis partout*, joined the Waffen-SS and won the Iron Cross while on the Eastern Front. Loustau later returned to France to fight invading Allied forces in June 1944.[105] Loustau was not representative of the intellectual collaborationist milieu. The most fervent ideologues – Brasillach, Drieu La Rochelle, Rebatet – preferred the pen to the sword. Secondly, Frenchmen could volunteer to fight in the Légion des Volontaires Français contre le Bolchevisme (LVF). The LVF was founded shortly after Hitler's invasion of the Soviet Union in 1941 and it marked a rare moment of consensus amongst collaborationists. A range of groups declared their support for the LVF, including the RNP, the PPF, the MSR, the Francistes and the Parti National Collectiviste. At the summit of the associations, Deloncle presided over a team of collaborationist leaders on a central committee. An additional 'Committee of Honour' included prominent political, intellectual and religious personalities. Cardinal Baudrillart stated publicly that the soldiers of the LVF were 'the Crusaders of the twentieth century...helping to prepare the great French renaissance'. LVF propaganda likewise stressed the link between the modern struggle against Bolshevism and the medieval Christian crusades. The first volunteers were deployed in Poland during October 1941.[106]

For its supporters, the LVF offered a means to cement Franco-German co-operation through shared endeavour on the battlefield. At a ceremony in Paris to honour the LVF's first volunteers in February 1942, Déat told the audience, 'this war is Europe's war. Europe is forging its unity and conquering its independence on the battlefields. France is still wretchedly hesitant and divided, still unable to break with the past. Fortunately, an elite of men answered history's call and threw themselves into battle in the name of France'. Doriot – the LVF's most famous volunteer – spoke at the ceremony, too. Fresh from his first tour of duty, he recounted proudly his experience: 'the tricolour flag, thanks to the volunteers [of the LVF], has flown alongside the German colours...We are engaged in a battle that we cannot afford to lose. We must win or be destroyed'.[107] The rank-and-file of the collaborationist movements did not share the enthusiasm of a Déat or a Doriot for the LVF. After two years, only 12,000 men had enrolled; this figure was several thousand short of the number that Abetz had wanted. Less than half of these men were declared fit for service.[108] Vichy forbade recruitment in the South though Pétain's position on the group was ambiguous; in January 1943, Laval recognized the group and appointed de Brinon head of its central committee. The response in North Africa was disappointing with only 800 men joining by the end of 1942.[109] Those recruits who made the grade were not all French Nazis. The German authorities believed that up to 60 per cent of volunteers held little ideological commitment to collaboration. Rather, unemployment and difficult personal circumstances had led them to join.[110] The soldiers of the LVF were a mix of political idealists, romantic adventurers – some of whom looked forward to having their sexual needs satisfied by grateful women liberated from Bolshevism – and those who saw the posting simply as a 'meal ticket'.[111]

Figure 13 *Collaborationist Philippe Henriot sees off a contingent of LVF volunteers in June 1944. The graffiti on the train carriage reads 'Long Live Doriot', 'Long Live the Legion', 'Long Live Henriot' and 'Long Live France'. Photo by Photo 12/ UIG/Getty Images.*

In sum, up to 40,000 French volunteered to fight in the Wehrmacht, the Waffen-SS or the LVF during the Second World War. France was not alone in providing soldiers for the Third Reich: 6,000 Danes, for example, volunteered to serve on the Eastern Front with the Waffen-SS.[112] Twelve thousand French saw combat while 10,000 served in units behind the frontlines. The remainder of the volunteers lacked the requisite physical fitness for service. By November 1944, the 7,600 French soldiers remaining in German uniform were amalgamated into the 33rd SS Charlemagne division. Ninety of these men fought to the bitter end of the Third Reich in Berlin, days after Hitler's suicide.[113]

Conclusion

Collaboration during the Second World War comprised a variety of behaviours and motivations. With regard to the collaboration between the Etat Français and the Occupier, we must distinguish between collaboration as cohabitation or accommodation, and collaboration as a matter of policy. Some form of cohabitation was inevitable given the presence of German military and security forces in France. A working relationship was essential in order to maintain the continued operation of the French government and its public services. This form of collaboration was not necessarily neutral from a political point of view. When, for example, French police arrested 'enemies' such as Jews and communists, they did so in the name of both professional service and the ideological goals of Vichy and Nazi Germany. Cohabitation and accommodation could therefore entail acts that served political ends.

Collaboration as foreign policy amounted to subservience to Germany. Vichy persistently sought a permanent peace treaty with Berlin. Progress towards this goal (or lack thereof) decided the fate of several governments. Advocates of collaboration hoped that a willingness to co-operate with, and concede to, German demands would bring concessions in return. Hitler was interested in France only as far as the country could fund and supply his broader war aims; a normalization of relations between the two countries was not on the Nazis' agenda. Collaboration thus implicated Vichy in German war crimes while achieving little tangible result for the French.

The French public's attitude to collaboration depended greatly on the context of the war and the likely success of the policy. Vichy's surveillance of the postal service revealed fluctuations in public backing for collaboration. During 1 September 1941–10 October 1941, between 20 and 30 per cent of letters that referred to collaboration approved of the policy. As the German campaign in the Soviet Union gathered pace during November–December 1941, approval evidenced in personal correspondence rose as high as 35 per cent. From early 1942, enthusiasm declined to as low as 11 per cent. Prefectural and police reports confirmed this downward trend.[114]

Attitudes to daily forms of 'collaboration' were more complex. Female relations with the Occupier were interpreted according to understandings of sexual honour. Thus, prostitutes sold their bodies with little fear of reprisals while French women with German lovers took great risks to their personal safety.[115]

The policy of collaboration provided the context in which collaborationism developed. There were certainly fascist sympathizers at Vichy who desired that the regime take a more radical approach to the National Revolution. Yet men such as Pétain and Laval were not Nazis even if their conciliatory policies towards Germany provided a legitimizing context for closer engagement. The beating heart of collaborationism was in Paris. Collaborationists such as Déat and Doriot hoped to force Vichy into ideological alignment with Berlin. The RNP and the PPF aimed to connect the people with the regime in the style of a fascist single party. Personal jealousies and political competition divided the collaborationist movement, limiting its effectiveness. This situation satisfied the Occupier who was content to use the collaborationists as a stick with which to beat Vichy yet who did not desire to see a French fascist government in power. The political importance of the collaborationist parties surpassed their numerical significance.

4

Resistance

On 18 June 1940, a little-known general named Charles de Gaulle broadcast to the French from the BBC in London. His speech was 'jerky and peremptory' but his tone was reassuring and defiant: 'the cause of France is not lost... the flame of French resistance must not and shall not die'.[1] De Gaulle claimed that with its Empire, its alliance with Great Britain and the support of the United States, France could win the war. He urged his fellow countrymen to join him in London to continue the fight.[2] This speech, known as the 'Appel du 18 juin' (Appeal of the 18 June), assumed huge symbolic significance; De Gaulle cited it as the beginning of 'La France Libre' or 'Free France', his movement to liberate the French from Nazi subjugation. Yet until D-Day in June 1944, Free French resistance operated largely beyond the borders of France and only 400 of de Gaulle's agents dropped into the country between June 1940 and June 1944.[3] The Free French offered a form of resistance *external* to the mainland.

Within France, there was not one resistance but many. Two types of organized group existed. Resistance *movements* attempted to mobilize public opinion against the Occupier through the means of propaganda and direct action. Resistance *networks* gathered intelligence on, and undertook operations against, the enemy in conjunction with Allied secret services. Movements and networks represented a broad spectrum of political opinion from the extreme left to the extreme right yet all desired to see the German Occupier evicted from France. Their attitudes to the Vichy regime were more complicated. While a hostility to the Etat Français characterized many movements and networks, some maintained a cautious respect for Pétain and his National Revolution, even working for the regime itself. The means of opposition also divided resisters. After the invasion of the Soviet Union in June 1941, communist groups mounted violent attacks on German troops and officers. This tactic drew severe reprisals against French civilians. Other resistance groups proceeded more cautiously, preferring to try and persuade the public with propaganda. Resistance was also a fractured phenomenon, a fact that stemmed from the conditions under which early resisters operated. Secrecy was paramount, with information and recruitment restricted to a small number of activists. Movements and networks necessarily worked in isolation from each other. Only during 1943 did the resistance groups begin to co-ordinate their struggle in conjunction with each other and with the Free French yet they still maintained their individual structures. It is therefore important to recognize that resistance was never the work of a single and disciplined entity.[4] Besides the activities of organized movements and networks, there were thousands of individual acts of defiance from ordinary French. These acts, many of which went unrecorded, were of little military significance yet they formed part of the moral fight against the Occupation.

Resistance was a global phenomenon. Until mid-1943, de Gaulle's most significant source of legitimacy and power lay in French Equatorial Africa and Cameroon. These territories declared their loyalty to the Free French in August 1940; the first street named after the General appeared that year in Yaoundé, Cameroon. On 27 October 1940 – three days after Pétain shook Hitler's hand at Montoire – de Gaulle established the Conseil de Défense de l'Empire (Empire Defence Council) in French Equatorial Africa. From this base, he issued a manifesto in which he declared, 'Millions of French people, of French subjects have decided to continue the war until liberation...I shall exercise my powers in the name of France...I call to war, that is to say to combat or to sacrifice, all the men and all the women of the French territories which have rallied to me'.[5] If in June 1940, de Gaulle had called a handful of French to resistance from London, four months later from Brazzaville he urged millions to go to war. Resistance, inspired by de Gaulle and drawing on local histories of dissent, developed throughout the overseas possessions: in the Antilles, for example, the memory of slavery on the islands informed reactions to Vichy's authoritarianism.[6] To 'de-centre' our understanding of resistance from its traditionally Eurocentric focus is to appreciate the scale of the worldwide battle to free France.[7]

This chapter examines the histories of the Free French and the internal resistance movements from July 1940 until the foundation of the Comité Français de Libération Nationale (French National Liberation Committee, CFLN) – de Gaulle's de facto provisional government – in June 1943. It describes and explains the major features of the resistance while taking into account not only the diversity of the fight against Vichy and the Nazis but also the diversity of the fighters themselves. The dominant post-war story of the resistance as a (male) military endeavour left little room for women. Likewise, the emphasis on the *Frenchness* of resisters ignored the contribution of foreigners and colonial peoples to the struggle.[8] We know now that women and non-French people had a significant involvement in the resistance. According to Olivier Wieviorka, given the social and political obstacles to women's participation in public life, '[i]t is not women's under involvement but rather their overinvolvement [in the Resistance] that should be stressed'.[9] Furthermore, almost half of the estimated 73,000 Free French members were neither French nationals nor citizens. There were approximately 3,800 non-French Europeans and 30,000 colonial subjects in de Gaulle's movement while thousands more around the world supported the Free French morally and financially.[10] Just as Vichy's project to remake France echoed around the world, the struggle to liberate France likewise assumed global dimensions.

De Gaulle and the Free French

In the historiography of the French who fought to free their country, the Free French have received relatively short shrift in comparison with resisters based within France itself. Jean-François Murraciole describes de Gaulle's followers as the 'other resistance', and claims that historians have largely ignored these fighters (if not the organization itself) in their work on France and the Second World War.[11] Free France and its 'Free French Forces' (Forces Françaises Libres or FFL) were the political and military organizations under the command of de Gaulle (Free France was renamed 'Fighting France' or 'La France Combattante' in July 1942). De Gaulle was born in Lille in November 1890. He attended the French officer academy at Saint-Cyr, passing out in 1912 and subsequently assuming the rank of a sous-lieutenant under Colonel Philippe Pétain's command. De Gaulle served as a captain during the First World War. He was wounded three times and taken prisoner on 2 March 1916 at Douaumont. After the war, de Gaulle benefitted from the patronage of Pétain (now a Marshal) and rose quickly through the ranks. A brief period spent at the General Secretariat of National Defence during 1931 allowed him to reflect upon modern military doctrine and he authored several books on the topic. In particular, his 1934 *Vers l'armée de métier* recommended the maintenance of a professional standing army and the use of armour and tanks in modern warfare. During the battle of France in 1940, he saw combat at Montcornet before Reynaud called him into government as Under-Secretary of State for National Defence and War. Upon hearing of Reynaud's decision to resign on 16 June – a move that favoured the defeatist faction in government – de Gaulle took a plane to London. He did not return to mainland France until 14 June 1944.[12]

The response to de Gaulle's Appel du 18 juin was disappointing. De Gaulle was not widely known in France. Even amongst those men and women who joined the Free French in 1940, 88 per cent claimed that they had not heard of the General prior to joining his movement.[13] With the Germans in a seemingly unassailable position, de Gaulle's speech from London drew derision from some French: Agnès Humbert's neighbour dismissed the General as a 'crackpot'.[14] In any case, the broadcast reached few French. Léon Werth only heard the speech for the first time when the BBC rebroadcast the appeal on 18 June *1944*. Werth recalled that in 1940, with millions in France on the move, the '[n]oise of the road and incoherent snatches of false news items were all that came to me, through a poor radio connected to a car battery. So on June 18, 1940, I did not hear de Gaulle'.[15] By September 1940, de Gaulle had attracted only about 2,000 people from France to his English base. As Jackson writes, 'there was no one of any importance [with de Gaulle in London]...no prefects or ambassadors, no academicians or professors, no top civil servants or politicians'.[16] The majority of French men in Britain with military experience – soldiers, sailors and pilots evacuated from France – preferred to return home; of the 1,600 French housed at a makeshift camp at the White City stadium in London, only 152 chose to remain in England.[17] By autumn 1940, the London-based Free French were small in number with only about 7,200 having rallied to the cause.[18]

De Gaulle's position of weakness was *relative*, not absolute. On 28 June 1940, British Prime Minister Winston Churchill recognized de Gaulle as leader of all French who opposed the Occupation. On 7 August, London granted financial and military support to the movement. There were

Figure 14 *De Gaulle in Carthage, Tunisia, 1943. General de Gaulle, accompanied by General Mast, saluting as the band plays the Marseillaise outside the summer palace of the Bey of Tunis. Photo in the public domain (Wikimedia Commons).*

many moments of tension in the Franco-Allied alliance. De Gaulle bridled at his exclusion from Allied military planning. When on 8 November 1942 he received news of the Allied landings in North Africa, he raged, 'I hope the Vichy people throw them back into the sea'.[19] The General's perceived arrogance rankled the British. At the Casablanca conference in January 1943, tempers were lost: 'If you get in my way, I will liquidate you!' Churchill famously thundered in broken French at the General. American President Roosevelt harboured a legendary dislike of de Gaulle for he feared that the Frenchman nurtured dictatorial desires. Roosevelt instead preferred General Henri Giraud, an officer famous for having escaped from a German prison in spring 1942.[20] The United States manoeuvred to appoint Giraud as the representative of the French after the invasion of North Africa in November 1942. Meanwhile, American military planners intended to maintain an occupation force in France after its liberation until free elections could be held, heading off any pretensions to power that de Gaulle may have had.[21]

The military weakness of the Free French was exposed in September 1940. On 23 September, an Anglo-French force attacked Dakar, the port-capital of French West Africa. De Gaulle hoped to depose Governor-General and Vichy loyalist Boisson and make Dakar the capital of the Free French Empire.[22] A combined force of French soldiers and Royal Marines expected little resistance as they set sail for western Africa from Liverpool. However, forces loyal to Vichy successfully defended the city and Pétain's regime exploited the victory in its propaganda. The embarrassing failure seemed to confirm the impotence of the nascent Free French movement; the Allies did not consult de Gaulle again in military matters regarding France. The Dakar debacle further undermined Free French recruitment efforts. Until November 1942, the FFL struggled to win followers to its cause; in the year between October 1941 and September 1942, only 2,500 members were recruited.[23] De Gaulle seized upon small victories, such as the FFL defeat of Rommel's forces at Bir Hakeim in June 1942, yet his celebration of this battle as 'one of the finest pages of glory' for France served only to underline that such successes were rare.[24]

The Free French possessed a navy and an air force. In June 1940, de Gaulle had eight submarines at his disposal. The *Narval* had escaped France and docked at Malta while seven others were docked in British ports and shipyards at the time of the surrender. The submarines took part in operations in the Atlantic, the Mediterranean and the waters off the coast of Norway. The Free French Air Force (Forces Aériennes Françaises Libres or FAFL) was likewise small. De Gaulle allowed French pilots to fight in the Battle of Britain but their contribution was relatively minor: only thirteen French pilots flew. By mid-1943 the FAFL could call upon approximately 500 pilots; nearly half of these men died in combat operations. In total, Free French pilots downed 213 enemy planes during 1940–1945.[25]

Figure 15 *Charles de Gaulle, leader of the French Free Forces, inspects French colonial troops during his visit to a military base in Great Britain on 24 January, 1941. Photo by AFP/Getty Images.*

Clandestine warfare within France offered another course of action for the Free French. Under André Dewavrin (codenamed Colonel Passy), the Free French espionage and intelligence services – amalgamated into the Bureau Central de Renseignement et d'Action (BCRA) in June 1942 – worked with the British Special Operations Executive (SOE) to drop agents into mainland France. The SOE's F section, under Maurice Buckmaster, likewise parachuted agents into France but this section operated outside Gaullist control. Despite a lack of resources and recruits, BCRA agents contributed to some important wartime successes for the Allies, not least the British sinking in May 1941 of the *Bismarck*, one of the German Navy's most feared ships.[26]

The BBC afforded de Gaulle and his comrades the opportunity to broadcast for five minutes each evening. Vichy tried to deter citizens from listening to the broadcasts, punishing those found guilty of doing so to between five and fifteen years of hard labour. Nevertheless, 3 million French regularly tuned in.[27] Radio broadcasts allowed the Free French not only to fight Vichy propaganda on the airwaves but also to instigate public acts of resistance in France. During 1941, Free French broadcasters urged their compatriots to descend into the street and gather in silent protest on 11 May (the feast day of Joan of Arc), 14 July and 11 November. Thousands responded, demonstrating in large urban centres such as Lille, Nantes and Bordeaux. Radio broadcasts nurtured a connection between Free France and the internal resistance in the early years of the war, fostering a sense of shared community.[28]

European members of the Free French were typically male, aged between twenty-three and twenty-five years, and unmarried at the point of recruitment. Orphans and so-called 'wards of the state' were over-represented in the movement. This was a symptom both of the huge losses suffered during the First World War and the fact that a lack of family ties made life in exile easier. In terms of social class, the educated bourgeoisie dominated. Over 40 per cent of members originated from a family in the higher socio-professional strata, the sons of high civil servants, industrialists and businessmen, managers, lawyers, professors and doctors as well as military officers (these men accounted for only 4 per cent of French in the 1930s).[29] There were over sixty nationalities in the Free French Forces. Non-French nationals numbered approximately 3,000, with the largest proportion from Spain.[30]

There were opportunities for women to join the Free French. On 17 November 1940, de Gaulle founded a Corps Auxiliaire Féminin (Auxiliary Feminine Corps), which was also known as the Feminine Corps of the FFL. The Corps comprised a handful of women, both escapees from France and residents of England, under the leadership of Simone Mathieu (Hélène Terré later took over the group). On 16 December 1941, these women were incorporated into the FFL in the new Corps des Volontaires Françaises (French Women Volunteers Corp or the CVF). In some respects, the CVF echoed the practices of their male counterparts. A 'cult of war heroines' developed in the body's publications and barracks were named after fallen female comrades.[31] Yet the founding statutes of the CVF stipulated that its purpose was to 'free up [male] combatants from jobs that can be performed by women' rather than to train female soldiers.[32] Volunteers were not permitted to hold military ranks in the CVF and were referred to simply as madame or mademoiselle. Recruits received lessons in firing guns yet they mainly fulfilled administrative roles. The aim of the CVF was to enrol women without 'distorting' their womanliness. Free French propaganda emphasized the femininity of the women volunteers. Images combined appeal to patriotism with depictions of elegant women with delicate facial features and discrete makeup – an 'altered femininity', according to Luc Capdevila. Concomitantly, the moral standing of recruits was of concern to the Free French authorities. Article Three of the decree of 16 June 1941 stipulated that female recruitment should depend on a positive outcome to both a physical and moral examination of the volunteer. On 11 January 1944, prostitutes were excluded from membership.[33] Male comrades often sniggered at these women volunteers 'playing soldiers' yet CVF members considered themselves military personnel capable of complementing the role of men in the FFL.[34] The number of women in the CVF swelled to several hundred after the Allied invasion of North Africa in November 1942. Women joined from newly liberated lands as well as from colonies loyal to de Gaulle and North and South America.[35] Aside from the CVF, women in the Free French worked as drivers, medics, nurses, mechanics and even pilots. Several women were parachuted into France on missions for the BCRA. Rosette Szekany, previously an au pair living in Britain, joined the FFL in June 1941. Szekany joined the air arm of the Corps and subsequently saw action from Omaha beach in June 1944 to Berlin in 1945. Three women died in uniform: Marie Hackin, Valentine Malaroche and Césarine Bigerel.[36]

There were proportionally fewer women in the Free French than the domestic resistance movements. Women accounted for 2.2 per cent (approximately 1,160 members[37]) of the total membership of the FFL; women made up 16 per cent of members of the resistance group Défense de la France.[38] The military character of the movement perhaps deterred more women from joining. Moreover, joining a domestic movement did not require leaving one's family and friends behind. In any case, women's disadvantaged social and political position presented further obstacles: women in the FFL could rise to the rank of commandant yet they were never trusted with leadership roles as in the movements and networks based in France itself.

It is difficult to discern a single reason why men and women rallied to de Gaulle. Few seem to have understood the political sense of the struggle: when asked, 'Did you read the speeches of General de Gaulle?' nearly 58 per cent of respondents replied 'never' or 'rarely or very rarely'. Indeed, Free French leaders took no great pains to provide recruits with a political education. Free French leaders considered membership a military engagement and the FFL maintained the tradition of political neutrality characteristic of the French army. Members understood broadly the cause for which they were fighting. They were fiercely loyal to de Gaulle and espoused a 'visceral rejection of the political collaboration and military attentisme of the Etat Français'.[39] Perhaps the best explanation for joining the Free French is found in Murraciole's 2009 book on the topic:

> Spontaneity, chance, the weight of emotions, the influence of an education, so much data imperceptible to the historian, surely counted more than a cold assessment of the situation. These observations take nothing away from the patriotic fire of the great majority of Free French. They show simply that engagement in a military cause at the risk of one's life as one leaves behind adolescence arises from a complex alchemy of convictions, emotions and chance as much as from reason.[40]

The General himself was a highly potent symbol. As Léon Werth wrote in May 1943: 'The figure of de Gaulle is far away. But Gaullism means all forms of Resistance, whatever they may be'.[41]

The global Free French

For much of the war, the Free French's greatest asset lay in central Africa. During 26–28 August 1940 – later known as the 'three glorious days' – French Equatorial Africa (comprising Chad, Oubangui-Chari, French Congo and Gabon) and Cameroon declared their loyalty to de Gaulle (an act termed 'ralliement' or 'rallying'). While these territories comprised 6 million people and 3,000 kilometres of land, they were considered the 'weakest' and 'most backward' of the French colonies.[42] Chad's capital, Fort Lamy, was 'a collection of huts and shacks, with corrugated iron roofs, dirt roads, [and] a smell of latrines competing with the smell of rotting meat', according to one member of the Free French.[43] However, we should not underestimate their strategic importance. In the north, French Equatorial Africa acted as a launching pad for attacks on Italian-held Libya and Ethiopia. The territories provided a link between the British-ruled Nigeria, the Belgian Congo and the Anglo-Egyptian Sudan. Allied planes could use airstrips in the Free French colonies to refuel on journeys from the Gulf of Guinea to the Nile and

Figure 16 *A Free French infantryman of the Chad colony, who was awarded the Croix de Guerre, 1942. Photo in the public domain (Wikimedia Commons).*

the Indian Ocean; 20,000 flights passed through French Equatorial Africa during the war. Most importantly within the context of 1940, these colonies' loyalty to de Gaulle lent legitimacy to his embryonic movement, not to mention a large pool of human and material resources. Jennings describes the area as 'the first hotbed of French resistance' and contemporaries agreed: Jacques Soustelle wrote that 'Free France was African'.[44] For the Gaullists, Brazzaville was 'the capital of legitimate France' and African place names took on huge symbolic importance. On 2 March 1941, when General Leclerc raised the French flag at Kufra in Libya following a Free French victory over Italian forces, he asked his soldiers to swear that they would not lay down their arms until the tricolour flew once again over Strasbourg cathedral. The so-called 'Kufra Oath', like the victory at Bir Hakeim in June 1942, entered Free French mythology.[45]

It is important to qualify the so-called rallying of Free French Africa. The term conjures the romantic image of a groundswell of popular opinion in favour of joining the Free French. Colonial leaders consulted neither the European settler nor indigenous African populations. Generally, the decision lay with a handful of men at the summit of the colonial administrations. When one considers that in 1941 the population of French Equatorial Africa and Cameroon comprised 8,881 European settlers and over 6 million indigenous peoples, to 'rally' to the Free French was not a democratic decision.[46] No single factor explained the decision to commit to the cause. Pragmatism informed some decisions to follow the General. Administrators in Chad feared the onset of famine if they followed Vichy into international isolation from Britain; loyalty to the Free French ensured the continued viability of supply lines from British Nigeria.[47] In the case of the Côte Française des Somalis, business interests – notably the Compagnie Ferroviaire du Franco-Ethiopien and the local branch of the Banque d'Indochine – forced a change of sides.[48] The loyalty of troops in French Equatorial Africa stemmed in part from a personal commitment to their officers and units, and in part from the proud service of their ancestors during the First World War. However, the same reasons explained the commitment of African soldiers to Vichy in French West Africa.[49]

Local factors likewise determined the engagement of colonial subjects elsewhere. In Chad, the fear of isolation and food shortages motivated some colonial administrators to consider a break with Vichy and an alliance with the British. The risk of famine spreading to the white population further prompted moves towards Britain.[50] In the French Antilles, hunger motivated dissidence as much as sympathy for the Free French. The British blockade of the islands between 1940 and 1943 cut food supplies and caused a near famine and some islanders resolved to escape to the nearby British possessions of Dominica and Saint Lucia. Yet the belief that hunger alone motivated these escapees likely derived from British reports of the way these refugees voraciously gobbled up plates of sandwiches on their arrival.[51] Such accounts fed the idea that whites resisted for principled reasons of ideology while indigenous resistance emerged only from material circumstances. In Guadeloupe, for example, food shortages, combined with a rejection of Vichy, motivated the development of a separatist movement to declare Guadeloupe an independent state under American protection.[52] Like their white settler counterparts, indigenous peoples chose dissent based on a range of factors, of which hunger was just one.

Colonial populations in Free French colonies did not unanimously support de Gaulle. Pro-Vichy and even pro-German voices were raised in objection. In Chad, loyalism to Pétain was strong yet the Marshal's followers chose to flee to French West Africa, fearing a mass uprising from the indigenous population should they make plain their opposition.[53] In rare instances where the authorities consulted with locals on the decision to back de Gaulle, the results were heartening if not overwhelming. A referendum in August 1940 in French Polynesia saw an overwhelming vote in favour of de Gaulle: 5,564 against eighteen. Yet the vote was limited to the European population, the Catholic members of which abstained on the orders of the local clergy.[54] Following the Free French seizure of Saint-Pierre et Miquelon, a small island off the coast of Canada, in December 1941 a plebiscite was staged. Sixty-three per cent of voters cast a ballot in favour of supporting de Gaulle while only 1 per cent favoured Vichy and collaboration. However, 18 per cent of ballots were blank or spoiled and a further 18 per cent of eligible voters abstained.[55]

The African territories that opted to turn their backs on Vichy did not cast off the shackles of colonial rule. As Jennings writes, '[i]f Free France was African...Africa was not free'.[56] Under Governor of Chad Félix Eboué, forced labour intensified – as it did under Vichy in French West Africa. Colonial slave drivers exploited men, women and children, as well as prisoners and the sick, for the collection of natural resources such as rubber in Cameroon. In Gabon, physical abuse was common in the gold mines and wages were often withheld when workers failed to fulfil their quotas. Only French citizenship could set one free from the injustices of colonial rule yet between August 1940 and March 1943, all requests for citizenship received a refusal. Overall, in French Equatorial Africa and Cameroon, indigenous peoples built nearly 10,000 kilometres of road and increased production in foodstuffs, lead, zinc, leather and precious metals. In the Free French Empire, as in all empires, such achievements owed to the blood, sweat and tears of the colonized.[57]

Indochina, France's most important possession in Asia, remained, beyond de Gaulle's grasp. In part, the colony's distance from France – it took one month to reach by sea – meant that resistance had to develop independently of de Gaulle. Yet the Free French gave little consideration to the colony: in the archives of the BCRA, there is no mention of the colony between 1940 and 1944, despite the fact that the Free French declared war on Japan on 9 December 1941.[58] In January 1943, a representative from the Indochinese Levain resistance network arrived in Algiers to establish formal contact with the Free French. Over a year later, in February 1944, de Gaulle informed the head of the resistance in Indochina that 'only through our armed and concrete participation in the liberation of Indochina will we be able to re-establish the plenitude of our rights'.[59] In July, de Gaulle – anxious to secure his control of the colony as France teetered on the brink of Liberation – sent the first Free French agents to Lang Son to organize guerrilla warfare on the French model, that is, assassinations, derailments and sabotage. Arms, explosives and medical supplies followed only in January and February 1945.[60] By mid-1944, the British SOE had trained French units in sabotage operations; they were men of French and Vietnamese nationality, based at Calcutta under Lieutenant-Colonel Jean Boucher de Crèvecoeur.[61] Free French intervention in the territory thus arrived at a late stage in the Japanese occupation. For the 34,000 Europeans in Indochina, the General was a 'distant personality' for much of the war.[62] As few as one in 50,000 inhabitants of Indochina joined the Free French.[63]

Beyond the borders of France and its Empire, the Free French waged a global propaganda campaign. To the diaspora communities of non-belligerent countries such as Portugal, propagandists distributed Free French brand consumer goods: pencils, playing cards, bookmarks, post cards, blotting paper, postage stamps, calendars, brooches and even records at Christmas. Products were circulated in schools and public places such as cinemas.[64] By June 1942, Free French delegates operated in cities such as Ottawa, Washington, Mexico City, Havana, Bogota, Lima, Montevideo, Reykjavik, Moscow, Tehran, Cairo, Jeddah, Pretoria and Sydney.[65] Meanwhile, private initiatives attracted expatriate French and Francophiles who wished to lend moral and material support to the General. In August 1940, Franco-American industrialist Eugène Houdry founded the 'France Forever' committee in Philadelphia. By June 1944, these committees claimed 15,000 members from San Francisco to New York via Santa Fe, Saint Louis and Nashville. In Canada, the citizens of Saskatoon paid $12,600 to purchase a tank for the Free French. The tank, bearing the city's name and coat of arms, took part in the Allied campaign in North Africa in 1943.[66] This global campaign achieved a modicum of success: by 1944, there were approximately 20,000 members of Free French committees around the world.[67]

On 25 September 1941, de Gaulle established the CFLN. This committee took on 'the appearance of a provisional government' for it purported to be 'the sole representative of France and the Empire'.[68] Such claims were patently untrue. Public opinion in France had not yet turned decisively against Vichy while the imperial possessions remained largely under Pétain's control. Foreign sympathy abroad was little match for boots on the ground. The disaster at Dakar undermined the attractiveness of the Free French for both the Allies and the French population. By September 1941, the Free French had recruited only 17,730 men and women (excluding the colonial territories) and it would be another year until the movement made a serious impact on the war.[69] Most seriously, de Gaulle was still uninformed about resistance movements within France despite the work of his agents in the territory to gather information. Yet de Gaulle's fears that the Allies would carve up France once Vichy fell meant that he simply had to present the CFLN as the only representative of the French nation, as a kind of 'state in exile', with whom Churchill and Roosevelt would be forced to deal at liberation.[70] Happily for the General, the fortunes of the Free French were about to change. On 20 October 1941, Jean Moulin, a former prefect of the Vichy regime, arrived in England with the information about the domestic resistance movements that de Gaulle and his comrades so desperately lacked.

Defining resistance

Before examining the French resistance organizations, we must address an important question: what is 'resistance'? While we may identify those men and women who belonged to resistance movements and networks as resisters, it is more difficult to label the actions of the French who did not belong to an organization but who risked much by committing acts of dissent and disobedience. Strikes, food riots and the black market posed serious challenges to the French and German authorities yet they did not necessarily stem from opposition to the Occupation. There are therefore many definitions of resistance in the historiography of France and the Second World War. Most definitions, however, centre on three elements: the act itself, the intention behind the act, and the hoped-for or likely consequences of the act.

Robert Paxton and John Sweets stand at opposite ends of the definitional spectrum. In 1972, Paxton proposed a narrow conception of resistance. He limited the number of resisters to the 400,000 men and women who belonged to the movements and networks, arguing that though the majority of French 'longed to lift the German yoke, [they] did not want to lift it by fire and sword'.[71] Paxton thus defined a resister as a member of an organization who was prepared to fight to evict the Occupier from France. This was a highly gendered view of resistance for it privileged paramilitary action as the pinnacle of rebellion. Resistance organizations rarely afforded women the opportunity to commit violence by fire or by sword. In 1986, John Sweets proposed a broader definition of resistance. He emphasized the 'massive and widespread popular complicity' that nurtured opposition after 1943, even if only a minority of French men and women made the decision to take up arms for the cause.[72] Sweets called this the 'phenomenon of resistance', made up of 'isolated acts of opposition' some of which were highly risky, such as listening to the BBC or sabotaging tanks and planes destined for the Wehrmacht.[73] Guéhenno described the effect of such small acts of defiance on 14 July 1941. He noted that some women in Paris were wearing the colours of the French flag to mark the national holiday: 'The blue shoes, white stockings, and red dress of one woman. The red jacket, blue purse, and white gloves of another'. Guéhenno explained that these displays of solidarity contributed to 'the joy of a communion' of like-minded French.[74]

Recent histories have acknowledged the complexity and diversity of French behaviour during the war. Focusing on the internal resistance, Wieviorka acknowledges that 'the infinite variety of modes of engagement [in resistance] and of lived experience makes any generalization misleading'.[75] He proposes several 'general contours' of resistance. Firstly, resistance involved action: 'to do battle concretely with the German occupier, and even its Vichy ally'. It was not enough merely to hold an opinion favourable to resistance: resistance was 'an engagement embodied before all else in practices'.[76] Secondly, a conscious desire to oppose the status quo motivated this action. Finally, resistance involved transgression: '[it stood] opposed to the legality imposed by the Reich and its Vichy accomplice', and it carried the risk of paying the ultimate price.[77] Like Wieviorka, Robert Gildea proposes an outline of the content and forms of resistance action: '[resistance] meant refusing to accept the French bid for the armistice and the German Occupation, and a willingness to do something about it that broke the rules and courted risk'.[78] It could entail: the military resistance of the Free French; the 'spontaneous, sporadic and symbolic' isolated acts of many citizens; and 'Resistance with a capital "R",' defined as 'activists organised into small groups with sustained activity and a material contribution to the war effort'.[79] Wieviorka and Gildea offer a means to conceptualize resistance between the extremes of Paxton and Sweets.

Acts of disobedience and dissent extended beyond the ranks of the movements and networks. The motives of such acts were manifold and complex, and influenced not least by the course of the war. Such acts, if not committed with the aims of 'resistance' in mind, could have political consequences. Selling meat on the black market, for example, could deny supplies to German troops.[80] Not all acts could be interpreted in this way. Food and fuel shortages rendered daily life a struggle and to hoard, pilfer or purchase supplies illegally could be a matter of survival first, and resistance second.[81] The historian's task is to understand and explain, not to pass judgement. A gulf existed between those who believed in resistance and those who were prepared to act. Public discontent developed unevenly, in part thanks to the geography of the Occupation. In the North, hostility to collaboration took hold by the end of 1940; by spring the following year, even the figure of the Marshal was tarnished. In the South, Vichy's propaganda and the absence of German troops before November 1942 saw support for Pétain's regime last longer than in the Occupied Zone. Nevertheless, public support was fragile and sceptical. In the spring of 1942, 'Down with Pétain!' graffiti was no longer an unusual sight in southern towns.[82] The few who chose to act were certainly brave; those who did nothing were not necessarily cowards.

Definitions generally conceive of the phenomenon as action undertaken in opposition to either the *German* Occupier or the metropolitan Vichy regime or both. Such an approach obscures opposition in the Italian and Japanese zones of occupation. In these areas, forms of defiance could mirror those witnessed in the German Occupied Zone: if in the North of France, women wore patriotic colours as an act of defiance, in the Italian Zone a piece of macaroni worn ostentatiously on one's clothes signalled opposition.[83] Local circumstance could condition responses, too: on Corsica, where many residents held dual French and Italian citizenship, matters of identity complicated notions of resistance.[84] In Indochina, the French intelligence service, the Service de Renseignement Intercolonial, transmitted information about Japanese military positions to the Chinese, the British in Singapore and the Americans in Manilla. Networks such as Graille in the north and Maupin in the south developed in military circles that were reluctant to accept the defeat. Civilians such as Jean Tricoire in Haiphong and Lucien Plasson in Phnom-Penh established links to the Allied powers, passing on information and aiding the escape of POWs.[85]

Histories of resistance to *French* persecution informed the wartime behaviour of outsider groups. Gypsies had long attempted to circumvent the restrictions of Republican law through the falsification of identity papers and the exploitation of legal loopholes and travellers continued to use such practices to escape Vichy's discrimination.[86] In colonies under Vichy's control, peculiar national circumstances and traditions, as well as long histories of colonial domination, led to idiosyncratic responses that jar with notions of resistance as understood in the metropolitan context. In the case of French West Africa, rebellion drew on old traditions of illegality. Indigenous peoples sold contraband and intelligence to the British via long-established smuggling routes to nearby colonies. For African smugglers who held French citizenship, such activity may have stemmed from opposition to Vichy's anti-assimilationist stance.[87] On the other hand, acts of dissidence and disobedience were mapped onto older conceptions of resistance to colonial rule and resulted in a rejection of both Vichy and the Free French in the 'war of the Whites'.[88]

In Free French Africa, notions of resistance were complex. How should we understand indigenous opposition to the Free French regime in the territories of French Equatorial Africa and Cameroon? Is it possible to draw an equivalency between a scheme such as the STO in metropolitan France and the abusive treatment of African workers under Free French colonial governance? If so, we might apply the term 'resistance' to the actions of those colonial subjects who refused to work for the Free French or who fled to neighbouring countries; these people were colonial réfractaires.[89] Such examples illustrate the difficulty that one encounters in using the term 'resistance' – and the values bound up within it – in the colonies. As Ginio argues in the case of French West Africa, 'resistance' (and its counterpart 'collaboration') is irrelevant categories.[90] This is a conclusion that applies to practically all French possessions beyond the borders of the mainland.

Movements and networks

In the early days of the Occupation, few people knew how to resist. Improvisation was the order of the day as small groups of like-minded French explored the possibilities for action. In July 1940, Agnès Humbert and her colleagues resolved to 'meet on agreed days to exchange news, to write and distribute pamphlets and tracts, and to share summaries of French radio broadcasts from London'. Humbert had little hope for the practical impact of their activities; rather, 'keeping our sanity will be success of a kind... it will be a way of keeping our spirits up'.[91] In the summer of 1940, there were few opportunities for more meaningful resistance.

Mass organized resistance movements were slow to emerge in France. The difference in conditions between the zones affected the development of opposition and the Demarcation Line ensured that unity of action was initially impossible. In the Northern Zone, resistance faced the double threat from Vichy's police and the German Occupation forces. In the South, resisters were freer to operate than their northern counterparts yet they faced the problem of public complacency. It was by no means clear to many French that Vichy was the enemy. Resisters themselves held complex attitudes to Vichy: Henri Frenay, leader of Combat, wrote in November 1940 of his commitment to Marshal Pétain and Vichy's reform agenda. At the time of Frenay's writing, the regime had begun to discriminate against Jews.[92]

The first organized groups emerged from the early resisters' social and professional networks, namely their friends and colleagues. In the North, the Musée de l'Homme group developed amongst the librarians and researchers of the Parisian museum of anthropology (from which the group took its name). These resisters operated initially as a *network*. Networks had 'specific military objectives – the collection of information, sabotage [and] organizing escape routes' – and were in touch with Allied intelligence services.[93] The Musée de l'Homme operatives soon diversified their action, printing the newssheet *Résistance* between December 1940 and March 1941. The group was betrayed at the end of 1941 and several of its leading members – Germaine Tillion, Agnès Humbert and founder Yvonne Oddon – were deported. The group's co-founders Boris Vildé and Anatole Lewitsky were executed.[94]

Networks existed in the South, some of them at the very centre of Vichy. These were the so-called 'resisto-Vichyists' who looked to use the apparatus of the state in operations *against* Germany. Their action ranged from espionage to the stockpiling of weapons for an eventual renewal of hostilities with Berlin. Shortly after the foundation of the regime in July 1940, Georges Loustaunau-Lacau, a former army officer with extreme right-wing political tendencies, set up the Alliance network. Marie-Madeleine Méric (later Fourcade) took over the leadership of the network when Loustaunau-Lacau was deported to Mauthausen. Fourcade and her comrades helped Giraud to reach a British submarine after his escape from Germany. The British – to whom Alliance passed its intelligence – considered the network one of their most valuable assets.[95] Pétain was prepared to tolerate such behaviour as long as it did not jeopardize the policy of collaboration.[96]

Personal acquaintances were likewise central to the beginnings of the resistance *movements*. Movements poured their energy into propaganda activities. Their 'priority was to target the French population: to shake it out of its lethargy and eventually organize for action'.[97] Philippe Viannay, a philosophy student at the Sorbonne in Paris, founded Défense de la France with the help of student and academic acquaintances. The movement published an eponymous newspaper from August 1941.[98] In the Unoccupied Zone, former naval officer Emmanuel d'Astier de la Vigerie made contact with history teacher Lucie Samuel in Clermont-Ferrand. With Samuel's engineer husband, Raymond, and her college friend Jean Cavaillès, they founded the small Dernière Colonne cell; this would later become the very important Libération-Sud movement.[99]

An underground press encouraged the development of the movements. Some newspapers were short-lived and existed without a movement behind them; Raymond Deiss's *Pantagruel* published sixteen issues before the arrest and execution of its founder in October 1941.[100] Other movements successfully employed a newspaper to expand their reach beyond the immediate membership: Défense de la France had only seventy members when it produced the first print run of 3,000 copies of its first edition.[101] Lack of paper and ink meant that groups could at first distribute only small numbers of crudely produced bulletins and tracts. Combat's Claude Bourdet wrote that 'at the start so few copies were printed that you heard rumours of them more than you read them'.[102] Yet publication figures in fact masked the true potential readership of the resistance press. Bulletins and newssheets were intended to be read once and left for someone else, whether on a bus, in a cinema or in the foyer of a building. Paxton estimated that up to 2 million people read the resistance press in this way.[103]

June 1941 marked a turning point in the history of the resistance. Hitler's invasion of the Soviet Union in that month saw the French communists join the struggle against the Occupation. Given Moscow's non-aggression pact with Hitler, there was no communist resistance before the summer of 1941. The party had found itself in a difficult situation in the wake of the Armistice, walking a precarious path of neutrality between its condemnation of conservative Pétainism in the South and its rejection of the war as an imperialist enterprise in the North. At the same time, communists denounced de Gaulle as a reactionary and a crypto-fascist. In the wake of Operation Barbarossa, the French party advocated violent opposition to the Occupier. Communist newspaper *L'Humanité* recommended that readers, 'kill the boches and traitors', specifying that 'it's not individual boches that must be killed but tens of them, hundreds of them'.[104] Yet the party only claimed responsibility for its violence from summer 1942, possibly wary of alienating public opinion. The Communist Party's principal instrument in the armed struggle was the Francs-Tireurs et Partisans (FTP), founded in April 1942. Franck Liaigre's study of the group uncovered 1,051 FTP attacks and incidents of sabotage in the Paris region alone between 21 June 1941 and 15 August 1944. The main target of the group's assassins were *French* collaborators: eighty-two collaborators were killed in the Paris region, compared with just six German casualties.[105]

De Gaulle rejected the use of violence against Occupation troops at this stage in the war. He admitted that in invading and occupying France, German soldiers had put themselves in harm's way. Yet in the wake of the communist assassinations in Nantes and Bordeaux, he told listeners to the BBC, 'The war of the French people must be waged by those to whom that responsibility falls, namely, myself and the National Committee... at present, the instructions I have given for the occupied territory are not to kill Germans openly'. The General explained that with French civilians at the mercy of occupying forces, the risk of retaliation for such attacks was too high.[106] Privately he remarked that a 'river of blood is necessary, collaboration will be drowned in it'.[107]

The majority of non-communist resistance movements likewise prohibited armed attacks against German soldiers. Their rejection of violence stemmed from a number of factors. Some Christian and left-wing resisters rejected violence on ethical grounds. Other resisters refused to use violence for they considered that their goal was to restore democracy, not to replace one dictatorship with another. Non-violent methods were necessary, too, from a tactical perspective. Without a defined territorial base, the movements had to persuade the public to join their cause and any attempt to mobilize support through terror risked being counter-productive. Furthermore, resistance attacks drew reprisals from the Germans in the form of hostage taking and executions (attacks on Italian troops were met with mass arrests and internment).[108] This practice was not unique to France: in Greece, German forces killed over 70,000 civilians as punishment for resistance violence.[109]

The armed struggle against the Occupation widened during 1943 to include the non-communist resistance groups. Groups targeted infrastructure such as railways and property like mines and arms stores.[110] The resistance press presented these acts of sabotage as proactive steps on the road to Liberation. Propaganda claimed that such damage could be a more effective contribution to the war effort even than Allied bombing raids: '[t]o cut a train line, stop a locomotive, put a factory out of action, sabotage always and everywhere: it's a little step closer to victory, [it renders] a bombing raid unnecessary and furthermore [it saves] French lives'.[111] Violence remained unpopular with the public and Vichy and the Occupation authorities condemned resistance 'terrorists'. Consequently, if historians have generally classified the resistance's armed struggle according to military or paramilitary categories such as 'urban guerrilla', 'partisan warfare', 'subversive warfare' and 'civil war', the French public generally understood resistance violence as terrorism.[112]

At the mid-point of the war, the resistance map of France was drawn; few new groups subsequently emerged. The largest movement in the North was Christian Pineau's Libération-Nord. The group grew from the publication of the newspaper *Libération*, which first appeared in December 1940. Pineau had co-authored the 'Manifesto of the Twelve', a statement of defiance from a number of trade unions, distributed in both the North and the South. Libération-Nord reflected this left-wing politics. In 1940, Maurice Ripoche founded the right-wing Ceux de la Libération (CDLL). The movement focused on military action and intelligence gathering, publishing a newspaper only in May 1943. The Organisation Civile et Militaire (OCM) emerged in December 1940 from a fusion of two smaller resistance cells. The OCM was organized on military lines and concentrated its action on intelligence gathering for the Allies. In the South, Combat and Libération-Sud were the two largest formations. Combat appeared in December 1941 when Henri Frenay's Mouvement de Libération Nationale fused with François de Menthon's Liberté. It developed into a fully fledged movement with a welfare service, military training courses and a newspaper with a circulation of 300,000 by 1944. The left-wing Libération-Sud arose out of the Dernière Colonne cell. It began with small-scale acts of sabotage and propaganda. In July 1941, it published the first edition of its bulletin, *Libération*.[113]

The resisters

Evidence suggests that the majority of resisters were young. Approximately 75 per cent of members of Franc-Tireur in the South were aged under forty years old. In the North, 62 per cent of members of Défense de la France were aged thirty years and under. The qualities of youth – 'ardour, selflessness, self-sacrifice' – and the fact that young people were less conscious of the risks of resistance prompted many to join the networks and movements. Not all young resisters were unmarried and childless and some risked their family's lives as well as their own in the name of liberation.[114]

Resistance was generally an 'interclass phenomenon'. A major portion of resisters came from working- or middle-class backgrounds. Workers may have responded to the call of the resistance because of repression in the workplace or to combat schemes such as the STO. The communist resistance mobilized established networks of supporters, many of whom had experience in working-class opposition and disobedience during the interwar years. Members of the petty bourgeoisie – shopkeepers, small manufacturers, salaried employees, artisans, merchants and civil servants – were likewise over-represented in resistance formations. This social stratum traditionally identified with Republicanism. Yet nothing predisposed these people towards resistance; they made up the bulk of collaborationist groups, too.[115]

Non-French European combatants made a significant contribution to the struggle against the Occupier. Wieviorka tells of a 'massive [foreign] presence in the resistance', because many immigrants had fled to France to escape fascism and Nazism during the 1920s and 1930s.[116] One of the most famous examples of the immigrant resistance was the 'Manouchian' group, a squad of twenty-three resisters (twenty-two men and one woman), under the leadership of Armenian poet Missak Manouchian. The Manouchian group was affiliated to the communist FTP under the directorship of Romanian communist Baruch Bruhman (later known as Boris Holban). Between autumn 1942 and November 1943, Bruhman directed 230 attacks, including the assassination of Julius Ritter, head of the STO.[117] Manouchian's group was arrested in late 1943 and executed the following February. Members of the group featured on the infamous 'Affiche Rouge' or 'Red Poster', which was distributed throughout France. The poster drew attention to the foreignness of the resisters, naming among others, 'Grzywacz, Polish Jew'; 'Elek, Hungarian Jew'; 'Fontanot, Italian communist'; and finally, 'Manouchian, Armenian'. The poster described the group as the 'Army of Crime'.[118]

France's colonial subjects also found a place in domestic resistance groups. The Musée de l'Homme network included the Madagascan architect Andriamihaingo who, thanks to his seat on Vichy's committee for overseas prisoners of war, helped captives escape from La Réunion and Madagascar.[119] Some colonial resisters had served as soldiers during the Battle of France. The German authorities redoubled security at the Frontstalags during June and July 1944, anticipating large defections to resistance movements.[120] After the war, ten Tirailleurs Sénégalais won the Ordre de la Libération, an honour reserved for men and women who had made a significant contribution to the struggle to Free France. Fifty more received the Médaille de la Résistance for acts of courage and bravery.[121] The names of dozens of North African subjects appear on the lists of arrestees of Vichy's anti-terrorist police. In particular, these men and women belonged to communist movements and networks; many had long-standing links to the French extreme left.[122] Beyond these cases, it is difficult to estimate the size of the involvement of colonial volunteers in resistance groups. The post-war narrative of a *French* (and predominantly white) resistance has obscured the contribution of men and women from the imperial territories to the struggle for Liberation.

In overseas territories under Vichy's control, the Allied war against Germany motivated some to resist. Fearing Hitlerian racism, Antillais islanders represented their resistance as an opposition to what they saw as the islands' Nazi-backed puppet regime. The colonial administration's preferential treatment of the békés (descendants of the first generation of European settlers), combined with the apparent racism of French officials on the islands, fed the indigenous population's resentment of the regime.[123] Islanders' resistance in some ways resembled that of the mainland French:

Vichy's propaganda posters were slashed; hats were not removed for the singing of the *Marseillaise*; drivers honked their horns to the rhythm of 'V' (for Victory) in the Morse code alphabet. Dissidence developed, too, in ways consonant with local circumstance and tradition. Black resisters portrayed opposition as a fight against the return of slavery to the territory. A popular rumour in Martinique held that 'General de Gaulle is a black general desiring, like Toussaint Louverture, to liberate people of colour from the yoke of the white owners'. In imitation of the escape of the fugitive slaves (marrons) of the past, up to 5,000 Antillais fled on makeshift dinghies to the nearby British islands of Dominica and Saint Lucia.[124]

At the Liberation, only six women received the Ordre de la Libération when over 1,000 men received the same honour.[125] If this fact gives the impression that few women joined resistance groups, the reality was very different. Women were present at all levels of the movements and networks. A number of prominent female resisters are well known. Ethnographer Germaine Tillion was a principal member of the Musée de l'Homme group. She was arrested in August 1942 and deported to Ravensbruck (which she survived). In February 2014, Tillion's remains were interred at the Panthéon in Paris (the French state's secular temple reserved for heroes of the nation), along with General de Gaulle's niece, Geneviève de Gaulle-Anthonioz, and male resisters Pierre Brossolette and Jean Zay. Berty Albrecht worked with Frenay to produce the newssheet *Les Petites Ailes*, and later joined him in Combat. On Albrecht's suggestion, the movement set up a service to aid the families of arrested resisters. She was betrayed to the Gestapo and arrested on 28 May 1943; a week later Albrecht killed herself. Lucie Samuel (codenamed Aubrac) was one of the very few women afforded the opportunity to lead a movement (Libération-Sud) and to take part in combat. On 21 October 1943, Aubrac and a resistance commando attacked a prison van in Lyon, freeing her husband Raymond and a dozen other resisters.[126]

Men and women did not join the resistance in equal numbers. Only 16 per cent of the Défense de la France membership was female, while less than 10 per cent of Franc-Tireur members were women.[127] However, given that the position of women in France amounted to no less than exclusion from public life (women were not afforded the right to vote until after the Second World War), these figures signify an over-representation.[128] Women performed a number of essential functions. Firstly, women resisters acted as propagandists: Agnès Humbert typed 'Vive le général de Gaulle' on five-Franc notes in the knowledge that her message would be passed from French to French as no one could afford to destroy money.[129] Secondly, female members acted as liaison agents, carrying messages and arms between the underground and its operatives. Women were particularly valuable for they could access places that men could not. The fact that they were women – and thus considered unsuited to combat roles – allowed them to slip past

German soldiers and police unhindered. Furthermore, female members of the Red Cross were permitted to visit POWs in the Frontstalags and they helped prisoners to establish links to resistance groups outside the prisons.[130] Thirdly, military action was not beyond the reach of some female resisters. Paula Schwartz describes the case of 'Claude' who was wined and dined by a Gestapo officer at the famous Parisian restaurant Maxim's. Upon leaving the restaurant, they took a taxi; in the back of the cab, Claude shot the officer dead. The driver (Claude's comrade) dropped her off in the centre of Paris and she made her way home.[131] Finally, a handful of women rose to positions of leadership. In such cases, their identity as women was often subsumed into that of the 'boss', their male comrades considering them a leader first and a woman second. Women could be complicit in this practice, knowing that to be 'one of the boys' assured the exercise of their authority.[132]

Determining the motives for joining the resistance is no easy task. It is not possible to settle upon a single factor that prompted people to act. As Gildea explains, the '[a]wakening to a consciousness that resistance was necessary took place in thousands of minds …. Sometimes this awakening was explained by patriotism, sometimes by idealism, sometimes by contingency. Often a family story of honour or shame or revolt was drawn upon to make sense of the impulse to resist'.[133] Mark Mazower's overview of life in Occupied Europe likewise cites motivations that can be difficult to pin down: 'For most of those involved [in resistance] it was a question of pride, and a demonstration that the rule of force had not succeeded in crushing the spirit of freedom. It involved enormous courage, and for those engaged from the start a refusal to accept the "realities" of 1940, when German domination of the continent seemed unassailable.'[134] For the communities in France threatened with repression or deportation – foreigners, French and foreign Jews, escaped POWs, colonial prisoners and veterans – resistance meant survival. For downtrodden colonial populations, dissidence and escape could likewise make a difference between life and death. It is difficult to pigeonhole the actions of groups and individuals when their actions drew on diverse sources of inspiration and held multiple meanings. We must recognize the diversity and plurality of responses to Vichy and its colonial administrations, as well to the various nations with troops stationed on French territory.

1943: Uniting the resistance

The drive to unite the resistance inside and outside France began in October 1941 when Jean Moulin met General de Gaulle in London. Moulin is probably the best known of all French resisters; on 19 December 1964, his ashes were interred in the Panthéon under the eyes of de Gaulle, then President of France. When Germany invaded in May 1940, Moulin was working as a prefect in the Eure-et-Loir. He refused a German order to sign a declaration that falsely implicated Senegalese troops in the rape and massacre of civilians. Beaten and imprisoned for his defiance, Moulin slit his own throat rather than submit (he survived the injury). Dismissed from his post as prefect in November 1940, he set about gathering information on the developing resistance movements and took what he learned to London. He first met with de Gaulle on 25 October 1941.[135]

De Gaulle sent Moulin back to France in January 1942 as his official representative in the South. Moulin had persuaded the General that the resistance movements could make a military contribution to the war effort under the leadership of the Free French. His mission now was to convince domestic resisters of this strategy and he had cash on hand to help achieve his goal. Over the following months, resistance leaders travelled to London to meet de Gaulle. The drive to unite the groups in the North – with whom de Gaulle had made contact through the figure of former socialist party member Pierre Brossolette – and the South now proceeded apace.[136]

The unification of movements under de Gaulle was not an easy task. Resistance leaders themselves were concerned at a potential loss of independence. D'Astier and Frenay even accused Moulin of an attempted power grab that would 'destroy' the resistance.[137] The suspicions of the resistance leaders were justified for London would provide financial aid only under certain conditions. In the first instance, de Gaulle required that the relatively meagre paramilitary wings of the principal southern groups – Libération-Sud, Combat and Franc-Tireur – unite into an 'Armée Secrète' ('Secret Army') that would operate separately from the movements. In this way, De Gaulle hoped to deprive the political resistance of its military potential. London put the Armée Secrète under the command of General Charles Delestreint.[138] Delestreint clashed with Frenay over the intended use of the armed force. The latter wanted to deploy the troops in a national uprising to coincide with the expected Allied invasion of France. Delestreint countered that all thoughts of insurrection should be subordinated to an Allied-led liberation. Only once the Allies had established a foothold on the continent should the French take up arms.[139] In order to strengthen the position of the resistance movements in relation to London, on 26 January 1943 Frenay, d'Astier and Jean-Pierre Lévy (leader of Franc-Tireur) founded the Mouvements Unis de la Résistance (MUR). So unhappy was Frenay with London's plan that he sought independent contacts with the Americans too.[140]

Opposition to de Gaulle's designs arose in the North, too. In April 1942, Brossolette arrived in London with information about several resistance groups in the Occupied Zone.[141] De Gaulle asked Brossolette to return to northern France in January 1943 in a bid to co-ordinate the movements. In March, resistance leaders founded the 'Co-ordinating Committee of the Occupied Zone' upon which sat the OCM, Ceux de la Résistance (CDLR), Libération-Nord and the communist Front National. Like their southern counterparts, Brossolette and the northern leaders clashed with

Moulin on several issues, not least the inclusion of former political parties in a proposed Conseil National de la Résistance (National Council of the Resistance, CNR).[142] Furthermore, they feared submersion by the larger and better-developed southern formations on the proposed council.[143]

Moulin's plan for the CNR prevailed. Divisions between the movements proved a major weakness in their challenge to London. In the North, the co-ordinating committee had left Défense de la France in the cold because De Gaulle had wanted to limit membership of the body to groups with a publication, an armed wing and an intelligence gathering apparatus. These requirements excluded Viannay's movement despite the fact that by 1944, 440,000 French read its newspaper.[144] Brossolette's claim to have united the northern movements was thus untenable. In the South, differences between the groups of the MUR – primarily over Frenay's American contacts – simmered beneath the surface. Moulin was able to stage the first meeting of the CNR on 27 May 1943. On the council sat delegates from the main movements in the North – the OCM, CDLR, CDLL, the Front National and Libération-Nord – the three southern groups of the MUR, and a number of political parties (the socialists and communists, the right-wing Fédération Républicaine and the centre-right Parti Démocrate Populaire and the Alliance Démocratique) and France's two largest trade unions (the Confédération Générale du Travail and the Confédération Française des Travailleurs Chrétiens).[145] Frenay, d'Astier and Lévy were absent from the inaugural gathering. The movements of the North and the South now acknowledged de Gaulle's leadership of the resistance inside and outside France.[146]

The CNR's recognition of de Gaulle in May 1943 bolstered the General's claim to the leadership of resistance France. De Gaulle's position was not yet secure. Since the Allied invasion of North Africa in November 1942, the General had faced competition for this title from General Henri Giraud. The Allies had designated Giraud the man to take control of Vichy forces once the North African territories had surrendered. For a time, de Gaulle and Giraud worked together, though with great reluctance. The two men had disagreed over the military use of tanks during a two-year posting together in Metz prior to the war.[147] Their handshake at the Casablanca conference in January 1943 was reportedly so brief that photographers required a second attempt. The two generals devised a working relationship as co-presidents of the CFLN (the de facto provisional government) founded on 3 June 1943. Relations were not always smooth and could result in a duplication of roles. In September 1943, Giraud led a force from North Africa to land on Corsica following an uprising on the island. De Gaulle sent his own representatives to Corsica and he and Giraud argued about the details of the French landings.[148]

An unexpected development during 1943 saw the emergence of a new resistance phenomenon: the 'maquis'.[149] The introduction of the STO in February 1943 sparked the flight of thousands of young men to the countryside to escape transport to Germany.[150] These réfractaires lived in makeshift camps in rural locations, earning them the name maquis after the hardy vegetation that grows on scrubland in southern France. As many as 13,000 men lived in the maquis camps across France.[151] The camps provided a home for all fugitives, not just those of the STO: in the Vercors, fifty-two Senegalese lived amongst their French comrades after escaping from a POW camp.[152] Maquis groups comprised a number of nationalities: three-quarters of the camp in Oisans in the French Alps were non-French; they hailed from Indochina, Morocco, Poland, Russia and Spain.[153] Women were discouraged from joining the maquis lest the French public perceive their camps as places of loose morals.[154]

Life was difficult for the 'maquisards'. Cold, hunger, illness and boredom afflicted these young men. A small maquis group of fifteen in Saint-Adjutory in the Corrèze suffered from boils and scabies. The men of the Glières maquis whiled away their hours playing cards, singing songs and doing crosswords.[155] Maquis groups concentrated their efforts on guerrilla-style attacks. While such a tactic contributed little to the eventual liberation of France, the maquisards were a thorn in the side of the Occupier and Vichy and they ran constant risk of arrest and death. In late March 1944, German and French forces killed 210 maquisards who had set up camp on the Glières Plateau.[156]

Figure 17 *Mountain-dwelling maquisards. Photo by Hulton-Deutsch Collection/ CORBIS/Getty Images.*

The maquis had a dual reputation. On the one hand, the maquisards gained a reputation as romantic outlaws and 'righters of wrongs'; they requisitioned goods and money from farmers whom they believed had profited from the war.[157] On the other hand, they were characterized as thieves and bandits who stole from impoverished farmers and peasants. Vichy played on citizens' fears of the maquis 'bandit-terrorist'. Guéhenno noted in his diary, 'We've actually reached the point where these young "volunteers," [the maquis] who are saving the honor of us all, have to justify themselves, argue their case, and prove their common honesty'.[158] The Allies and the Free French learned with surprise of the maquis's existence in summer 1943. Relations between the young partisans and London could be tense at times. Maquisard Eugène Chavant described the Free French leadership as 'criminals and cowards', who had little knowledge of the daily struggles of resistance.[159] Still, a number of channels of communication opened between the maquis and the Free French in both London and Algiers. By autumn 1943, Allied military planners began to take into account a maquis contribution to the coming invasion of France.

Conclusion

Resistance to Vichy and the Occupier (whether German, Italian, Japanese or, in the colonies, French) was multi-faceted and diverse. De Gaulle succeeded in transforming the Free French from a very modest organization in 1940 to a large political and military force with a global reach by summer 1943. Men and women, whether from France, Europe or further afield, contributed in a multitude of ways from propaganda work and intelligence gathering to armed operations. Networks allowed members to work internationally while friendly societies provided moral and material aid. In sum, 2,254 European and 170 foreign Free French recruits died; 222 BCRA agents were also killed.[160] De Gaulle owed much to the commitment of colonial territories. Over 30,000 of French overseas subjects joined de Gaulle and hundreds of these volunteers died in the service of La France Libre.[161] Between August 1940 and summer 1943, the 'heart of Free France' lay in Africa, not in London.[162] African place names such as Kufra and Bir-Hakeim became hugely symbolic in the history of the Free French's campaign as did Dakar, the site of the humiliating reversal in September 1940.

Resistance within France was fragmented during 1940–1943. Resisters 'of the first hour' had to contend with newly installed repressive regimes in various zones of occupation as well as a shell-shocked population. The groups remained distinct thanks to differing political loyalties and the necessities of an existence that required secrecy. Modes of resistance were diverse from the printing of newspapers, leaflets and posters to armed action and sabotage. These were acts that left traces; we must be aware that many individual acts of defiance and resistance are now lost to the historian. Public discontent developed unevenly. In the North, hostility to collaboration took hold by the end of 1940; by spring the following year, even the figure of the Marshal was tarnished. In the South, Vichy's propaganda and the absence of German troops before November 1942 saw support for Pétain's regime last longer than in the Occupied Zone. But, public support was fragile and sceptical.

It is difficult to establish reliable membership figures for the resistance groups for the keeping of membership lists was dangerous. Some resisters worked sporadically while others belonged to several different movements at once. Colonel Passy estimated that there were 65,000 members across the three movements of the MUR (16,000 in Franc-Tireur; 23,000 in Libération-Sud; 26,000 in Combat).[163] However, given that the resistance leaders frequently inflated the number of their followers, any reliable estimate is difficult to ascertain. Outright resistance was the practice of a minority; as Guéhenno reported, 'all [the French] think about is "getting through" without harm, as if all the great mass of this country cared about was to live at all costs'.[164] Wieviorka estimated that there were between 300,000 and 500,000 members of a resistance movement or network, a figure that amounts to less than 2 per cent of the population.[165] As many as 35,000 resisters or 7 per cent of the membership died.[166]

To what extent did French resistance contribute to the Allied victory? We must bear in mind that resistance was a 'minority phenomenon' in all the territories of occupied Europe. In Belgium, approximately 2 per cent of the population belonged to a group. Between 1 and 2.5 per cent of Danes were recruited to the resistance. Only in countries such as Poland, where living conditions were far harsher than in Western Europe, did larger proportions of the population resist.[167] Mazower concludes that 'with the exception of the Eastern Front, where extensive partisan activity really did worry the Germans, there were few places or moments in the occupation of Europe when the Germans were seriously troubled for very long'.[168] Lynne Taylor concurs: 'The clandestine organizations simply did not have the resources with which to make a significant impact on the German war effort'.[169] The importance of resistance lay elsewhere. In moral and political terms, the French resistance sustained a nation under Occupation; 'the very fact of resistance was sufficient to make the point and, thus, morally defeat the Germans'.[170]

5

Persecution

The shadow of the Holocaust hangs over the history of France during the Second World War. Few other governments in Hitler's Europe provided more help in resolving the 'Jewish Question' than Vichy.[1] Persecution of the Jewish community was an immediate priority in the wake of the Armistice. From 1 July 1940, Raphaël Alibert, Vichy's future Minister of Justice, began preparing a legal text on France's Jewish 'problem'. The subsequent 'Jewish Statute' of October 1940 was the first French law to discriminate explicitly against a defined racial group. It was not the last: between July 1940 and August 1944, the Jewish population of France was subjected to 400 discriminatory legal acts and directives. Vichy's discriminatory policies applied to French and foreign-born Jews alike yet the latter group – the 'dregs' according to Laval – were treated with particular disdain.[2] Vichy and the German Occupier deported 75,721 Jews from France to the East; 14 per cent of deportees were aged under eighteen years. Only 2,500 of these men, women and children survived their ordeal. A further 4,000 Jews died in custody on French soil, the victims of cold weather, poor sanitation and malnutrition in the regime's 'death camps'.[3]

Vichy's discrimination against Jews represented only one side of its persecution. The renovation of France through the National Revolution required the purging of all 'anti-French' elements. The hammer of repression fell on Freemasons, gypsies, communists, resisters, blacks, colonial peoples and teachers, to name but a few of the regime's targets. 'Soon the Etat Français will have neither enough prisons nor police officers to hold its victims', wrote former Republican minister Anatole de Monzie in 1943.[4] The following year marked a 'catastrophic peak' in both French and German repression: 42 per cent of state-sanctioned executions occurred in 1944, while one-third of all deportations happened after the Allied landings in June.[5] French officials and police carried out much of this work themselves. The regime considered the ability to maintain domestic law and order *without* outside intervention an important expression of its sovereignty.⁶ The policy of collaboration subsequently led to French police 'doing the Nazis' dirty work for them...[allowing] the Germans to occupy France with the minimum deployment of German police and military resources'.⁷ Consequently, if anything defined the complex world of Vichy, it was the relentless persecution of its presumed enemies.⁸

Vichy's repression did not end at the borders of France. Overseas governments kept a close watch on their subjects and imprisoned dissenters without hesitation.⁹ The regime's anti-Semitic laws came into force around the world from October 1940. The effects of this legislation were devastating to the large Jewish communities in North Africa. However, while state officials generally prosecuted the policy of the mainland with assiduity, the dictates of local circumstances could lessen the severity of some measures. In the Moroccan and Tunisian protectorates, where Jews remained the subjects of the Sultan and the Bey respectively, the indigenous authorities made gestures of solidarity with the Jewish community. Such gestures, however, stemmed from concerns for the independence of indigenous governments rather than for the well-being of Jewish people.¹⁰

This chapter examines exclusionary policies and practices in France and its imperial dependencies. The first part of the chapter focuses on the maintenance of law and order. French police forces functioned much as they had done under the Third Republic and Vichy meddled rarely with their structure and composition. By 1944, the paramilitary Milice increasingly took the lead in fighting resisters. The judiciary loyally served the regime and ensured that French prisons and internment camps overflowed with prisoners. The second part of the chapter explores discrimination against minority groups, namely gypsies, homosexuals and blacks. The French government's policies on these groups reflected indigenous prejudices that diverged in some respects from those of the Occupier. Finally, the chapter addresses Vichy's persecution of French and foreign-born Jews and the efforts made by this community to escape the worst excesses of persecution. The desire to relegate Jews to the status of second-class citizens drew on a well-established tradition of anti-Semitism in France. Combined with the self-deluding logic of collaboration, it culminated in the deaths of thousands of men, women and children in the extermination camps of Eastern Europe.

Law and order

The occupying powers installed their own security forces in their respective territories. In the German Occupied Zone, the Militärbefehlshaber in Frankreich (Military Authority in France, MbF) worked with the French police and judicial powers until 1942. The MbF vigorously pursued resistance fighters. Between August 1941 and May 1942, it delivered 493 death sentences; 377 of the men and women convicted were executed.¹¹

From June 1942, German responsibility for law and order passed to the Sicherheitsdienst (SD) (an organization that included the Gestapo) and the SS. The Gestapo relied on French informers to root out opponents; to fall into its hands was to disappear without trial.[12] The SS, under Karl Oberg, took over the lion's share of policing in the Occupied Zone. Oberg negotiated a settlement with head of the French police René Bousquet to limit German interference in domestic affairs. In return, Bousquet promised the swift arrest, prosecution and punishment of resisters by the French authorities. Vichy's jealous regard for its sovereignty therefore blurred the line between the French and Germans in matters of repression.[13] The majority of French, however, remained untroubled by German military and state police forces. The Occupier sought to foster 'a certain complicit resignation' in the public. As long as only 'real' criminals (Jews, communists and resisters) were arrested, normal life could proceed unhindered.[14]

Citizens in the Italian Zone lived under the perpetual threat of legal sanction and abuse. In December 1942, Italian police tortured a woman from Séez for two weeks in a cellar for the illegal purchase of a pair of boots from an Italian soldier. In May the following year, with the war turning against the Axis powers, the civil commissioner outlawed public expressions of frivolity including the wearing of swimming costumes and listening to music. The Organizzazione per la Vigilanza e la Repressione dell'Antifascismo (OVRA) led the fight against the resistance. Its agents imprisoned opponents in places such as the infamous Villa Lynwood in Nice, the Marbeuf barracks in Bastia and the Battesti barracks in Ajaccio. Italian jailers 'had as good a record' as the Gestapo when it came to the mistreatment of prisoners.[15] Joint operations with the German intelligence services were common: during April–May 1943, for example, the OVRA and the Gestapo worked together to arrest the leadership of the MUR and its intelligence services in the departments of the Var and the Alpes-Maritimes.[16]

Following the removal of the French administration in Indochina on 9 March 1945, Japanese military and police forces conducted a merciless war against resistance networks. Occupation troops arrested and executed approximately 3,500 French and indigenous opponents. A further 3,000 resisters were imprisoned in camps such as the notorious concentration camp at Pakson and the forced labour camp of Hoa Binh. The Kenpeitai police managed these camps and inflicted atrocious torture on prisoners. Captives were housed in sweltering bamboo cages riddled with mosquitoes and tropical insects. Food and water were scarce and the prisoners slowly starved. So terrible were the conditions that resisters referred to their Kenpeitai guards as the 'Gestapo-Jap'.[17]

Vichy had a wealth of means at its disposal to repress its enemies. The regime left the police force of the defunct Third Republic intact; as few as two hundred men lost their jobs in 1940.[18] It hoped that continuity in policing would shore up the public's acceptance of the regime. A culture of obedience within the police, along with offers of improved pay and working conditions and a celebration of law and order, secured the loyalty of the majority of police officers at least until late 1942. Disenchantment set in thereafter, thanks in part to Vichy's failure to make good upon its promises. Furthermore, increased resistance activity led to longer working hours and a greater risk of suffering injury or death on the job. From 1943, Vichy relied increasingly on German troops to arrest political dissenters.[19]

The battle against the 'Anti-France' ensured that policing was central to the implementation of the National Revolution. The Etat Français founded a number of specialized police bodies to serve its ideological objectives: the Police des Questions Juives (Police for Jewish Questions), the Service des Sociétés Secrètes (Service for Secret Societies) directed against Freemasons and the Service de Police Anticommuniste (Anti-Communist Police Service), later the Service de Répression des Menées Antinationales (Service for the Repression of Anti-National Activities).[20] In Paris, the BS1 Special Brigade was founded in March 1940 to target communists. A second BS2 Brigade charged with hunting immigrant communists was established in 1942. The Brigades worked closely with the Gestapo, arresting opponents and torturing detainees; of the 3,200 men and women arrested between August 1941 and August 1944, 216 died at the hands of German executioners.[21] These special squads operated alongside the gendarmerie and the local and national police forces. Vichy had substantial means at its disposal to repress its enemies and persecute its victims.

Vichy's police forces worked alongside paramilitary groups in France and its foreign dependencies. In December 1941, the SOL paramilitary force emerged from within the ranks of the veterans' Légion. The SOL was the creation of a hardcore of political extremists under the leadership of Darnand. Darnand and his comrades had grown frustrated with the perceived lack of dynamism amongst the ageing veterans of the Légion. According to its co-founder Jean Bassompierre, the SOL sought to recruit 'the youngest and most dynamic elements [and] to provide them with political training [and] a physical education of a type to make them into a paramilitary group in the service of the government, ready to support the police in case of insurrection'.[22] The SOL's 'Twenty-One Points' manifesto left few in doubt about what the group stood for: 'Against Jewish leprosy. For French purity'; 'Against democracy. For authority'; 'Against Gaullist dissent. For French unity'; 'Against Bolshevism. For nationalism'.[23] Members wore a uniform of a khaki shirt, blue beret, black tie and SOL insignia.

From January 1943, Vichy's principal tool of terror was the Milice Française. The Milice evolved out of the SOL. Milice chief Darnand hoped to use the body to stamp out opposition to the regime and promote a radical version of the National Revolution. Collaborationist Lucien Rebatet celebrated the Milice as 'the union of French national-socialists'.[24] The group recruited approximately 30,000 members, many of whom were young men aged between sixteen and twenty-five years old. Diverse motives prompted men to sign up. Membership was doubtless attractive to collaborationists yet some men joined for the steady income, bed and board on offer. When Darnand took control of the French police in December 1943, the Milice assumed a central position in the regime's repressive apparatus. Equipped with German weapons, miliciens mercilessly hunted resisters, Jews and dissidents.[25]

Censorship of the press, the radio and the cinema was common practice in France and its overseas territories. In the Northern Zone, the German Press Agency and the Propaganda-Abteilung vetted all publications. In the South, the French Information Office did likewise. This Office further instructed newspapers to focus on particular issues and ignore others, according to the dictates of the regime's political agenda.[26] Vichy's political police, the Renseignements Généraux, collated information on public opinion into weekly reports. From Paris to Senegal, the regime's prying gaze spared few areas of daily life. Undercover police recorded the reactions of cinema audiences to newsreels and propaganda films. When catcalling and booing became commonplace in movie theatres, the lights were turned up to deter offenders.[27] Meanwhile, the Secretary of State for War oversaw the surveillance of the postal service: officials opened and read between 350,000 and 370,000 letters *per week*.[28] During December 1943 alone, agents read 2,448,554 private letters, eavesdropped on 20,811 telephone calls and intercepted 1,771,330 telegrams.[29] To some extent, French citizens policed themselves. Anonymous letters of denunciation informed the authorities of suspected anti-national behaviour. Punishments were severe; a disparaging remark about the Marshal could land a person in prison.[30] Yet denunciations usually stemmed more from personal jealousies than political loyalty to the regime and few accusations stood up to the scrutiny of police investigation. Nevertheless, the practice was so widespread as to cause concern within Vichy about its effect on national unity.[31]

Judges and magistrates faithfully applied the laws of the regime and in fact only a single judge refused to take the mandatory oath of loyalty to Pétain.[32] There was little resistance from the judiciary when in August 1941 Vichy founded 'Special Sections' attached to the appeal courts to try communist and anarchist crimes.[33] On 5 June 1943, the remit of the Special Sections expanded to include acts that promoted or encouraged 'terrorism, communism, anarchy, social or national subversion', as well as 'rebellion against the established social order'. Indictment for 'social crimes' went back to the anti-anarchist laws of the 1890s; during the interwar years, the authorities regularly charged communists with similar offences.[34] Wartime Minister of Justice Maurice Gabolde justified such an intervention with the warning that growing resistance activity had rendered civil war a real possibility. Men and women convicted in the Special Sections could expect imprisonment, forced labour, or death; forty-five capital sentences were handed down and twelve executions carried out.[35]

The judgements of the Special Sections did not fall evenly on all groups. Communists bore the most severe punishments, frequently receiving hard labour for their crimes. Gaullists were treated comparatively lightly. This difference in treatment in part stemmed from the courts' perceptions of each group. Communists had appeared before French judges throughout the interwar years and magistrates had grown accustomed to thinking of them as a category of incorrigible extremists. Conversely, Gaullists hailed from diverse social, economic and political backgrounds and were therefore less likely to be treated according to type.[36] From 20 January 1944, all resisters suspected of terrorism were rendered liable for court martial. The courts afforded the accused neither a defence lawyer nor a right of appeal. The guilty were shot immediately, with no other sentence but death available to the courts. Two hundred death sentences were delivered in the final six months of the Occupation.[37]

In September 1940, Vichy installed a military court at Gannat (Allier) to deal specifically with dissidence in the empire. The move, which came in the wake of the attack on Dakar, signalled a shift in the regime's attitude to Gaullists abroad. Up to that point, Vichy had treated such offenders as misinformed and misled, under the spell of de Gaulle and his English allies. The establishment of the court at Gannat now recognized these lost sheep as enemies of France.[38] In French West Africa, Boisson took advantage of special legislation to crackdown on Gaullist dissidents. He used the law of September 1939 that had put the empire in a state of siege to charge resisters with threatening state security. The military authorities, rather than the civilian judiciary, now tried suspected Gaullists at a court in Dakar.[39] In Indochina, Decoux established camps for the purpose of housing Gaullist resisters. Indochinese courts condemned these political prisoners to years of forced labour in camps such as Nui-Bara and Long-Xuyên, both in Cochin-China.[40]

Vichy's enthusiastic repression of its opponents pushed the prison system to breaking point. The number of prisoners in French jails increased from 18,000 in 1939 to 59,000 by 1944. The regime's offer in April 1943 to grant a suspended sentence in return for labour service in Germany did little to reduce the size of the prison population.[41] Communist prisoners accounted for a large proportion of inmates: 60 per cent of men imprisoned for acts of resistance at Eysse prison were communists as were 96 per cent of political prisoners in Vichy's prison for women in Rennes.[42] The penal infrastructure strained under the weight of numbers and living conditions in overcrowded jails were intolerable. Tuberculosis and malnutrition were endemic. So appalling was the quality of food that in November 1941 Vichy allowed the Red Cross into its prisons to help feed detainees.[43] Conversely, the regime used starvation as a means of punishment and this had damaging effects on prisoners' health. Incarcerated at the Cherche du midi prison in Paris, Agnès Humbert recounted: 'The hunger is unbearable...I gather that I am being more or less deprived of my soup rations, of the soup that forms our staple diet. The other prisoners have large bowls that hold a litre; I have just a plate and a beaker about the size of a teacup...they are trying to weaken me physically'.[44] The death-rate of prisoners rocketed: at the prison in Riom, 120 prisoners died during the first four months of 1942; prior to 1940, the average number of *annual* deaths stood at four.[45] The situation was no better in Algeria. By May 1942, the prison in Algiers was operating at over three times its capacity. In overcrowded cells, prisoners slept on top of each other. Malnutrition and typhus were rife.[46]

A network of internment camps housed thousands more detainees. Many of the camps dated from the late 1930s when the Republic had interned Spanish Republican refugees, foreign 'undesirables' and communists.[47] By spring 1939, 330,000 inmates languished in French camps on the mainland. The first camps in Algeria opened in March 1939 when the surrender of Madrid sparked a seaborne exodus from Spain to North Africa.[48] The precise number of Vichy's camps is difficult to determine. There were at least thirty in the Southern Zone and over a dozen in the Northern Zone. Across North Africa, more than thirty camps housed units of the Groupements de Travailleurs Étrangers (GTE) forced labour gangs.[49] Vichy took charge of running all the camps except for those at Compiègne in the North and Struthof in the annexed region of Alsace. The population of the camps grew from September 1940 when the law permitted the internment of 'all individuals representing a danger to national defence or public security'. Up to 5,000 communists alone fell victim to this legislation prior to mid-1941.[50] In October 1940, the camp population grew further when the regime rendered all foreign Jews liable for detention. In total, Denis Peschanski estimates that approximately 60,000 prisoners passed through Vichy's camp system during the Occupation; 75 per cent of internees were foreign Jews.[51]

Internees lived in appalling conditions: by March 1941, one-third of people in southern camps were suffering from malnutrition and gastro-intestinal complaints.[52] At the Drancy camp near Paris (where mainly Jews and foreigners were housed), a report in August 1941 noted that many prisoners had lost up to 20 kilograms in weight due to a diet that consisted of two thin soups per day while dysentery was rife. Following an inspection of the camp in October 1941, German officials ordered the immediate release of 900 prisoners due to their ill health.[53] In the North African camps at Djelfa and Djenien-Bou-Rezg, inmates suffered routine torture, overwork and starvation.[54] The Saharan camp of Colomb Béchar lacked adequate food and clothing; scorpion and snake infestations presented further dangers for its prisoners.[55] So hard was life for the GTE at Hadjerat M'Guil in Algeria that inmates nicknamed the camp the 'French Buchenwald'.[56]

Colonial governments applied mainland repressive legislation to the territories under their authority. In Madagascar, Governor Annet transposed the repressive features of the National Revolution onto the island, pursuing with vigour communists, trade unionists and recalcitrant indigenous nationalists. Seven of the regime's opponents were executed.[57] On the island

Figure 18 *Children held prisoner at the Rivesaltes internment camp in May 1941. Photo by Everett Collection Inc./Alamy Stock Photo.*

of La Réunion, Vichy's law against Freemasons of 13 August 1940 took immediate effect and officials seized and sold off masonic property. Within two years, all Freemasons in primary education had lost their jobs.[58] In addition to grafting metropolitan legislation onto colonial lands, Vichy's governors tailored their repression to local circumstance. In the Antilles, the French authorities targeted the consumption of rum, the carnival tradition and the bals populaires, deeming that all would likely undermine the morality of the new France.[59] The proximity of French West Africa to both the Gaullist French Equatorial Africa and British imperial possessions saw Boisson expand the colony's police forces. Several new bodies emerged. The Service Menées Antinationales (Antinational Activities Agency) worked with the Ministry of Colonies to investigate dissenters. The General Security Service assumed authority over the police in Dakar and for security services in the other regions of the colony. The Direction des Affaires Politiques et Administratives (Directorate of Political and Administrative Affairs) monitored public opinion in the colony and adjacent territories.[60] In addition to such innovations, in all colonies Vichy's repression mixed with long-established forms of colonial control; the Etat Français was simply less concerned than its democratic predecessor to mask the brazen exploitation of indigenous subjects.[61] In French West Africa, Vichy's use of forced labour and its payment of starvation wages built on long-established Republican precedent.[62] The indigénat – the arbitrary system of laws applied to colonial subjects – remained in force as it had done under the Republic.[63] Consequently, if fresh measures aimed to punish the new enemies of the French state, colonial governments could rely on much older forms of repression to keep the indigenous population in line.

Vichy was not a police state but it was 'a highly policed society'.[64] The repressive apparatus of the Etat Français and its colonial governments sought to eliminate the Anti-France, ensure popular loyalty to the regime and remove all obstacles to the reconstruction of the nation. Censorship and surveillance closely monitored the population, aiming to nip dissent in the bud. The professional culture of policing and promises of better salaries ensured the loyalty of officers in 1940. Specialist police forces, together with new paramilitary formations, rooted out ideological and ethnic undesirables. The judiciary adapted easily to the repressive requirements of the new regime and, from 1941, its Special Sections punished resister-terrorists with assiduity. Given both the regime's long list of opponents and victims and the diverse repressive means at its disposal, it is small wonder that prisons and internment camps soon reached capacity.

Gypsies, homosexuals and blacks

Long-established French prejudices underscored much of the regime's thinking with regard to its persecution and discrimination. This fact ensured that in certain areas French repression developed in directions different to that enforced in Nazi Germany. Vichy's policy on gypsies illustrates this point. The regime established a special camp for the Roma and Sinti traveller population at Salier (Bouches-du-Rhône). The close surveillance of travellers built on Republican precedent: the law of 1912 had required that all travelling salespersons and traders (a thinly veiled euphemism for gypsies) carry a special identity card upon which was recorded a number of the bearer's physical features (Republican authorities kept similar information on criminals). Later, on 6 April 1940, the Reynaud government required all gypsies to reside in a designated area under police surveillance under the pretext of national security concerns.[65]

Following the defeat, the Nazi authorities in the North ordered the internment of all gypsies (the law of 4 October 1940). In January 1941 all travelling professions were outlawed, a measure that saw the rate of internment increase substantially. In the Southern Zone, prefects were empowered to intern traveller populations or impose upon them compulsory residence orders to ensure that they did not venture beyond defined geographic boundaries.[66] Compulsory residence orders paid little heed to their victims' family, professional or personal circumstances. Families were torn apart as the authorities assigned spouses without marriage certificates to different areas while the prefect rarely granted permission to work outside the residence zone. Some gypsies were forced to sleep in the open air for the residence orders did not provide housing. Police made numerous arrests for infractions of the orders and the courts treated gypsies with undue severity.[67]

During the course of the war, Vichy interned as many as 6,500 gypsies. Living conditions in the gypsy camps were poor. Food and water were scarce and sanitary facilities inadequate while the French guards regularly beat inmates.[68] The internment of the traveller population served two ends. Firstly, the segregation of gypsies from society pleased those French who lived near gypsy encampments. Locals had long complained about the alleged criminal behaviour of gypsies who were associated with acts of petty theft. Secondly, the policy of internment sought to assimilate gypsies into the nation while erasing traveller culture. Internees received an education in the values of the National Revolution to nurture and develop their 'Frenchness'. Travellers did not blithely accept internment. Protests and riots within the camps occurred. Escape attempts were frequent: 66 per cent of internees at the Rivesaltes camp escaped at least once.[69] Vichy responded to these challenges with imprisonment and re-internment, rather than execution. The regime understood its 'gypsy problem' in cultural terms that differed from Berlin's racial conception of the issue; Germany deported approximately 20,000 travellers to the Auschwitz-Birkenau death camp.[70]

Vichy's policy on homosexuality likewise differed from that of the Third Reich. The Etat Français's campaign against so-called immoral practices inspired the law on homosexuality of 6 August 1942. This legislation provided for the punishment of 'unnatural' or immoral sexual acts with a minor of the same sex aged under twenty-one years. Offenders could expect up to two years' imprisonment. Homosexual relationships between *adult* French remained beyond the purview of the law and Vichy did not systematically persecute adult gay citizens.[71] A certain ambiguity characterized German policy on French homosexuality in northern France. The Occupation authorities deported twenty-three Frenchmen for soliciting sex with German troops; six of these men died in concentration camps. Yet the famous Select gay bar in Paris remained open though soldiers were not permitted to frequent it. In the annexed regions of Alsace and the Moselle, approximately 350 people were prosecuted for homosexuality. One hundred prosecutions resulted in expulsion to the Southern Zone of France; the remainder were imprisoned and twelve died while in custody. These numbers are certainly deplorable but they are low in comparison with the scale of persecution in the wider Reich. The Reichzentrale zur Bekämpfung der Homosexualität und der Abreibung was responsible for the repression of homosexuality in Germany. In 1938 alone, 8,562 people fell victim to its persecution. Meanwhile, up to 15,000 concentration camp inmates wore the pink triangle of homosexuality. SS guards singled out these men for brutal treatment and 60 per cent of such prisoners died.[72]

Historians have rarely broached the question of Vichy's treatment of black citizens and subjects. The German Occupier imposed its own restrictions. Black women could not work in brothels that served the German army.[73] Black people were unable to cross the Demarcation Line freely into the North until May 1941. It is unclear whether this directive originated from the Occupier or the French administration. A number of colonial parliamentarians protested the measure directly to Pétain yet the Marshal, though expressing regret, did nothing to resolve the issue.[74] It is more difficult to discern a distinctly 'anti-black' agenda at Vichy: the Etat Français did not enact explicitly discriminatory legislation against people of colour as it did against Jews. In some cases, black subjects enjoyed privileges denied to Jews. In French West Africa, it was still possible for indigenous subjects to become naturalized French citizens; this option was not available to Jews. Nevertheless, only five West Africans were naturalized in 1942; in 1939, the corresponding number stood at thirty-eight.[75] Moreover, some incidents of apparent French racism originated with the Occupier. When in July 1941, Vichy announced the liberation of all prisoners of the 'white race' remaining in France, black prisoners directed their anger at the French state. This was in fact a German decision merely endorsed by Vichy. Similarly, the German decision in November 1941 to release 10,000 colonial soldiers, the majority of whom were North African, was also interpreted by black colonial prisoners as evidence of French racism.[76]

Vichy certainly treated non-whites according to its broader 'racialist world view' that assigned particular moral and physical characteristics to different races.[77] Vichy's colonial governments were more explicit in their racism than their Republican predecessors (the latter were at least required to dress up their racism in the language of universalism).[78] In French West Africa, the blatant racism of the new colonial authority shocked Africans, especially the educated elite who had enjoyed some small amount of privilege under Republican rule.[79] Administrators in Senegal studied a project to withdraw the citizenship of the so-called privilégiés, the indigenous peoples who received automatic citizenship from the French state. The plan was abandoned for fear that it would gift a propaganda victory to the Free French. On the island of La Réunion, there was a 'redoubling' of racism under Admiral Robert while Admiral Rouyer (Robert's delegate in the Antilles) demanded the resignation of a number of black civil servants on apparently racial grounds.[80]

Jennings perceives racist motivations behind two pieces of Vichy's legislation. Firstly, on 27 August 1940, the regime abrogated the so-called 'Marchandeau Law' of 21 April 1939. This law repressed religious and racial defamation in the press. While the deletion of the law permitted Vichy to pursue freely its anti-Semitic campaign, all races and religions were now vulnerable to attack. Secondly, the law of 17 April 1942 authorized the withdrawal of French citizenship from any former subject who had committed a criminal offence. Denaturalization rendered the offender subject once again to the indigénat. By this measure, Vichy hoped to deter colonial peoples from joining the Free French. The arbitrary manner with which French administrators dealt with overseas subjects left the law open to abuse and no naturalized French citizen was safe.[81]

Vichy's treatment of French colonial POWs hints at an attitude to blacks that was at least ambiguous. Firstly, on 16 November 1940, the French negotiated the release of all POWs who were fathers of large families. This provision did not apply to colonial soldiers, 60 per cent of whom had at least four children. While Scheck points out that, in any case, many colonial soldiers lacked the documentation to prove their fatherhood, the exemption of colonial soldiers spoke to Vichy's equivocal position on non-whites.[82] Secondly, from September 1941, the Commissariat Général au Reclassement des Prisonniers de Guerre lobbied employers to retain soldiers' jobs for them while they remained in captivity and provided support to prisoners' families. Once again, colonial POWs found themselves exempted and there was no such body for them. Martin Thomas therefore concludes that Vichy's 'crude racialism' was plain; '[the regime] attached greater importance to the lives of French prisoners than to those of its colonial troops'.[83]

Vichy's policies on gypsies, homosexuals and non-whites exposed the regime's cultural, sexual and racial prejudices. Discrimination drew on French precedent and prejudice rather than imitation of the Nazi regime. Republican governments had long monitored the gypsy population of France and attempted to restrict the movements of these 'undesirables'. Wartime measures on homosexuality similarly emerged from older concerns about the effect of same-sex relationships on public morality. French permissiveness ensured that the Nazi persecution of homosexuals was not imported to regions under Vichy's authority. As for blacks, Vichy's racism fell broadly in line with contemporary French and European attitudes to non-whites.

Vichy's anti-Semitism: Aims and origins

During July 1940–1942, legal and bureaucratic discrimination against Jews characterized Vichy's anti-Semitic policy. The regime's two 'Jewish Statutes' (passed on 3 October 1940 and 2 June 1941) defined Jewishness and introduced a host of restrictions and exclusions across France and its Empire. During this first phase of persecution, large-scale arrests were exceptional and confined mainly to the Occupied Zone: during August 1941, for example, raids in the North saw almost 9,000 Jews of mainly foreign origin interned.[84] Vichy's intention was to steadily strip Jews in France of their political, civil and professional rights in order to reduce them to second-class citizens.

The second phase of French anti-Jewish persecution began in July 1942. In the wake of the conference at Wannsee in January 1942 (at which the Nazi leadership approved the murder of the Jewish population of Europe), pressure came to bear on Vichy to provide Jews for deportation to the

East. Germany demanded an initial quota of 28,000 Jews; arrests began in Paris on 16 July 1942. This operation – codenamed Spring Breeze – was the responsibility of the French police; Jews had become an important bargaining chip in matters of sovereignty. Nine thousand officers captured nearly 16,000 Jews.[85] Eight thousand Jews, including 4,000 children, languished for several days in the city's indoor sports stadium, the Vélodrome d'Hiver.[86] Deportation to Auschwitz awaited the prisoners. The 'Vél d'Hiv' roundup has come to symbolize France's involvement in the Holocaust. In sum, seventy-nine convoys of trains took 75,721 Jews from France to their death in Eastern Europe. Several thousand more died from mistreatment or execution in France itself.[87] By 1945, approximately 80,000 Jews – 24 per cent of France's pre-war Jewish population – were dead.[88]

The Nazi Occupier did not require the Etat Français to implement anti-Semitic legislation. Rather, the regime acted autonomously, tapping into a long tradition of French anti-Semitism, on the left and right. Left-wing anti-Semitism connected capitalism with Jewish control of French finances, a position articulated in Alphonse Toussenel's 1847 *Les Juifs, rois de l'époque* and the journal, *La Revue socialiste*. During the 1880s, radical right-wing groups discovered the potential of anti-Semitism to mobilize public opinion against the Republic. Attacks on Jews drew on theories of national identity popularized in the works of intellectuals such as Maurice Barrès who argued that Israélites, as a 'rootless' people, could never be truly French. The developing fields of anthropology, psychology and sociology further fed anti-Semitic prejudice. Anthropologist Georges Vacher de la Pouge blamed interracial breeding for what he perceived to be the degradation of the French race. Psychologist Jules Soury pitted the Aryan French against the inferior Jewish 'species'. In 1886, anti-Semitic journalist Edouard Drumont published *La France juive*, a book that synthesized contemporary popular hatreds and prejudices regarding Jews. Drumont's book helped to normalize debate about the 'Jewish problem' in France, bringing it into the mainstream political arena. The book proved wildly popular and underwent 200 re-editions in fifteen years.[89]

Late nineteenth-century anti-Semitism reached fever pitch during the 'Dreyfus Affair'. In December 1894, Captain Alfred Dreyfus, a Jewish Frenchman from Alsace, was found guilty of passing military secrets to Germany and deported to Devil's Island, a penal colony off the coast of French Guiana.[90] The conviction, however, was far from safe and further investigation revealed that the case against Dreyfus rested on forged evidence; the real spy was in fact Major Ferdinand Esterhazy. The campaign to reopen Dreyfus's case gathered strength and the captain returned to France for a retrial in 1899. The case divided the country between Dreyfus's supporters (the Dreyfusards) and those who defended the position that the honour of the army could not be challenged (the anti-Dreyfusards). The anti-Dreyfusard campaign deployed anti-Semitism to its full extent in its defence of the military. During January and February 1898, sixty-six anti-Semitic disturbances occurred in cities throughout the country. This was 'an explosion of anti-Semitism without precedent in the history of contemporary France', according to Gérard Noiriel.[91] Later that year, Drumont's *La Libre Parole* newspaper launched a funding drive to support the widow of Colonel Hubert-Joseph Henry, the man who had forged the evidence against Dreyfus and who had subsequently committed suicide while awaiting prosecution. Donors made various proposals as to the solution to the 'Jewish problem', suggesting that Jews be poisoned, roasted, burned alive, guillotined, shot, boiled in oil and fed to cats and dogs. The campaign raised 131,110 Francs. It attested to the extent to which anti-Semitic diatribes in the press had whipped up popular hatred.[92]

After the First World War, the service of Jews in the French army changed some minds about the alleged traitorous nature of their 'race'. A more tolerant atmosphere prevailed; *La Libre Parole* collapsed in the mid-1920s. The respite from anti-Semitism was brief. During the 1930s, the immigration of refugees from Central and Eastern Europe, many of whom were Jews fleeing persecution, was met with hostility and xenophobia. Parties and leagues across the political spectrum decried the 'immigrant problem', the symptoms of which ranged from the prolonged economic crisis of the decade to the alleged interference of foreign spies and terrorists in French politics. Extreme right-wing groups such as the Action Française and the PPF took a stridently anti-Semitic position, connecting Jews with Republicanism and communism and demanding that France rid itself of both. With as many as 3 million members, La Rocque's right-wing PSF espoused a chauvinism that strayed at times into anti-Jewishness. Racist weeklies like *Candide* and *Gringoire* enjoyed readerships of approximately half a million each.[93] In response to this populism, successive Republican governments attempted to obstruct immigration with laws limiting immigrants' political and professional rights. Police gained new powers to arrest and expel illegal aliens. Internment camps sprang up across the south of the country to house refugees and 'undesirables'.[94] Ultimately, when the Republic fell in July 1940, 'the ground had been well prepared in advance' for anti-Semitism to flourish.[95]

1940–1942: Exclusion

In 1940, France's Jewish community numbered approximately 300,000 in a country of 43 million. Roughly half of the Jewish population was French; the remainder were immigrants who had sought work or refuge in the country. A significant number of Jewish citizens – 90,000 – came from families that had resided in France for generations. A further 60,000 had gained citizenship more recently, thanks to the Republic's relaxation of the law governing naturalizations during the 1920s.[96] Most French Jews considered themselves secular. In fact, of the 90,000 French Jews in Paris in 1939, only about 6,000 paid dues to the Parisian Consistory.[97] These Jews were less easy to identify with their faith than their foreign-born counterparts who wore traditional styles of dress, retained their accents and congregated in the Jewish quarter of Paris; this area was the first to be raided by Vichy's police.[98]

On 3 October 1940, Vichy issued its first Jewish Statute. The Statute was the first French law to delineate a racial group. Article One defined a Jew as any person with three Jewish grandparents, or two such grandparents if one's spouse was also Jewish. The statute considered a person Jewish even after conversion to another religion, a fact that exposed the French state's racial conception of Jewishness. The law disqualified Jews from holding political office as well as posts in the judiciary, the diplomatic service and the senior branches of French bureaucracy. It excluded them from management positions in radio, film and the print media. In an indication of the cultural, rather than essentially racial, basis of Vichy's first Statute, a single exemption applied to Jews who had served during the First World War or distinguished themselves during the campaign of 1940.[99] A second Jewish Statute on 2 June 1941 expanded both the definition of Jewishness and the list of proscribed occupations forbidden to Jews.

Vichy's Minister of Justice Raphaël Alibert drafted the first Statute. Historians once believed that Pétain had little input into the project. However, a document discovered in 2010 showed that the Marshal amended the draft of the text to ensure that a greater number of Jews were subject to the legislation. He further broadened the range of professions from which Jews were excluded.[100] Pétain intervened further in the matter of Jews living in Algeria. In this territory, the first Jewish Statute was swiftly followed on 7 October by the suspension of the Crémieux decree of 1870, the law that had granted French citizenship to all Jews in Algeria. Pétain paid special attention to this matter: he remarked to Weygand in October 1940 that the 'Jewish question' in Algeria required a solution if the regime was to put an end to the Jews' 'harmful political activity' there.[101]

On 4 October 1940, a new law targeted foreign-born Jews in France. The legislation empowered prefects to intern Jewish immigrants without charge. This measure was not the first to discriminate against foreigners. The law of 17 July 1940 excluded naturalized French from posts in government. On 22 July 1940, all cases of citizenship granted since 1927 were placed under review; over 15,000 people (of whom roughly 6,000 were Jewish) were subsequently stripped of their nationality and interned. In August and September 1940, further laws restricted access to the medical and legal professions to those with French fathers only. Restrictions were applied with particular rigour to Jews.[102]

The German Occupation authorities implemented their own measures in the Northern Zone, beginning on 27 September 1940 with the requirement that all Jews register for an identity card carrying the word 'Juif'.[103] Jewish businesses were ordered to display a sign in their window informing customers that they were in an 'Entreprise juive' or a 'Jewish Business'. On 18 October 1940, the Germans placed such businesses under the responsibility of an administrator charged with transferring the business to Aryan ownership (a process known as 'Aryanization').[104] Expulsions accompanied these economic sanctions. On 23 October 1940, 7,700 Jewish refugees from Bade, Palatinatt and the Sarre were expelled from the North to the South. Vichy interned these people at a camp in Gurs; the majority of these refugees were women, elderly people and the very young, Conditions in the camp were so atrocious that within two months inmates were dying at a rate of twelve per day. Six hundred perished in total during the winter of 1940.[105]

Historical and ideological anti-Semitism explains only in part the French regime's agenda. The logic of collaboration influenced the Etat Français in this area, too. The Jewish population offered leverage in French efforts to retain control of domestic affairs. The establishment of Vichy's Commissariat Général aux Questions Juives (General Commissariat for Jewish Questions, CGQJ) – a 'virtual ministry of state anti-Semitism'[106] – in March 1941 arose from this concern. When Abetz intimated to Darlan that the Germans would establish a 'Jewish office' in the North, the deputy Prime Minister acted quickly to take the matter out of German hands.[107] Xavier Vallat took charge of the new CGQJ. A former right-wing deputy, Vallat was an intransigent anti-Semite who believed that 'anti-Semitism has never been aroused by anything but the Jews' unsociability and their intrinsically

Figure 19 *Notice in a restaurant window banning Jews from entering, German-occupied Paris, July 1940. Photo by The Print Collector/Alamy Stock Photo.*

inassimilable nature'.[108] Vallat oversaw the extension of Aryanization to the Southern Zone in July 1941, ensuring simultaneously that the French managed the process in both zones. By May 1944, the French and German authorities had stolen 42,277 Jewish businesses with nearly a quarter sold on to Aryans. The CGQJ epitomized the Vichy leadership's approach to relations with the Germans; as Michael Marrus and Robert Paxton concluded, 'by internalizing parts of the German project, stamping them "made in Vichy" and extending them to the Unoccupied Zone, they seem to have hoped that they could both extend French authority and diminish the German grip over the Occupied Zone'.[109]

The response of the French public to Vichy's anti-Semitism during 1940–1942 was muted. According to prefects' reports on public opinion, few French reacted openly to the publication of the first Jewish Statute. Only four out of forty-two prefects reported an unfavourable response. Similar indifference greeted the second Statute. The shortages of wartime and the struggle to survive concerned the French more than the fate of the Jews. Daily miseries revived and reinforced age-old anti-Semitic prejudices. It was rumoured that Jews were hoarding resources, making money from the black

Figure 20 *Opening of the Institute of Jewish Questions and the arrival of a portrait of Marshal Petain in Paris, May 1941. Photo by Roger Viollet/Getty Images. The text in the photograph reads: 'The Jews are like an Asiatic colony in France. They live among us like in a foreign land, three times foreign, for they are neither French, nor Christian, nor even European'.*

market, and profiting from the war.[110] Some French took advantage of the regime's hostility towards Jews for their own ends. A family in Limoges sought the help of Vichy's Police for Jewish Questions to evict tenants from their rented property. It was common for similar material concerns to trump political motivation in instances of ostensible public anti-Semitism.[111] Vichy's policy seemed reasonable to many French who remembered the refugee crises of the 1930s. The public were thus generally favourable to the sanctions that befell foreign Jews but officials had to exercise more caution in the case of French Jews. However, anti-Semitic discrimination left most French unmoved.[112]

Jews responded in diverse ways to Vichy's persecution. Native Jewish organizations were slow to react to the threat from Vichy. The leaders of the French Jewish community had long held their tongue on the persecution of Jews abroad, fearful that this would provoke an anti-Semitic backlash in France. In November 1940, the Parisian Consistory reacted to the first Jewish Statute by blaming 'foreign elements who had not assimilated themselves to the national spirit' and citing 'an understandable anti-Semitism' misdirected at French Jews. Unity between the Consistory and immigrant Jewish groups only came on the eve of the Liberation.[113] Still, the Jewish community took advantage of long-established social and cultural networks in its attempt to blunt the force of discrimination. The vulnerability of foreign Jews was greater than that of their indigenous counterparts yet they too could rely on political and social organizations. These 'networks of complicity' provided support when Jews lost their jobs or needed a hiding place.[114]

There were multiple individual responses. Within weeks of the first Jewish Statute, journalist Jacques Biélinky learned of seven suicides of Jews in Paris.[115] Other individuals chose to make public statements of defiance. A handful of Jewish shopkeepers in the Northern Zone displayed posters such as 'Veteran of 1914–1918, war wounded. French shop' and 'Owner volunteered for the war of 1914–1918; his two employees [are] veterans of 1939–1940', alongside the mandatory 'Entreprise juive' sign.[116] Following the introduction of the yellow star in the North on 1 June 1942, Jewish teenage Hélène Berr made the following entry in her diary:

> [We met] at Mme Jourdan's and we talked about the meaning of the insignia. At that point I was determined not to wear it. I considered it degrading, proof of one's submission to the Germans' laws. This evening I've changed my mind: I now think it is cowardly not to wear it, vis-à-vis people who will. Only, if I do wear it, I want to stay very elegant and dignified at all times so that people can see what that means. I want to do whatever was most courageous. This evening I believe that means wearing the star. [117]

Defiance was idiosyncratic.

Anti-Semitism overseas

Vichy's overseas governments implemented the regime's anti-Semitic legislation with varying degrees of zeal. Anti-Semitic sentiment was generally sharper in Algeria than on the French mainland. The 117,000-strong Jewish population's apparent loyalty to Republicanism angered the French settler community whose sympathies laid with fascism.[118] Pétain himself recognized that the Jewish question was 'very sensitive' in North Africa.[119] General Maxime Weygand oversaw the implementation of anti-Jewish measures in Algeria during October 1940 to November 1941. To a certain extent, Algerian anti-Semitism mirrored that of the French regime. The Jewish Statutes and the Aryanization process were applied soon after their introduction in France, much to the satisfaction of European settlers. Regional peculiarities also developed. The Service des Question Juives (Service for Jewish Questions) directed the regime's discrimination in the place of the CGQJ, which did not operate in the territory. In autumn 1942, Governor-General Yves Châtel examined a project to require all Algerian Jews to wear a yellow armband displaying the six-pointed star; Vichy had rejected this course of action in January that year. The Allied invasion in November 1942 halted Châtel's plan.[120] Still, the French authorities proceeded cautiously in the realm of anti-Semitic propaganda for they feared that a more virulent campaign against Jews would win indigenous Arabic subjects over to Nazism rather than the National Revolution.[121]

In the French Moroccan protectorate, where approximately 200,000 Jews resided, the Sultan approved anti-Jewish 'dahirs' (royal decrees). The dahirs drew inspiration from the first Jewish Statute but they contained an important exception: a Moroccan who was born Jewish and who had subsequently converted to another faith was no longer subject to discrimination.[122] Restrictions on Jewish life reflected those of mainland France. The government introduced a quota system to limit the proportion of Jews in certain professions; ceilings of 2 per cent applied to the medical and legal professions with a 10 per cent limit in secondary school teaching. Further regulations required Jews resident in European neighbourhoods to move into Jewish ghettoes. Discrimination pleased the settlers but Vichy's commander in Morocco, General Noguès, was concerned above all with the maintenance of order in the protectorate. He ordered the censorship of a number of anti-Semitic publications lest they provoke violent pogroms against the Jewish community. A similar concern motivated his decision to detain 7,700 Jewish refugees in rural internment camps while they awaited transport to the United States and Palestine. Forced labour camps at Agdz and Bou Denib housed 'politically suspect' Jewish residents.[123]

The presence of a large Italian Jewish population obstructed the enactment of Vichy's anti-Semitic laws in Tunisia. Resident General Admiral Jean-Pierre Estéva did not wish to provoke Italian intervention in the territory (which Mussolini had long coveted) with policies that targeted the entirety of the territory's 90,000 Jews.[124] Estéva promulgated both of Vichy's Jewish Statutes in the name of the Bey yet only one further piece of racial legislation subsequently came into force before 1942. Aryanization remained partial in order to avoid the seizure of Italian Jewish businesses and property. Anti-Semitic repression gathered pace after March 1942 when Estéva came under renewed pressure from CGQJ representative in Tunisia, François Hayaux du Tilly, to act more forcefully. However, many of the subsequent decrees lacked the necessary legal ratification to make them into law. Vichy's racial legislation in Tunisia thus 'lagged significantly behind that of the metropole and never saw full implementation'.[125] This state of affairs arose from the complexity of the colonial situation rather than from any concern for the protectorate's Jews. Indeed, throughout French North Africa, the exclusionary essence of Vichy's anti-Semitism remained intact. By the end of 1941, Jews in the Maghreb were second-class citizens.[126]

Beyond France's possessions in North Africa, the Jewish population under French rule was very small. A census conducted in summer 1941 found 140 Jews in Indochina, 26 in Madagascar, and none on the island of La Réunion; the Jewish community of the empire was only a 'drop in the ocean' of the broader population.[127] Still, on 15 March 1941, Vichy decreed that colonial governments should apply the first Jewish Statute. By the end of that same year, colonial minister Admiral Platon had prepared the way for the implementation of the second Statute throughout the empire. In French West Africa, Boisson removed or demoted Jews working in the French administration; 68 of the 287 civil servants sanctioned according to Vichy law were Jewish.[128] On Madagascar, the imperial government persecuted its Jewish subjects with assiduity: Jews lost their jobs and suffered the same political and professional restrictions as their mainland counterparts.[129] In Indochina, Decoux pursued the handful of Jews with fervour despite the fact that the small European settler elite was vital to his defence of French rule against Japanese intrusion. Jews found themselves excluded from numerous professions and universities applied quotas to their intake of Jewish students.[130] Meanwhile, in the Antilles, Robert and Sorin even scuppered a plan to deport foreign Jews from mainland France to their islands.[131] Vichy loyalists helped to export the anti-Semitic demonology of the National Revolution around the world. Such actions, undertaken free from the threat of German intervention, provided further proof, if any were needed, of the French roots of Vichy's anti-Semitism.

1942–1944: France and the Final Solution

In January 1942, senior Nazi officials met at Wannsee to decide upon the 'Final Solution' to the 'Jewish Question': the murder of the Jewish population of Europe. German policy towards Jews in France subsequently fell in line with this broader strategy. In May 1942, Reinhardt Heydrich notified Vichy's police chief Bousquet of the German decision to deport foreign Jews from the Occupied Zone to Eastern Europe. The following month, Theodor Dannecker – Adolf Eichmann's representative in France – informed Vichy of the number required: 40,000 Jews aged between sixteen and forty years. Thirty thousand of this total would be taken from the North while the French were required to make up the remainder from the internment camp population in the South. Dannecker insisted that 40 per cent of deportees be of French nationality.[132]

Laval – who had returned as Head of Government in April 1942 – baulked at the proposal to deport French Jews. His reluctance to deport French nationals stemmed less from any humanitarian concern than from the likely negative effect on public opinion.[133] In conjunction with Bousquet, Laval came to a compromise agreement, ratified by Oberg on 2 July. Arrests would be limited to foreign Jews including children under sixteen (a special request from Laval himself). French police would conduct the entire operation.[134] Arrests began in Paris on 16 July 1942 with the Vél d'Hiv roundup. Berr's diary gives a vivid account of the fear amongst the Jewish community of Paris in the wake of the arrests. Rumours abounded: 'a whole family, the father, the mother, and five children, gassed themselves to escape the roundup'; '[o]ne woman lost her mind and threw her four children out of the window'; '[w]omen are giving birth right there [in the Vél d'Hiv]. No medical help'; 'Mme Carpentier saw two goods trains at Drancy in which men and women had been stacked like cattle, without even any straw, for deportation'.[135] French police began arresting Jews in the South during August. For Laval and his ministers, the sacrifice of Jewish immigrants was a price easily paid to maintain French sovereignty over the operation. The arrests therefore spoke to Vichy's twisted logic of collaboration. In total, 40,000 Jews left France for the East during 1942.[136]

French anti-Semitism subsequently spiralled in a radical direction. Head of the CGQJ, Louis Darquier de Pellepoix (who had replaced Vallat in April 1942) applied himself with zeal to his role. His interest in race science led to the founding of several intellectual bodies devoted to the study of such questions, such as the Institute of Anthropo-Sociology and the Institute for the Study of Jewish and Ethno-Racial Questions under Georges Montandon.[137] Montandon acted as an ethnological expert for the CGQJ, examining citizens to determine their Jewishness. His investigations encompassed a subject's family history and a physical examination to determine the degree to which their stature, complexion, facial features and – in the case of men – their penis resembled those of a Jew. Montandon's judgements varied from 'not specifically Jewish', 'a little Jewish' to 'could pass for very Jewish'.[138]

The radicalization of Vichy's anti-Semitism shook some French from their apathy. Prefects noted a public reaction during summer 1942 especially in the departments that bordered the Demarcation Line and

Figure 21 *Jewish deportees in the Drancy transit camp, their last stop before the German concentration camps, c. 1942. Photo by AFP/Getty Images.*

to which many Jews fled from the North. Refugees did not receive a great deal of sympathy from their new neighbours. On the contrary, with Jews now on the doorstep of many southern French, some responses were hostile. Nevertheless, the arrests of women and children undermined official explanations that the deportees were going to work in the East. Scenes of panic, chaos and misery in the streets as police tore Jews from their beds and manhandled them into trucks raised concerns. Protestant leaders publicly aired their concerns. On 23 August 1942, a letter from Archbishop Jules Saliège of Toulouse was read aloud in the churches of his diocese. It called on Christians to recognize their common humanity with the Jews: 'They are our brothers like so many others'. The following month, Pastor Marc Boegner, leader of the Protestant Federation, likewise condemned the discrimination and arrests in a public letter. Catholic and protestant clergy hid Jews, rescuing thousands.[139] The decline in support for Vichy's anti-Semitism weakened the regime's resolve and Laval eventually withdrew full French co-operation. From spring 1943, German Occupation forces took charge of the arrests. With Berlin in command, Vichy's distinction between French and foreign Jews ceased to matter and 17,069 Jews of all nationalities were deported that year. By the Liberation, a further 14,833 Jews had left for the East as the Nazis, in conjunction with the Milice, searched for more victims.[140]

The Italian-occupied zone offered a form of refuge for Jews seeking to escape persecution. Since June 1940, Rome had persistently frustrated Vichy's sovereignty in the South while nurturing its own project to annexe portions of the French Riviera. In December 1942, Italy refused a French order to evacuate all Jews from the southern coastline to internment camps in France.[141] On 2 March 1943, General Avarna di Gualteri informed Admiral Platon that all Jews, foreign and French, were now under the protection of Italy. In matters other than criminal offences, only Occupation soldiers were now permitted to carry out arrests.[142] As the rumour spread that the Italian Zone offered protection, the Jewish population in the Alpes-Maritimes rose to approximately 30,000 by 1943, double its pre-war level.[143] Rivalry between the French and Italian authorities had worked to the benefit of the Jewish community, much to the incomprehension (and no little suspicion) of the Germans. However, it would be a mistake to regard Italy's attitude to the Jews as an example of noble humanitarianism for, while the occupation authorities refused to deport Jews from the south east, it proceeded to intern suspect aliens – and Jews. Police-Inspector General Guido Lospinoso, who was, from 19 March 1943, responsible for policy towards the Jews in Italian occupied-France, delivered lists of German Jews under Italian authority, to the SS in Marseille.[144]

Developments in the war meant that this situation could not last indefinitely. In the wake of the Italian Armistice with the Allies on 8 September 1943, German forces arrived in Nice. SS officer Alois Brunner led a special commando, with the support of the PPF, to arrest Jews in the southeast. Between 10 September 1943 and 14 December 1943, 1,189 Jews were transported to Drancy. This number fell far short of the 25,000 that Brunner had hoped to capture. A shortage of troops and a lack of French co-operation thwarted the organization of arrests and deportations. In addition, many Jews hid or made the crossing into Italy.[145]

Did Vichy know of the fate that awaited the men, women and children deported to Eastern Europe? German explanations were replete with euphemism and half-truths about the transferral of Europe's Jews to eastern labour colonies. These explanations were not entirely implausible: during the 1930s, proposals to establish a colony to house Jewish refugees and immigrants were widely discussed, with Madagascar proposed as a possible destination. If the arrests of 1942 aroused some suspicions, the reports of mass killings seemed too horrifying to be true. In July 1942, Laval informed his ministers: 'The German government's intention seems to be to create a Jewish state in the East of Europe. I would not feel dishonoured if I one day sent to that Jewish state the countless foreign Jews who are in France'. In the same meeting, he referred to foreign Jews as 'rubbish sent here by the Germans themselves'. Burrin concludes that, while the industrial extermination of the Holocaust was unimaginable when deportations began in earnest in 1942, 'it certainly was easy to imagine the appalling nature of the future reserved for a population deported like cattle in the middle of a war'.[146] Yet Germany was helping to rid France of a foreign nuisance and Vichy was not interested in pressing the Nazis on the issue.[147]

Survival

Over 75 per cent of the Jewish community in France survived the Second World War. Thirty-thousand Jews remained in Paris, the capital of collaborationism, for the duration of the Occupation, seemingly undisturbed.[148] Only in Denmark and Italy were a greater proportion of Jews spared. In the Netherlands, on the other hand, the Jewish population was devastated: 78 per cent of Jews were deported.[149] After the war, Vichy's apologists cited the relatively high survival rate of Jews in France as evidence of the regime's efforts to protect French Jews from destruction on an even greater scale. Such attempts to rescue the reputation of the Etat Français ignored the many ways in which Vichy persecuted the Jewish community and facilitated the Germans' project to deport thousands. Yet, the survival of so many Jewish people requires explanation.

Aid organizations helped a number of Jews to weather the hardships of the Occupation. The Commission Centrale des Organisations Juives d'Assistance, founded under American impetus in October 1940, offered relief to Jews inside and outside Vichy's camps. Non-Jewish groups such as the ecumenical Amitiés Chrétiennes, the YMCA and the Red Cross provided support in the form of food and medical assistance, as well as education for Jewish children.[150] In August 1942, police in Clermont-Ferrand netted 'only' fifty-nine Jewish people out of a targeted 226; they suspected that those who fled had received a warning from someone in the Red Cross.[151] Jewish immigrants in the Northern Zone established the Comité Amelot to bring legal and social aid to the persecuted. Its members rescued and hid numerous Jews before the Germans shut down the group in late 1943. In the Southern Zone, associations such as the Fédération des Sociétés Juives de France and the Mouvement de la Jeunesse Socialiste operated with relative freedom, providing information and false papers to fugitives and refugees. Clandestine groups such as the Armée Juive and the Children's Relief Organisation procured forged identity documents and arranged for Jews to escape from France.[152] The Jewish scout movement, the Eclaireurs Israélites de France, provided false papers and hid children in its network of rural homes.[153] Charitable associations and private aid networks therefore provided a number of means for Jews to flee French and German repression.

In November 1941, Vichy established an official umbrella organization for all Jewish associations called the Union Générale des Israélites de France (UGIF). The founding of the UGIF caused concern amongst French Jewish leaders who were suspicious of the organization's affiliation to the CGQJ. Vichy countered that the UGIF's attachment to the CGQJ ensured that the association remained under French authority rather than becoming a Nazi-style Judenrat. In any case, French Jewish notables were confident that the regime did not intend to persecute the *native* Jewish community. The UGIF undertook a range of aid activities from the organization of social services to the provision of financial support. Its workers took charge of children whose parents had left France for the East: between July and November 1942, the UGIF placed over a thousand orphaned children in private homes and shelters.[154]

The UGIF maintained a strict legalism in its operations for it did not wish to draw unwelcome attention to the French Jewish community with obstructionism. Consequently, when arrests began in mid-1942, the UGIF continued with its relationship with the government in an effort to fend off greater repression. So concerned was it to retain the good favour of the regime that, having learned on 1 July 1942 of the plan to arrest Jews in the North, the UGIF waited two weeks before warning the Jewish communities under threat.[155] The fact that the arrests initially targeted foreign Jews alone informed the UGIF's actions. Like the Parisian Consistory, the UGIF distinguished between French and foreign Jews, believing that 'Jewish immigrants had compromised the future of French-born citizens of France'.[156] Ultimately, while the UGIF unquestionably provided important social services and legal assistance to Jews in France, it practised legalism 'to the point of self-delusion', and its mistakes and attitude to foreign Jews cost lives.[157]

Resistance groups generally responded to the persecution of Jews in France with caution. Sporadic references to anti-Semitic repression appeared in resistance propaganda. Jacques Duchesne, a French producer in charge of the 'Français parlent aux Français' BBC broadcast, condemned on the radio on 20 October 1942 what he termed 'the persecution of the Jews that has begun in France'. However, the resistance considered little difference between Jews in France and war victims such as the French residents of Alsace.[158] Some leading resisters even recognized the existence of a so-called 'Jewish problem'. Maurice Ripoche of CDLL wrote that the task ahead was to 'complete the work of liberation by ridding the Nation of inept and blowhard politicians (good or bad) [and] of stateless Jews'.[159] Neither de Gaulle's Free French nor the internal resistance movements were willing to risk wholesale association with the Jewish cause, lest Vichy and the Nazis draw propaganda value from it.

Once the roundups commenced, Vichy's opponents were more incisive in their criticism. Yet the Free French Comité Exécutive de Propagande focused more on the inhumane treatment of detainees than on the political aspects of anti-Semitism. Its aim was to appeal to the human sentiments of all French (even anti-Semites) and its propaganda posed the Jews as victims of a broader policy to brutalize the entire French nation. After October 1942, references to the Jews in France disappeared from both Free French radio broadcasts and the underground press. Reports about the fate of the Jews in

Eastern Europe still appeared yet, in the French context, 'deportation' now meant forced labour service in Germany rather than a death sentence in the East.¹⁶⁰ The reality was that the aim of the resistance and the Free French was to liberate the country; all other matters were secondary.

Many ordinary French helped Jews to flee. There are numerous stories of friends, acquaintances, neighbours, police officers and strangers providing food, shelter and escape routes to Jewish fugitives. By 2017, almost 4,000 French had received the honour of the 'Righteous Among Nations', a title bestowed by the State of Israel on people who helped to save Jews during the Second World War. Only Poland and the Netherlands can claim more such awards than France.¹⁶¹ Many more gestures of solidarity probably went unrecognized. The argument that small acts of kindness shown to Jews helped to save thousands from deportation has recently gained traction in the historiography: Wieviorka concluded that '75 per cent of the French Jewish community was saved by ordinary people acting in spontaneous ways'.¹⁶² Jacques Semelin has likewise argued that the charity of the average French person was central to a 'non-conformist, disobedient, even resistant social tissue, at the heart of which, like other pariahs and enemies of the Occupier and Vichy, [Jews] were able to hide and survive'.¹⁶³ This 'social connection between Jews and non-Jews was crucial to counteracting the genocidal project' in France.¹⁶⁴ The survival rate of Jews in France is certainly striking: 90 per cent of French Jews and 60 per cent of foreign Jews survived, as did 86 per cent of all Jewish children, French *and* foreign. However, to cite the benevolence of ordinary citizens as the primary factor in the survival of so many Jews is not only inaccurate but also irresponsible for it skirts perilously close to exonerating the French.

There are a number of factors to consider if we are to understand the survival of the majority of France's Jewish population. Firstly, Jewish and non-Jewish aid organizations hid and sheltered many fugitives: the Children's Relief Organisation alone rescued up to 9,000 children.¹⁶⁵ Secondly, personal wealth, education, status and social networks could determine one's fate.¹⁶⁶ In order to procure false papers, not only one needed to know where to get them but also one needed to have the financial means to pay the cost. Thirdly, the fact that the persecution of the Jewish community intensified at a moment when the French population began to turn away from the regime facilitated their concealment.¹⁶⁷ Fourthly, in some circumstances, it was possible for Jews to hide in plain sight and to coexist with the French State. The pluralist nature of the regime, the disparity between policy implementation at the centre and in the provinces, and the contradictions inherent to numerous policies and projects meant that, though marginalized, some Jews could participate in the very institutions of the National Revolution, such as the Chantiers de la Jeunesse.¹⁶⁸ Finally, the policy of the Occupier towards France was highly significant to the survival of the Jews. In Eastern Europe, the extermination of the entire Jewish population was a prerequisite to Hitler's plan to expand Germany eastward. Concomitantly, some occupied territories in Western Europe, such as the Netherlands, were considered 'Germanic' regions, and prepared for full-scale Nazification. France, on the other hand, was not reserved for German settlement. The liberation of the country during 1944 spared the Jewish population the radicalization of the Final Solution in the final year of the war.[169] Between April and November 1944, 7,534 Jews from France arrived at Auschwitz. In the same period, over 400,000 Hungarian Jews were transported to this camp.[170] Overall, Jewish survival in France did not depend on the goodwill of the French alone.[171]

Conclusion

Vichy's programme of repression, persecution and discrimination was multifaceted. The success of the National Revolution depended on both the renovation and reconstruction of France and the removal of so-called enemies and undesirables. The exclusionary apparatus of the Etat Français state built in part on Republican precedent, not least in the democratic regime's construction of a network of internment camps during the 1930s. Furthermore, in the final decade of the Third Republic, police officers, lawyers, magistrates and judges had grown used to discriminating against so-called undesirables. Vichy thus encountered little problem in enforcing tougher sanctions against the 'Anti-France'. Yet the regime's repressive policies extended far beyond the bounds of those of its democratic forerunner. The Special Sections, for example, were just one of a host of areas in which Vichy innovated. The repression of resistance was bloody. German firing squads executed 4,000 people. Eighty-eight thousand civilians were deported on grounds other than their race; 35,000 of these deportees perished in Nazi concentration camps.[172]

The enforcement of legislation in the lands of the French Empire ensured that Vichy's repression had a global reach. The racist imperial project had long used coercion and violence to repress dissent and put down rebellion. Vichy cast off the universalist rhetoric of the Republic in the name of the National Revolution and exploitation remained the order of the day. Colonial administrators pursued the so-called enemies of France in foreign lands, tailoring persecution to local contexts. This appreciation of local circumstance sometimes resulted in an uneven application of repression in France's overseas possessions. Nevertheless, Pétain's repressive crusade fell on people worldwide.

Vichy's anti-Semitism drew on French tradition. Since the late nineteenth century, anti-Semites had popularized anti-Jewish bigotry. The economic depression of the 1930s and the arrival of foreign refugees into France revived anti-Semitism in mainstream politics, convincing many that a solution to this 'problem' was the most pressing issue of the day. The Etat Français took advantage of these prejudices and few French protested against its discriminatory Jewish Statutes. As the regime's persecution radicalized in tandem with the Nazis' plan to commit genocide, opposition grew. Yet the public's indifference to the awful treatment of Jews in France – and of foreign Jews in particular – bordered on complicity, providing a broadly compliant environment in which a more radical anti-Semitism could operate.

In pondering the survival of so many Jews in France, we must not lose sight of the scale of the regime's persecution or, as Paxton puts it, 'how Vichy made it worse'.[173] Few other collaborationist regimes provided as much help to the German authorities in their mission to destroy European Jews as Vichy. It is unlikely that even a quarter of France's Jewish population would have died without the co-operation of the Etat Français. Vichy sought to exclude Jews from national life rather than to exterminate them yet its actions, set within the warped reasoning of collaboration, aided and abetted Hitler's genocide.[174] Jews in France endured years of suffering, anxiety and loss – of family, friends, property, status and lives. French Jewish author Léon Werth's account of living under the rule of the Gestapo illustrates the state of perpetual anxiety in which some lived: 'I have given the Gestapo a timetable. They once came into the town at nine thirty, another time at four in the morning. When I get up in the morning, I tell myself: "It's past four in the morning, I can relax until nine thirty." And after nine thirty I tell myself, *they* won't come today, at least'.[175]

6

Liberation

Shortly after midnight on 6 June 1944, 18,000 Allied paratroopers dropped into northwestern France to secure vital strategic locations. Hours later, nearly 7,000 ships launched an amphibious assault on the beaches of the French Channel coast. The invasion of Normandy, codenamed Operation Overlord, had begun. An Allied landing in the southeast of the country (Operation Dragoon) took place on 15 August 1944. On 19 August, French resistance forces – now amalgamated into the Forces Françaises de l'Intérieur (FFI) – staged an uprising in Paris. Five days later, General Philippe Leclerc's Deuxième Division Blindée (Second Armoured Division, 2DB) entered the capital with American General George Patton's army close behind. On 25 August, de Gaulle arrived in the City of Light. He delivered a speech at the Hôtel de Ville in which he declared that Paris had been, '[l]iberated by itself, liberated by its people with the help of the French armies, with the support and the help of all France, of the France that fights, of the only France, of the real France, of the eternal France!'[1] The Second Battle of France was not yet over. Allied forces continued to push westwards and the First French Army under General Jean de Lattre de Tassigny helped to defeat German troops in Alsace in February 1945. The final surrender of Nazi forces in France came three days *after* VE Day when, on 11 May, stubborn German soldiers surrendered in the western port of Saint-Nazaire. The war had cost approximately half a million French lives, as many as 200,000 more casualties than the British suffered.[2]

As the Allied grip tightened on France during late summer 1944, Vichy's ministers fled. In September, Germany transferred the French government to the castle at Sigmaringen on the banks of the Danube. Pétain and Laval both refused to govern in exile. Fernand de Brinon, a fervent collaborationist who had served as Vichy's official contact with Germany in the Occupied Zone, assumed power. With France in the hands of the Allies, there was very little for de Brinon to do. His administration fell into factional infighting as ministers prepared their post-war defences. When Allied forces advanced on the castle in April 1945, its inhabitants tried to escape. Laval took a German plane to Spain, from where he was eventually extradited to France. British forces arrested Darnand in Italy. Déat fared better: he and his wife took refuge in a convent near Turin. Condemned to death in absentia, he lived out the rest of his days there. Doriot enjoyed no such long retirement: he was killed in February 1945 when Allied planes strafed the car in which he was travelling. As for Marshal Pétain, he gave himself up at the Franco-Swiss border.[3] On 23 July 1945, the trial of the former head of the Etat Français opened in Paris.

De Gaulle worked quickly to establish his grip over France. On 2 June 1944, the CFLN became the Gouvernement Provisoire de la République Française (Provisional Government of the French Republic). The General appointed eighteen 'Commissars of the Republic' to act as 'super prefects' in newly liberated regions. Each Commissar had the power to appoint local officials, commute death sentences and even suspend the law where necessary. The Commissars worked to entrench Gaullist authority, taking charge of matters that otherwise could have fallen into Allied hands. This network of administrators allowed the General to begin to rebuild the state without the consent of Washington and London.[4] However, de Gaulle did not easily supplant the authority of the resistance. The CNR had appointed Comités Départementaux de Libération (Departmental Liberation Committees, CDL) of local resisters, politicians, trade unionists and war victims such as women and former POWs. The CDLs had significant influence over the local press, police and provincial local judicial system, providing a counterweight – and a potential challenge – to Gaullist designs.[5] The Communist Party, by virtue of its role in the armed resistance, held a substantial number of seats on the CDLs, offering the party a means to consolidate a local power base independent of the Gaullists.[6] Yet if a dual power existed in some places, the strength of the committees depended much on local circumstances and personalities. Most functioned simply as holding operations until the state could reassert its control.[7] In any case, the CDLs declined in power as the country returned to normality. Local resistance groups found themselves deprived of some of their most dynamic elements when de Gaulle incorporated the FFI into the regular army in September 1944. By spring 1945, once-obstructionist committees had been neutered.[8]

The resistance groups of the CNR formulated their own plans for the renovation of France. These plans were expressed in the 'Programme of Action for the Resistance' of 15 March 1944 otherwise known as the CNR Charter. This document called for the re-establishment of democratic government, the nationalization of major industries and financial institutions, and the expansion of social security provision for workers. However, political divisions between the resistance groups and parties ensured that more far-reaching proposals were excluded from the Charter; the Radical Party, for example, refused to countenance the inclusion of voting rights for women. The CNR guaranteed an expansion of political and social entitlements to imperial subjects but stopped far short of demanding decolonization. With its basis in well-established left-wing economics and its eschewal of genuinely progressive political reforms, Wieviorka ultimately concludes that the plan 'did not look very revolutionary to contemporaries'.[9]

The first part of this chapter examines the experience of liberation in France and its Empire. The D-Day landings and the emancipation of Paris are the best-known episodes in the final months of the Occupation yet they provide only a partial picture of the Liberation. It is in fact more accurate to speak of 'liberations', for the freeing of the French from their wartime subjugation was not a single event.[10] Liberation took place at different times, in different locations, and happened according to different methods throughout France and its colonial holdings. The experience was both joyous and dangerous. Aerial bombardment and ground fighting presented great risks to civilian lives while Allied soldiers at times behaved more like conquering louts than liberating heroes. The second part of this chapter investigates the punishment of the guilty during and after the Liberation. Spontaneous violence and the summary execution of collaborators took place in some regions of France. Women who had had love affairs with German soldiers suffered head shavings and public humiliation. It took some time for the Provisional Government to initiate legal proceedings against the hundreds of thousands of suspected collaborators. When the courts began to sit, the demands of reconstruction and reconciliation often trumped the popular desire for justice, and the post-war purge gave rise to great public frustration.

Liberations

To gain a fuller picture of the Liberation, we must reconsider the geographic terms of France's exit from the war. By summer 1944, a number of French overseas possessions were already free from Vichy and Axis control. On 12 November 1940, an Anglo-French force took Gabon after several days of fighting. Free French Forces landed on the archipelago of Saint-Pierre-et-Miquelon in the northern Atlantic on 24 December 1941. The island's police offered no resistance and within days a referendum confirmed Gaullist control of the islands. Operation Torch, launched on 8 November 1942, cut France's North African territories from mainland control. If one considers (as contemporaries did) that Algeria was an integral part of France, liberation began not on the beaches of Normandy but on those of Algeria and Morocco. Madagascar, La Réunion and French West Africa all slipped from Vichy's grasp by the end of 1942. Guadeloupe and Martinique were freed in mid-1943. Yet liberation from Vichy's control did not always mean liberation from Pétainist authority. Admiral Darlan continued to govern in North Africa until his assassination on 24 December 1942. Boisson remained in charge of French West Africa until 7 July 1943, over six months after he had negotiated a settlement with the United States. In French West Africa, as in North Africa, Vichy's legislation remained in force as late as March 1946.[11] Other regions of the empire had to wait considerably longer for their liberation. In Indochina, the Japanese occupation lasted until September 1945 (Tokyo took full control of the territory in March 1945). Living conditions steadily worsened under Japanese domination. While France celebrated its freedom, settlers and indigenous peoples in France's eastern possession suffered internment, abuse, and forced labour. Japanese executioners beheaded scores of French officers and subjected some to public crucifixion.[12] To expand the geographical terms of the Liberation thus prompts a reconsideration of its temporal terms.

The level of French participation in their own liberation varied. De Gaulle was not privy to Allied discussions of Operation Overlord. It was only upon the General's dogged insistence that the Allies permitted a handful of French to take part in the D-Day landings: 177 French naval commandos (under British command) crossed the Channel with 156,000 Allied soldiers.[13] De Gaulle could call upon a substantially stronger force within France itself: the FFI. Established in February 1944, the FFI combined the combat wings of the resistance movements, notably the communist FTP and the Armée Secrète. Under the command of General Pierre-Marie Koenig, the FFI numbered 100,000 by June 1944; it grew to a size of 400,000 by the end of the year.[14]

The size of the FFI's contribution to the Liberation was not negligible. Resisters mounted operations to support Allied action in the weeks either side of D-Day. They attacked roads, bridges and railways, and harassed Occupation troops. Breton resisters sabotaged communications networks and transport infrastructure to prevent the German reinforcement of the region. FFI forces sabotaged the railway line between Paris and Toulouse eight hundred times during June 1944 alone. French units freed a number of southern departments as well as large cities such as Grenoble and Limoges, capturing 13,000 German prisoners in the process.[15] However, such victories were not representative of French action overall. Departments in the southwest may have fallen under resistance control but in sum, only 16 per cent of French towns, villages, and cities were freed by French action alone.[16] Furthermore, once Hitler sounded the general retreat on 16 August 1944, German armies were able to withdraw in an orderly manner, saving the majority of their military material and ensuring that the war would last for nine more months. The contribution of French forces was undoubtedly significant in some places – and 24,000 brave FFI volunteers died in the battle for France during 1944–1945 – yet the Third Reich did not fall in France.[17]

The Allies adopted a cautious attitude to arming the French. Washington and London hoped that French fighters would wage a guerrilla war against the Germans, and military instructors parachuted into France to better coordinate local resisters with Allied plans. These were the so-called Jedburgh teams and ninety-three entered France in June 1944.[18] This conception of the potential contribution of French combatants influenced the types of weapons supplied to France. Light arms made up the majority of those weapons dropped into France from American and British planes: 86,000 Sten guns, 62,000 rifles, and 290,000 grenades but only 900 bazookas. Most supplies arrived *after* D-Day, once Allied leaders were confident that resisters could play a meaningful role in the fighting. Domestic resisters received 50,000 containers of military material during July–September 1944 compared with 3,000 containers during the whole of 1943. If the resistance had hoped to spark a national insurrection, Allied strategy ensured that it lacked the weapons to do so.[19]

Allied military action prised some of France's overseas lands from Vichy's grasp. Fighting in North Africa saw the deaths of 1,368 Vichy French and 453 Allied soldiers. Yet it was 'a funny kind of liberation', for it involved neither Free French troops (among the 110,000-strong invasion army) nor Axis forces. Rather the Allies liberated this portion of territory *from* the French.[20] The accords signed between Darlan (subsequently installed as High Commissioner for North Africa) and US General Mark W. Clark on 22 November 1942 secured American military authority while permitting the Pétainist administration to remain in place. Darlan subsequently founded an imperial council made up of Vichy's former African governors, Noguès, Châtel and Boisson. The council continued to pursue the goals of the National Revolution in what Jacques Cantier calls, 'a Vichyism under American tutelage'.[21] Nonetheless, citizens and subjects of French North Africa were now implicated in the war against the Axis and on 24 November 1942, eligible men were mobilized for the campaign against Germany in Tunisia.[22] Following Darlan's assassination on 24 December 1942, General Henri Giraud took charge. Giraud's conservative politics chimed with those of Vichy and it was only on 14 March 1943 – and under considerable pressure from the United States – that he stated his intention to democratize the territory. Giraud gradually unravelled Vichy's legislation though he refused to reinstate the Crémieux decree. Jews in Algeria only reacquired the rights of citizenship on 20 October 1943 under the impetus of de Gaulle and the CFLN.[23]

Allied soldiers likewise freed Madagascar through force of arms. Japan's conquests in Asia during spring 1942 prompted an Allied reconsideration of the strategic importance of the island. Madagascar offered a potentially useful position for the British defence of the Indian Ocean should the Japanese continue to advance southward.[24] In May 1942, British forces attacked and occupied the port city of Diego-Suarez on the island's northernmost tip. London immediately opened negotiations with Annet about a transfer of power. Much to his annoyance, De Gaulle was excluded from the talks. On 10 September, with the situation deadlocked, British troops – mainly South and East African imperial units – moved south. Vichy forces – a combination of French, Senegalese and Madagascan soldiers – put up a robust defence, holding out until 6 November.[25] General Paul Legentihomme, a veteran of French colonial government, landed on the island on 7 January 1943 to exercise power in the name of de Gaulle as High Commissioner of French Possessions in the Indian Ocean.

Japanese military intervention 'liberated' Indochina from Vichy's control on 9 March 1945 when a coup toppled Decoux's administration. Up to that point, the Governor had enjoyed an uneasy relationship with the Occupier while carefully maintaining a modicum of French sovereignty. In early 1945, Tokyo came to believe that American landings were likely in south Indochina and that only total control of the colony could effectively obstruct the invader from advancing on Japanese positions in the north. In March 1945, some 50,000 colonial French soldiers attempted to resist the takeover yet they were soon beaten. Japan subsequently declared independence in Vietnam, Cambodia, and Laos, intending to use these puppet states to foster indigenous nationalist sentiment and so curry favour with the locals. Following an agreement at the Potsdam conference (July–August 1945), British and Chinese forces entered Indochina to rout the Japanese. Britain and China jointly managed the territory until French control was re-established in March 1946.[26]

Other territories escaped Vichy's authority in a more peaceful fashion. In November 1942, on the island of La Réunion, Aubert declared Saint-Denis an open city following light shelling from the Free French ship *Léopold*. In Guadeloupe and Martinique, popular discontent spilled over into protests and even armed resistance during spring 1943. When on 18 June 1943 police refused Robert's order to put down a demonstration, the writing was on the wall for Vichy's regime. Sorin and Robert soon left for France under US protection.[27] In French West Africa, a demonstration on 18 June 1943 voiced popular animosity towards Boisson, a Governor who had implemented with assiduity all of Vichy's legislation. To the regret of the American authorities, the Governor left his post on 7 July 1943; the Gaullist Pierre Cournarie succeeded him as Governor-General.[28]

For France's overseas possessions, liberation from the wartime regime did not mean liberation from colonial rule. A Free French conference at Brazzaville during January and February 1944 did raise some hopes for reform. The meeting sent a message to both Vichy and the Allies that the future of the French Empire lay with the Gaullists. The programme of the conference hinted at a new relationship between the colonizer and its subject peoples through the recognition of 'African parties' with a role to play in a commonwealth-style federation, the expansion of educational provision, new funds for investment and the widening of participation in politics for colonial peoples. Yet delegates – among whom there was not a single indigenous representative – also espoused a conservative view of the future of the empire in which France would continue to pursue its mission to 'raise up' the colonized races. The prohibition of forced labour practices and the abrogation of the indigénat were postponed until five years after the end of the conflict.[29] Moreover, de Gaulle neglected to ensure that colonial governors made good on the promises at Brazzaville and Free French administrators implemented only the reforms that they determined suitable for their colony. Indigenous leaders were thus disappointed. Even Vichy recognized that the Brazzaville conference did not mark a decisive break with the colonial past, stating that the Gaullist imperial vision was 'situated on a political line that has already been well trodden'.[30]

In the aftermath of liberation, the exploitation and bloody repression of subject peoples continued. In Madagascar, Free French rulers abused indigenous labour: islanders spent three times as many days in forced labour service than under Annet and the authorities continued to forcibly requisition crops and foodstuffs. These practices did little to endear islanders to the re-establishment of French colonial governance once the war was over and insurrection broke out in March 1947. In Morocco, demonstrations against the French authority in January and February 1944 saw up to 150 protesters killed in the cities of Rabat, Salé and Fez. In Algeria, the arrest of nationalist Messali Hadj sparked demonstrations in May 1945. Forty-seven Europeans were killed during violent outbursts in Sétif, Guelma and Kherrata. In retaliation, settler mobs killed over 1,000 Algerians, burying many of them in unmarked mass graves. In the same month, Syrian protests against the French presence in Damascus led to rioting during 19–29 May 1945. The Provisional Government in Paris responded with aerial bombardment, killing 641 Damascenes on 29 May alone. Thomas is correct to conclude that '[b]y 1945 there was a stark contradiction between the restoration of liberty in France and the provisional government's stubborn refusal to act upon earlier promises of reform...the superstructure of [settler] privilege remained intact'.[31] For many colonial peoples, the notion of liberation was meaningless.

Experiencing Liberation

The D-Day landings in June 1944 dangled the prospect of freedom before the French and liberation could not come fast enough. Léon Werth wrote that after four years of imagining the Allied invasion of Europe, the event itself was an anti-climax: 'For us, everything is just as it was. No more than if they had landed on some Pacific island. We're disconcerted by the contrast. It's a tremendous event, but it is only a mental object.'[32] Guéhenno described a sense of longing among the public: 'We live with just one thought. Time is long and short, both. Every minute goes by with infinite slowness, but the days with incredible rapidity.'[33] The trials of everyday survival still preoccupied many French. Years of shortages and the disruption of food supply networks in the wake of the Allied invasion had produced a virtual pre-industrial economy beholden to the weather, local circumstance, and conflict between the people and the State.[34] Black market prices remained prohibitive: in Paris, the price of a litre of oil rose to 1,000 Francs in spring 1944, twenty times its legal price, while a kilogramme of butter, at 600 Francs, cost nearly eight times its shop value.[35] When freedom arrived, there was 'an unparalleled sense of elation and relief' and people took to the streets to dance, a transgressive act in itself for the ban on public dancing remained in place until the end of the war.[36] In Paris, an atmosphere of permissiveness reigned and many celebrated with alcohol and sex.[37] Living conditions were, however, slow to improve. The government removed the bread ration in November 1945 only to reinstate it in January 1946 due to a shortage of flour, much to the anger of the public.[38] A poll in January 1946 saw more than half of respondents cite the search for food as the 'most important problem' facing their family. In May 1946, an amazing three-quarters of French surveyed stated that the last twelve months had been 'disappointing' for them.[39] Restrictions on foodstuffs remained in force until mid-1949 when only imported products such as sugar and rice were still subject to rationing.[40]

For the French living and working in Germany, liberation arrived much later than it did for their families at home. Until spring 1945, millions of French languished in the ruins of the Third Reich: 950,000 POWs, 735,000 labourers (mainly STO workers but including approximately 200,000 volunteers), and 150,000 concentration camp inmates (resisters, hostages, political prisoners, Jews and racial deportees, and criminals). The majority of these people were repatriated during the 'Great Return' of 12 April–15 May 1945 when the US Air Force flew over 25,000 French a day from Germany to Paris. The Ministry of Prisoners, Deportees and Refugees organized money, clothing, medical care and free holidays for the returnees, though the volume of cases soon brought the system under intense pressure.[41] The government faced, too, the problem of rehoming huge numbers of displaced persons within France itself. Municipal councils and charities struggled to provide adequate food and shelter for these domestic refugees: in the Loire-Inférieure alone, there were still 100,000 displaced men, women and children by October 1945.[42]

The Liberation was a time of danger for many ordinary citizens even if it is true that France did not descend into civil war in summer 1944. On the one hand, fewer French were prepared to fight for Vichy even if Marshal Pétain could still draw large crowds to his personal appearances. On the other hand, resistance remained a minority phenomenon though groups did welcome so-called eleventh hour resisters, some of whom were former collaborators hoping to hide in plain sight.[43] Nevertheless, the absence of civil war did not diminish the sacrifice and suffering of many citizens during the final months of the Occupation. Arrests, imprisonments, deportations and killings continued.[44] The Milice and the SS hunted down Jews with zeal. Joseph Antignac – who had taken over the CGQJ in May 1944 – was preparing new legislation on the Aryanization of Jewish businesses as late as 4 August 1944.⁴⁵ The repression of the resistance persisted unabated. Over 200 maquis died on 26 March 1944 when French miliciens and German soldiers attacked an encampment on the Glières plateau (Haute-Savoie).⁴⁶ Meanwhile, Occupation forces committed acts of extreme violence against French civilians. On 10 June 1944, the SS Panzer Das Reich division murdered 642 men, women, and children at Oradour-sur-Glane (Haute Vienne) as they searched the town for resistance weapons. Other mass killings of civilians took place at Ascq, Maillé, Tulle and in the Saulx Valley.

Allied bombing raids terrorized the public, at home and abroad. In general, French public opinion during 1940–1943 had been tolerant of American and British air attacks. Civilians recognized the importance of bombing to the broader war effort against Germany. However, the air campaign intensified during 1944: of the 9,436 Allied raids over France during the Second World War, 7,482 occurred in the final year of the Occupation.⁴⁷ The new intensity of the bombing threatened to undermine French goodwill. Léon Werth noted on 21 April 1944, '[The people] were firm, and they used to say, "That's war." But the bombings, the fires, the ruins, and the dead are making them waver.'⁴⁸ The Allied attack on Tunisia the previous year had harbingered the destructive power of the bombing raids over France: by mid-1943, fighting had caused an estimated $200 million of damage to urban areas and left 1 million Tunisians homeless.⁴⁹

Figure 22 *Residents of Dunkirk evacuate the town in September 1944 to escape the fighting. Photo by Bettmann/Getty Images.*

The inaccuracy of some raids, particularly those carried out by the US Air Force, sparked anger. Resisters argued that their own sabotage operations were more effective against enemy targets than the American practice of high-altitude bombing. In May 1944, a report for the CFLN stated, 'The clumsiness of American airmen...[has] done more to sow doubt and scepticism in French hearts than three years of propaganda from Berlin and Vichy'.[50] Of course, the Luftwaffe bombed enemy positions in France and civilians died in these raids, too: on the night of 26 August 1944, 200 Parisians perished in a German raid as the city celebrated its liberation.[51] Yet Allied raids seemed more likely to cause significant human and material damage. In a single day (7 July 1944), over 2,000 tonnes of bombs fell on Caen, destroying nearly three-quarters of the town. Allied planes dropped leaflets to warn civilians that the bombers were coming but many of them simply blew away in the wind before they could reach their destination.[52] Vichy's propaganda made much of Allied air raids and the destruction left in their wake. The dead and injured – elevated to the status of martyrs – were pictured in the press. When Rouen was bombed in April 1944, propaganda posters compared the English devastation of the city to the burning of Joan of Arc.[53] Even American journalist Andy Rooney noted of the French in the battle zone, 'It was true that [the French] were being freed but at the cost of the total destruction of everything they had'.[54]

In sum, Allied planes dropped 570,730 tonnes of bombs on France between 1939 and 1945. In comparison, Germany attacked Britain with 74,172 tonnes of bombs and rockets during the conflict. The bombs that fell over France represented over 20 per cent of the total number of all explosives dropped on Axis territories in Europe. French casualties from Allied bombings were therefore high: between June and September 1944, raids killed over 20,000 civilians. People living in the war zones in the north of France were particularly vulnerable; 7,000 people died during the twelve days after the D-Day landings.[55] Colonial POWs were likewise exposed to attack as they worked in war factories, near airfields and in train stations, all of which presented prime targets for bombers.[56] In total, 54,631 civilians died in Allied raids, 38,158 of them during 1944.[57]

On the ground, French civilians lived in close proximity to the liberating armies; by the end of July 1944, Allied troops numbered 1.5 million in Normandy alone. The first sight of an Allied soldier could elicit anxiety. Teenager Jacques Bailleul remembered, '[The soldiers] looked a little strange – stressed and wary, very wary – but more than anything they looked scary, with their knives and packs of clips, not to mention the huge magazines on their rifles. Some even had bloodstains on their uniforms and others were soaked to the waist!'[58] On the other hand, many civilians were grateful to US troops in particular for bringing them cigarettes, chocolate and chewing gum. Later, soldiers realized that they could trade these commodities for alcohol and sex. Civilians complained about the yobbish behaviour of soldiers who drank too much and engaged in rowdy behaviour. One angry

Frenchman contrasted the recently departed 'well-behaved' German soldiers to the newly arrived American 'pigs'.[59] While such an opinion was rarely voiced, the French authorities recognized that the behaviour of American soldiers was harming relations with civilians. In August 1945, the Mayor of Rambervillers went as far as to ban the sale of alcohol to US troops, 'with the goal of stopping the incidents that happen every day and in order to re-establish good order in the town'.[60] The American military authorities shared French concerns. In a brochure entitled, 'Welcome to the Riviera-Bienvenue sur la Côte d'Azur' – a tourist guide for US soldiers on leave in Nice – readers were warned that the Military Police patrolled the area; their aims were to 'prevent trouble, assist you in every possible way and to make arrests only when any other solution is impossible'. Soldiers were subject to a 2am curfew and no members of the opposite sex were permitted in army hotels.[61] Yet the comportment of some FFIs was little better. Near Nantes, these young men were known for 'drinking, womanizing, looting farms and villages... hijacking vehicles, having fatal accidents with firearms or selling them to racketeers behind the lines in the luxury restaurants and brothels of [the town]'.[62]

The sexual harassment of French women was a further source of conflict. Prior to D-Day, US army propaganda – notably the popular servicemen's publication *Stars and Stripes* – had portrayed the invasion of France as a story of virile American knights liberating grateful French damsels from both the barbarous German and their effeminate French husbands. Such a picture fitted easily into the average soldier's idea of France as a country of easy sex while it conflated US war aims with soldiers' sexual desires.[63] Basic French lessons in the US army thus included the phrases: 'Are you married?', 'Would you like to go for a walk?' and 'I will miss you'.[64] Yet such linguistic advice was not limited to the Normandy campaign. A book produced for American soldiers in *North Africa* also included phrases for men looking for romance: 'Do you like pictures?'; 'Would you like to have a drink?'; 'Where can we go to dance?'; 'Come to the restaurant with me'; 'When can I see you again?'[65] In the aftermath of the Normandy landings, French women brought rape charges against scores of American troops. Rumour served to heighten the fear that liberation had simply replaced one abusive military power with another. The fact that many of the accused soldiers were black saw racial prejudices come to the fore. In the upheaval and fear of wartime a 'rape hysteria' spread throughout rural northern France.[66]

Women did not experience the Liberation solely as victims. By the time of the invasion of North Africa in November 1942, 400 women belonged to the Free French Corps des Françaises Libres. The Corps provided female recruits to the land army, the navy and the air force, though few served in the traditionally masculine combat zone. The number of female recruits swelled to 3,100 as further territories rallied to the Allied war effort throughout 1943 and 1944. On 26 April 1944, all-women's sections in the CVF, the FFL, and the FFI were amalgamated into the Arme Féminine de l'Armée de Terre (AFAT). Women continued to fulfil roles away from the frontline in support roles better to free up men for combat duty. By September 1945, there were 14,000 women in the AFAT.[67]

A handful of women risked their lives at the frontline as nurses and ambulance drivers in the so-called Groupe Rochambeau. This group was founded in the United States on the initiative of American Florence Conrad. During 1943, Conrad arrived in Casablanca with fourteen women recruited in New York and ten ambulances. She was successful in convincing a sceptical Leclerc to incorporate her group of frontline nurses into the 2DB. After serving in North Africa, the Groupe Rochambeau landed on Utah Beach in June 1944 and supported French forces throughout their campaigns in France and Germany. These remarkable women – of whom there were sixty-five by the end of the war – faced scorn and derision from their male comrades. Nicknamed the 'Rochambelles', the women 'had to prove that a woman's courage could equal that of a man', according to member Rosette Peschaud.[68] Decades after the war, the Rochambeaus received the Légion d'Honneur, the highest French order of merit.

The soldiers of the Free French Forces experienced the Liberation as a time of disappointment and bitterness. The state of ruin in France shocked many of de Gaulle's men, whether it was their first visit to France or their return to the land of their birth. Their memoirs recalled the poverty, fear and mob justice that apparently reigned in the country. Relations between the soldiers of the Free French and the men of the domestic FFI were often strained. Free French troops – who were used to military discipline and training – scorned the amateurish resisters who seemed to hold ranks that they did not deserve. Many perceived an immense ingratitude on behalf of resisters and civilians who had remained in France. Furthermore, the privileges reserved for returning deportees and resisters were not forthcoming to the demobilized combatants of the Free French. These men received simply 'a voucher for a shabby-looking suit, a meal, a Metro ticket, and a thanks for everything'. Destitution awaited some veterans of de Gaulle's army.[69]

Like their French counterparts, Free French colonial troops experienced similar feelings of bitterness at the Liberation. The subject peoples of France's Empire fought in the liberation of both France and Europe. So important were they to the invasion of Corsica that Driss Maghraoui claims the 'only thing French in the Corsican campaign was the names of the [ships]' used to transport men and materiel from North Africa.[70] The invasion of southern France in August 1944 similarly relied on a significant contingent of French colonial forces in support of the US Seventh Army. Imperial subjects comprised over half of the total manpower in General Jean de Lattre de Tassigny's Army B (130,000 soldiers).[71] These men – North Africans, black Africans, and islanders from the Antilles, Nouvelle-Calédonie, Polynésie and Nouvelles-Hébrides – helped to liberate the south of the country.[72] As late as April 1945, soldiers from French Equatorial Africa and Somalia fought at Pointe de Grave where the last remaining Nazi forces were holding out. At

Royan, nearly 600 African soldiers fought alongside their French comrades against a force of 13,000 Germans.[73] Three-quarters of the French army at the Liberation hailed from Africa; half of all soldiers were indigenous subjects of the empire.[74]

During autumn 1944, black colonial soldiers were removed from the French fighting forces in a process known as 'blanchiment' or 'whitening'. In August 1943, Leclerc had suggested that white troops begin to replace their black comrades in the ranks of the Free French. Leclerc planned that 1,500 French and 2,370 North African troops would take the place of soldiers from France's black African colonies who, he claimed, were unsuited to combat in colder European climes. This was the first blanchiment.[75] The Allies later selected Leclerc's 2DB to be the first armoured force to enter Paris in 1944. The proportion of non-white soldiers in the 2DB was lower than that of any other divisions (approximately 25 per cent compared to a 40 per cent average).[76] In late 1944, de Gaulle ordered the replacement of black African soldiers in the French armies with young white Frenchmen. The General desired both to give young French a taste of a victory that he hoped would shore up future national unity and to place potentially volatile FFI combatants under military authority. Indigenous soldiers left the frontline almost immediately; the First Free French Division lost 6,000 Africans and 300 Oceanians by the end of the year.[77] Stripped of their weapons and their uniforms, these men were housed alongside colonial former POWs in poorly supplied makeshift transit camps while they waited to be shipped home. The first contingent of men repatriated to French West Africa arrived at a camp at Thiaroye near Dakar in Senegal. Such was their anger at their treatment that a riot broke out during which thirty-five African veterans died.[78]

The purge of collaborators

As the Vichy state collapsed, the punishment of collaborators assumed a central position in the concerns of many French. Resisters had called for vengeance against collaborators throughout the Occupation and, in March 1944, the CNR's 'Programme of Action for the Resistance' demanded 'the punishment of traitors and the eviction from the administration and professional life of all those who have dealt with the enemy or have actively associated themselves with the policy of the government of collaboration'.[79] The épuration or purge of collaborators at the Liberation tapped into a public desire for revenge against men and women who had betrayed France. It spoke also to a wish for national renovation, a sweep of the broom through the country before post-war reconstruction could begin.[80]

The purge took two forms. Firstly, in areas where the machinery of the state was yet to be re-established, resisters took matters into their own hands and delivered summary justice to the guilty. Shortly after the liberation of

Paris, for example, police fished twenty-eight bodies from the river Seine; each had a bullet in the head and was weighted down with a rock.[81] This form of extra-legal punishment is often called the 'épuration sauvage' or 'wild purge'. To describe this form of purging as 'wild' is problematic for two reasons. Firstly, the label lends credence to the claims of Vichy's post-war apologists that the violence of the liberation resulted in tens of thousands of murders. The true number of deaths was likely much lower. Secondly, the label creates an artificial juxtaposition between an apparently reckless and unofficial first phase of the purge and a second legal phase. On the one hand, violence was just one aspect of the 'wild' purge; resisters also spent this period compiling evidence that was later used in the trials of collaborators. On the other hand, violent attacks on collaborators persisted into 1945, once the courts had taken charge of matters. Megan Koreman prefers the term 'local purge' to describe this form of unofficial justice; this is the term used here.[82]

Secondly, from September 1944 proceedings began in French courts to try collaborators. This was the 'épuration légale' (legal purge) or national purge. The Haute Cour de Justice (High Court of Justice) tried the leaders and high functionaries of the Vichy regime, including Marshal Pétain. The Cours de Justice (Courts of Justice) heard the cases of mid-level and junior civil servants. The Chambres Civiques (Civic Chambers) examined the collaboration of ordinary French. In addition to these courts, independent commissions investigated and punished members of the professional and business world. The sheer volume of cases meant that progress was slow and the public expressed much dissatisfaction with the effectiveness of the process. Furthermore, French who had suffered at the hands of Vichy's henchmen were equally dismayed at the apparent clemency of sentencing. The purge courts quickly gained a reputation as 'ateliers de blanchisserie' or whitewashing workshops.[83] As a result, attempts to purge collaborators at the local level continued to operate in tandem with the national legal process.

The local purge

It is difficult to quantify the scale of the violence committed against collaborators during local purges. In the post-war years, critics of the resistance (mostly recalcitrant former Vichyites) put the number killed at over 100,000 French. French government inquiries in 1948 and 1952 found that at most 10,822 people died. Historians' estimates vary considerably. Aron proposed a median figure of between 30,000 and 40,000 deaths while Vinen contended that in the months either side of the Liberation up to 5,000 people fell victim to resistance murders or fighting with the police and the Milice.[84] A lack of evidence and the chaotic conditions of hasty executions mean that we are unlikely to ever know the true figure. Lethal violence was nevertheless an exceptional form of punishment.[85]

It is important to recognize that the violence perpetrated during local purging was not solely attributable to the wartime division between resisters and collaborators. Mobs of so-called faux maquis (false maquis) committed armed robberies under the guise of requisitioning food stuffs and supplies for the resistance. Organized criminal gangs continued to ply their trade. Rumours of fifth columnists – traitorous men and women prepared to undo the resistance and return Vichy and the Nazis to power – spread quickly in an environment where reliable news was hard to come by. The atmosphere of fear and suspicion led to lethal violence committed in error as in the case of a police detective who was mistaken for a member of the Milice and murdered. The newspaper *La Liberté de l'Est* speculated that violence had become a way of life in France: 'It becomes natural to insult, to curse, to slander, to calumniate, as it becomes natural to pillage, to steal, to punish or to kill. There is a furor to harm that surpasses the imagination.'[86]

The targets of resistance violence were generally men and women who had persecuted or betrayed resisters during the Occupation. Local people acted upon pent-up grievances against known collaborators, and their punishment was framed as a debt paid to the martyrs and heroes of the resistance.[87] Former members of the Milice were particularly vulnerable; 'The Milicien was worse than the Boche', reported one newspaper in the south. Those French charged with membership of the Milice were subject to trial by court martial and summary execution.[88] Miliciens often faced their charges in public before the men, women and children of the local community. Spectators loudly called for the death of these men who had betrayed, tortured and killed resisters. In some cases, mobs lynched the guilty and mutilated their bodies.[89]

Violent purging was more common in the south where an absence of Allied troops allowed local justice to operate. The French forces of order were often impotent to prevent acts of violence. Police officers who had worked under Vichy went into hiding or refrained from taking action for fear of being purged themselves.[90] They were right to fear retribution: resisters had promised to wreak bloody vengeance on all servants of Vichy and the police were amongst the most visible.[91] In the absence of legal order, chaos and confusion allowed for the settling of scores between people for reasons of little political import.[92] Violent mobs targeted those in whom they perceived a difference: fifteen of the sixty North African inhabitants of the Morbihan were executed. It is unlikely that such a high proportion of this community was involved in collaboration.[93] As one witness to the Liberation recalled, 'jealousy, rancor, acrimony, covetous desire, resentment, contemptible acts, and vengeance' reigned.[94]

Some of the most striking images from the local purge concern the treatment of women allegedly guilty of 'horizontal collaboration' with German soldiers. Journalist Charles Wertenbaker described the punishment

Figure 23 *A young man executed for acts of collaboration in Grenoble. Photo by Three Lions/Stringer/Getty Images.*

of several such women in Chartres on 18 August 1944, captured on film by photographer Robert Capa: 'The patriots were bringing in women collaborators, old ones who had helped the Germans or operated black markets and younger blowsy ones who had sold themselves to the Germans. They were lined up against a wall, some with their hair already clipped close to the skull, and in the centre of the courtyard was a pile of grey and blond hair. In the corner of the courtyard a woman and a boy were selling red wine by the glass'.[95] This was a shearing or 'tonte' and the women concerned were known as 'femmes tondues' or shorn women. The public nature of the event was vital to its function as an act of scapegoating: the punishment of the few absolved the guilt of the many. The wide dissemination of images of the shavings in the press spoke to a similar national concern to punish the bad apples.[96] Men carried out the attacks; sometimes fathers shaved the heads of their daughters. The tontes served to put right the gendered hierarchy of power that the war had disrupted; they were 'a reassertion of patriarchy after the occupation and all the humiliations it represented for French masculinity'.[97] Up to 20,000 women received such a punishment.[98] Local authorities channelled a number of women into the court system in order to protect them from the tontes. The courts did not shrink from punishing horizontal collaboration: a woman in Cantal lost her political and civil rights for twenty years for her 'crime'.[99] Head shavings continued into 1946. Yet, with collaborators on trial now in the courts, the tontes became less public ritual than criminal assaults.[100]

Violent purging played out in the context of specific environments. What had happened in a particular town or village during the war was of great significance at the Liberation. Citizens knew who was guilty – or they thought they knew – and took punishment into their own hands. Violence filled the retributive void until a formal legal process to try collaborators took shape. Summary executions of known collaborators and the shearings of 'guilty' women sated the community's appetite for justice. Yet, summary justice did not end with the re-establishment of judicial authority. Resisters unhappy with the courts' decisions painted swastikas on the houses of collaborators, sent them death threats and even committed murder against those who had

Figure 24 *A group of femmes tondues, one carrying her baby, in Chartres, 25 August 1944. Photo by Bettmann/Getty Images.*

apparently escaped justice. During the Great Return of spring 1945, the desperate state of the returnees revived popular anger against those deemed responsible and police recorded twelve bomb attacks per day against the homes of former collaborators.[101]

The national purge

The legal punishment of French collaborators commenced prior to the liberation of the French mainland. In May 1943, the CFLN appointed a special commission in Algiers to try Pierre Pucheu, Vichy's former Minister of the Interior. Pucheu had travelled to North Africa following the Allied conquest of the territory to seek the protection of General Giraud. He arrived in Casablanca on 8 May 1943 to find that the Gaullists had gained the upper hand. Judges sentenced the former minister to death and, in a message to the Vichy regime, de Gaulle refused to commute the sentence. Pucheu was executed in March 1944.[102]

Pucheu was not the only collaborator tried on Algeria soil. On 18 August 1943, a purge commission began to prosecute alleged traitors. The first wave of purges between August 1943 and March 1944 saw 998 cases tried. The commission imposed legal sanctions on 507 occasions. The second wave of trials commenced in July 1944. The courts in Alger, Oran and Constantine subsequently tried 14,056 men and women for acts of collaboration, convicting 6,898 of the accused.[103] In other overseas possessions, political expediency took precedence over punishment. In French West Africa, a shortage of European administrators and a desire to maintain the prestige of the colonial government resulted in a rather limited purge in the immediate aftermath of the colony's rallying to the Allies. The governors of Togo, Dahomey, Senegal and Guinée were 'retired' yet the épuration got underway only in May 1945.[104]

In September 1944, the criminal justice system began proceedings against collaborators in France. The courts faced a significant problem from the outset. Collaboration was not a crime under French law. Other former occupied territories encountered a similar dilemma. In Denmark, the Netherlands and Norway, the liberation governments introduced retroactive legislation to prosecute collaborators and they re-established the death penalty to punish this crime. France chose not to punish the guilty retrospectively. Instead, the courts tried collaborators according to existing legislation on the sharing of intelligence with the enemy and the perpetration of acts detrimental to national security. Where jurists deemed the existing legal provision on treason unsuitable, collaborators stood accused of 'indignité nationale' or national unworthiness, an offence introduced on 26 August 1944 (Denmark, the Netherlands and Norway employed similar measures). Indignité nationale pertained to a person who had, 'directly or indirectly, voluntarily aided Germany or her allies, or harmed the unity of the nation or the liberty and equality of Frenchmen'.[105] The law sought to punish antinational activity of various sorts that did not relate to an pre-existing criminal offence to a specific crime. The guilty received a sentence of 'dégradation nationale' or national degradation, a penalty that amounted to the deprivation of a number of civic and political rights including the right to vote and run for political office. Convicts could no longer work in the media, finance, teaching and law. An amendment to the legislation in September 1944 provided for the confiscation of the guilty party's property.[106]

The legal purge involved a number of different courts. The Haute Cour de Justice (created on 18 November 1944) tried men from the upper echelons of the Vichy regime before three magistrates and twenty-four jurors selected from a consultative assembly in Algeria. The cases rested on the essential illegitimacy of the regime itself. René Cassin, lawyer and member of the Free French, argued that the circumstances in which deputies and senators had met in July 1940 meant that parliamentarians had voted under duress. Cassin further claimed that these deputies and senators had possessed no legal right to delegate statutory power to Pétain. The Marshal's revision of the constitution was therefore illegitimate.[107]

The trial of Pétain opened in Paris on 23 July 1945 and lasted three weeks. Privately, de Gaulle had hoped that Pétain would not be present at proceedings. The Marshal, though, was keen to face his accusers and he handed himself into French authorities in April 1945. The public still harboured a certain amount of sympathy for the Victor of Verdun: an opinion poll in October 1944 found that 58 per cent of respondents believed that Pétain should receive no punishment for his conduct during the Occupation.[108] The trial commenced with a long address from Pétain during which he refused to recognize the authority of the court. He went on to claim that he had acted only to protect France from the horrors of Nazism while de Gaulle had worked from abroad to free the nation. The case against Pétain focused on the Marshal's agreement to the armistice and the Vichy regime's relations with the Third Reich. The crimes committed against the residents of France – including those of the Jewish faith – remained beyond the purview of proceedings. On 15 August, the jury returned a guilty verdict and Pétain received a capital sentence. In the aftermath of the trial, an opinion poll found that 72 per cent of French now believed that Pétain deserved punishment[109], with 37 per cent believing that a life term was the most suitable penalty.[110] De Gaulle agreed and he commuted the sentence to life imprisonment. Pétain subsequently lived in exile in the Fort de Pierre-Levée, a prison on the Ile d'Yeu, a small island off the west coast of France. He died on 23 July 1951 at the age of ninety-five.

No such lingering retirement was in store for Laval. Condemned to death on 9 October 1945, the former premier was executed at the prison at Fresnes six days later. Darnand was shot in the same month. Flandin, who headed the Vichy government in the winter of 1941, received a suspended sentence of national degradation. Vallat, one time head of the Légion and Vichy's CGQJ, was sentenced to a prison term of ten years. Darquier de Pellepoix, Vallat's successor at the Commissariat, managed to escape to Spain, where he lived out his days under the protection of the Franco regime despite a death sentence delivered in absentia in the French courts. Overall, the Haute Cour heard 108 cases. It condemned sixty-six of the accused, sentencing eight to death; only three executions were carried out.[111]

The fate of Vichy's principal colonial administrators varied. Admiral Platon (Secretary of State for the Colonies from September 1940 until April 1942) was executed in August 1944, a victim of the local purge.[112] The governors of Madagascar, Cayla (August 1940–April 1941) and Annet (April 1941–November 1942) received sentences of five years' imprisonment and national degradation, respectively. Admiral Robert (High Commissioner of the French Antilles) received ten years' hard labour. Boisson (Governor-General of French West Africa) was condemned to national degradation. Governor of Indochina Decoux was acquitted. Sorin, Governor of Guadeloupe (April 1940–July 1943), escaped prosecution and he fought in the Free French campaign in Alsace.

The Cours de Justice (created on 26 June 1944) and the Chambres Civiques (created on 26 August 1944) tried low-level servants of the regime along with ordinary French accused of acts harmful to national defence and security. In the Cours de Justice, selection for a jury depended on evidence of one's patriotic sentiments; they included women, which was a novelty for France at this time.[113] This court heard the cases of those charged with promoting the enemy through propaganda, belonging to an enemy organization, perpetrating acts injurious to France or simply acting in a favourable way towards the Occupier.[114] In total, 58,000 citizens stood trial; 47,560 received a prison term or a capital sentence.[115] The Chambres Civiques were empowered to deliver the sentence of national degradation to punish the crime of indignité nationale. In severe cases, convicted parties forfeited their property and were subject to orders banning them from living in a certain place; the Chambres sentenced 46,230 French to this penalty.[116]

When considering the scale of the purge in France, we must bear in mind that no other semi-autonomous government co-operated as fulsomely with the Nazi authorities as did the Vichy regime. In this respect, some aspects of the purge appeared light. In Paris, the cases of only 400 police officers made it to trial out of some 4,000 investigations; seven trials resulted in a death sentence.[117] The weight of justice did not fall evenly on all sectors of society. Men and women were not equal before the liberation courts. One in four people who appeared before the courts was female yet 40 per cent of convictions went to women. Furthermore, where women stood trial, their moral conduct during the Occupation came under greater scrutiny than that of men charged with similar offences.[118] With regard to the world of business, a special commission examined 1,342 cases, delivering only 191 convictions.[119] The government confiscated the Renault automobile manufacturer and the Paris Metro company.[120] The purge of French business was relatively limited given the huge sums of money that companies had earned from German manufacturing and construction contracts. Conversely, journalists, intellectuals and writers received severe punishments: their guilt was plain for all to see in black and white. Georges Suarez, who had edited the collaborationist newspaper *Aujourd'hui*, was the first journalist to face justice. The prosecution drew on over 600 of Suarez's editorials that called for the violent punishment of resisters, Jews and the Free French.[121] Suarez was executed in November 1944.

There was much public dissatisfaction with the legal process. The courts simply could not work quickly enough. The sheer volume of cases caused a logjam and complaints about the glacial pace of progress grew.[122] Moreover, the process of prosecuting offenders was fraught with difficulties: a judiciary tainted by its Vichy past, overworked magistrates and prosecutors, cases based on scant evidence and unreliable testimony, and public intimidation of jurors to arrive at the 'right' sentence.[123] There was a tension, too, between the public expectation of justice and the attitude of de Gaulle. The French wanted the courts to make good on the wartime promises of the timely punishment of, and vengeance against, collaborators. De Gaulle's priority was to stabilize the state, heal societal divisions and move the country forward. To achieve this end, the Provisional Government needed to maintain the integrity of state institutions severely compromised by their association with Vichy, not least the judiciary, where three-quarters of the judges and magistrates who sat in the purge courts had practised under the Vichy regime.[124] Furthermore, de Gaulle's claim that the 'true' France had supported the resistance would not stand up to scrutiny if the judicial system punished wholesale the accused. Many French were dismissive of the punishment of national degradation, considering it 'no more than a derisory slap on the wrist'.[125] For those who had suffered under the Occupation, the apparent clemency of the courts was incomprehensible.[126]

Conclusion

As de Gaulle proclaimed the liberation of Paris on 25 August 1944, Guéhenno concluded his wartime diary: 'Freedom – France is beginning again'.[127] For him at least, summer 1944 brought the promise of both liberty and renovation. For many thousands more French citizens and subjects, liberation was not quite so straightforward. There were various moments of liberation, from the earliest rallying of territories such as Saint-Pierre-et-Miquelon in December 1941 to the final eviction of the Japanese from Indochina in September 1945. Modes of liberation were equally numerous, including Allied military intervention, resistance uprisings and even referenda. There were also pseudo-liberations; for French POWs and their families, the freeing of France in 1944 had little impact. Civilians experienced the Liberation as a time of danger and thousands suffered loss, injury, homelessness and abuse. In French African territories, freedom from Vichy's government did not necessarily mean the rollback of the National Revolution. Meanwhile, throughout the empire, the demise of the Etat Français saw the resumption of an equally exploitative colonial regime whether under the wartime Free French or the Liberation-era Provisional Government. In France, ethnic diversity characterized the liberating armies yet the 'whitening' process soon removed soldiers of colour from the frontline.

The desire to punish the guilty united many French. The violence of the local purge occurred in the context of the collapse of the Vichy state after years of anger and shame. Lawlessness was not general. The CDLs and de Gaulle's Commissars worked to keep the peace in their departments and regions. Where police were absent, resistance law and order reigned. Men enforced this order and exacted justice against their enemies, frequently (though not always) with violence. There were few more painful reminders of the humiliation of 1940 than the sight of French women consorting with the enemy. Sex with the invader constituted not only a slight on a woman's sexual honour but also a 'betrayal of the nation, on the symbolic battlefield in wartime France'.[128] The shearings served to reassert male power in Liberated France. Even the presence of Allied troops did not generally guarantee social peace: the tontes could take place under the gaze of Allied soldiers, who were ordered not to interfere in local matters.[129]

In total, the French courts examined 311,263 cases of collaboration, involving as many as 350,000 people. Approximately 60 per cent of those men and women under investigation did not ultimately face charges. The courts convicted 100,000 French; approximately half of the guilty were sentenced to national degradation while 40,000 received prison terms. Almost 7,000 French received the death sentence, with 3,910 delivered in absentia. Ultimately, 767 executions were carried out. De Gaulle commuted the remainder of the capital sentences. The fundamental difference between public expectations of justice and the actions of the purge courts gave rise to tension and conflict. As Koreman writes: 'The purge of collaborators revealed popular aspirations for a multifaceted and subtle justice that responded to community grievances. It also revealed that the national government neither shared the local definition of justice nor had any intention of providing it'.[130] Post-war amnesties in January 1951 and August 1953 ensured that a number of those purged were able to return to their previous profession. The last collaborator was released from prison in 1964.

7

History and memory

The experience of the French during the Second World War left deep scars. Historians have described France's difficult relationship with the period in the post-war decades as a long process of 'coming to terms' with the past.¹ The trauma of the defeat and the Occupation, the shame of collaboration, the costly campaign of the resistance and the Free French, and the global ramifications of the wartime struggle have defied simple explanation. Since 1944, competing narratives of the war have developed, undergoing processes of evolution, adaptation and episodic convulsion. These narratives have often spoken to the needs of the time in which they emerged. In the difficult aftermath of the Liberation, the notion of a people united in resistance under de Gaulle provided grounds for national reconciliation and it quickly came to dominate national memory. Numerous public parades and commemorations reinforced this heartening story: on 11 November 1945, for example, a ceremony brought together the bodies of fifteen resisters at Fort Mont Valérien outside Paris where hundreds of resisters suffered execution during the war. The proceedings placed the resistance to the fore, connecting the heroes of 1940–1944 with the fallen of 1914–1918. The following year, René Clément's 1946 film *La Bataille du rail* depicted a people united in defiance in the story of Gaullist and communist railway workers; Clément later won the Palme d'Or at the Cannes Film Festival. Meanwhile, the names of the heroes of the war came to adorn metro stations in Paris and roads and squares throughout France and the empire.²

This representation of the war – the 'Gaullist resistancialist myth', according to Henry Rousso – dominated the memory of Vichy until the late 1960s. The myth did have a basis in historical fact. Yet it concealed inconvenient truths, writing and rewriting the pasts of heroes and villains. De Gaulle assumed the proportions of a providential leader (in particular after his accession to the presidency of the Fifth Republic in 1958) who had led the French against the Nazis since the Appel du 18 juin. Pétain became a nobly heroic figure who held the line against Hitler at Vichy while London prepared the counter-attack. The figure of the resister *him*self – for his depiction was usually male – was a white French military combatant accepting of the Gaullist leadership. This representation confined to the margins the actions of men and women who did not conform to the political, gendered or ethnic orthodoxy. Such groups often did not possess the political, social or cultural capital to make their voices heard.

Under the pressure of historical investigation and shifts in culture and society at the end of the 1960s, not least the resignation of de Gaulle in 1969, the legend of the French nation of resisters began to crack. The following decade, the Gaullist story of the war was smashed (almost) beyond repair. The French embarked on a period of self-flagellation as the truth of collaboration and France's role in the Holocaust exploded into history books, political debates, the courts and onto cinema screens. Marginalized groups (women, Jews, and foreigners, to name but a few) asserted their own claims on the memory of the war. Ceremonies, monuments and commemorative plaques memorialized forgotten heroes, ordinary people and the crimes of Vichy. In recent years, scholarly research has expanded as historians have begun to investigate a plethora of new avenues as well as reassessing old conclusions.

The memory of the Second World War in France has thus long existed as a stake in the political, social and cultural battles of the present and historians have used vivid imagery to depict this persistent 'presence of the past'. In 1987, Henry Rousso described Vichy as a corpse that was still warm and upon which the French were not ready to operate.[3] Richard J. Golsan entitled his 2000 book on the memory of the regime *Vichy's Afterlife*, suggesting that though the Etat Français was long since dead, the nation continued to feel its (supernatural?) manifestation like a 'body in the basement'.[4] To paraphrase Rousso and Eric Conan, Vichy is a 'past that has not passed'.[5]

This chapter examines the history and memory of the Vichy years. Historians usually approach post-war understandings and representations of the Dark Years by dividing the years since 1944 into a number of phases, delineated according to the narratives that dominated in successive periods. These narratives expressed themselves in the 'carriers' of collective memory, that is, the reconstructions and representations of the war in, for example, official discourses and symbols such as ceremonies and monuments; organized movements and activities; cultural productions such as films and literature; and scholarly outputs and educational curricula.[6] This chapter divides the post-war years into three phases. Firstly, during the years 1944–1969, the Gaullist resistance myth gradually took root in the popular consciousness, reaching its fullest strength during de Gaulle's tenure as president from 1958 to 1969. Secondly, from the early 1970s, the 'nation of resisters' myth gave way to an examination of the darker aspects of French behaviour as well as to the emergence of 'forgotten' histories, not least that of the Etat Français's involvement in the Holocaust. Finally, from the turn of the millennium, memory of the period has diversified thanks to the influence on the field of approaches to everyday life, as well as new interests in the contribution of colonial peoples to the French war effort. At the same time, reassessments of long-established historiographical orthodoxies have emerged, some of them unwelcome.

We must make two caveats before proceeding to examine these phases. Firstly, while historians like to divide history into manageable and broadly coherent chunks, we must acknowledge that what appear to be watershed moments from the present are rarely perceived in so straightforward a way in the past. Contemporaries do not always recognize change from one period to the next and attitudes to history do not transform overnight. Secondly, while my focus is largely on historiography, historians' writings on this topic – on *any* topic – represent but one carrier of collective memory and few works of history have the power to alter memory single-handedly. Scholarly research takes a long time to filter into the popular consciousness (if this happens at all). Even the most notable historical works on Vichy France owed their impact to their interaction with broader political, social and cultural factors that ultimately rendered them 'timely'. We must therefore pay attention, too, to the connection between the historian and his or her society. Historians may strive for objectivity yet they are products of their time; the world in which they live influences their historical writing.

Mythologizing the resistance: 1944–1969

During his celebratory speech at Paris's Hôtel de Ville on 25 August 1944, de Gaulle referred to France ten times, Paris nine times and the Allies once. He made no mention of the resistance. Rather, he extended the act of resistance to the nation at large. In doing so, he stripped the resisters of their unique contribution to the war effort. This was the foundation stone of the Gaullist resistancialist myth, that of a nation of resisters (embodied in the figure of the General) and locked in a noble struggle against Nazism.[7] The myth did not deny the existence of collaboration yet it confined such behaviour to a few fanatics and criminals. This ostensibly inclusive narrative contained an inherent exclusionism for it framed resistance as a male and military activity. De Gaulle subsumed resisters into the history of the French military struggle against Germany, a thirty years' war beginning in 1914. Women who had fulfilled vital roles without firing a bullet found themselves on the margins.[8]

It took time for the Gaullist narrative to take root in the French consciousness; the General's resignation from government in January 1946 obstructed its development somewhat. However, a number of factors facilitated the germination of the resistancialist myth. Firstly, it is difficult to underestimate the deep trauma caused by the defeat of 1940 and the four years of Occupation that followed. The shame of the disaster of 1940 was such that its commemoration was repressed and veterans of the failed

French campaign were forgotten.[9] The majority of French chose to muddle through the war years rather than commit to the cause of either resistance or collaboration. Still, they experienced hardship in numerous ways from the daily demand of putting food on the table to giving up a son, father, uncle or brother to forced labour in Germany. The vast majority of the nation may have remained estranged to the violent struggle of the activist minority but French society nonetheless emerged from the war profoundly troubled. In this context, de Gaulle's narrative was a decidedly comforting portrayal of recent history. It exonerated those French who had simply not acted at all, providing a focal point for national reconciliation in the uncertain moments of the Liberation.

Secondly, parties and movements in the political arena drew upon the heritage of the resistance to legitimate their own claims to the leadership of France. There was no 'resistance party' because the political divisions of the movements continued into peacetime. De Gaulle himself assumed the premiership of the Provisional Government on 13 November 1945 while a constituent assembly hammered out the constitutional proposals for the new Fourth Republic. Yet the General resigned on 20 January 1946, unhappy at what he considered to be the reestablishment of the divisive parliamentary politics of the Third Republic. De Gaulle subsequently founded the Rassemblement du Peuple Français (RPF). The movement presented itself as the continuation of the wartime struggle to re-establish French grandeur and it depicted de Gaulle as a messianic figure ready to save France for a second time. However, the centre-left and conservative parties that dominated parliament shut the Gaullists out from power. That other great party of the resistance, the Communist Party, was likewise estranged from government. The communists styled themselves as the party of the '75,000 martyrs', a figure that both exaggerated the actual number of communist war deaths and deftly elided the party's period of neutrality prior to June 1941. Communist deputies participated in the first government of the Fourth Republic under Paul Ramadier yet the onset of the Cold War in the wake of the Truman Doctrine speech in March 1947 saw communist ministers evicted from power two months' later.[10]

Thirdly, the development of the bipolar world order focused minds on the global role of France. In Europe, Paris's desire to maintain Germany in a position of subjugation eventually gave way to America's drive to strengthen the West German state against communism. Apparent American interference in French domestic affairs caused consternation and threw into question the very meaning of Frenchness. When in the late 1940s the Coca-Cola Company applied to the government for permission to begin production of the beverage at a plant in Marseille, opponents lined up to denounce the pernicious cultural influence of a fizzy drink that epitomised the American way of life.[11] Attempts to ban the product from France ultimately failed but the affair attested to a desire to protect a sense of identity undermined seriously during the Occupation and further threatened in the bipolar world.

A similar concern prevailed in the successful campaign to ban Tarzan comics of the early 1950s.[12]

As for the French Empire (rebranded the French Union in the constitution of the Fourth Republic), Paris did not intend to surrender its colonies. The Union represented an important symbol – perhaps the only symbol – of French power and prestige and the promises made at Brazzaville in 1944 were not allowed to endanger colonial control. In May 1945, French troops massacred thousands of Algerians at Sétif in order to put down a nationalist rising. Brutal repression soon followed in other territories from the Middle East to Madagascar. In Indochina, French forces engaged Ho Chi Minh's nationalists in armed struggle for almost a decade. France formally withdrew from the territory following negotiations in Geneva in July 1954. The retreat revived painful memories of 1940.

The first histories of the Dark Years emerged in this context. Former resisters established themselves as the foremost authority of the history of the period. They published their accounts largely under the leadership and guidance of former teacher and resister Henri Michel and his Comité Français de la Deuxième Guerre Mondiale (the French Committee for the Second World War, founded by de Gaulle in 1946 as the Comité d'Histoire de l'Occupation et de la Libération [the Historical Committee of the Occupation and the Liberation] and renamed in 1950). The committee sought to establish an archive of the resistance by means of recording interviews with former combatants. The methods of the interviewers, in many cases former resisters themselves, lay far from the careful approaches of contemporary oral historians and it is likely that they edited or redacted some accounts.[13] Given the huge moral legitimacy that resisters enjoyed, it was difficult to challenge the testimonies of these witnesses. Michel himself stated in 1958 that 'the uniqueness of the Resistance fight [was] such that only those who took part in it could properly recount it'.[14] The Gaullist myth dominated these sacrosanct testaments, erecting them into 'Bastilles of memory'.[15] As a result, the history of the resistance dominated the output of the committee's journal, the *Revue d'histoire de la Deuxième Guerre mondiale*. Between 1949 and 1975, for example, the *Revue* published only five articles on the Allied involvement in the Liberation.[16] Few could challenge the growing dominance of this Gaullist history. The communist memory of the war fell apart during the 1950s as Moscow purged a number of former resisters during its reconfiguration of European communist parties between 1948 and 1952.[17] Meanwhile, the prejudices of the time meant that research and writing focused inordinately on the activities of white French men at the expense of groups such as women and ethnic minorities.[18]

The climate of Cold War anti-communism helped conservatives and recalcitrant former Vichyites to rehabilitate themselves and their right-wing politics. Men from Pétain's entourage such as Henri du Moulin de Labarthète and ex-ministers like Yves Bouthillier authored works that sought to absolve themselves of blame. Several former colonial governors used post-war memoirs to recast themselves as loyal servants of France and minimize their commitment to the National Revolution. Admiral Decoux in fact devoted only twenty of the more than 500 pages in his memoir to wartime domestic policy in Indochina.[19] Even Laval spoke from beyond the grave to set the record straight: a collection of notes penned during his incarceration was published as *Laval parle* in 1948. According to such works, Pétain had acted as a shield that spared the French the excesses of Nazi barbarism and resistance to the Occupation ran throughout the regime itself. The legal rehabilitation of the regime and its supporters was not long in coming. Parliament approved the first amnesty for people punished during the purge on 16 April 1946. By the mid-1950s, a series of amnesties had reduced to under 100 the number of prisoners serving prison time for collaboration.[20] French memories seemed decidedly short: a Gallup poll in May 1947 found that 63 per cent of respondents did not know where Marshal Petain was currently residing in exile.[21]

The most significant historical work to appear in the decade after the Liberation was Robert Aron's 1954 *Histoire de Vichy*. This 700-page work drew upon transcripts from the trials of ex-ministers at Vichy – including former deputy Prime Minister Flandin, former Ministers of Justice Alibert and Gabolde and former Minister of the Interior Peyrouton – as well as numerous secretaries of state and other functionaries such as Annet, Bousquet and Cayla. Aron also consulted many other documents and testimonies from both Vichy's supporters and its opponents. His account was rich in detail yet there were stark omissions from the work, not least Vichy's persecution of the Jewish population. The book is most famous for its reliance on the so-called 'sword and shield' thesis. According to Aron, Pétain and his government undertook the painful task of protecting the independence of France and its population while de Gaulle strove to free the country from abroad: 'Both were equally necessary to France', Aron maintained, because, '[t]he Marshal was the shield, [and] the General [was] the sword'.[22] There was of course no such 'collaboration' between Vichy and London but, in the context of the 1950s, the idea was an attractive one.

In 1956, Aron's conclusions received the prestigious endorsement of political scientist André Siegfried. Siegfried distinguished between a 'Vichy of Pétain' and a 'Vichy of Laval'. The 'real Vichy' was that of Pétain; it existed between 10 July 1940 and 18 April 1942 (the date upon which Laval returned to power). Siegfried located Pétain's political convictions in the tradition of the Catholic and paternalist right, summed up in the regime's triptych 'Travail, Famille, Patrie'. Yet more important than the Marshal's political convictions was his temperament: Pétain was a man who, faced with defeat, looked for reconciliation while limiting the potential damage of the Occupation. On the other hand, Siegfried portrayed Laval as an opportunist and a manipulator. He blamed the former parliamentarian for the destruction of democracy in 1940, 'Pétain being nothing but an instrument in his hands'.[23] Laval's goal was to integrate France into Hitler's New Order, an objective that he pursued vigorously from spring 1942. Siegfried concluded that if Laval's priority was collaboration, Pétain's was to practise a noble 'double game': 'to limit the [effects of] the debacle in accepting the defeat, [and] to use it to nurture recovery'.[24] In the Vichy regime, as in the nation at large, the excesses of the Occupation were attributable to a few bad apples.

De Gaulle's accession to the leadership of France in 1958 cemented the centrality of the resistance myth to French memory of the war. The General's return after more than a decade away from frontline politics came amid the deepening crisis in Algeria. On 31 October 1954, Algerian nationalists in the Comité Révolutionnaire d'Unité et d'Action (which would later become the Front de Libération Nationale, the FLN) demanded independence from France and insurrection broke out the following day. Deputies in Paris granted the government special powers to re-establish order and successive Prime Ministers increased the military presence in the territory. The FLN waged a guerrilla campaign against soldiers and settlers while French forces responded with repression, summary executions and torture. When on 13 May 1958, parliament invested Pierre Pflimlin as Prime Minister – a man whom many expected to seek conciliation with Algerian nationalists – Generals Raoul Salan and Jacques Massu established a Committee of Public Safety in Algiers. The Committee demanded that General de Gaulle assume the leadership of the French government. Panicked at the prospect of a military dictatorship in Algeria, President René Coty appointed de Gaulle as Prime Minister on 29 May 1958. On 1 June, the National Assembly approved the General's appointment by 329 votes to 224.[25] Desirous to shift power away from parliament and into the office of the executive, on 28 September 1958 de Gaulle submitted a new constitution to a public referendum; 79 per cent of voters approved. On 21 December 1958, de Gaulle became president of the new Fifth Republic.

With the 'man of 18 June' in power, the Gaullist resistancialist myth gained renewed impetus. It served several contemporaneous agendas. At home, the myth provided a unifying narrative to heal the divisions exposed during the Algerian conflict and provide the new regime with an aura of legitimacy; Michel's 1962 *Les courants de pensée de la résistance* concluded that if the ideas of the resistance had taken a hiatus during the Fourth Republic, they had experienced 'a sudden resurrection many years later, in the Constitution of the [Fifth] Republic'.[26] In the context of decolonization, de Gaulle recalled in 1958 that his promises at Brazzaville had 'opened to the Africans the road that led them to their freedom'. He thus cast France's retreat from its empire as a long process with its roots in the Free French struggle and its ultimate outcome in his own return to grant Africa its freedom.[27]

De Gaulle missed few opportunities to reinforce and propagate his reading of the past. On 18 June 1960, he inaugurated a new 'Mémorial de la France combattante' at Mont Valérien. The date of the ceremony and the monument itself – a cross of Lorraine over an excerpt from the Appel du 18 juin – brought the Gaullist reading of history to the fore.[28] In 1964, the televised interment of the remains of Jean Moulin in the Panthéon, France's temple for national heroes, saw the Gaullist myth reach its zenith. Writer and former resister André Malraux delivered a speech that celebrated de Gaulle's singular ability to unite the diverse resistance groups in the name of France.[29] The image of the resister as a 'soldier in the army of shadows' under the noble leadership of the Free French reigned supreme.[30] These ceremonies encouraged the nation at large to identify with the Gaullist wartime struggle. The equation was simple: 'the Resistance equal[led] de Gaulle; de Gaulle equal[led] France; hence the Resistance equal[led] France'.[31]

Two works of history published at the close of the 1960s hinted at a change of focus in the study of Vichy France. In 1968, Harvard University professor Stanley Hoffmann published an article-length enquiry into collaboration and collaborationism. Hoffmann noted the dearth of work on the subject in the years since the war, citing only two books to have investigated collaboration since 1944: Michèle Cotta's study of the press, *La collaboration, 1940–1944* (1944) and Maurice-Yvan Sicard's sympathetic *Histoire de la collaboration* (1964). Hoffmann wondered if historians had shied away from the topic because of the inconvenient truth that 'the cancer which was gnawing at France's sense of national identity had spread much beyond the narrow confines of the "Paris traitors".'[32]

Figure 25 *Jean Moulin's remains in the Panthéon, 1964. President de Gaulle and Prime Minister Georges Pompidou pay their respects. Photo by Keystone-France/ Gamma-Keystone/Getty Images.*

Eberhard Jäckel took collaboration as his focus in *Frankreich in Hitlers Europa* (1966, published in French in 1968 as *La France dans l'Europe de Hitler*). Based predominantly on German sources, Jäckel revealed that Vichy had at times gone further down the path of collaboration than the Occupier had required. The book was received positively in France. Literary critic for *Le Monde* Yves Florenne noted Jäckel's 'detachment' from his subject (despite his German nationality) as well as his 'copious' and 'painstaking research', all supported with 'precise references'.[33] In his review for the *Annales*, historian Jean Sigmann noted the 'calmness' with which Jäckel approached the subject, something that the reviewer believed derived from the author's age: born in 1929, Jäckel had been neither a witness to nor an actor in the events of the war, unlike his French and German counterparts.[34] Jäckel's important research pre-empted much later work on Vichy and collaboration. Yet *La France dans l'Europe de Hitler* did not break the orthodox Gaullist reading of Vichy and the Dark Years. It was simply not the right time: with de Gaulle in the Elysée and Moulin in the Panthéon, the moment to challenge the resistancialist interpretation was yet to come. Whether walking through the place du Colonel Fabien (named in 1945, formerly the place du Combat), crossing the Bir Hakeim bridge (named in 1949, formerly the pont de Passy) or alighting the metro at Guy Môquet (named in 1946 after the young communist martyr, formerly Marcadet-Balagny), the myth of a 'national' resistance was ubiquitous.

Inconvenient truths: 1971–1995

The decisive moment for the Gaullist narrative of the war arrived in the early 1970s. In 1972, Robert Paxton published *Vichy France: Old Guard and New Order*. The book was not the American's first on France and the Second World War; his 1966 *Parades and Politics at Vichy* had taken the French officer corps as its focus. In *Vichy France*, Paxton turned his attention to Vichy's programme for domestic reform while following Jäckel's example in consulting German sources on the wartime relationship between France and Germany. His conclusions were damning. Firstly: 'Collaboration was not a German demand...[it] was a French proposal'.[35] Pétain's regime made strenuous efforts to secure for itself a partnership with Germany, much to the indifference of Hitler. Secondly: 'Everything done at Vichy was in some sense a response to fears of decadence...the defeat gave cause and opportunity for more radical measures designed to reverse that long moral decline'.[36] The regime was no mere holding operation or 'shield': it espoused a far-reaching political project to remake the nation according to deeply rooted French political prejudices. Paxton admitted that fascism played a 'relatively restricted role' at Vichy yet he concluded that if one defines fascism as '[h]ard measures by a frightened middle class...[then] Vichy was fascist'.[37] Thirdly: 'the overwhelming majority of Frenchmen, however they longed to lift the German yoke, did not want to lift it by fire and sword'. Paxton estimated that the number of active resisters never grew to more than 400,000 French or 2 per cent of the adult population.[38] Paxton reserved his most incriminatory accusation for the French nation: 'Even those [French] who grumbled at the regime without doubting its basic legality or doing anything positive against it helped swell the tide of acquiescence... from lukewarm to fervent, [they] were "collaborators" in a functional sense.'[39] If the resistance myth had comforted many who had supported the struggle in spirit alone, Paxton now condemned the same people for enabling the regime to survive. The 1973 French publication of Paxton's book (entitled *La France de Vichy*) caused a scandal in France. Critics, many of whom were right-wing Vichyites, lined up to condemn this 'young American' for having the temerity to write a book on France; a foreigner could not possibly understand the French experience of the war years. Reaction from the *academic* community in France ranged from unadulterated praise (Marc Ferro and Jean-Pierre Azéma) to barely concealed envy at the popularity of the book (Janine Bourdin) and a jealous desire to protect one's own area of scholarship from the intrusion of a foreign historian (Henri Michel).[40]

In the decades since the publication of *Vichy France/La France de Vichy*, Paxton's conclusions have permeated the field both in France and beyond. Historians now recognize the 'Paxtonian Revolution' as a watershed moment in the history and memory of Vichy. Rare are the history books that change the way historians approach a subject; rarer still are those that change the way a nation understands its past. Yet why, if Jäckel's 1968 *La France dans l'Europe de Hitler* foreshadowed a number of Paxton's arguments, do historians not celebrate the 'Jäckelian Revolution' in Vichy studies? As Moshik Temkin argues, Paxton's book had such a profound impact because it 'appeared in the right place at the right time; it caught a generation eager to find fault with their fathers and elders'.[41] Paxton's *Vichy France* was just the latest, though surely the most powerful, blow to the Gaullist resistancialist myth. The presidential election of 1965 undermined de Gaulle's status as a figure of consensus. Though the General won the second-round run-off ballot comfortably, the campaign had forced him to reveal his conservatism against left-winger François Mitterand. Three years later, civil unrest throughout the country undermined further the prestige of President de Gaulle. A younger generation of students and activists had taken to the streets to air their dissatisfaction with what they perceived to be an authoritarian and sclerotic political establishment and education system. Paxton himself cited the climate of protest at the time of the Vietnam War as one of his major influences, for it 'sharpened [his] animosity to nationalist conformities of all sorts'.[42] In 1968, French student protesters frequently directed their anger at de Gaulle: protest placards pictured caricatures of the president under the cross of Lorraine while they depicted police as SS foot soldiers. For some young French, the General was the ultimate symbol of the war generation, of their parents' generation, at once discredited and out of touch.⁴³ De Gaulle ultimately re-established order yet his prestige and authority never recovered. On 27 April 1969, he was defeated in a referendum on relatively benign amendments to the constitution. Opposition parties had framed the ballot as a vote of confidence in the president and the day after the defeat, the General resigned. Little more than eighteen months later, on 9 November 1970, Charles de Gaulle died.

Immediately prior to the publication of *Vichy France*, Marcel Ophüls's 1971 documentary film *Le chagrin et la pitié* exposed cinema audiences to a less heroic picture of the French wartime experience. The film featured interviews with leading statesmen such as Pierre Mendès-France and Anthony Eden as well as prominent resisters like Georges Bidault and Emmanuel d'Astier de la Vigerie. Yet the focus of the documentary – and undoubtedly the viewing that was most uncomfortable for French audiences – was an investigation of the town of Clermont-Ferrand during the Occupation. Interviews with local inhabitants told less a reassuring tale of resistance than a humiliating account of venal and shabby behaviour. The unflattering image of the French that emerged from the film prompted the French state television regulator, the ORTF, to forbid its broadcast. According to ORTF head Arthur Conte, the film 'destroys the myths that the French still need'.⁴⁴ This was not the first time that the censor had intervened to protect French sensibilities. In 1956, Alain Resnais's documentary about wartime deportation, *Nuit et brouillard*, had featured an image of a gendarme watching over prisoners at the Pithiviers internment camp. Censors required that Resnais obscure the gendarme's iconic hat lest the audience comprehend the truth of French complicity in Nazi deportation.⁴⁵ As for *Le chagrin et la pitié*, French audiences could watch the film in a cinema in Paris's Latin Quarter; 600,000 cinemagoers saw the film during its 87-week run. Only in 1981 did the French state permit the television showing of the documentary and 15 million French tuned in.⁴⁶

The Paxtonian Revolution opened a new period of scholarly and popular interest in the Vichy regime and collaboration. Pascal Ory's 1977 *Les collaborateurs* and Bertram M. Gordon's 1980 *Collaborationism in France during the Second World War* shed new light on the darker aspects of French conduct under the Occupation. In cinemas Louis Malle's *Lacombe, Lucien* painted a complicated picture of the choice between collaboration and resistance. The film told the story of Lucien Lacombe, a disaffected teenage peasant who, in 1944, joins the French collaborationist police and betrays the local resistance leader to the Nazis. Its portrayal of the choice between collaboration and resistance was anything but the black-and-white image of the Gaullist years. The young Lucien is not a fascist ideologue or Nazi sympathiser. Rather, he stumbles into collaboration after initially experiencing rejection from the resistance due to his young age. His chance encounter with the collaborationists who draw him into their circle could have befallen any French.

The focus on Vichy's crimes facilitated the emergence of the regime's victims into public consciousness. In 1981, Paxton's third book on Vichy – *Vichy France and the Jews/Vichy et les Juifs*, co-authored with Canadian historian Michael R. Marrus – was published in both English and French. In the decades since the war, historians had largely ignored the fate of the Jews of France and only the Centre de Documentation Juive Contemporaine had sponsored serious academic research into the subject.[47] Marrus and Paxton's book was therefore the most comprehensive assessment to date of the regime's systematic persecution of the Jewish community and its complicity in the Final Solution. The novelty of the work lay in its examination of the roots of Vichy's anti-Semitism, which Marrus and Paxton located squarely in French political and cultural tradition stretching back to the nineteenth century. This long history of anti-Semitism, combined with the use of French and foreign Jews as bargaining chips with Germany, resulted in an indigenous and autonomous programme of anti-Jewish legislation and abuse.[48] Indeed, amongst the semi-independent states in Hitler's Europe, only Bulgaria volunteered to deliver foreign Jews from unoccupied territories as Vichy did.[49] As for the French population at large, indifference characterized the reaction of the majority. Only after the round-ups began in summer 1942 did the French concern themselves with the treatment of the Jews and some voices were raised in protest.[50] *Vichy France and the Jews/Vichy et les Juifs* stands today as a landmark in the historiography of wartime France. Along with Serge Klarsfeld's monumental studies, *Le calendrier de la persécution des Juifs de France* (1983) and the two-volume work *Vichy-Auschwitz* (1985), it facilitated the entry of the Jews into the mainstream historiography of Vichy.

The 1980s saw the integration of women into the French narrative of the war years. The Gaullist myth had allowed for the celebration of several individual women regarded as heroes of the resistance: Berty Albrecht, for example, was named with five other women among the Compagnons de la Libération and she was buried at Mont Valérien. Furthermore, early works of history such as Elisabeth Terrenoire's *Combattantes sans uniforme. Les femmes dans la Résistance* (1946) and Edith Thomas's contribution on Albrecht to a 1947 collection on resisters demonstrated that women were not entirely absent from the historical record of resistance.[51] Still, the dominant representation of the resister as a male soldier left little room for the many thousands of women who had resisted either as members of movements or in their daily life.[52] Under the influence of the feminist movement of the 1970s and several high-profile publications such as Lucie Aubrac's best-selling memoir *Ils partiront dans l'ivresse* (1984, translated as *Outwitting the Gestapo*), women resisters gradually began to emerge into the historiographical and popular consciousness. Academic conferences – notably the 1975 colloquium on 'Les Femmes dans la Résistance' – and publications explored women's contribution to resistance.[53] Films that centred on women's resistance activity entertained cinema audiences, from

Claude Berri's 1997 *Lucie Aubrac* (a dramatization of Aubrac's memoir) to Jean-Paul Salomé's 2008 *Les Femmes de l'ombre* (renamed *Female Agents* for its English-language distribution).

A string of high-profile trials during the 1980s and 1990s ensured that the issues of collaboration and resistance remained firmly in the public consciousness. The 1985 trial of Klaus Barbie, former head of the Gestapo in Lyon, raised few eyebrows. Known as the 'Butcher', and implicated in the death of resistance hero Jean Moulin, Barbie's guilt was plain. Convicted of crimes against humanity, he died in prison in 1991. The indictment of several *French* for crimes against humanity drew for the first time the attention of the courts to French involvement in the Holocaust. In 1979, Jean Leguay, formerly a representative of Vichy police chief Bousquet (and thus implicated in the infamous round-up of Jews in Paris in July 1942), was charged with crimes against humanity. Legal wrangling over his trial lasted until Leguay died in 1989. In 1983, Maurice Papon, a civil servant in the Gironde during the war, was charged with organizing the deportation of a number of Jews from his department. In 1998, a court convicted Papon of complicity in crimes against humanity and sentenced him to ten years' imprisonment. In 1989, former head of Vichy's Milice in Lyon Paul Touvier was charged for his role in the round-up and execution of seven Jews in summer 1944. In 1994, Touvier became the first Frenchman convicted of crimes against humanity. Finally, Bousquet himself was indicted for crimes against humanity in 1991; he was murdered in 1993 before he could be brought to trial.[54] In a sense, Bousquet, Papon and Touvier acted as proxies for both the Vichy regime and France itself and the criminal cases sparked 'an orgy of collective repentance for France's guilt in the Holocaust'.[55]

The criminal trials revealed the closeness of the post-war French state to former collaborators. Papon had escaped the purges of the 1940s to enjoy a stellar career in the French police. During 1958–1965, he had served as prefect of the Paris police and had notably overseen the brutal repression of Algerian nationalism in the city during the early 1960s. Touvier, on the other hand, had received two death sentences, delivered in absentia, in 1946 and 1947. Arrested in Paris in 1947, he managed to escape his captors and subsequently went on the run. The capital sentences lapsed in 1967 yet he remained subject to several minor penalties. In November 1971, the fugitive Touvier received a pardon from president Georges Pompidou thanks largely to the former's connections with the Catholic Church, whose clergy were sheltering him. The president's decision sparked a scandal. Pompidou's response to his critics caused surprise: 'Hasn't the time come to draw a veil over the past, to forget a time when Frenchmen disliked one another, and even killed one another?'[56] At a time when the Gaullist resistancialist myth was under intense pressure, the president had badly misread the national mood.

Like Touvier, Bousquet had received a legal punishment in the immediate post-war years: in 1949, the Haute Cour sentenced him to five years' indignité nationale and disqualification from holding public office. He subsequently pursued a career in the press and worked for the 1974 presidential campaign of François Mitterrand, with whom he became friends. The two men continued to meet during the 1980s when Mitterrand was president. Mitterand's own Vichy past was complex. The president had worked as a functionary at Vichy until 1943 when he sided with the resistance. During his time working for the Etat Français he had won the honour of the francisque medal, a fact that suggested that Mitterand had held some sympathy for the National Revolution. As president between 1981 and 1995, he refused to recognize the complicity of the French nation in wartime anti-Semitism, twice refusing to apologize for Vichy's persecution of the Jews on the grounds that Pétain's regime was an aberration that had little to do with the Republican nation.[57] The controversy over Mitterrand's attitude to Vichy's anti-Semitic acts persists today: the website of the Institut François Mitterrand contains a detailed rebuttal to the accusations of his detractors.[58]

The electoral breakthrough of Jean-Marie Le Pen's Front National (FN) during the early 1980s offered a stark warning that some French had not abandoned the politics of Vichy. Founded in 1972, the FN provided a haven for unrepentant Vichyites; banners at its first congress borrowed the regime's 'Travail, Famille, Patrie' slogan.[59] The party enjoyed its first real electoral success when in March 1983 Le Pen won a seat on the municipal council of Paris, having run on an anti-immigration platform. Further minor gains at the polls followed and the party took thirty-five seats in the elections to the National Assembly of 1986. In 1987, during a television interview, Le Pen described the Nazi gas chambers as merely a 'detail' (*point de détail*) in the history of the Second World War and cast doubt on their importance in the murder of the Jews. A civil court censured Le Pen for trivializing the Holocaust but he subsequently repeated the insult on several occasions. The desecration of a Jewish cemetery at Carpentras in May 1990 saw the FN accused of inciting racial hatred, though no party members were involved in the crime.[60]

The year 1995 marked a turning point in France's relationship with its wartime past when Jacques Chirac became the first French president to admit French responsibility in the deportation of Jews. Speaking at a ceremony to mark the fifty-third anniversary of the Vél d'Hiv roundup, he said: 'These dark hours forever sully our history and are an insult to our past and our traditions...Yes, the criminal folly of the occupiers was seconded by the French, by the French state'.[61] He broke with the policy of his predecessor Mitterrand who, though being the first president to attend the commemoration in 1992, had steadfastly refused to recognize the responsibility of France in such crimes. However, Chirac's admission was qualified. The president attributed the survival of three-quarters of the Jewish population of France to the several thousand French who risked their lives to save Jews, the so-called 'Righteous Among Nations'. These brave few, so Chirac claimed, had acted according to values of freedom, justice and tolerance, French qualities shared by the nation at large.[62]

Historian John Sweets has compared the change in collective understandings of wartime France during the 1970s and 1980s to the motion of a pendulum swinging from resistance to collaboration. This 'pendulum of interpretation', Sweets contends, 'swung further than the historical evidence [warranted]', replacing the Gaullist version of history with a Paxtonian counterpart, the 'nation of collaborators'.[63] Historians had not cast off Aron's conclusions wholesale: Henri Amouroux's popular 1976 history of the Second World War restated much of the arguments made over twenty years' previous. The resistance, too, continued to provide fruitful grounds for research: HR Kedward's 1978 *Resistance in Vichy France* is a classic study of its kind.[64] However, the image of the resistance tarnished as stories of the infighting between supposed wartime comrades emerged. Henri Frenay's 1976 memoir laid bare his opposition to the Gaullist leadership and accused Jean Moulin of spying for the Soviets.[65] The revival of interest in Vichy's victims and the trials of Frenchmen accused of war crimes ensured that the dark history of the war years remained fixed in the public consciousness.

Diversification and revisionism: 2000 to present

A move away from the study of collaboration and resistance has characterized scholarship on Vichy since the 1990s. The study of everyday life, in the style of the German school of *Alltagsgeschichte*, has come to influence a growing body of work on Second World War France. This approach was not entirely new. Pioneering work by Sweets and Pierre Laborie during the 1980s had tried to shift attention away from the high politics of the regime and towards the daily tribulations of the average citizen.[66] Since 2000, a number of historians have turned to the grass roots of Vichy society and the daily worries and concerns of people who were perhaps less affected by the drama of events than a historian would like to admit. This approach simultaneously brings the individual back into history, valorizing their capacity to effect, or at least contribute to, historical change. The history of the everyday prompts the historian to consider the humanity of the subjects under study, to situate them within their familial relationships and friendship groups and within the spaces and places that they live, bringing 'emotional empathy' to research.[67] Everyday life approaches have helped to further integrate the experiences of minority groups into mainstream historiography: Shannon L. Fogg's 2009 *The Politics of Everyday Life in Vichy France*, for example, drew gypsies into the history of Vichy's persecution. They have revealed, too, new aspects of familiar topics. Daniel Lee's *Pétain's Jewish Children* (2014) focused on

Jewish involvement in the regime's Chantiers de la Jeunesse youth association. Lee's book typifies the complexity of experience uncovered via a focus on everyday experience. Lindsey Dodd and David Lees's recent collection of essays on everyday life in Vichy France attests to the vibrancy of this subfield of Vichy studies and the sheer range of topics and groups to which it speaks: 'bosses, civil servants, women, police, universities,... Jews, prison, asylums, gypsies in camps, colonies, [and] deportees', to name but a few.[68]

Oral history approaches are central to several works on everyday life. Robert Gildea's *Marianne in Chains* (2002) used oral interviews and testimonies to reconstruct a diverse array of experiences in occupied Tours. Likewise, Dodd's 2016 *French Children under Allied Bombs* made use of interviews to reveal the experience of the youngest French during wartime. The use of oral history as a research tool is not to everyone's taste. Paxton, still the most eminent scholar of Vichy France, has questioned the scholarly value of post-war testimonies: 'Memory... is the shakiest of all human constructions; the documents in the archives, on the other hand, don't change'.[69] With the gradual disappearance of the generation that witnessed the war, Paxton declared in 2016 that 'the time of the historians has come' and 'the subject [is now] firmly [in] the hands of scholars and their sources'.[70] For Paxton, nothing can replace the paper documents of the archives.

Filmmakers have brought to the fore the ethnic and religious diversity of the men and women who fought to free France. Rachid Bouchareb's 2006 *Indigènes* (entitled *Days of Glory* for its English-language release) tells the story of four North African soldiers in the French army as they fought to liberate France after 1943 in the face of racial discrimination from their comrades and superiors. Bouchareb told *Time* magazine that his desire to recount the experience of the indigènes ('native') soldiers arose from a contemporary concern: 'These kids from the banlieue,[71] having re-examined this history, are going to get back the pride and dignity. And [the rest of the] French will see why these people are just as French as they are'. Three weeks of rioting in the ethnically mixed and deprived areas of the banlieues had struck France during autumn 2005. According to Michael F. O'Riley, the film was 'an explicit attempt to bring together pieces of the repressed history of these colonized soldiers' service in such a way as to instil in the spectator a much larger sense of Frenchness'.[72] The political impact of the film was immediate. Prior to the film's release in September 2006, President Chirac announced that the government would bring the service pensions of France's colonial soldiers in line with those of French soldiers; the government had frozen the pensions of at least 80,000 soldiers in 1959.[73]

Robert Guédiguian's *L'armée du crime* (2009, in English: *The Army of Crime*) examined the resistance activities of the Manouchian group, an organization of migrants led by Armenian poet Missak Manouchian and affiliated to the immigrant worker section (Main-d'oeuvre immigrée – MOI) of the FTP. The final scene depicts a humiliating photo-shoot in the aftermath of the group's arrest in November 1943. The photographs later appeared on the infamous 'Affiche Rouge', which mocked the resisters as an 'Army of Crime'. The film begins and ends with a roll call of the Manouchian group, a device that serves to demonstrate the 'foreignness' of this resistance group. The film presents a stark contrast between the immigrant resistance and native French collaboration (*French* resisters are absent from the film). If in the pages of *Le Monde*, historians Sylvain Bouloque and Stéphane Courtois criticized Guédiguian for producing a hagiography, the film was a much-needed exposé of the 'outsiders' in the resistance.[74]

While historians of the Dark Years generally use films and novels as both barometers of popular attitudes to the history of the Occupation and carriers of memory, they ignore the home entertainment market. This situation surely cannot last. Videogames reach global markets. Those games that take a historical perspective have as much potential to influence public understandings of the past as cinema, especially those that offer immersive experiences such as the first-person shooter genre. Wartime France has featured in several editions of Activision's multi-billion dollar franchise *Call of Duty*. Significantly, female resisters feature prominently among the French characters in the franchise. The 2006 *Call of Duty 3* featured a non-playable woman maquis fighter named Isabelle DuFontaine. Her in-game description stated, 'Once a simple farm girl, any innocence Isabelle once had has been kicked out of her. She is ready to die for the cause as long as she takes down three or four Germans with her'. The character dies during an attack on a Nazi armoured car. In 2017 *Call of Duty: WWII* further recognized the role of women in the French resistance with the playable character Camille 'Rousseau' Denis (voiced by actress Ludivine Sagnier in the French edition). Rousseau joined the maquis (eventually rising to the rank of leader) following the murder of her family at the hands of the Nazis. Players can help Rousseau avenge the deaths of her loved ones by killing SS Commander Heinrich. *Call of Duty: WWII* was 2017's best-selling videogame in the United States with global revenues of over $1 billion. In France, the game sold over 1 million copies, making it the second-bestselling title of 2017 behind *FIFA*. In comparison, Quentin Tarantino's 2009 film *Inglourious Basterds* sold 2.8 million tickets in France and topped the charts for four weeks during 19 August–9 September 2009; *L'armée du crime* sold approximately 400,000 tickets in the same year. Most recently, the French resistance figured in 2019's *The Resistance* Community Event, a time-limited special edition of *Call of Duty* that provided online subscribers with new weapons, character 'skins' and bonuses. The webpage that advertised the event featured *The Resistance* written in the colours of the French tricolour next to a Cross of Lorraine.[75]

Several historical works on the French Empire have brought a global dimension to the study of Vichy. Early accounts of the war in the empire took up the familiar tropes of the Gaullist myth and they celebrated the loyalty of imperial subjects to the French homeland and the General.[76] Historians began to turn their attention to France's overseas possessions during the 1990s when the importance of the empire to Vichy's domestic propaganda and economic policy came under investigation.[77] Study of Pétainist imperialism shifted to the colonies the following decade. Eric Jennings's *Vichy in the Tropics* (2004) explored the implementation of the National Revolution in Guadeloupe, Indochina and Madagascar. In the same year, Jennings and Jacques Cantier brought together historians of the empire in *L'Empire colonial sous Vichy* (2004). This book aimed to demonstrate that the 'colonial mirror' could reveal much about Vichy for it was in these lands that loyalists were free to pursue policy away from German interference.[78] Subsequent research has blossomed in areas as diverse as colonial sports and leisure policy, family and race policy, and anti-Semitism.

Jennings's 2014 book *La France libre fut africaine* (published in English in 2015 as *Free French Africa in World War II*) was a highly significant contribution to the history of the empire at war. Jennings demonstrated convincingly that the people of Chad, Cameroon, Oubangui-Chari, French Congo and Gabon were due no small thanks for their role in the French war effort. After the war, these combatants did not receive due recognition for their service. Only eleven combatants and five indigenous African civilians were named amongst the 1,038 members of the Order of the Liberation.[79] The French state erected few plaques and monuments to these fighters of the first hour. In 2011, the press greeted with little fanfare the death of the last surviving African fighter at Kufra in March 1941, Joseph Djemakangar. Jennings was therefore right to conclude 'the wartime sacrifices of FEA and Cameroon remain scarcely known in France', despite the fact that '[i]nstead of a beret-coiffed white maquisard in the Alps, the archetypal early French resistance fighter between 1940 and 1943 was, in fact, black and hailed from Chad'.[80]

Alongside the diversification of historical research, historians have not abandoned long-established tenets of the historiography. Contemporary fascination with the resistance is nowhere more evident than in the recent works of two heavyweights of the field: Wieviorka's *Histoire de la résistance* (2013) and Gildea's *Fighters in the Shadows* (2015). The subsequent translations of each work attest to the unrelenting appetite for the topic. Wieviorka's aim was to offer a comprehensive history of the domestic resistance organizations free from the 'form of self-censorship' that had characterized previous accounts of the subject.[81] Gildea sought to bring to light the diversity of resisters and their experiences through the use of personal accounts, both in written and oral form.[82] These well-worn subjects have thrown up new angles for research, too. Valerie Deacon's 2016 *The Extreme Right in the French Resistance* explored the trajectories of several extreme right-wingers who, though located at the heart of Vichy, sought to resist the Nazis. Deacon prompted the reader to consider these otherwise unsavoury characters as heroes and patriots.

The Vichy past continues to rear its head in contemporary French politics. In 2007, conservative president Nicolas Sarkozy chose the day of his inauguration, 16 May, to visit the site in the Bois de Boulogne where Occupation forces had shot thirty-five resisters in August 1944. The ceremony that accompanied the visit saw a high school pupil read aloud the last letter of seventeen-year-old Guy Môquet, a communist executed for acts of resistance in 1941. Sarkozy heralded the defiance of resisters such as Môquet, whose actions derived from a belief in a 'human freedom [opposed] to everything that threatens to subjugate it', and the example that such acts set for young people in the present: 'I want schools to teach our children to hear and understand this cry'. Sarkozy's framing of the Resistance hardly spoke to the diversity of the phenomenon: his speech mentioned 'man' or 'men' six times and there were no references to women.[83] The president's decision to require the reading of Môquet's letter in all French schools aroused opposition from teachers and unions that decried Sarkozy's intrusion into the classroom.[84] Furthermore, Sarkozy's hard-line policy on illegal immigration and immigrant crime drew comparisons with Vichy's own xenophobia.[85]

At a ceremony to mark the seventieth anniversary of the Vél d'Hiv arrests in 2012, Sarkozy's successor, socialist François Hollande, was categorical in his admission of French complicity in the deportation of Jews: 'the truth is that not a single German soldier, not one, was mobilised for the whole of this operation. The truth is that the crime was committed in France, by France'.[86] Hollande's opponents countered with some familiar criticisms of the president's position. Left-winger Jean-Pierre Chevènement reprised the argument that 'the French State of Vichy was neither the Republic nor France'. Rachida Dati, former Minister of Justice in Sarkozy's administration, attacked Hollande's association of the Vichy regime with the nation at large, stating that '[n]ot all French were complicit in this barbarism'.[87] Four years later, in 2016, Hollande acknowledged the 'great responsibility' of the French in the internment of thousands of Roma gypsies during 1940–1944.[88] The irony of Hollande's statement was that in 2012 he had pursued his predecessor's policy of razing Roma camps to the ground and deporting their inhabitants, actions that the European Commission described as a 'disgrace'.[89]

On 16 July 2017, President Emmanuel Macron once again reaffirmed French responsibility for the arrest of Jews in Paris in July 1942: 'France ... organized the round-up, subsequent deportation and, consequently, for almost all of them, the death of the 13,152 French Jews dragged from their homes on 16 and 17 July 1942. More than 8,000 were taken to the Vél d'Hiv before being deported to Auschwitz. Among them were 4,115 children aged between 2 and 16 years'.[90] He mentioned unnamed 'French political leaders prepared to trample on the truth' and framed his speech as a retort to these 'counterfeiters'. Macron was referring to Marine Le Pen, current president of the FN (now renamed the Rassemblement National) and daughter of Jean-Marie. During a television interview in April 2017, Marine Le Pen had stated, 'I think that France was not responsible for the

Vél d'Hiv [round up]. If anyone is guilty it is those who were in power at the time, it is not France. Really, we have taught our children that they have many reasons to criticise [France], to see in it perhaps only the darkest parts of its history. I want them to be proud once again to be French'.[91]

Le Pen's provocative statement was not so out of step with current attitudes to French involvement in the Holocaust as one might imagine. Rose Bosch's 2010 film *La rafle* (*The Roundup*) was a heartening depiction of French attitudes to the plight of the Jews. Set against the background of the Vél d'Hiv arrests, the film tells the story of Joseph Weismann, a young Jewish boy who survived the ordeal but whose family did not. Bosch presented the film as a model of cinematic historical authenticity, employing no less than Serge Klarsfeld as historical adviser. History teachers attended special screenings and 11,000 schools received educational dossiers to accompany the film's release.[92] Historian Annette Wieviorka severely criticized the film's depiction of numerous acts of French benevolence towards the Jews. Wieviorka wrote scathingly of the closing scene (in which Joseph is reunited with his angelic younger brother Nono at the Liberation): 'If by chance, sensitive to the melodramatic, you had shed a few tears [during the film], you can, at the film's end, wipe them away and leave [the cinema] relieved by this happy ending... *La Rafle* does not confront the French with their past. It reconciles them to it'.[93] It is difficult to disagree. French audiences doubtless found the story of Weismann's survival comforting. It was, however, extraordinary. French police arrested thousands of Jewish children in July 1942; the vast majority of these children died at the hands of the Nazis.

The history of French complicity in the Holocaust is currently the subject of historical revisionism. In his 2012 *Vichy et la Shoah*, Alain Michel was unequivocal in his aim: '[I] propose to show how Vichy, voluntarily, delivered foreign Jews to the Nazis, on the one hand, and succeeded in protecting the majority of French Jews "[who had been in the country] pre-1920" on the other hand'.[94] Michel depicted himself as a challenger to the 'official' history (founded by Marrus and Paxton) that ignored the complexity of French behaviour in favour of black-and-white conclusions that had become the 'dogma' of the historiography.[95] Michel's attitude to the Vichy leadership was far from negative: 'It's certain that [the leaders] made mistakes, and even [committed] crimes. But it seems an equally reasonable statement that their action had in the end more positive than negative consequences'.[96] Vichy's role in the Final Solution was thus 'ambiguous' because the regime had acted 'at once [as] executioner and saviour'.[97] Paxton dismissed Michel's work: 'You cannot write what he wrote if you have read Vichy's [anti-Semitic] texts and recent work on the application of these texts'.[98] *Vichy et la Shoah* enabled further attempts at historical revisionism, namely, Eric Zemmour's best-selling *Le Suicide français*, a right-wing analysis of the decline of France since the 1960s in which the author claimed that Pétain and Laval had saved French Jews. Zemmour attacked Paxton's work as a political defence of multi-culturalism.[99]

In 2013, Jacques Semelin likewise challenged Marrus and Paxton's thesis. Semelin pointed to what he termed 'a French enigma' (Michel had called it a 'paradox'): 'if twenty-five per cent of Jews in France were killed, how was it possible that three quarters of the Jewish community escaped death?'[100] This comparatively high rate of survival prompted Semelin to look for the 'factors unique to France that could have allowed the obstruction of the genocidal process' in order to provide a 'more balanced' view and bring 'a new historiographical impulse' to the subject.[101] Semelin's research uncovered what he termed a 'non-conformist, disobedient, even resistant social tissue, at the heart of which, like other pariahs and enemies of the Occupier and Vichy, [Jews] were able to hide and survive'.[102] So many Jews had survived in France because ordinary French had helped them. French benevolence ensured that the Holocaust in France was a 'semi-failure'.[103]

Renée Poznanski, historian of the Jewish community in France, has rebuked the revisionism of the likes of Michel and Semelin. Poznanski criticized the latter's emphasis on 'nice stories relating ordinary acts of rescue', describing his conclusions as 'simplistic explanations' that 'get a good press', but that ultimately do little to explain the survival of the majority of the Jewish population.[104] Marrus and Paxton also responded to Semelin in the preface to their 2015 update of *Vichy et les Juifs*. They wrote that far from being the 'average French person' (as Semelin argued), those men and women who saved Jews were 'exceptional human beings'.[105] Marrus and Paxton chastised those historians who had focused on the supposed goodwill of the French with regard to their Jewish neighbours: 'Instead of asking how so many Jews survived in France, we should ask why so many perished, given the potential in the country to help or hide the victims. The loss of 25 per cent of Jews in France is not a total to boast about'.[106] Semelin hit back at his critics in the 2018 revised and abridged version of his book, revealingly entitled *La survie des Juifs en France* (published in English as *The Survival of the Jews in France*). Semelin noted that Marrus and Paxton had devoted only forty lines to the '75 per cent' in their classic 1981 work; 'That is to say that they totally concealed it', he added.[107] He reframed his work as 'the history and memories of the *non-deportation* of the Jews from France' and underscored once again that the 'social connection between Jews and non-Jews was crucial to counteracting the genocidal project'.[108] Semelin's question about the 'French enigma' is a valid one yet his conclusions, couched in exceptionalist terms, amount to a quasi-exoneration of the French nation.

Conclusion

The zombie Vichy has stalked the political and cultural life of France since the Liberation. It is an ever-present corpse periodically reanimated to serve the needs of the present. The Gaullist resistancialist myth provided the basis for post-war unity after years of Franco-French conflict. In the new world order of the Cold War, it reinforced French claims to a seat at the victors' table. The myth showered resisters with glory, minimized the misdeeds of collaborators and allowed the French who had done nothing to hold their head high. The Gaullist narrative prioritized unity and homogeneity; it necessarily effaced difference and marginalized groups that did not conform to its representation. With de Gaulle in power during the 1960s, few could challenge the president's reading of the war years.

By the 1970s, the Gaullist myth collapsed under the weight of historical enquiry and the emergence of a new generation ready to question society's established truths. Paxton's transformative work laid the foundation stone of all subsequent research into Vichy while Ophüls's documentary exposed the French public to the inconvenient and hidden truths of its past. The dark side of Vichy now came into view as the victims of the regime's repression staked a claim to their own versions of the past. The nation put itself on trial as collaborators returned to French courtrooms. Meanwhile, groups that had remained marginal to mainstream historiography (not least women) broke their silence, laying the foundations for the diversity that characterizes contemporary Vichy studies.

Since 2000, research into Vichy has continued to expand. Historians have followed important avenues of research into the daily experience of the French. The empire has come into focus within both the context of metropolitan France and the global reach of the National Revolution. Resistance and collaboration continue to fascinate researchers and the public and, thanks to the appreciation of the ethnic, religious and gendered diversity of the 'French' of the war years, one can study the history of the struggle to liberate France in all its complexity. However, the continued debate about the complicity of the French nation in the Holocaust shows that revisionism is not always welcome, especially when framed in terms of national exceptionalism. Ultimately, the debate between the revisionists and their critics speaks to the continued relevance of the Vichy past in France today.

8

Conclusion

Few moments in the history of France have broken into Anglophone popular consciousness in quite the same way as the defeat and Occupation of France. Why? A widespread belief in the cowardly surrender and the shameful collaboration of the French serves to aggrandize both the British myth of the Second World War – that of the plucky island nation that stood alone against Hitler – and its American equivalent – according to which the white knights of the 'Greatest Generation' arrived like the cavalry to save the day. The tale of Vichy's treachery also serves as a handy stick with which to periodically beat the French. On 1 November 1990, British tabloid rag *The Sun* printed its famous 'Up Yours Delors' front page, a Francophobic piece aimed at then-President of the European Commission Jacques Delors. Along with a host of French 'crimes' against Britain (including the banning of British beef and the jeering of Margaret Thatcher during a visit to Paris), the newspaper reminded readers that '[The French] GAVE IN to the Nazis during the Second World War when we [the British] stood firm'.[1] In a 1995 episode of the US animated comedy show *The Simpsons*, Scottish school janitor Groundskeeper Willie stands in for the French teacher, greeting pupils with 'Bonjoooouuurrr, ya cheese-eatin' surrender monkeys!' Several American newspapers later used the phrase 'surrender monkeys' to lambast the French over President Jacques Chirac's reluctance to involve his country in the second Iraq War.[2] The condescending inaccuracy that the French have not yet confronted the darkest corners of their own past accompanies such ridicule; Jackson observed as much in 2001.[3] In December 2015, for example, the *Daily Express* revealed that the French government had *finally* unlocked files on France's involvement in the Holocaust. 'The secret archives were opened as France faces up to its Nazi shame', the newspaper claimed. It was true that the French government had at that time decided to declassify a number of documents from the period of the war. However, by 2015 a mountain of literature existed on France's 'Nazi shame', and a decade had passed since the opening of the Holocaust museum in central Paris (conversely we still await British popular recognition of the brutal violence committed for centuries in the name of their empire).[4] Unfortunately, anti-French prejudices are deeply rooted in Anglophone culture: I have lost count of the number of times someone has lectured me, a historian of twentieth-century France, on 1940 and 'when all the French ran away'.

What explains this continued fascination with the Dark Years in Anglophone popular culture? It is unclear whether the interest lies in genuine historical interest or a disaster-porn-style attraction that prompts the imagining of the consequences of a Nazi victory in one's own country. Whatever the case, the Occupation has provided an artistic backdrop for numerous English-language cultural productions that, if not entirely satisfactory from a historical point of view, have at least helped to sensitize Anglophone audiences to the wartime history of France. Several examples follow, though there are many more. The popular BBC comedy series *'Allo! 'Allo!* (1982–1992) contrasted the wily French café owner René Artois and his resistance contact Michelle Dubois with the bumbling German authorities and the hapless British. René walked a fine line between accommodating the local Nazi officers – and appearing outwardly as a collaborator – and aiding the resistance. The English-language translation of Némirovsky's *Suite Française* (ranked the fifth best novel of the 2000s by *The Times*) and its 2015 film adaptation brought both the Exode and the intricacies of life and love during the Occupation to Anglophone audiences (though the film was not released in theatres in the United States).[5] Quentin Tarantino's typically bombastic 2009 *Inglourious Basterds* provided glimpses into the dangers that some French encountered in Occupied France. In the most memorable and terrifying scene of the film (for this historian of France, at least), Mélanie Laurent's Jewish character, Shoshanna Dreyfus, escapes a Nazi search of the house in which she and her family are hiding.[6] Still, the most popular war films in Britain in recent years, Joe Wright's *Darkest Hour* (2017) and Christopher Nolan's *Dunkirk* (2017), barely acknowledged the fact that, as British narrowly avoided tragedy in 1940, France stumbled headlong into the abyss of defeat. The latter film featured few French soldiers, an absence that French reviews of the film noted.[7] Happily, the BBC's 2019 miniseries *World on Fire* did include soldiers of the French army, from Senegal, no less.

Readers of *France in the Second World War* will recognize that attempts to simplify French history between 1940 and 1944 lie not in the historians' craft but in Hollywood caricaturing at best and, at worst, in nationalist idiocy and the scoring of chauvinistic cheap shots. However, readers may find the complexity of the subject daunting and some form of summary is now required. This conclusion summarizes the key themes that have emerged in this book with a view to informing and organizing readers' own research. These themes are: (a) collaboration and resistance; (b) persecution; (c) gender and ethnicity. In addition, it is important that, when researching France in the Second World War, we consider: (a) chronology – what was happening in France, its Empire and the wider war at the particular point under investigation; and (b) geography – where in the world did the events take place and what was the influence of local factors.

Collaboration or resistance? The eternal question

A minority of French chose to collaborate. Military men, politicians and civil servants at Vichy looked to secure a future for France in Hitler's New Order through co-operation in founding that very Order. The delusion that Berlin would reward such co-operation with concessions informed the logic of state collaboration. In Paris, the collaborationist groups strove to strengthen the bonds between France and Nazism while positioning themselves as the primary conduit (in the style of a fascist single party) between the people and the government. Collaboration and collaborationism were most popular in the early stages of the Occupation when Britain's defeat looked inevitable. As the war turned against the Third Reich, collaborators and collaborationists clung to the hope of an Allied reversal even as their support slipped away. The increasingly desperate situation at home and abroad prompted some fanatics (and not a few men and women who sought only to maintain a steady income) to join the Milice or to volunteer to fight communism in the East.

A minority of French chose to resist. Resistance developed in patchwork fashion during 1940 and 1941 as people developed diverse ways to respond to the Occupation in the North and Vichy in the South. Established professional and social networks provided like-minded people with a basis from which to work; their actions centred mainly on the production of propaganda and the passing of intelligence to the Allies. The entry of the Communist Party into resistance, Moulin's missions between London and France, and the turn of the tide of the war against Germany all encouraged resistance movements and networks to grow and diversify their methods of action. Unification came in 1943 with the foundation of the CNR. Despite the political differences that remained between the groups, the CNR ensured the representation of the Resistance at the Liberation and beyond. In sum, no more than 500,000 French or 2 per cent of the population participated in a movement or network, a figure broadly in line with those of other Western-occupied territories.[8] This figure included non-French fighters who fought to free their adopted country.

Even fewer French (and their imperial subjects) – certainly fewer than 50,000 – joined the Free French. From inauspicious origins in London and Brazzaville, de Gaulle and his supporters nurtured the Free French into a global and multi-ethnic force. By 1943, the Free French could claim to be an international body with pseudo-diplomatic representation in countries around the world. Free French soldiers fought alongside Allied troops in the Liberation of France and provided an important basis for the re-establishment of a French army.

Problems arise when we seek to apply the terms 'collaboration' and 'resistance' to men and women beyond the groups outlined above. It is impossible to understand the behaviour of these French in black-and-white terms. Repertoires of defiance were varied and acts such as strikes and food riots, with limited and often economic aims, do not easily fit into the category of resistance to the political and ideological status quo. Moreover, daily life consisted of a series of choices and negotiations. Just as there were motives to resist and to collaborate, there were compelling reasons for doing nothing, not least one's own survival and the survival of one's family. Only in exceptional circumstances did people choose to resist or collaborate in an active sense. Rather, the struggle to put food on the table and heat one's home dominated the everyday life of millions of French.

Moving beyond the relationship between French and Germans further complicates notions of collaboration and resistance. In the Italian-occupied zone, Rome refused French demands – and, by extension, German demands – to deport foreign Jews to camps within France. Yet one would hardly describe such an act as resistance. In Indochina, the French administration co-operated with the Japanese authorities in an attempt to maintain French sovereignty; in this instance, 'collaboration' was not tinged with its inherent association with Nazism. When we confront the territories of the French Empire the Eurocentric basis of the labels fully reveals itself. Collaboration and resistance carried different meanings in the lands of the empire where the French regime was the occupying power. The absence of German forces in France's distant imperial holdings meant that, beyond the shipping of resources to mainland France for German consumption, collaboration – understood as co-operation with the Nazis – was meaningless. Likewise, resistance here meant the defiance of the French administration and often drew on long-established traditions of anti-colonial dissidence. The re-examination of collaboration and resistance in a colonial context underscores the narrowness of the Eurocentric reading of these transnational phenomena.

Nevertheless, we cannot abandon the terms entirely for the very reason that contemporaries used them: Marshal Pétain chose the 'path of *collaboration*' in 1940, while dissident groups self-consciously identified themselves as the resistance, not least in the title of their representative body, the CNR. At the Liberation, collaboration and resistance carried legal connotations. To be found guilty of collaboration (or, more accurately, acting in the service of a foreign power), whether in a state court or a locally sanctioned resistance trial, could entail the loss of civil rights, imprisonment and, in the worst cases, execution. Meanwhile, resisters received medals and could use such honourable credentials to accede to public office. The words further carried moral connotations that became deeply rooted in French society. Those attached to resistance were not always positive: some French still treated resisters (particularly communist resisters) as 'terrorists' even decades after the war. Attitudes to collaboration were no less complex, as illustrated by the case of the femmes tondues. In the historiography, disagreements over the definitions of each word and their attendant moral implications have brought a further level of complexity to their use.

Whether the French resisted or collaborated is an eternal question because one cannot arrive at an answer that satisfies everyone; the circuitous discussions in the classrooms of many universities prove this contention. It is unsafe to use these labels to describe the action of men and women beyond a very small number of historical actors. Terms such as 'defiance' and 'accommodation' better characterize the actions of French outside the Vichy-collaborationist and resistance-Free French mainstream. They certainly carry less political and moral baggage.

Persecution: Vichy's raison d'être

The drive to exclude the perceived enemies of France was present from the first day of the regime until its last. The establishment of the Etat Français provided an outlet for many years of pent-up hatred against the principal groups on Vichy's blacklist, namely Jews, Freemasons, communists and foreigners. On the one hand, the policy of collaboration in part influenced this discriminatory agenda for, in doing the Germans' dirty work, successive governments calculated what such action could win for France in terms of concessions and sovereignty. On the other hand, the violence committed against minorities did not stem solely from callous pragmatism. Vichy and the Third Reich held shared hatreds for the same groups and the renovation of France and its Empire proposed in the National Revolution required the political, social and cultural, if not physical, elimination of these groups. The regime fully directed its energies into undoing the 'damage' inflicted on France during the country's years of democracy. Persecution was therefore Vichy's raison d'être. By the final year of the war, with resistance growing and Germany retreating throughout Europe, the regime's terrorist policies had reached the fullest extent of their radicalism.

Vichy's exclusionary legislation owed something to Republican precedent. The governments of the democratic regime did not explicitly single out certain political and ethnic groups for exclusion yet one does not have to look very far to find harbingers of French wartime persecution in the decades before 1940: the laws against communism, anarchism and terrorism of 1941 and 1943 built upon legislation against 'social crimes' from the 1890s; the 1912 law on travelling salespersons and traders targeted gypsies; the so-called 'immigrant problem' of the 1930s prompted parliamentary action to limit and restrict the professional and political rights of non-French, many of whom were Jewish refugees; internment camps established during the late 1930s housed suspect foreigners, notably Spanish Republican exiles.

In its imperial territories, France had long subjected indigenous inhabitants to discrimination based on the idea of a French national community defined as white, European and Christian. Racism, forced labour, arbitrary punishment and extreme violence were common currency in the empire. In colonies under Free French control, the need to fuel the Allied war effort, financially and materially, saw repression intensify and the brutal treatment of the indigenous inhabitants was commonplace. Ultimately, in the lands of the French Empire built discrimination upon Republican tradition. One wonders if colonial peoples noticed any difference between their treatment before and after 1940.

French involvement in the Holocaust is undeniable. Vichy was an anti-Semitic regime that persecuted Jewish residents from its earliest days. Anti-Semitism radicalized as indigenous racism combined with the fallacious logic of collaboration to bring France into Hitler's schedule for the extermination of Europe's Jewish population. French anti-Semitism may have lacked the biological core of its German counterpart (for Vichy based its discrimination on cultural lines) yet for those mainly non-French Jews who fell afoul of the law deportation and gassing awaited. Geography affected the severity of discriminatory measures. Jews in the Occupied Zone suffered under both Vichy and Germany's persecution; Jews in the South escaped this double penalty at least until November 1942. The Italian-occupied zone offered something of a safe haven for Jewish refugees when Rome refused to hand over non-French Jews to Vichy. Yet these same Jews were subject to surveillance and arrest within the Italian zone itself.

It is true that a number of organizations and brave individuals sheltered Jews from the authorities. We must not ignore such risky acts of selflessness. Yet to attribute the survival of 75 per cent of Jews in France to French generosity is unwise. This view may comfort those who wish to cleanse the reputation of France from its association with the Holocaust yet it is, at best, a politically suspect contention. Marrus and Paxton were ultimately right to argue that the question should not centre on how so many Jews survived but on how so many more Jews *could have* survived without French complicity in the Nazis' project. To frame the wartime experience of Jews in France as primarily one of survival is little short of outrageous.

A pluralist historiography

The most recent shift in the historiography of France and the Second World War – what we might term the latest phase of the Vichy Syndrome – has seen a proliferation of work on gender and minorities. This work valorizes the pluralism of the French experience.

Notions of gender were central to the politics and action of the Vichy regime as well as to the movements that opposed it. The National Revolution sought to combat an alleged decline in the quality and quantity of the French nation (which it blamed on Republican decadence) through a gendered appeal to parenthood. This appeal reinforced the traditional boundaries between the sexes, maintaining the distinctness of the feminine private sphere and the masculine public sphere (Republicans had expressed a similarly gendered view of society). Propaganda cast women as dutiful mothers in the home while men were strong fathers, ready to do their duty to France and their family through siring a child or going to work in Germany. Legislation repressed or curtailed threats to the integrity of the family, from women's work and divorce to abortion. Youth movements looked to create a new generation of morally and physically fit French unfettered by flabby democratic ideas of individualism and equality. Imperial governors likewise tried to mould indigenous peoples to Vichy's vision, though their transformation depended less on a drive for improvement and more on racial prejudices about the 'natural' abilities and mentalities of certain non-white peoples.

Gendered thinking informed women's methods of resistance. Women were present at all levels of resistance organizations, even if they were fewer in number than their male counterparts. Women were generally prohibited from involvement in military and paramilitary action yet a few women did commit acts of violence. A handful also ascended to positions of leadership in movements and networks. Female resisters concerned themselves in the main with propaganda and communications work, message-carrying, administrative tasks and care-giving, that is, activities considered suited to a woman's 'inherent' abilities. Women could use gender stereotypes to their advantage, for example, slipping unsuspected past enemy checkpoints. Furthermore, some repertoires of defiance – the food riot, for example – depended solely on female participation and their exploitation of the traditional image of the homemaker. Ideas about feminine qualities governed the scope for action of female collaborationists, too. Women acted as surrogate mothers (or marraines, godmothers) and pen pals for the few men who volunteered to fight Bolshevism in the east and they provided social services in collaborationist parties and Vichy's Milice.

Gendered readings of appropriate behaviour influenced responses to the women who had sexual relations with German soldiers. Double standards were rife: prostitutes and French men were free to engage in sex with Germans yet women who took German lovers faced ostracism and punishment at the Liberation. For French men humiliated by the defeat and occupation of France, the sight of the invaders cavorting with French women was both an insult to their male pride and an analogy for the Nazi rape of the motherland. In 1944, the ceremonies that saw these women shorn of their hair re-established French male dominance over their female counterparts.

Vichy's policy to non-white peoples was rooted in decades of racialist thinking. Within France, black residents were subject to special restrictions and colonial POWs felt that the regime privileged the liberation of their white comrades over their own freedom. Abroad, the subjects of the French Empire experienced daily discrimination, not least in the rationing system. Yet it is difficult to determine the extent that this racism was specific to the Vichy period. The French Empire had long been a 'system of racial oppression'.[9] It is more likely the case that Vichy was simply less concerned to dress up its racism in the hollow universalist rhetoric of the Republic. The Free French likewise continued to abuse indigenous peoples in the colonies 'liberated' from Pétain's rule. Yet black African fighters were integral to the foundation of the Free French in 1940 while troops from North Africa distinguished themselves in the invasion of Southern Europe. De Gaulle saw fit to reward these men with their abrupt replacement with white French soldiers (the blanchiment). The responses of colonial subjects to the conflict were complex, conditioned by local politics and history. Caribbean islanders, for example, opposed what they considered to be the Hitlerian racism of the Vichy puppet state, fearing a return to slavery, but West Africans considered the global conflict as a war between white men in which they should not become embroiled.

The proliferation of research on the role of minority groups in the history of France and the Second World War represents a new phase in the historiography. Historians have come to address the history of the period in all its diversity and it is no longer tenable for a researcher to ignore gender or race in their work. This focus on groups heretofore absent from the historiography owes something to the development of the history of everyday life and its reliance on sources that lay beyond the archives. It is a history that has thrown up new and complex questions as much about the identity of the French today as those in the past. In 2017, when Marine Le Pen expressed her desire to see an end to the nation's self-flagellation for historical wrongdoing, Henry Rousso claimed that the FN president had 'reopened the file on Vichy'. It had never really been closed.

GLOSSARY

Abetz, Otto (1903–1958): German ambassador to France between August 1940 and July 1944.

Albrecht, Berty (1893–1943): Albrecht was a resister and among the founder members of Combat. She died in prison in May 1943, probably as a result of suicide. Albrecht is one of six women named as a Compagnon de la Libération and her remains were interred at the Mémorial de la France combattante at Mont Valérien.

Alibert, Raphaël (1887–1963): Minister of Justice during July 1940–February 1941.

Alliance: Under the leadership of Georges Loustaunau-Lacau and Marie-Madeleine Fourcade, Alliance was one of the principal resistance networks in Occupied France with up to 3,000 operatives.

Annet, Armand (1888–1973): Governor-General of Madagascar between December 1940 and November 1942.

Armée Secrète (AS): A combat organization formed in September 1942 from the paramilitary wings of Combat, Libération-Sud and Franc-Tireur. Its first head was General Charles Delestraint between October 1942 and June 1943. The AS merged with the FFI in February 1944.

Astier de la Vigerie, Emmanuel d' (1900–1969): Resister and co-founder of Libération-Sud.

Aubert, Pierre-Emile (1888–1972): Governor of La Réunion between December 1939 and December 1942.

Aubrac, Lucie (1912–2007): Real name Lucie Samuel, née Bernard, Aubrac was a resister and co-founder of Libération-Sud.

Aubrac, Raymond (1914–2012): Real name Raymond Samuel, Aubrac was a resister and co-founder of Libération-Sud.

Auxiliary Feminine Corps: Also known as the Feminine Corps of the FFL, the Auxiliary Feminine Corps was founded on 17 November 1940 for female volunteers to the Free French. The Corps was incorporated into the Corps des Volontaires Françaises in December 1941.

Barbie, Klaus (1913–1991): Named head of the Gestapo in Lyon in February 1943, Barbie – nicknamed the 'Butcher' – was responsible for the deaths of dozens of resisters and Jews. After years on the run, he was brought to trial in France in 1987 and convicted of crimes against humanity.

Barthélemy, Joseph (1874–1945): Minister of Justice between January 1941 and March 1943.

Bloch, Marc (1886–1944): Historian and founder of the Annales school of historiography, Bloch wrote *L'Etrange Défaite* (1946), his account of the fall of France, during July–September 1940. Bloch was executed in 1944 for acts of resistance.

Blum, Léon (1872–1950): Leading socialist and Prime Minister of

France during June 1936–June 1937 and March 1938–April 1938. Vichy put Blum on trial at Riom for his alleged role in the defeat of France. He was deported to Buchenwald in 1943.

Boisson, Pierre (1894–1948): High-Commissioner for French Africa (French West Africa, French Equatorial Africa, Cameroon and Togo) between June 1940 and July 1943.

Bonnard, Abel (1883–1968): Minister of Education between April 1942 and July 1944.

Bousquet, René (1909–1993): Head of the French police between April 1942 and December 1943, Bousquet oversaw the arrest and deportation of thousands of Jews, organizing the infamous Vél d'Hiv roundup in July 1942. After the war, he grew close to future French President François Mitterand. Bousquet was murdered in 1993 as he awaited trial for crimes against humanity.

Bouthillier, Yves (1901–1977): Minister of Finance between June 1940 and April 1942.

Brinon, Fernand de (1885–1947): Principal delegate of the Vichy government in the Occupied Zone between November 1940 and August 1944.

Brossolette, Pierre (1903–1944): A resister who worked with the Musée de l'Homme group, Libération-Nord and the OCM, Brossolette joined the Free French in spring 1942, becoming one of de Gaulle's principal operatives in France. Arrested in February 1944, Brossolette committed suicide the following month.

Bureau Central de Renseignement et d'Action (BCRA): The intelligence arm of the Free French, founded in July 1940.

Cayla, Léon (1881–1965): Governor-General of Madagascar between July 1940 and April 1941.

Ceux de la Libération (CDLL): A right-leaning resistance movement in the Occupied Zone and a member of the CNR, the CDLL took shape in summer 1940 when industrialist Maurice Ripoche and chemist Roger Coquoin began to collect intelligence to be transmitted to the Allies.

Ceux de la Résistance (CDLR): The CDLR was founded in early 1943 by Jacques Lecompte-Boinet, Pierre Arrighi and Jean de Vouguë. It gathered intelligence for the Allies and was a member of the CNR.

Chantiers de la Jeunesse: Vichy's system of youth camps in the Southern Zone and North Africa for men aged twenty years, under the command of General Joseph de la Porte du Theil.

Châtel, Yves (1865–1944): Governor-General of Algeria between November 1941 and January 1943.

Combat: The largest resistance movement in the Southern Zone and a member of the CNR. Henry Frenay and Berty Albrecht founded the Mouvement de Libération Nationale (MLN) in Lyon in summer 1940. The MLN subsequently spread throughout the Southern Zone, merging with the Liberté network in 1941, to create Combat.

Commissariat Général aux Questions Juives (CGQJ): Created in March 1941, the CGQJ directed and implemented Vichy's anti-Semitic discrimination.

Comité Français de Libération Nationale (CFLN): The CFLN was founded on 3 June 1943 when de Gaulle's France Libre united with Giraud's North African Commandement en Chef

Français Civil et Militaire. The Comité functioned as a provisional government-in-exile until June 1944 when it became the Gouvernement provisoire de la République Française.

Compagnons de France: A voluntary organization for youths aged between fifteen and twenty years old. Full-time members lived in camps. Members' activities included outdoor labour and social work and all were heavily infused with the propaganda of the National Revolution. Founder Henry Dhavernas served as the association's president until February 1941. Guillaume de Tournemire succeeded Dhavernas, serving until 1944.

Conseil National de la Résistance (CNR): A national co-ordinating body for resistance action founded in May 1943 under the aegis of Jean Moulin. A number of resistance movements and political parties sat on the council: the OCM, CDLR, CDLL, the communist Front National and Libération-Nord (from the North); Combat, Libération-Sud and Franc-Tireur (from the South); the socialists and communists, the right-wing Fédération Républicaine and the centre-right Parti Démocrate Populaire and the Alliance Démocratique, and France's two largest trade unions, the Confédération Générale du Travail and the Confédération Française des Travailleurs Chrétiens.

Corps des Volontaires Françaises (CVF): A quasi-military unit of the Free French for female recruits, founded in December 1941.

Daladier, Edouard (1884–1970): A politician from the Radical Party and three times Prime Minister of France (January–October 1933; January–February 1934; April 1938–March 1940). Daladier was imprisoned in Germany from April 1943.

Darlan, François (1881–1942): An Admiral in the French Navy, Darlan served as deputy Prime Minister at Vichy between February 1941 and April 1942. He also acted as Foreign Minister, Minister of the Interior, Minister of Defence and Minister of Information. Following the Allied invasion of North Africa in November 1942, Darlan assumed the title of High Commissioner for France in Africa and led a Vichyite administration in the Allied-occupied territory. He was assassinated on 24 December 1942.

Darnand, Joseph (1887–1945): A veteran of the interwar extreme right, Darnand founded the Service d'Ordre Légionnaire (SOL) in August 1941 and led the Milice Française from January 1943. He was appointed Secretary General for the Maintenance of Order in January 1944 and Secretary of State for the Interior in June 1944. In October 1945, the High Court of Justice sentenced Darnand to death and he was executed by firing squad on 10 October.

Déat, Marcel (1894–1955): The former socialist Déat was the founder of the collaborationist Rassemblement National Populaire (RNP), a movement that advocated a close relationship with Germany in a new European economic order. He served as Minister for Labour and National Solidarity at Vichy during March–August 1944.

Decoux, Jean (1884–1963): Admiral and Governor-General of Indochina between June 1940 and March 1945.

Défense de la France: A resistance movement in the Northern Zone, founded by Philippe Viannay and his student acquaintances. Défense de la France published an eponymous newspaper from August 1941.

Deloncle, Eugène (1890–1944): An extreme right-wing activist and leader of the interwar Organisation Secrète d'Action Révolutionnaire Nationale, otherwise known as the Cagoule. Deloncle founded the collaborationist Mouvement Social Révolutionnaire (MSR) in 1940.

Dewavrin, André (1911–1998): Dewavrin directed the Free French Bureau Central de Reseignement et d'Action under the codename Colonel Passy.

de Gaulle, Charles (1890–1970): De Gaulle was the leader of Free France, a body that resisted Vichy and the Nazis outside France for the majority of the war. De Gaulle launched Free France with a speech on 18 June 1940 in which he called on the French to continue the fight against both French defeatists and the invader. De Gaulle positioned himself as the head of a de facto government in exile with the establishment of the Comité National Français in September 1941 and the subsequent Comité Français de Libération Nationale. The movements and parties of the CNR recognized de Gaulle's leadership of the French resistance in May 1943. At the Liberation of France, he assumed the presidency of the Provisional Government of the French Republic, a role from which he resigned in January 1946. In 1958, de Gaulle returned to frontline politics as the last Prime Minister of the Fourth Republic. The following year, he founded the Fifth Republic and became the new regime's first President.

Dhavernas, Henry (1912–2009): Founder of the Compagnons de France, Dhavernas was expelled from the group in February 1941 and later joined the Allies.

Doriot, Jacques (1898–1945): Doriot was the leader of the Parti Populaire Français (PPF). Expelled from the communist party in 1934, Doriot gravitated towards fascism and anti-Semitism during the late 1930s. He pursued a collaborationist line during the war years as he aimed to pose the PPF as a fascist-style single party. Doriot served on the Eastern Front as a recruit to the Légion des Volontaires Français contre le Bolchevisme. He was killed in February 1945 when fighter planes strafed the car in which he was travelling.

Eboué, Félix (1884–1944): Governor-General of French Equatorial Africa between November 1940 and May 1944 (formerly Governor of Chad).

Estéva, Jean-Pierre (1880–1951): Resident General of France in Tunisia from July 1940 until May 1943.

Fighting France: See France Combattante.

Flandin, Pierre-Etienne (1889–1958): Former Prime Minister of the Third Republic (November 1934–June 1935) and leading politician with the centre-right Alliance Démocratique, Flandin served as Vichy's deputy Prime Minister during December 1940–February 1941 as part of a triumvirate with Darlan and Huntziger. At the Liberation, Flandin was sentenced to indignité nationale and served two years in prison.

Forces Françaises de l'Intérieur (FFI): Formed in February 1944 when the military wings of the Resistance fused in preparation for the coming Allied invasion.

Fourcade, Marie-Madeleine (1909–1989): Fourcade (née Méric) led the Alliance resistance network following the arrest of Georges Loustaunau-Lacau.

France Combattante: On 13 July 1942, de Gaulle's France Libre assumed the name 'France Combattante', an umbrella term to describe the collaboration of the former France Libre with the internal resistance movements and networks.

France Libre: Founded on 18 June 1940, 'France Libre' – 'Free France' – was the name of de Gaulle's resistance movement that operated outside the borders of France. It was renamed 'France Combattante' in July 1942.

Francs-Tireurs et Partisans (FTP): The armed wing of the communist resistance, founded in early 1942 from the Organisation Spéciale and the Travail Particulier groups. The FTP co-founded the FFI in 1944.

Free France: See France Libre.

Frenay, Henri (1905–1988): Frenay co-founded the Combat resistance movement in 1941.

Front National: A communist resistance movement founded in mid-1941.

Gabolde, Maurice (1891–1972): Minister of Justice between March 1943 and August 1944.

Gamelin, Maurice (1872–1958): General Gamelin was the Supreme Commander of Allied forces in 1940. Prime Minister Paul Reynaud removed Gamelin from his post on 18 May 1940. The Vichy regime held Gamelin partially responsible for the defeat and he was interned until November 1942. German forces subsequently deported Gamelin to Germany where he resided in custody until May 1945.

Gaulle, Charles de (1890–1970): De Gaulle was the leader of Free France, a body that resisted Vichy and the Nazis outside France for the majority of the war. De Gaulle launched Free France with a speech on 18 June 1940 in which he called on the French to continue the fight against both French defeatists and the invader. De Gaulle positioned himself as the head of a de facto government in exile with the establishment of the Comité National Français in September 1941 and the subsequent Comité Français de Libération Nationale. The movements and parties of the CNR recognized de Gaulle's leadership of the French resistance in May 1943. At the Liberation of France, he assumed the presidency of the Provisional Government of the French Republic, a role from which he resigned in January 1946. In 1958, de Gaulle returned to frontline politics as the last Prime Minister of the Fourth Republic. The following year, he founded the Fifth Republic and became the new regime's first President.

Giraud, Henri (1879–1949): General, co-president of the Comité Français de Libération Nationale between June 1943 and November 1943, and rival of de Gaulle. Giraud succeeded Darlan as High Commissioner in North Africa following the assassination of the latter in December 1942. In February 1943, Giraud assumed the title of Civil and Military Commander in Chief; the following June, this role was amalgamated into the Comité Français de Libération Nationale.

Guéhenno, Jean (1890–1978): A left-wing political and cultural commentator, Guéhenno published his account of life under the Occupation in *Journal des années noires, 1940–1944* (1947). The work appeared in English in 2014 as *Diary of the Dark Years, 1940–1944*.

Hecker, Alphonse van (1890–1981): Head of the Chantiers de la Jeunesse in French North Africa between 1940 and 1942.

Henriot, Philippe (1889–1944): Henriot was an extreme right-wing polemicist who served as a deputy between 1928 and 1940. During the Occupation, Henriot was a collaborationist, a supporter of the SOL and a member of the Milice. He was a skilled propagandist and made regular radio broadcasts on Radio-Paris, attacking the resistance and General de Gaulle. Laval appointed Henriot Vichy's Secretary of State for Information and Propaganda in January 1944. A resistance commando unit assassinated Henriot on 28 June 1944.

Humbert, Agnès (1894–1963): An art historian and academic, Humbert was a founder member of the Musée de l'Homme resistance network. She was arrested in February 1941 and deported to Ravensbruck. Humbert published her wartime account, *Notre Guerre*, in 1946, published in English in 2008 as *Résistance: A Woman's Journal of Struggle and Defiance in Occupied France*.

Huntziger, Charles (1880–1941): General Huntizger was a member of the French Armistice delegation in June 1940. Huntziger subsequently served as head of the French Army and Minister of War.

Lamirand, Georges (1899–1994): Secretary of State for Youth between September 1940 and March 1943.

Lattre de Tassigny, Jean de (1889–1952): Tassigny was the youngest General in the French Army during the Battle of France in 1940. After the Armistice, he remained in his post until late 1942 when he was arrested for having opposed the total occupation of the Southern Zone. He escaped custody and rallied to Free France in 1943. Tassigny went on to command Allied forces in the Liberation of France and the invasion of Germany.

Laval, Pierre (1883–1945): Laval occupied a number of senior posts in the Republican governments of the interwar years, twice serving as Prime Minister between January 1931 and February 1932, and June 1935 and January 1936. In July 1940, he helped to convince parliamentarians to grant full powers to Pétain. The Marshal subsequently appointed Laval to the post of deputy Prime Minister and his designated successor. However, on 13 December 1940, Pétain removed Laval from the government due to the latter's inability to negotiate a permanent treaty with Berlin. Laval later returned to Vichy as Head of Government (April 1942–August 1944), a post that saw him assume great personal power. Laval was executed for the crime of treason on 15 October 1945.

Lebrun, Albert (1871–1950): President of the Third Republic between May 1932 and July 1940.

Leclerc de Hautecloque, Philippe (1902–1947): An infantry commander in the French Army, Leclerc joined de Gaulle in London in July 1940. He led Free French forces during several military operations in Africa, notably the capture of the oasis at Kufra in February 1941. Promoted to General in May 1943, Leclerc led a division in the battle for Normandy and the liberation of Paris in 1944.

Légion Française des Combattants: The Légion was established on 29 August 1940 when all existing First World War veterans' associations were fused into a single organization. Pétain tasked the Légion with spreading the ideals of the National Revolution amongst the populations of France and its overseas territories. The Légion had as many as 1.5 million members by the end of 1941, when non-veterans and women were allowed to join the group.

Légion des Volontaires Français contre le Bolchevisme (LVF): The LVF was founded shortly after Hitler's invasion of the Soviet Union in 1941. It recruited French volunteers to fight on the Eastern Front. A range of collaborationist groups declared their support for the LVF, including the RNP, the PPF, the MSR, the Francistes and the Parti National Collectiviste. LVF leader Eugène Deloncle presided over a team of collaborationists on a central committee. The first volunteers were deployed in Poland during October 1941.

Leméry, Henri (1874–1972): Minister for the Colonies between July 1940 and September 1940.

Libération-Nord: Founded in the Occupied Zone in 1940, Libération-Nord became one of largest resistance movements in the north of France. Libération-Nord maintained the leftist political line of its principal founder, the former banker and trade unionist Christian Pineau. The movement joined the CNR in 1943.

Libération-Sud: Libération-Sud grew out of the resistance activity of left-wingers Emmanuel d'Astier de la Vigerie and Lucie and Raymond Aubrac. The movement was one of the two largest resistance groups in the Southern Zone, with Frenay's Combat. Libération-Sud joined the CNR in 1943.

Maquis: The maquis resistance groups were founded in 1943 when young men called to work in Germany under the STO scheme fled to the countryside. The maquisards lived in camps situated in isolated rural locations and led partisan-style raids against German forces and French collaborators.

Marion, Paul (1899–1954): Secretary General for Information and Propaganda between August 1941 and 1944.

Milice Française: Founded in January 1943 under the leadership of Joseph Darnand, the Milice was Vichy's paramilitary police force that led a merciless war against the resistance.

Moulin, Jean (1899–1943): Moulin was prefect of the Eure-et-Loir when Germany invaded France in 1940. He continued as prefect under Vichy until November 1940 when his centre-left sympathies saw him removed from his post. Moulin subsequently collected information on resistance movements in France and took this information to de Gaulle in London in October 1941. Moulin returned to France as de Gaulle's delegate and succeeded in uniting the main resistance movements in the CNR under the General's leadership. In June 1943, Moulin was arrested at Caluire. Tortured at the hands of Gestapo chief Klaus Barbie, he died of his injuries at Metz railway station whilst in transit from Paris to Berlin. His remains were interred at the Panthéon in 1964. Moulin's account of his experiences between June and November 1940 was published in 1947 as *Premier Combat*; an English translation of the text appeared in Charles Potter's *The Resistance, 1940* (2016).

Mouvement Social Révolutionnaire (MSR): A Paris-based collaborationist movement under the leadership of Eugène Deloncle.

Mouvements Unis de la Résistance (MUR): An organization founded in January 1943 when the three non-communist groups in the Southern Zone (Combat, Libération-Sud and Franc-Tireur) merged. In December 1943, the MUR expanded to include Défense de la France and a number of other smaller movements.

Noguès, Charles (1876–1971): General of the French Army and Resident General of Morocco between 1936 and 1943.

Organisation Civile et Militaire (OCM): A resistance group founded in December 1940 when the Équipe Française d'Organisation du Redressement and the Confédération des Travailleurs Intellectuels merged. The OCM was organized on military lines and concentrated its action on intelligence gathering for the Allies. It joined the CNR in May 1943.

Papon, Maurice (1910–2007): In 1998, Maurice Papon was convicted of complicity in crimes against humanity for his role in the deportation of Jews from the Gironde where he had worked for Vichy between 1942 and 1944. He escaped punishment at the Liberation and went on to enjoy a career in the police and politics, notably serving as Prefect of the Paris Police during 1958–1965 and Minister for the Budget between 1978 and 1981.

Parti Populaire Français (PPF): An extreme right-wing collaborationist party founded in 1936 and led by Jacques Doriot.

Passy, Colonel: Codename of André Dewavrin.

Pellepoix, Louis Darquier de (1897–1980): Anti-Semite and veteran of interwar extreme right-wing politics, Darquier served as head of Vichy's Commissariat Général aux Questions Juives during May 1942–February 1944.

Pétain, Philippe (1856–1951): A Marshal of France (the country's highest military rank), Pétain served as Head of the French State between July 1940 and August 1944. A hero of the First World War known popularly as the 'Victor of Verdun' for his role in the French victory at Verdun in 1916, Pétain gained a reputation during the interwar years as a man largely disinterested in politics. He served briefly as Minister for War in 1934 before taking up the ambassadorship to Spain. Prime Minister Paul Reynaud recalled Pétain to government in June 1940 as deputy Prime Minister. The Marshal was a significant voice amongst the defeatist faction in the cabinet and his preference for an armistice ultimately prompted Reynaud's resignation. Pétain became the last Prime Minister of the Third Republic on 16 June 1940. He helped to destroy the democratic regime and accepted full powers to revise the constitution on 10 July 1940. On 11 July 1940, Pétain concentrated power in his own hands via the founding acts of the Etat Français. On 15 August 1945, the Haute Cour sentenced Pétain to death; de Gaulle commuted the capital sentence to life imprisonment two days later. Stripped of his military rank and honours, Pétain lived out his days in a prison on the Ile d'Yeu, an island off the French Atlantic coast.

Peyrouton, Marcel (1887–1983): Minister of the Interior between September 1940 and February 1941 and Governor-General of Algeria between January 1943 and June 1943.

Pineau, Christian (1904–1995): A former banker and trade unionist, Pineau authored the 'Manifesto of the Twelve' in November 1940, a document that set our trade unionist opposition to the Occupation. He co-founded Libération-Nord in October 1940 and edited its newspaper *Libération*. He was arrested in 1943 and deported to Buchenwald.

Platon, Charles (1886–1944): Admiral and Secretary of State for the Colonies between September 1940 and April 1942.

Porte du Theil, Joseph de la (1884–1976): Founder and head of the Chantiers de la Jeunesse.

Pucheu, Pierre (1899–1944): Secretary of State for Industrial Production during February–July 1941 and Secretary of State, then Minister, of the Interior during July 1941 and April 1942.

Rassemblement National Populaire (RNP): A collaborationist party founded by Marcel Déat in February 1941.

Reynaud, Paul (1878–1966): Prime Minister of the Third Republic between March 1940 and June 1940.

Robert, Georges (1875–1965): High Commissioner for French Overseas Territories in the West Atlantic.

Service d'Ordre Légionnaire (SOL): A paramilitary offshoot of the Légion, founded in Nice in December 1941 by Joseph Darnand. Its 'Twenty-One Points' manifesto promised to fight 'Jewish leprosy', democracy, 'Gaullist dissent' and Bolshevism.

Service du Travail Obligatoire (STO): Established in February 1943, the STO rendered all men aged between twenty and twenty-two years liable for two years' labour service in the Reich. Later amendments widened the scope of recruitment to include older men and women.

Sorin, Constant (1901–1970): Governor of Guadeloupe during 1940–1943.

SS Charlemagne Division: A motorized infantry division of the Waffen-SS comprised mainly of French volunteers.

Todt Organisation: A German civil and military engineering body that employed workers in occupied territories.

Touvier, Paul (1915–1996): Touvier led the Milice in Lyon. In 1995, Touvier became the first Frenchman convicted of crimes against humanity for his role in the execution of seven Jews during the Occupation.

Union Générale des Israélites de France (UGIF): Founded in November 1941, the UGIF was an official umbrella organization for all Jewish associations.

Vallat, Xavier (1891–1972): Secretary General for Veterans and responsible for the Légion during between September 1940 and March 1941, and head of the Commissariat Général aux Questions Juives between March 1941 and May 1942.

Viannay, Philippe (1917–1986): Philosophy student and founder of Défense de la France.

Werth, Léon (1878–1955): Writer and author of wartime account *Déposition, Journal 1940–1944* (1947), published in English in 2018.

Weygand, Maxime (1867–1965): General in the French Army and commander of North Africa between September 1940 and November 1941. Weygand was a forceful advocate of an armistice in 1940.

NOTES

Preface

1 Henry Rousso, *The Vichy Syndrome: History and Memory in France since 1944* (Cambridge, MA: Harvard University Press, 1991); Eric Conan and Henry Rousso, *Vichy. Un passé qui ne passe pas* (Paris: Fayard, 1994).
2 Pierre Laborie, *Le Chagrin et le vénin. Occupation, résistance, idées recues* (Paris: Gallimard, 2014), 10.

Chapter 1

1 David Reynolds, '1940: Fulcrum of the Twentieth Century?' *International Affairs* 66, no. 2 (1990): 325.
2 Jean Guéhenno, *Diary of the Dark Years, 1940–1944: Collaboration, Resistance, and Daily Life in Occupied Paris* (Oxford: Oxford University Press, 2014), 3.
3 Nicole Jordan, 'Strategy and Scapegoatism: Reflections on the French National Catastrophe, 1940', in *The French Defeat of 1940: Reassessments*, ed. Joel Blatt (Oxford: Berghahn Books, 1998), 13.
4 Marc Bloch, *L'Etrange défaite. Témoignage écrit en 1940* (Paris: Société des Éditions Franc-tireur, 1946). The version referred to in this chapter is *Strange Defeat: A Statement of Evidence Written in 1940* (New York: W. W. Norton, 1999).
5 William L. Shirer, *Berlin Diary: The Journal of a Foreign Correspondent, 1934–1941* (New York: Galahad Books, 1995), 434–442.
6 Jean-Baptiste Duroselle, *Politique étrangère de la France. La decadence 1932–1939* (Paris: Imprimerie Nationale, 1979).
7 Richard Carswell, *The Fall of France in the Second World War: History and Memory* (Cham: Palgrave Macmillan, 2019), 261.
8 Julian Jackson, *The Fall of France: The Nazi Invasion of 1940* (Oxford: Oxford University Press, 2003), 213.
9 Martin Thomas, *The French Empire at War, 1940–45* (Manchester: Manchester University Press, 2007), 12.
10 Karl-Heinz Frieser, *Le mythe de la guerre-éclair. La campagne de l'Ouest de 1940* (Paris: Belin, 2015), 247–248.
11 Peter Caddick-Adams, 'The German Breakthrough at Sedan, 12–15 May 1940', in *The Battle for France and Flanders: Sixty Years On*, ed. Brian Bond and Michael Taylor (Barnsely: Leo Cooper, 2001), 13.

12 Adam Tooze, *The Wages of Destruction: The Making and Breaking of the Nazi Economy* (London: Penguin, 2007), 379. On German concerns over the success of the invasion, see Alistair Horne, *To Lose a Battle: France 1940* (London: Macmillan, 1990), 267–268.
13 Jackson, *The Fall of France*, 39–42.
14 Jordan, 'Strategy and Scapegoatism', 15.
15 Tooze, *The Wages of Destruction*, 369.
16 Jackson *The Fall of France*, 105.
17 Guéhenno, *Diary of the Dark Years*, 1.
18 Philip Nord, *France, 1940: Defending the Republic* (New Haven: Yale University Press, 2015), 114.
19 Nord, *France, 1940*, 112–127.
20 Shirer, *Berlin Diary*, 419–425.
21 The full text of the Franco-German Armistice of 25 June 1940 may be found here: http://avalon.law.yale.edu/wwii/frgearm.asp (accessed 21 November 2019).
22 Giorgio Rochat, 'La campagne italienne de juin 1940 dans les Alpes occidentales', *Revue historique des armées* 250 (2008): 5.
23 Jordan, 'Strategy and Scapegoatism', 36.
24 See Richard Herbst, *The Politics of Apoliticism: Political Trials in Vichy France, 1940–1942* (Berlin: De Gruyter, 2019).
25 Bloch, *Strange Defeat*, 135.
26 Bloch, *Strange Defeat*, 142.
27 Bloch, *Strange Defeat*, 170.
28 Bloch, *Strange Defeat*, 157.
29 Jackson, *The Fall of France*, 13.
30 Nord, *France, 1940*, 33–35; Jackson, *The Fall of France*, 14.
31 Jackson, *The Fall of France*, 15; Nord, *France, 1940*, 33–35; Horne, *To Lose a Battle*, 217–220.
32 Tooze, *The Wages of Destruction*, 376; Frieser, *Le mythe de la guerre-éclair*, 83–84.
33 Tooze, *The Wages of Destruction*, 379.
34 Tooze, *The Wages of Destruction*, 371; Jackson, *The Fall of France*, 217.
35 Jackson, *The Fall of France*, 26–27; Ernest R. May, *Strange Victory: Hitler's Conquest of France* (London: I.B. Tauris, 2009), 118–120, 276, 288.
36 Horne, *To Lose a Battle*, 58–64.
37 Horne, *To Lose a Battle*, 530–531.
38 Tooze, *The Wages of Destruction*, 373; Nord, *France, 1940*, 80–81, May, *Strange Victory*, 455–456; Frieser, *Le mythe de la guerre-éclair*, 122–123.
39 Tooze, *The Wages of Destruction*, 377.
40 Karl-Heinze Frieser, 'La légende de la "Blitzkrieg"', in *Mai-juin 1940. Défaite française, victoire allemande, sous l'oeil des historiens étrangers*, ed. Maurice Vaïsse (Paris: Autrement, 2000), 79.
41 Frieser, *Le mythe de la guerre-éclair*, 442–443.
42 Frieser, 'La légende de la "Blitzkrieg"', 84; Frieser, *Le mythe de la guerre-éclair*, 15–17.
43 Martin S. Alexander, '"No Taste for the Fight?" French Combat Performance in 1940 and the Politics of the Fall of France', in *Time to Kill: The Soldier's Experience of War in the West, 1939–1945*, ed. Paul Addison and Angus Calder (London: Pimlico Books, 1997), 161.

44 *The Last Days of Paris* (1940), 163.
45 *The Last Days of Paris* (1940), 156.
46 For an excellent summary in English of the crisis of the 1930s, see Julian Jackson, *France: The Dark Years, 1940–1944* (Oxford: Oxford University Press, 2001), 65–81.
47 Robert Soucy, *French Fascism: The Second Wave* (New Haven; London: Yale University Press, 1995); Chris Millington, *A History of Fascism in France: From the First World War to the National Front* (London: Bloomsbury Academic).
48 Julian Jackson, *The Popular Front in France: Defending Democracy, 1934–38* (Cambridge: Cambridge University Press, 1990), 250–259.
49 Arthur Koestler, *Scum of the Earth* (London: Eland, 2006 [originally published London: Jonathan Cape, 1941]), 158.
50 Julian Jackson, *A Certain Idea of France: The Life of Charles de Gaulle* (London: Allen Lane, 2018), 87.
51 Jackson, *The Popular Front in France*, 256–257; William D. Irvine, 'Domestic Politics and the Fall of France in 1940', in *The French Defeat of 1940*, ed. Joel Blatt 85–99.
52 Daniel Hucker, 'French Public Attitudes towards the Prospect of War in 1938–1939: "Pacifism" or "War Anxiety"?', *French History* 21 no. 4 (2007): 431–449.
53 Alexander, 'No Taste for the Fight?', 170.
54 Frieser, *Le mythe de la guerre-éclair*, 277–282.
55 Alexander, 'No Taste for the Fight?', 172.
56 Alexander, 'No Taste for the Fight?', 170.
57 Rochat, 'La campagne italienne de juin 1940', 5–6; Richard Carrier, 'Réflexions sur l'efficacité militaire de l'armée des Alpes, 10–25 juin 1940', *Revue historique des armées* 250 (2008): 3–5.
58 Martin S. Alexander, '"Fighting to the Last Frenchman"? Reflections on the BEF Deployment to France and the Strains in the Anglo-French Alliance, 1939–40', in *The French Defeat of 1940*, ed. Joel Blatt 312.
59 Jackson, *The Fall of France*, 85.
60 Jackson, *The Fall of France*, 77.
61 Alexander, 'Fighting to the Last Frenchman?', 306–307.
62 Jackson, *The Fall of France*, 78; Alexander, 'Fighting to the Last Frenchman?', 308–309.
63 Alexander Werth, *The Last Days of Paris: A Journalist's Diary* (London: Hamish Hamilton, 1940), 179.
64 Alexander 'Fighting to the Last Frenchman?', 300.
65 Horne, *To Lose a Battle*, 650.
66 Reynolds, '1940', 328.
67 Horne, *To Lose a Battle*, 618–620; Frieser, *Le mythe de la guerre-éclair*, 531.
68 Jackson, *The Fall of France*, 138.
69 Frieser, *Le mythe de la guerre-éclair*, 241–243.
70 Tooze, *The Wages of Destruction*, 376–377.
71 May, *Strange Victory*, 451.
72 Jordan, 'Strategy and Scapegoatism', 28.
73 Jackson, *The Fall of France*, 269.
74 Jordan, 'Strategy and Scapegoatism', 23.
75 Jackson, *The Fall of France*, 179–180. Alexander states that 120,000 French soldiers died while 250,000 were wounded: 'No Taste for the Fight?', 174.

Tooze claims that 120,000 French died while 49,000 Germans were killed: Tooze, *The Wages of Destructions*, 370.
76 Reynolds, '1940', 327; Tooze, *The Wages of Destruction*, 376, 380.
77 Martin Thomas, *The French Empire between the Wars: Imperialism, Politics and Society* (Manchester: Manchester University Press, 2005), 12.
78 Horne, *To Lose a Battle*, 365n4.
79 Myron Echenberg, '"Morts pour la France": The African Soldier in France during the Second World War', *The Journal of African History* 26, no. 4 (1985): 363.
80 C. M. Andrew and A. S. Kanya-Forstner, 'France, Africa, and the First World War', *Journal of African History* 19, no. 1 (1978): 18–120.
81 Joe Lunn, 'Remembering the *Tirailleurs Sénégalis* and the Great War: Oral History as a Methodology of Inclusion in French Colonial Studies', *French Colonial History* 10, no. 1 (2009): 125–150.
82 Thomas, *The French Empire between the War*, 11.
83 Andrew and Kanya-Forstner, 'France, Africa, and the First World War', 20.
84 Thomas, *The French Empire between the Wars*, 317; Andrew and Kanya-Forstner, 'France, Africa, and the First World War': 14.msibalis@wlu.ca.
85 Francesca Bruschi, 'Military Collaboration, Conscription and Citizenship Rights in the Four Communes of Senegal and in French West Africa (1912–1946)', in *The World in World Wars: Experiences, Perceptions and Perspectives from Africa and Asia*, ed. Heike Liebau, Katrin Bromber, Katharina Lange, Dyala Hamzah and Ravi Ahuja (Leiden; Boston: Brill, 2010), 435n14.
86 Bruschi, 'Military collaboration', 435.
87 Echenberg, 'Morts pour la France', 364. Echnberg estimates 175,000 soldiers served.
88 Thomas, *The French Empire between the Wars*, 314.
89 Andrew and Kanya-Forstner, 'France, Africa, and the First World War', 22.
90 Thomas, *The French Empire between the War*, 31.
91 Thomas, *The French Empire between the War*.
92 See Raffael Scheck, *Hitler's African Victims: The German Army Massacres of Black French Soldiers in 1940* (Cambridge: Cambridge University Press, 2006), 104–112; Echenberg, 'Morts pour la France', 370; Bruschi, 'Military Collaboration', 451.
93 Jean Moulin, 'First fight', in *The Resistance, 1940: An Anthology of Writings from the French Underground*, ed. Charles Potter (Baton Rouge: Louisiana State University Press, 2016), 70.
94 Bruschi, 'Military Collaboration', 443n51.
95 Raffael Scheck, 'La Victoire allemande de 1940 comme justification de l'idéologie raciale nazie', in *La guerre de 1940: Se battre, subir, se souvenir*, ed. Stefan Martens and Steffen Prauser (Villeneuve d'Ascq: Presses universitaires du Septentrion, 2014), https://books.openedition.org/septentrion/7360 (accessed 31 July 2018). See also Scheck, *Hitler's African Victims*, 8–9.
96 Thomas, *The French Empire between the Wars*, 339.
97 Raffael Scheck, 'French Colonial Soldiers in German Prisoner-of-War Camps (1940–1945)', *French History* 24, no. 3 (2010): 420.
98 Scheck, 'French Colonial Soldiers': 424–425.
99 Armelle Mabon, 'La singulière captivité des prisonniers de guerre coloniaux durant la Seconde guerre mondiale', *French Colonial History* 7 (2006): 183.

100 Scheck, 'French Colonial Soldiers', 424–425, 435.
101 Guillaume Pollack, 'Résister sous les tropiques. Les réseaux de résistance en Indochine (1940–1945)', *European Review of History: Revue européenne d'histoire* 25, no. 2 (2018): 297; Eric Jennings, *Vichy in the Tropics: Pétain's National Revolution in Madagascar, Guadeloupe and Indochina* (Stanford: California University Press, 2001), 138–139.
102 Andrew Knapp and Claudia Baldoli, *Forgotten Blitzes: France and Italy under Allied Air Attack* (London: Bloomsbury, 2012), 3–4.
103 Jean-Luc Leleu, 'Une guerre "correcte"? Crimes et massacres allemands à l'Ouest au printemps 1940', in *La guerre de 1940: Se battre, subir, se souvenir*, ed. Stefan Artens and Steffen Prauser (Villeneuve d'Ascq: Presses universitaires du Septentrion, 2014), https://books.openedition.org/septentrion/7358 (accessed 20 July 2018). This number is a conservative estimate for Leleu counted only those instances where more than five civilians were murdered
104 Léon Werth, *33 Days* (Brooklyn: Melville House Publishing, 2015), 88.
105 Hanna Diamond, *Fleeing Hitler: France 1940* (Oxford: Oxford University Press, 2007), 150.
106 Agnès Humbert, *Résistance: A Woman's Journal of Struggle and Defiance in Occupied France* (New York: Bloomsbury, 2009), 1.
107 Shirer, *Berlin Diary*, 409–414.
108 Diamond, *Fleeing Hitler*, 65.
109 See Dominique Veillon, *Vivre et survivre en France, 1939–1947* (Paris: Editions Payot, 1995), 54–58.
110 Werth, *33 Days*, 9.
111 Humbert, *Résistance*, 5–6.
112 Veillon, *Vivre et survivre en France*, 57.
113 Andrew Shennan, *The Fall of France, 1940* (Harlow: Longman, 2000), 7.
114 Moulin, 'First fight', 49, 69.
115 Veillon, *Vivre et survivre en France*, 56.
116 Werth, *The Last Days of Paris*, 181–182.
117 Diamond, *Fleeing Hitler*, 68–78.
118 Charles Keith, 'Vietnamese Collaborationism in Vichy France', *The Journal of Asian Studies* 76, no. 4 (2017): 993.
119 Moulin, 'First Fight', 53.
120 Shennan, *The Fall of France*, 14.
121 Diamond, *Fleeing Hitler*, 18.
122 Miranda Pollard, *Reign of Virtue: Mobilizing Gender in Vichy France* (Chicago: University of Chicago Press, 1998), 26–27.
123 Elodie Jauneau, 'Des femmes dans la France combattante pendant la Deuxième Guerre mondiale: Le Corps des Volontaires Françaises et le Groupe Rochambeau', *Genre & Histoire* [online], 3 (2008), http://journals.openedition.org/genrehistoire/373 (accessed 13 November 2018); Jean-Francois Murraciole, *Les Français libre. L'autre résistance* (Paris: Tallandier, 2009), 47.
124 Luc Capdevila, 'La mobilisation des femmes dans la France combattante (1940–1945)', *Clio. Histoire, femmes et sociétés* 12 (2000): 2.
125 Tooze, *The Wages of Destruction*, 380.
126 Jordan, 'Strategy and Scapegoatism', 25. See also Frieser, *Le mythe de la guerre-éclair*, 249–250.

127 Géraud Létang, 'Traque impériale et repression impossible? Vichy face aux Français Libres du Tchad', *European Review of History: Revue européenne d'histoire* 25, no. 2 (2018): 280.
128 Jennings, *Vichy in the Tropics*, 37.
129 Jennings, *Vichy in the Tropics*, 85.
130 Reynolds, '1940', 346–350.

Chapter 2

1 Jackson, *The Dark Years*, 129.
2 Julian Jackson, 'Vichy and Fascism', in *The Development of the Radical Right in France: From Boulanger to Le Pen*, ed. Edward J. Arnold (Basingstoke: Palgrave, 2000), 155.
3 A number of parliamentarians were missing from both votes. Communist deputies were prevented from voting since the ban on the party introduced in August 1939. Twenty-seven parliamentarians – including Edouard Daladier, Georges Mandel, Jean Zay and Pierre Mendès-France – had boarded the *Massilia* at Bordeaux on 21 June to sail to North Africa with a view to continuing the fight from abroad.
4 The text of the these acts in French may be found here: http://mjp.univ-perp.fr/france/co1940.htm#1 (accessed 21 November 2019).
5 Nicholas Atkin, *The French at War, 1934–1944* (Harlow: Longman, 2001), 47.
6 Michele Cointet, 'Ligne de démarcation', in *Dictionnaire historique de la France sous l'Occupation*, ed. Michèle et Jean-Paul Cointet (Paris: Editions Tallandier, 2000), 452–453; Francois Marcot, 'Ligne de démarcation', in *Dictionnaire Historique de la Résistance: Résistance intérieure et France Libre*, ed. Francois Marcot, Bruno Leroux and Christine Levisse-Touze (Paris: Editions Robert Laffont, 2006), 262–263.
7 Rochat, 'La campagne italienne de juin 1940', 246–248.
8 Kenneth Mouré, 'Food Rationing and the Black Market in France (1940–1944)', *French History* 24, no. 2 (2010): 275.
9 Robert O. Paxton, *Vichy France: Old Guard and New Order* (New York: Alfred A. Knopf, 1972), 52–55; Sébastien Albertelli and Claire Levasseur, *Atlas de la France libre. De Gaulle et la France libre, une aventure politique* (Paris: Autrement, 2010), 25.
10 Mark Mazower, *Hitler's Empire: How the Nazis Ruled Europe* (New York: Penguin Press, 2008), 281, 287; H. R. Kedward, 'France', in *The Oxford Companion to World War II*, ed. I. C. B. Dear and M. R. D. Foot (Oxford: Oxford University Press, 2001), 309.
11 Kedward, 'France', 309.
12 Kedward, 'France', 309.
13 Jackson, *The Dark Years*, 298; Rod Kedward, *La vie en bleu: France and the French since 1900* (London: Allen Lane, 2005), 249; Mazower, *Hitler's Empire*, 271.
14 Olivier Wieviorka and Jacek Tebinka, 'Resisters: From Everyday Life to Counter-State', in *Surviving Hitler and Mussolini: Daily Life in Occupied Europe*, ed. Robert Gildea, Olivier Wieviorka and Annette Warring (Oxford; New York: Berg, 2007), 155.

15 Paxton, *Vichy France*, 53; Marcot, 'Ligne de démarcation', 262–263.
16 Paxton, *Vichy France*, 55; Mazower, *Hitler's Empire*, 199–201.
17 Jean-Louis Panicacci, *L'Occupation Italienne. Sud-Est de la France. Juin 1940-septembre 1943* (Rennes: Presses Universitaires de Rennes, 2010), 15, 22.
18 Panicacci, *L'Occupation Italienne*, 54–64; Diane Grillère, 'L'Occupation italienne en France de 1940 à 1943. Administration, souvraineté, rivalités', *Diacronie. Studi di Storia Contemporanea* 4, no. 3 (2010): 12–14.
19 Jackson, *The Dark Years*, 170–171; Philippe Burrin, *France under the Germans: Collaboration and Compromise* (New York: The New Press, 1996), 87–97.
20 Ruth Ginio, *French Colonialism Unmasked: The Vichy Years in French West Africa* (Lincoln: University of Nebraska Press, 2006), 20; James Giblin, 'A Colonial State in Crisis: Vichy Administration in French West Africa', *Africana Journal* 16 (1994) ['colonial rule was probably never as politically significant in any other period of French history as it was under Vichy']: 327.
21 Jean-Pierre Bertin-Maghit, *Les documenteurs des années noires. Les documentaires de propaganda, France 1940–1944* (Pairs: Nouveau Monde Editions, 2004), 126–127.
22 Evelyne Combeau-Mari, 'Les politiques de la jeunesse et des sports du régime de Vichy à la Réunion: 1940–1942', *Outremers* 91, no. 342–343 (2004): 142.
23 Robert Aldrich, *Greater France: A History of French Overseas Expansion* (Basingstoke: Palgrave, 1996), 120.
24 Léon Werth, *Deposition, 1940–1944: A Secret Diary of Life in Vichy France* (Oxford: Oxford University Press, 2018), 162.
25 Today's Mali.
26 Today's Burkina Faso.
27 The latter three provinces form today's Vietnam.
28 Jennings, *Vichy in the Tropics*; 'French Indo-China', in *The Oxford Companion to World War II* eds. I. C. B. Dear and M. R. D. Foot, 328–329.
29 Eric Jennings, 'La politique colonial de Vichy', in *L'Empire Colonial sous Vichy*, ed. Eric Jennings and Jacques Cantier (Pairs: Odile Jacob, 2004), 14–15; Robert O. Paxton, *Parades and Politics at Vichy* (Princeton: Princeton University Press, 1966), 149 and 149n18; Eric Jennings, *Free French Africa in World War II* (Cambridge: Cambridge University Press, 2015), 15.
30 Today's Congo-Brazzaville.
31 Today's Central African Republic.
32 In India: Pondichéry, Karikal, Mahé, Yanaon and Chandernagor. In the Pacific, Tahiti, Nouvelles-Hébrides and Nouvelle-Calédonie, the Marquesas; and Chinese treaty port of Kwangchowan.
33 Jackson, *The Dark Years*, 246–247.
34 Jennings, 'La politique colonial de Vichy', 14.
35 Phillip Thody, *French Caesarism from Napoleonto de Gaulle* (Basingstoke: Palgrave, 1989), 79.
36 Lindsey Dodd, 'Children's Citizenly Participation in the National Revolution: The Instrumentalization of Children in Vichy France', *European Review of History: Revue européenne d'histoire* 24, no. 5 (2017): 763–765. On Pétain's personality cult see Nicolas Atkin, *Pétain* (Harlow: Longman, 1998), 106–110.

37 Humbert, *Résistance*, 23.
38 Werth, *Deposition*, 58–59.
39 Jean-Pierre Azéma, 'La Milice', *Vingtième Siècle* 28 (1990): 85; Pascal Ory, *Les collaborateurs, 1940–1945* (Paris: Seuil, 1977), 248–249; Bertram M. Gordon, *Collaborationism in France during the Second World War* (Ithaca: Cornell University Press, 1980), 167–172; Pierre Milza, *Fascisme français. Passé et Présent* (Paris: Flammarion, 1987), 269–270.
40 Jennings, 'La politique colonial de Vichy', 21.
41 Jennings, 'La politique colonial de Vichy', 20–21.
42 Pierre Ramognino, 'L'Afrique de l'Ouest sous le proconsulat de Pierre Boisson (juin 1940-juin 1943)', in *L'Empire colonial sous Vichy*, eds. Jacques Cantier and Eric Jennings 79–81; Ginio. *French Colonialism Unmasked*, 50–52.
43 Guéhenno, *Diary of the Dark Years*, 172.
44 Jean-Paul Cointet, *La Légion Française des Combattants. La tentation du fascisme* (Paris: Albin Michel, 1995), 154–160.
45 Robert Aron, *Histoire de Vichy 1940–1944* (Paris: Librairie Arthème Fayard, 1954); André Siegfried, 'Le Vichy de Pétain, le Vichy de Laval', *Revue française de science politique* 6, no. 4 (1956): 737–749.
46 Werth, *Déposition*, 27.
47 Burring, *France under the Germans*, 74.
48 Paxton, *Parades and Politics*, 146.
49 Jackson, *The Dark Years*, 144–145, 175.
50 Burrin, *France under the Germans*, 75; Jackson, *The Dark Years*, 146.
51 Paxton, *Vichy France*, 114–115; Ruth Ginio, 'La propaganda impériale de Vichy', in *L'Empire colonial sous Vichy*, eds. Jacques Cantier and Eric Jennings 124–127.
52 Jackson, *The Dark Years*, 182–185; Paxton, *Vichy France*, 131–135.
53 Philippe Burrin, *La Dérive fasciste. Doriot, Déat, Bergery, 1933–1945* (Paris: Seuil, 1986), 438.
54 Jackson, *The Dark Years*, 213.
55 Jackson, *The Dark Years*, 215.
56 Atkin, *France at War*, 46; Milza, *Fascismes français*, 268.
57 Milza, *Fascismes français*, 273; Jackson calls this stage of Vichy a 'Milice state': *The Dark Years*, 529.
58 John Sweets, *Choices in Vichy France: The French under Nazi Occupation* (Oxford: Oxford University Press, 1986), 32.
59 Jackson, *The Dark Years*, 145.
60 In Martinique, Governor Louis Bressoles served until March 1941; Yves Nicol served during March 1941–July 1943. In Guyane, Robert Chot-Plassot and René Veber were governors.
61 Jennings, 'La politique colonial de Vichy', 14–15; Paxton, *Parades and Politics*, 149 and 149n18.
62 Atkin, *Pétain*, 110–111.
63 Jean-Pierre Azéma, 'Vichy', in *Histoire de l'extrême droite en France,* ed. Michel Winock (Paris: Seuil, 1993), 197.
64 Philippe Burrin, 'The Ideology of the National Revolution', in *The Development of the Radical Right in France* ed. Edward J. Arnold, 139–140.
65 Paxton, *Vichy France*, 147.
66 Guéhenno, *Diary of the Dark Years*, 47.

67 Jackson, *The Dark Years*, 142–166; Sweets, *Choices in Vichy France*, 51–52; Richard Vinen, *The Unfree French: Life under the Occupation* (London: Penguin, 2007), 71–73.
68 On the non-conformists, see Loubet Del Bayle, *Les Non-conformistes, Les non-conformistes des années 30. Une tentative de renouvellement de la pensée politique Française* (Paris: Seuil, 2001), 214.
69 Jean-Pierre Azéma, 'Vichy face au modèle républicain', in *Le modèle républicain*, ed. Serge Berstein and Odile Rudelle (Paris: Presses Universitaires de France, 1992), 348–350.
70 Gordon, *Collaborationism in France*, 290; Jackson, 'Vichy and Fascism', 168; Milza, *Fascisme francais*, 238, 268; Jackson, 'Vichy and Fascism', 168.
71 Milza, *Fascisme français*, 239; Tumblety, 'Revenge of the Fascist Knights', 18.
72 Alcalde, *War Veterans and Fascism*, 269–270.
73 Milza, *Fascismes français*, 234–235.
74 On Salazar's Portugal, see António Costa Pinto, 'Le salazarisme et le fascisme européen', *Vingtième Siècle* 62 (1999): 15–25.
75 Martin C. Thomas, 'The Vichy Government and French Colonial Prisoners of War, 1940–1944', *French Historical Studies* 25, no. 4 (2002): 660; Raffael Scheck, 'The Prisoner of War Question and the Beginnings of Collaboration: The Franco-German Agreement of 16 November 1940', *Journal of Contemporary History* 45, no. 2 (2017): 378.
76 An international organization founded in 1883 that aims to promote the French language and culture around the world.
77 Janet R. Horne, 'Global Cultural Fronts: The Alliance Française and the Cultural Propaganda of the Free French', *European Review of History: Revue européenne d'histoire* 25, no. 2 (2018): 222–241; Patricia E. Prestwich and Kenneth J. Munro, 'A Wartime Partnership: Establishing the Free French Movement in Canada, 1940–42', *European Review of History: Revue européenne d'histoire* 25, no. 2 (2018): 245.
78 Charles Keith, 'Vietnamese Collaborationism in Vichy France', *The Journal of Asian Studies* 76, no. 4 (2017), 990, 995.
79 Jérôme Cotillon, 'L'Empire français dans la Révolution nationale: l'exemple de la vision algérienne des entourages du maréchal Pétain (1940–1942)', *Outre-mers*, 91.342–343 (2004), 41.
80 Combeau-Mari, 'Les politiques de la jeunesse et des sports du régime de Vichy à la Réunion', 133.
81 Eric T. Jennings, 'Vichy à Madagascar. La "Révoluion nationale", l'enseignement et la jeunesse, 1940–1942', *Revue d'histoire moderne et contemporarine* 46, no. 4 (1999): 731.
82 Eric T. Jennings, 'La dissidence aux Antilles', *Vingtième Siècle* 68, no. 1 (2000): 58.
83 Jennings, 'Vichy à Madagascar', 730.
84 Pollard, *Reign of Virtue*, 6.
85 Sweets, *Choices in Vichy France*, 42.
86 Mary-Louise Roberts, *Civilization without Sexes: Reconstructing Gender in Postwar France, 1917–1927* (Chicago: University of Chicago Press, 1994).
87 Pollard, *Reign of Virtue*, 4; Francine Muel-Dreyfus, *Vichy and the Eternal Feminine: A Contribution to a Political Sociology of Gender* (London: Duke University Press, 2001), 9.
88 Pollard, *Reign of Virtue*, 21–26.

89 Luc Capdevila, 'The Quest for Masculinity in a Defeated France, 1940–1945', *Contemporary European History* 10, no. 3 (2001): 427–428; Jackson, *The Dark Years*, 144.
90 Sweets, *Choices in Vichy France*, 50 Dodd, 'Children's Citizenly Participation in the National Revolution', 753, 759–760.
91 Jackson, *The Dark Years*, 330–331.
92 Muel-Dreyfus, *Vichy and the Eternal Feminine*, 194–195.
93 Paula Schwartz, 'The Politics of Food and Gender in Occupied Paris', *Modern & Contemporary France* 7, no. 1 (1999): 39; Pollard, *Reign of Virtue*, 132–134.
94 Joan Tumblety, *Remaking the Male Body: Masculinity and the Uses of Physical Culture in Interwar and Vichy France* (Oxford: Oxford University Press, 2012), 213.
95 Pollard, *Reign of Virtue*, 51.
96 Jackson, *The Dark Years*, 334.
97 Pollard, *Reign of Virtue*, 174; Muel-Dreyfus, *Vichy and the Eternal Feminine*, 283.
98 Jackson, *The Dark Years*, 329–332; On abortion Muel-Dreyfus, *Vichy and the Eternal Feminine*, 279–285.
99 Christina E. Firpo, 'Lost Boys: "Abandoned" Eurasian Children and the Management of the Racial Topography in Colonial Indochina, 1938–1945', *French Colonial History* 8 (2007): 205, 213–214, 216.
100 Capdevila, 'The Quest for Masculinity', 427–428.
101 Paxton, *Vichy France*, 162–163; Atkin, *The French at War*, 47; Jackson, *The Dark Years*, 339; Sweets, *Choices in Vichy France*, 60–61.
102 Jacques Cantier, *L'Algérie sous le regime de Vichy* (Paris: Odile Jacob, 2002), 63.
103 Atkin, *Pétain*, 113; Sweets, *Choices in Vichy France*, 61–62.
104 Cantier, *L'Algérie sous le regime de Vichy*, 291–292.
105 Jackson, *The Dark Years*, 340.
106 Cantier, *L'Algérie sous le regime de Vichy*, 292–293.
107 Jérôme Cotillon, 'L'Empire français dans la Révolution nationale: l'exemple de la vision algérienne des entourages du maréchal Pétain (1940–1942)', *Outre-mers* 91, no. 342–343 (2004): 47–48; Cantier, *L'Algérie sous le regime de Vichy*, 294–296.
108 Combeau-Mari, 'Les politiques de la jeunesse et des sports du régime de Vichy à la Réunion', 140.
109 Jennings, 'Vichy à Madagascar', 742–743.
110 Tumblety, *Remaking the Male Body*, 206–207.
111 Pollard, *Reign of Virtue*, 86–87.
112 Jackson, *The Dark Years*, 340.
113 Tumblety, *Remaking the Male Body*, 208.
114 Jackson, *The Dark Years*, 340.
115 Cantier, *L'Algérie sous le regime de Vichy*, 64–65.
116 Jennings, 'L'Indochine de l'amiral Decoux', in *L'Empire colonial sous Vichy*, eds. Jacques Cantier and Eric Jennings 45.
117 Jennings, 'L'Indochine de l'amiral Decoux', in *L'Empire colonial sous Vichy*, eds. Jacques Cantier and Eric Jennings 45.
118 Evelyne Combeau-Marie, 'The Cult of Maréchal Pétain and the Enrolment of Youth under Governor Annet (1941–1942)', *The International Journal of the History of Sport* 28, no. 12 (2011): 1675–1682.
119 Vinen, *The Unfree French*, 71.

120 Vinen, *The Unfree French*, 76.
121 Kevin Passmore, *The Right in France from the Third Republic to Vichy* (Oxford: Oxford University Press, 2012), 351–352.
122 This point is made here: Fabrice Grenard, *La France du marché noir (1940–1949)* (Paris: Payot, 2008), 59; Mouré, 'Food Rationing', 262–263; Kenneth Mouré and Paula Scwartz, '*On vit mal*: Food Shortages and Popular Culture in Occupied France, 1940–1944', *Food, Culture & Society* 10, no. 2 (2007): 273; Veillon, *Vivre et survivre en France,* 127.
123 Grenard, *La France de marché noir*, 59; David Lees, 'Defining Everyday Frenchness under Vichy', in *Vichy France and Everyday Life*, eds. Lindsey Dodd and David Lees 230.
124 David Lees, 'Defining Everyday Frenchness under Vichy', in *Vichy France and Everyday Life*, eds. Lindsey Dodd and David Lees 230; Polymeris Voglis, 'Surviving Hunger: Life in the Cities and the Countryside during the Occupation', in *Surviving Hitler and Mussolini*, eds. Robert Gildea, Olivier Wieviorka and Annette Warring 16.
125 Ginio, *French Colonialism Unmasked*, 60; Schwartz, 'The Politics of Food and Gender in Occupied Paris', 35; See, for example, Kenneth Mouré, 'Black Market Fictions: *Au bon beurre, La traverse de Paris*, and the Black Market in France', *French, Politics, Culture & Society* 32, no. 1 (2014): 47–67.
126 Mouré, 'Food Rationing', 262.
127 Hanna Diamond, *Women and the Second World War in France,1939–1948: Choices and Constraints* (Harlow: Longman, 1999), 50–53.
128 Veillon, *Vivre et survivre en France*, 116–117, 121, 124–125.
129 Ginio, *French Colonialism Unmasked*, 62.
130 E. G. H. Joffé, 'The Moroccan Nationalist Movement: Istiqlal, the Sultan, and the Country', *Journal of African History* 26, no. 4 (1985): 304.
131 Grenard, *La France du marché noir*, 38.
132 Diamond, *Women and the Second World War in France*, 50–53.
133 Pollard, *Reign of Virtue*, 134–135. On queueing, see also Mouré and Schwartz, '*On vit mal*', 281–284.
134 Veillon, *Vivre et survivre en France*, 127.
135 Veillon, *Vivre et survivre en France*, 128.
136 Schwartz, 'The Politics of Food and Gender in Occupied Paris', 42.
137 Schwartz, 'The Politics of Food and Gender in Occupied Paris', 43.
138 Schwartz, 'The Politics of Food and Gender in Occupied Paris', 37–38.
139 Veillon, *Vivre et survivre en France*, 116–117, 121, 124–125.
140 Mouré, 'Food Rationing', 264; Mouré and Scwartz, '*On vit mal*', 264.
141 Voglis, 'Surviving Hunger', 21.
142 Milton Dank, *The French against the French: Collaboration and Resistance* (London: Cassell, 1978), 165; Mouré, 'Food Rationing', 272.
143 Mouré, 'Food Rationing', 272.
144 Grenard, *La France de marché noir*, 40.
145 Kedward, 'France', 309.
146 Dank, *The French against the French*, 167–168; Veillon, *Vivre et survivre en France*, 149–151.
147 Dank, *The French against the French*, 164–165; Mouré and Schwartz, '*On vit mal*', 275, 278.
148 Mouré and Schwartz, '*On vit mal*', 279.

149 Veillon, *Vivre et survivre en France*, 119.
150 Jennings, *Vichy in the Tropics*, 39.
151 Jennings, *Vichy in the Tropics*, 105–109.
152 Voglis, 'Surviving Hunger', 25.
153 Mouré and Scwartz, 'On vit mal', 266.
154 Sarah Fishman, *We Will Wait: Wives of French Prisoners of War, 1940–1945* (New Haven and London: Yale University Press, 1991), 60.
155 Mouré, 'Food Rationing', 263; Mouré and Scwartz, 'On vit mal', 266–267.
156 Mathieu Devigne, 'Coping in the Classroom: Adapting Schools to Wartime', in *Vichy France and Everyday Life: Confronting the Challenges of Wartime, 1939–1945*, ed. Lindsey Dodd and David Lees (London: Bloomsbury Academic, 2018), 40.
157 Diamond, *Women and the Second World War in France*, 67.
158 Jennings, *Vichy in the Tropics*, 221.
159 Jennings, *Vichy in the Tropics*, 141.
160 Jennings, *Vichy in the Tropics*, 39, 228.
161 Jennings, *Vichy in the Tropics*, 105–109.
162 Jennings, *Vichy in the Tropics*, 68–69.
163 Jennings, *Vichy in the Tropics*, 63–66.
164 Grenard, *La France de marché noir*, 154.
165 Grenard, *La France de marché noir*, 152–153; Lees, 'Defining Everyday Frenchness', 231.
166 Diamond, *Women and the Second World War in France*, 60.
167 Mouré and Schwartz, 'On vit mal', 269–271.
168 W. D. Halls, *The Youth of Vichy France* (Oxford: The Clarendon Press, 1981), 181; Diamond, *Women and the Second World War in France*, 60.
169 Diamond, *Women and the Second World War in France*, 59.
170 Grenard, *La France de marché noir*, 87–94.
171 Grenard, *La France de marché noir*, 46; Marcel Boldorf and Jonas Scherner, 'France's Occupation Costs and the War in the East: The Contribution to the German War Economy, 1940–1944', *Journal of Contemporary History* 47, no. 2 (2012): 299.
172 Boldorf and Scherner, 'France's Occupation Costs', 306.
173 Grenard, *La France de marché noir*, 47–58; Dank, *The French against the French*, 169–170; Mouré, 'Food Rationing', 277–278.
174 Pollard, *Reign of Virtue*, 135.
175 Grenard, *La France de marché noir*, 58–70.
176 Jennings, *Vichy in the Tropics*, 61–62, 84–85.
177 Mouré, 'Food Rationing', 281.
178 Mouré, 'Food Rationing', 270.
179 Mouré, 'Black Market Fictions', 58.
180 Denis Peschanski, '1939–1946, les camps français d'internement', *Hommes et Migrations*, 1175 (1994): 13.
181 Jennings, 'La politique coloniale de Vichy', 24.
182 Pollard, *Reign of Virtue*, 88.
183 Jackson, *The Dark Years*, 332.
184 Denis Peschanski, 'Vichy au singulier, Vichy au pluriel. Une tentative avortée d'encadrement de la société (1941–1942)', *Annales. Economies, Sociétés, Civilisations* 43, no. 3 (1988): 656.

Chapter 3

1. Guéhenno, *Diary of the Dark Years*, 30.
2. Jules Roy, *The Trial of Marshal Pétain* (New York: Harper & Row, 1968), 120.
3. Fabian Lemmes, 'Collaboration in Wartime France, 1940–1944', *European Review of History/Revue européenne d'histoire* 15, no. 2 (2008): 159.
4. Mazower, *Hitler's Empire*, 108–109.
5. Burrin, *France under the Germans*, 109.
6. Stathis N. Kalyvas, 'Collaboration in Comparative Perspective', *European Review of History-Revue européenne d'histoire* 15, no. 22 (2008): 109.
7. Vesna Drapac and Gareth Pritchard, *Resistance and Collaboration in Hitler's Empire* (London: Palgrave, 2017), 37.
8. Burrin, *France under the Germans*, 460–462.
9. Stanley Hoffmann, 'Collaborationism in France during World War II', *The Journal of Modern History* 40, no. 3 (1968): 376.
10. Paxton, *Vichy France*, 277.
11. Hoffmann, 'Collaborationism in France during World War II', 376–379.
12. Paxton, *Vichy France*, 117.
13. Burrin, *France under the Germans*, 120–121.
14. Atkin, *Pétain*, 147.
15. Burrin, *France under the Germans*, 121; Paxton, *Vichy France*, 117–131; Jackson, *The Dark Years*, 182.
16. Jackson, *The Dark Years*, 181.
17. Hoffmann, 'Collaborationism in France during World War II', 376.
18. Hoffmann, 'Collaborationism in France during World War II', 379.
19. Gordon, *Collaborationism in France*, 23.
20. Ariane Chebel d'Appollonia, *L'extrême droite en France. De Maurras à Le Pen* (Brussels: Edition Complexe, 1996), 173.
21. Hoffmann, 'Collaborationism in France during World War II', 381.
22. Kedward, *La Vie en Bleu*, 262.
23. Karine Varley, 'Entangled Enemies: Vichy, Italy and Collaboration', in *France in an Era of Global War, 1914–1945: Occupation, Politics, Empire and Entanglements*, ed. Ludivine Broch and Alison Carrol (Basingstoke: Palgrave, 2014), 161, 164–165. Varleu in C and B, 164–165.
24. John E. Dreifort, 'Japan's Advance into Indochina, 1940: The French Response', *Journal of South-East Asian Studies* 13, no. 2.2 (1982), 279–295.
25. Pierre Jautée, 'Les camps japonais en Indochine pendant la Seconde Guerre mondiale', *Mémoire vivante, bulletin trimestriel de la Fondation pour la Mémoire de la Déportation* 52 (2007): 2–3.
26. Combeau-Mari, 'Les politiques de la jeunesse et des sports': 134.
27. Léo Elisabeth, 'Vichy aux Antilles et en Guyane: 1940–1943', *Outre-mers* 91, no. 342–343 (2004): 148.
28. Ginio, *French Colonialism Unmasked*, 90–91.
29. Ginio, *French Colonialism Unmasked*, 123–124.
30. Ginio, *French Colonialism Unmasked*, 123–124.
31. Jennings, *Free French Africa*, 274.
32. Modus vivendi is Jennings's term: 'L'Indochine de l'amiral Decoux', 33–37; Ralph B. Smith, 'The Japanese Period in Indochina and the Coup of 9 March 1945', *Journal of South-East Asian Studies* 9, no. 2 (1978): 268–301.

33 Jean-Pierre Azéma and Olivier Wieviorka, *Vichy, 1940–1944* (Paris: Perrin, 1997), 101; Vinen, *The Unfree French*, 164–165; 291; 299.
34 Robert Gildea, Dirk Luyten and Julian Fürst, 'To Work or Not to Work', in *Surviving Hitler and Mussolini: Daily Life in Occupied Europe*, ed. Robert Gildea, Olivier Wieviorka and Annette Warring (Oxford: Berg, 2006), 48. See also Lemmes, 'Collaboration in Wartime France': 164, 166.
35 Robert Gildea, *Marianne in Chains* (London: Macmillan, 2002), 85, 308; Peschanksi, '1939–1946, les camps français d'internement': 16; Jackson, *The Dark Years*, 298.
36 Vinen, *The Unfree French*, 117.
37 Cantier, *L'Algérie sous le regime de Vichy*, 166.
38 Jackson, *The Dark Years*, 215.
39 Jackson, *The Dark Years*, 297.
40 Mabon, 'La singulière captivité des prisonniers de guerre coloniaux durant la Seconde guerre mondiale': 183; Scheck, 'French Colonial Soldiers in German Prisoner-of-War Camps (1940–1945)', 426–427; Gildea, *Marianne in Chains*, 308; Peschanksi, '1939–1946, les camps français d'internement', 16.
41 W. D. Halls, 'Young People in Vichy France and Forced Labour in Germany', *Oxford Review of Education* 4, no. 3 (1978): 297–300.
42 Jackson, *The Dark Years*, 530.
43 Paxton, *Vichy France*, 322; 370; Mazower, *Hitler's Empire*, 301–302.
44 Mouré and Scwartz, *'On vit mal'*, 266–267.
45 Wieviorka and Tebinka, 'Resisters: From Everyday Life to Counter-state', 159.
46 Annette Warring, 'Intimate and Sexual Relations', in *Surviving Hitler and Mussolini*, eds. Robert Gildea, Olivier Wieviorka and Annette Warring 90.
47 Paxton, *Vichy France*, 311.
48 Burrin, *France under the Germans*, 184.
49 Burrin, *France under the Germans*, 199.
50 Julian Jackson, 'Homosexuality, Collaboration and Resistance in Occupied France', *Contemporary French Civilization* 31, no. 2 (2007): 62.
51 Vinen, *The Unfree French*, 158.
52 Warring, 'Intimate and Sexual Relations', 113.
53 Warring, 'Intimate and Sexual Relations', 113.
54 Vinen, *The Unfree French*, 162–163; Gildea *Marianne in Chains*, 71–79; Jackson, *The Dark Years*, 334.
55 Burrin, *France under the Germans*, 207.
56 Vinen, *The Unfree French*, 160.
57 Warring, 'Intimate and Sexual Relations', 92–93, 102.
58 Vinen, *The Unfree French*, 162.
59 Simon Kitson, 'From Enthusiasm to Disenchantment: The French Police and the Vichy Regime, 1940–1944', *Contemporary European History* 11, no. 3 (2002): 374.
60 Koreman, *The Expectation of Justice: France, 1944–1946* (Durham, NC: Duke University Press, 1999), 94.
61 Warring, 'Intimate and Sexual Relations', 113.
62 Pollard, *Reign of Virtue*, 67–69.
63 Burrin, *France under the Germans*, 204–205; Gildea, *Marianne in Chains*, 76–79.
64 Vinen, *The Unfree French*, 300–307.
65 Diamond, *Women and the Second World War in France*, 138.

66 Vinen, *The Unfree French*, 334–335; Claire Duchen, 'Crime and Punishment in Liberated France: The Case of *les femmes tondues*', in *When the War Was Over: Women War and Peace in Europe, 1945–1956*, ed. Claire Duchen and Irene Bandhauer-Schoeffmann (London: Leicester University Press, 2000), 241.
67 Jackson, 'Homosexuality, Collaboration and Resistance': 62, 68.
68 Jackson, 'Vichy and Fascism', 155.
69 Roger Bourderon, 'Was the Vichy Regime Fascist? A Tentative Approach to the Question', in *Contemporary France: Illusion, Conflict, and Regeneration*, ed. John C. Cairns (New York; London: New Viewpoints, 1978), 205.
70 Owen Anthony Davey, 'The Origins of the Légion des Volontaires Français contre le Bolchevisme', *Journal of Contemporary History* 6, no. 4 (1971): 39–40; James G. Shields, 'Charlemagne's Crusaders: French Collaboration in Arms, 1941–1945', *French Cultural Studies*, 18, no. 1 (2007): 86.
71 Denis Peschanski, 'Vichy au singulier, Vichy au pluriel. Une tentative avortée d'encadrement de la société (1941–1942)', *Annales. Economies, Sociétés, Civilisations* 43, no. 3 (1988): 651.
72 Peschanski, 'Vichy au singulier', 647.
73 Jackson, 'Vichy and Fascism', 164; Peschanski, 'Vichy au singulier', 652; Cointet, *La Légion Française des Combattants*, 130–131, 154–160.
74 Milza, *Fascisme français*, 249, 253; Ory, *Les collaborateurs*, 58; Jean-Paul Brunet. *Du communisme au fascisme* (Paris: Balland, 1986) 323.
75 Ory, *Les collaborateurs, 1940–1945*, 20–24, 122, 127; Hoffmann, 'Collaborationism in France during World War II', 383–384; Tumblety, 'Revenge of the Fascist Knights', 11–20.
76 Samuel M. Osgood, *French Royalism under the Third and Fourth Republics* (The Hague: Martinus Nijhoff, 1960), 166.
77 Sean Kennedy, *Reconciling France against Democracy: The Croix de Feu and the Parti Social Francais, 1927–1945* (Montreal: McGill-Queen's University Press, 2007), 225–259.
78 Azéma, 'Vichy', 206.
79 Keith, 'Vietnamese Collaborationism in Vichy France', 988–1000.
80 Henri Michel, *Paris Allemand* (Paris: Albin Michel, 1981), 93.
81 Ory, *Les collaborateurs*, 113; Azéma estimates that up to 100,000 men and women were collaborationists: Azéma, 'Vichy', 208. Lemmes estimates 250,000: Lemmes, 'Collaboration in Wartime France', 160–161; Gordon, *Collaborationism in France*, 327, estimates 100–200,000.
82 Ory, *Les collaborateurs*, 117.
83 Ory, *Les collaborateurs*, 97; Gordon, *Collaborationism in France*, 135.
84 Ory, *Les collaborateurs*, 28.
85 Marcel Déat, 'Mourir pour Dantzig?' *L'Oeuvre*, 4 May 1939, pp. 1 and 4; Gordon, *Collaborationism in France*, 46; Cointet, *La Légion Française des Combattants*, 30–31.
86 Burrin, *La Dérive fasciste*, 386; 389.
87 Ory, *Les collaborateurs*, 109; Gordon, *Collaborationism in France*, 125.
88 Burrin, *La Dérive fasciste*, 410; 417.
89 Gordon, *Collaborationism in France*, 109, 114–115.
90 Burrin, *La Dérive fasciste*, 389; Ory, *Les collaborateurs*, 106, 112; Milza, *Fascisme français*, 257. On the array of smaller collaborationist groups, see Gordon, *Collaborationism in France*, 357–360.
91 Gordon, *Collaborationism in France*, 100.

92 Ory, *Les collaborateurs*, 113; Burrin, *La Dérive fasciste*, 393, 409–413. On the RNP's estimated membership, see Gordon, *Collaborationism in France*, 99, 119–121; Milza, *Fascisme français*, 259.
93 Georges Loustaunau-Lacau, *Mémoires d'un Français rebelle* (Paris: Laffont, 1948), 121.
94 Brunet, *Jacques Doriot*, 9; Soucy, *The Second Wave*, 210–211; Brunet, *Jacques Doriot*, 14–15. Burrin gives date of dismissal as 27 July: *La Dérive fasciste*, 163–164, 174–175.
95 Burrin, *La Dérive fasciste*, 434–441.
96 Burrin, *La Dérive fasciste*, 426.
97 Burrin, *La Dérive fasciste*, 428.
98 Ory, *Les collaborateurs, 1940–1945*, 103.
99 Burrin, *La Dérive fasciste*, 438.
100 Milza, *Fascisme français*, 254; Brunet, *Jacques Doriot*, 359.
101 Burrin, *La Dérive fasciste*, 401–403.
102 Paul Jankowski, *Communism and Collaboration: Simon Sabiani and Politics in Marseille, 1919–1944* (New haven and London: Yale University Press, 1989), 75.
103 Burrin, *La Dérive fasciste*, 449.
104 Shields, 'Charlemagne's Crusaders': 93–94.
105 Ory, *Les collaborateurs*, 237–238.
106 Davey, 'The Origins of the Légion des Volontaires Français contre le Bolchevisme', 33–35, 44; Philippe Carrard, 'From the Outcasts' Point of View: The Memoirs of the French Who Fought for Hitler', *French Historical Studies*, 31, no. 3 (2008): 485; 492–493; Ory, *Les collaborateurs*, 243–245.
107 '"Le bolchevisme est un ennemi qui ne pardonne pas"', *Le Matin*, 2 February 1942, 1 and 4.
108 Lemmes, 'Collaboration in Wartime France', 162; Gordon, *Collaborationism in France*, 245, 250. Davey, 'The Origins of the Légion des Volontaires Français contre le Bolchevisme', 32, 38, 40–41; Burrin, *La Dérive fasciste*, 431; Shields, 'Charlemagne's Crusaders', 87, 91; Ory, *Les collaborateurs*, 242.
109 Thomas, *The French Empire at War*, 238.
110 Lemmes, 'Collaboration in Wartime France, 1940–1944', 162.
111 Carrard, 'From the Outcasts' Point of View', 485, 492–493; Ory, *Les collaborateurs*, 136–138.
112 Warring, 'Intimate and Sexual Relations', 90.
113 Ory, *Les collaborateurs*, 267.
114 Peschanski, 'Vichy au singular', 656.
115 Warring, 'Intimate and Sexual Relations', 118.

Chapter 4

1 Humbert, *Résistance*, 7.
2 Charles de Gaulle, *The Call to Honour, 1940–1942. War Memoirs Volume One. Documents*, trans. Jonathan Griffin (London: Collins, 1955), 11–12.
3 Olivier Wievioka, *The French Resistance* (Cambridge, MA: The Belknap Press, 2016), 130–133.

4   Matthew Cobb, *The Resistance* (London: Simon & Schuster, 2009), 4.
5   De Gaulle, *The Call to Honour,* 46–47.
6   Jennings, 'La dissidence aux Antilles'.
7   Charlotte Faucher and Laure Humbert, 'Introduction – Beyond de Gaulle and beyond London: The French External Resistance and Its International Networks', *European Review of History: Revue européenne d'histoire* 25, no. 2 (2018): 195–221.
8   Robert Gildea, *Fighters in the Shadows: A New History of the French Resistance* (London: Faber & Faber, 2015), 458; 468–471.
9   Wieviorka, *The French Resistance*, 408.
10 Murraciole, *Les Français libres*, 27–28; 36; Jennings, *Free French Africa in World War II*, 4.
11 Murraciole, *Les Français libres*, 26.
12 Jackson, *A Certain Idea of France*, 97–125.
13 Albertelli and Levasseur, *Atlas de la France Libre*, 10; Wieviorka, *The French Resistance*, 27; Murraciole, *Les Français libres*, 194.
14 Humbert, *Résistance*, 7.
15 Werth, *Deposition*, 284.
16 Jackson, *The Dark Years*, 390.
17 Jackson, *A Certain Idea of France*, 137.
18 Albertelli and Levasseur, *Atlas de la France Libre*, 10.
19 Jackson, *A Certain Idea of France*, 245.
20 Wieviorka, *The French Resistance*, 177.
21 Cobb, *The Resistance*, 146.
22 Jacques Cantier, 'Les horizons de l'après-Vichy. De la "Libération" de l'Empire aux enjeux de la mémoire', in *L'Empire colonial sous Vichy,* eds. Jennings and Cantier, 338.
23 Murraciole, *Les Français libres*, 137.
24 Albertelli and Levasseur, *Atlas de la France Libre*, 39.
25 Albertelli and Levasseur, *Atlas de la France Libre*, 47–50; Murraciole, *Les Français libres*, 143; G. H. Bennett, *The RAF's French Foreign Legion: De Gaulle, the British and the Re-Emergence of French Airpower, 1940–5* (London: Continuum, 2011), 226.
26 Wieviorka, *The French Resistance*, 130–133.
27 Wieviorka, *The French Resistance*, 9–15.
28 Raphaële Balu, 'Pour une histoire des liens entre Français libres, maquis de France et Alliés (1943–44): acteurs et réseaux d'une coopértaion oubliée', *European Review of History: Revue européenne d'histoire* 25, no. 2 (2018): 342.
29 Murraciole, *Les Français libres*, 51–60; 65, 69; 95; 108.
30 Albertelli and Levasseur, *Atlas de la France libre*, 14; Murraciole, *Les Français libres*, 50–60.
31 Capdevila, 'La mobilisation des femmes dans la France combattante': 6–7.
32 Elodie Jauneau, 'Images et représentations des premières soldates françaises', *Clio. Femmes, Genre, Histoire* 30 (2009): 240.
33 Jauneau, 'Images et représentations', 245.
34 Elodie Jauneau, 'Des femmes dans la France combattante pendant la Deuxième Guerre mondiale: Le Corps des Volontaires Francaises et le Groupe Rochambeau', *Genre & Histoire* 3 (2008), http://journals.openedition.org/genrehistoire/373 (accessed 21 November 2019).
35 Jauneau, 'Des femmes dans la France combattante'.

36 Murraciole, *Les Français libres*, 47–48.
37 Cited in Murraciole, *Les Français libres*, 45–49.
38 Wieviorka, *The French Resistance*, 403.
39 Murraciole, *Les Français libres*, 189–194.
40 Murraciole, *Les Français libres*, 208.
41 Werth, *Deposition*, 209.
42 Jennings *Free French Africa*, 18.
43 Jackson, *A Certain Idea of France*, 151.
44 Jennings *Free French Africa*, 2; 49.
45 Jackson, *A Certain Idea of France*, 171.
46 Jennings, *Free French Africa*, 45.
47 Létang, 'Traque impériale et repression impossible?', 280–281.
48 Murraciole, *Les Français libres*, 207.
49 Murraciole, *Les Français libres*, 62–64.
50 Létang, 'Traque impériale et repression impossible', 280–281.
51 Elisabeth, 'Vichy aux Antilles', 163–164.
52 Jennings, 'La dissidence aux Antilles', 64, 68–69.
53 Létang, 'Traque impériale et repression impossible?', 282.
54 Murraciole, *Les Français libres*, 206.
55 Albertelli and Levasseur, *Atlas de la France libre*, 30.
56 Jennings, *Free French Africa*, 5.
57 Jennings, *Free French Africa*, 79, 102, 195–196, 208, 221–222; Albertelli and Levasseur, *Atlas de la France libre*, 22.
58 Pollack, 'Résister sous les tropiques. Les réseaux de résistance en Indochine (1940–1945)', 301–305; Sylvain Cornil, 'La repression de la Résistance en Indochine', http://www.france-libre.net/repression-resistance-indochine/#1 (accessed 27 July 2018).
59 Jautée, 'Les camps japonais en Indochine'.
60 Pollack, 'Résister sous les tropiques', 304–305.
61 Thomas, *The French Empire at War*, 206–207.
62 Pollack, 'Résister sous les tropiques. Les réseaux de résistance en Indochine (1940–1945)', 301–305; Sylvain Cornil, 'La repression de la Résistance en Indochine'.
63 Murraciole, *Les Français Libres*, 61.
64 Helena Pinto Janeiro, 'Salazar et les trois France (1940–1944)', *Vingtième Siècle* 62, no. 2 (1999): 43.
65 Albertelli and Levasseur, *Atlas de la France libre*, 36; Murraciole, *Les Français libres*, 31–33.
66 Prestwich and Munro, 'A Wartime Partnership', 243.
67 Albertelli and Levasseur, *Atlas de la France libre*, 37.
68 Jackson, *The Dark Years*, 395.
69 Murraciole, *Les Français libres*, 135–137.
70 Jackson, *A Certain Idea of France*, 280.
71 Paxton, *Vichy France*, 294–295.
72 Sweets, *Choices in Vichy France*, 224.
73 Sweets, *Choices in Vichy France*, 224; 227.
74 Guéhenno, *Diary of the Dark Years*, 101.
75 Wieviorka, *The French Resistance*, 2.
76 Wieviorka, *The French Resistance*, 3.
77 Wieviorka, *The French Resistance*, 3.

78 Gildea, *Fighters in the Shadows*, 62.
79 Gildea, *Fighters in the Shadows*, 62.
80 Wieviorka and Tebinka, 'Resisters: From Everyday Life to Counter-State', 170.
81 Wieviorka and Tebinka, 'Resisters: From Everyday Life to Counter-State', 156.
82 Burrin, *France under the Germans*, 180–182.
83 Mazower, *Hitler's Empire*, 476.
84 Karine Varley, 'Between Vichy France and Fascist Italy: Redefining Identity and the Enemy in Corsica during the Second World War', *Journal of Contemporary History* 47, no. 3 (2012): 507–527.
85 Pollack, 'Résister sous les tropiques': 297–298.
86 Lise Foisneau and Valentin Merlin, 'French Nomads' Resistance (1939–1946)', in *Roma Resistance during the Holocaust and in Its Aftermath*, ed. Angela Kóczé and AnnaLujza Szász (Budapest: Tom Lantos Institute, 2018), 71–74.
87 Ginio, *French Colonialism Unmasked*, 63.
88 Ginio, *French Colonialism Unmasked*, 156.
89 Jennings, *Free French Africa*, 231–241.
90 Ginio, *French Colonialism Unmasked*, xv.
91 Humbert, *Résistance*, 11–12.
92 Charles Potter, *The Resistance, 1940: An Anthology of Writings from the French Underground* (Baton Rouge: Louisiana State University Press, 2016), 143–159; Wieviorka, *The French Resistance*, 76–79.
93 Jackson, *The Dark Years*, 408.
94 Wieviorka, *The French Resistance*, 66; Jackson, *The Dark Years*, 408; Potter, *The Resistance, 1940*, 107–118.
95 Cobb, *The Resistance*, 141–143; Valerie Deacon, *The Extreme Right in the French Resistance: Members of the Cagoule and the Corvignolles in the Second World War* (Baton Rouge: Louisiana State University Press, 2016), 87.
96 Wieviorka, *The French Resistance*, 79–87. See also Deacon, *The Extreme Right in the French Resistance*.
97 Jackson, *The Dark Years*, 408.
98 Wieviorka, *The French Resistance*, 60.
99 Wieviorka, *The French Resistance*, 60.
100 Wieviorka, *The French Resistance*, 65.
101 Wieviorka, *The French Resistance*, 60.
102 Wieviorka, *The French Resistance*, 99.
103 Paxton, *Vichy France* 295.
104 Franck Liaigre, *Les FTP. Nouvelle histoire d'une résistance* (Paris: Perrin, 2015), 87.
105 Liaigre, *Les FTP*, 277–281; 324.
106 Jackson, *A Certain Idea of France*, 193.
107 Jackson, *A Certain Idea of France*, 193.
108 Pnaicacci book, 222.
109 Wieviorka and Tebinka, 'Resisters: From Everyday Life to Counter-State', 169.
110 Wieviorka, *The French Resistance*, 250.

111 '"Terrorisme" et insurrection nationale', *Libération. Organe du Mouvement uni de la résistance*, 38 (30 October 1943), 1–2; G. Le Mainois, 'Terrorisme or résistance', *Défense de la France. Organe du Mouvement de la Libération Nationale. Edition de Paris*, 15 December 1943, 1–2.
112 Chris Millington, 'Were We Terrorists? History, Terrorism and the French Resistance', *History Compass* 16, no. 2 (2018): e12440–e12440; Pierre Laborie, *L'Opinion française sous Vichy* (Paris: Seuil, 1990), eds. Jacques Cantier and Eric Jennings, 300–301.
113 On the Resistance movements, see Wieviorka, *The French Resistance*, 55–88.
114 Wieviorka, *The French Resistance*, 401–403.
115 Wieviorka, *The French Resistance*, 386–390.
116 Wieviorka, *The French Resistance*, 393–394.
117 Gavin Bowd, 'Romanians of the French Resistance', *French History* 28, no. 4 (2014): 544.
118 Cobb, *The Resistance*, 107–109.
119 Armelle Mabon, 'Solidarité nationale et captivité coloniale', *French Colonial History* 12, no. 1 (2011): 203–204.
120 Scheck, 'French Colonial Soldiers in German Prisoner-of-War Camps', 442.
121 Éric Deroo and Antoine Champeaux, 'Panorama des troupes coloniales françaises dans les deux guerres mondiales', *Revue historique des armées* 271 (2013): 11.
122 Ludivine Broch, 'Colonial Subjects and Citizens in the French Internal Resistance, 1940–1944', *French Politics, Culture & Society* 37, no. 1 (2019): 6–31.
123 Laurent Jalabert, 'Les Antilles de l'amiral Robert', in *L'Empire colonial sous Vichy*, 57.
124 Jennings, 'La dissidence aux Antilles', 58–69.
125 Jackson, *The Dark Years*, 490.
126 Wieviorka, *The French Resistance*, 153; Potter, *The Resistance, 1940*, 107–119.
127 Wieviorka, *The French Resistance*, 403.
128 Wieviorka, *The French Resistance*, 408.
129 Humbert, *Résistance*, 33.
130 Mabon, 'Solidarité nationale et captivité coloniale', 201–205.
131 Paula Schwartz, '*Partisanes* and Gender Politics in Vichy France', *French Historical Studies* 16, no. 1 (1989): 130.
132 Wieviorka, *The French Resistance*, 407–408; Schwartz, '*Partisanes* and Gender Politics in Vichy France', 136.
133 Gildea, *Fighters in the Shadows*, 57.
134 Mazower, *Hitler's Empire*, 516.
135 Wieviorka, *The French Resistance*, 140–141; Potter, *The Resistance, 1940*, 11–104.
136 Jackson, *The Dark Years*, 427–432.
137 Gildea, *Fighters in the Shadows*, 272; Jackson, *The Dark Years*, 454.
138 Gildea, *Fighters in the Shadows*, 263–264.
139 Gildea, *Fighters in the Shadows*, 270–271; Cobb, *The Resistance*, 150–151.
140 Gildea, *Fighters in the Shadows*, 272.
141 Jackson, *The Dark Years*, 431–432.

142 Cobb, *The Resistance*, 156; Gildea, *Fighters in the Shadows*, 261.
143 Gildea, *Fighters in the Shadows*, 275.
144 Cobb, *The Resistance*, 156.
145 The Wieviorka, *The French Resistance*, 259–265.
146 Gildea, *Fighters in the Shadows*, 275–276; Cobb, *The Resistance*, 158–159.
147 Jackson, *A Certain Idea of France*, 95.
148 Wieviorka, *The French Resistance*, 310–314.
149 Cobb, *The Resistance*, 170–184.
150 H. R. Kedward, *In Search of the Maquis: Rural Resistance in Southern France* (Oxford: Oxford University Press, 1994).
151 Cobb, *The Resistance*, 172.
152 Mabon, 'La singulière captivité des prisonniers de guerre coloniaux', 185.
153 Deroo and Champeaux, 'Panorama des troupes colonials françaises', 8.
154 Schwartz, '*Partisanes* and Gender Politics', 139.
155 Wieviorka, *The French Resistance*, 309–310.
156 Wieviorka, *The French Resistance*, 323–328.
157 Vinen, *The Unfree French*, 234.
158 Guéhenno, *Diary of the Dark Years*, 248.
159 Raphaële Balu, 'Pour une histoire des lines entre Français libres, maquis de France et Alliés (1943–44): acteurs et réseaux d'une coopértaion oubliée', *European Review of History: Revue européenne d'histoire* 25, no. 2 (2018): 334.
160 Murraciole, *Les Français libres*, 268.
161 Murraciole, *Les Français libres*, 268.
162 Jennings, *Free French Africa*, 2.
163 Jackson, *The Dark Years*, 437.
164 Guéhenno, *Diary of the Dark Years*, 251.
165 Wieviorka, *The French Resistance*, 411.
166 Murraciole, *Les Français libres*, 286.
167 Wieviorka and Tebinka, 'Resisters: From Everyday Life to Counter-State', 153.
168 Mazower, *Hitler's Empire*, 516.
169 Lynne Taylor, *Between Collaboration and Resistance: Popular Protest in Northern France, 1940–1945* (New York: St Martin's Press, 2000), 157–158.
170 Taylor, *Between Collaboration and Resistance*, 158.

Chapter 5

1 This point is made most forcefully in Michael R. Marrus and Robert O. Paxton's classic *Vichy France and the Jews* (New York: Basic Books, 1981). A second edition, published by Stanford University Press in 1995, included a foreword from Stanley Hoffmann. A revised and updated edition is to appear in 2019. The notes in this chapter refer to the 1981 English edition.
2 Jacques Adler, 'The Jews and Vichy: Reflections on French Historiography', *The Historical Journal* 44 (2001): 1067, 1069, 1069n24, 1070n27.

3   Jackson, *The Dark Years*, 362; Paula Hyman, *The Jews of Modern France* (Berkeley: University of California Press, 1998), 161; Burrin, *France under the Germans*, 157.
4   Anatole de Monzie, *La saison des juges* (Paris: Flammarion, 1943), 8.
5   Wieviorka, *The French Resistance*, 428.
6   Jackson, *The Dark Years*, 182.
7   Kitson, 'From Enthusiasm to Disenchantment', 373–375.
8   Jackson, *The Dark Years*, 151.
9   Ginio, *French Colonialism Unmasked*, 110.
10 Colette Zytnicki, 'La politique antisémite du regime de Vichy dans les colonies', in *L'Empire colonial sous Vichy,* eds. Jacques Cantier and Eric Jennings 163.
11 Wieviorka, *The French Resistance*, 416.
12 Gildea, *Marianne in Chains*, 267, 280–281.
13 Burrin, *France under the Germans*, 133.
14 Burrin, *France under the Germans*, 187.
15 Panicacci, *L'Occupation Itallienne*, 228.
16 Panicacci, *L'Occupation Itallienne*, 228–229, 247–249.
17 Pollack, 'Résister sous les tropiques', 305–306; Jautée, 'Les camps japonais en Indochine'; Guillaume Zeller, *Les cages de la Kempetaï. Les Français sous la terreur japonaise. Indochine mars-août 1945* (Paris: Tallandier, 2019).
18 Kitson, 'From Enthusiasm to Disenchantment', 377.
19 Kitson, 'From Enthusiasm to Disenchantment', 382.
20 Wieviorka, *The French Resistance*, 421; Burrin, *France under the Germans*, 155.
21 Jackson, *The Dark Years*, 216; Wieviorka, *The French Resistance*, 421.
22 Jean-Pierre Azéma, 'La Milice', *Vingtième Siècle. Revue d'histoire* 28 (1990): 85.
23 Jackson, *The Dark Years*, 231.
24 Ory, *Les collaborateurs,* 254; Azéma, 'Vichy', 211–212.
25 Jean-Louis Panicacci, 'Une section modèle? La Légion des Alpes-Maritimes', *Annales du Midi. Revue archéologique, historique et philologique de la France méridionale* 116, no. 245 (2014): 104; Azéma, 'La Milice', 91; Pierre Giolitto, *Histoire de la Milice* (Paris: Perrin, 2002), 72–73; Azéma, 'La Milice', 103.
26 Jackson, *The Dark Years*, 254.
27 Ginio, *French Colonialism Unmasked*, 40.
28 Peschanski, 'Vichy au singulier', 656.
29 Marrus and Paxton, *Vichy France and the Jew*, 181.
30 Vinen, *The Unfree French*, 93.
31 Jean-Marie Guillon, 'La Légion française des combattants ou comment comprendre la France de Vichy', *Annales du Midi. Revue archéologique, historique et philologique de la France méridionale*, 116, no. 245 (2004): 11–16; Sweets, *Choices in Vichy France*, 23, 73–75.
32 Jackson, *The Dark Years*, 262.
33 Burrin, *France under the Germans*, 133.
34 See Virginie Sansico, *La justice déshonorée, 1940–1944* (Paris: Editions Tallandier, 2015).
35 Virginie Sansico, 'Le terrorisme, vie et mort d'une notion juridique (1930–1945)', *Archives de la Politique Criminelle* 38, no. 1 (2016): 37–39; Wieviorka, *The French Resistance*, 416.

36 Sansico, *La justice déshonorée*, 446–448.
37 Sansico, *La justice déshonorée*, 489–534.
38 Létang, 'Traque impériale et repression impossible?', 287; Sansico, *La justice déshonorée*, 104–105.
39 Létang, 'Traque impériale et repression impossible?', 285.
40 Jennings, *Vichy in the Tropics*, 143–144.
41 Sansico, *La justice déshonorée*, 428–429.
42 Corinne Jaladieu, 'Les résistantes dans les prisons de Vichy: l'exemple de la centrale de Rennes', 89 (2002): http://journals.openedition.org/chrhc/1547
43 Corinne Jaladieu, 'Eysses. Une prison dans la Résistance', https://criminocorpus.org/fr/expositions/prisons/eysses/prisons-resistance/ (accessed 21 November 2019)
44 Humbert, *Résistance*, 76.
45 Corinne Jaladieu, 'Document no. 1: L'inflation carcérale sous Vichy', https://criminocorpus.org/fr/expositions/prisons/eysses/complements/linflation-carcerale-sous-vichy/ (accessed 21 November 2019).
46 Cantier, *L'Algérie sous le regime de Vichy*, 346–347, 352–353.
47 Shannon L. Fogg, *The Politics of Everyday Life in Vichy France: Foreigners, Undesirables and Strangers* (Cambridge: Cambridge University Press, 2009), 114–115.
48 Cantier, *L'Algérie sous le regime de Vichy*, 77.
49 Christine Lévisse-Touzé, 'Les camps d'internement d'Afrique du Nord, politiques répressives et populations', in *L'Empire colonial sous Vichy*, 183.
50 Wieviorka, *The French Resistance*, eds. Jacques Cantier and Eric Jennings 419.
51 Peschanski, '1939–1946, les camps français d'internement', 11–19 [check this number].
52 Peschanski, '1939–1946, les camps français d'internement', 15.
53 Vinen, *The Unfree French*, 143.
54 Cantier, *L'Algérie sous le regime de Vichy*, 346–347, 352–353.
55 Lévisse-Touzé, 'Les camps d'internement d'Afrique du Nord', 184.
56 Zytnicki, 'La politique antisémite du regime de Vichy', 168.
57 Jennings, 'Vichy à Madagascar', 730.
58 Combeau-Mari, 'Les politiques de la jeunesse et des sports', 133.
59 Jennings, 'La dissidence aux Antilles', 59.
60 Ginio, *French Colonialism Unmasked*, 28.
61 Jennings, 'Vichy à Madagascar', 735.
62 Thomas, 'The Vichy Government and French Colonial Prisoners of War', 664.
63 Ginio, *French Colonialism Unmasked*, 28–29.
64 Jackson, *The Dark Years*, 259.
65 See Foisneau and Merlin, 'French Nomads' Resistance', 57–103.
66 Foisenau and Merlin, 'French Nomads' Resistance', 61–62.
67 Foisenau and Merlin, 'French Nomads' Resistance', 66–67.
68 Shannon L. Fogg, '"They Are Undesirables": Local and National Responses to Gypsies during World War II', *French Historical Studies* 31, no. 2 (2008): 350; Foisenau and Merlin, 'French Nomads' Resistance', 69.
69 884 out of 1,334 internees: Foisneau and Merlin, 'French Nomads' Resistance', 79.
70 Sybil H. Milton, '"Gypsies" as Social Outsiders in Nazi Germany', in *Social Outsiders in Nazi Germany*, ed. Robert Gellately and Nathan Stoltzfus

(Princeton and Oxford: Princeton University Press, 2001), 212–233; Nikolaus Wachsmann, *KL: A History of the Nazi Concentration Camps* (New York: Farrar, Straus and Giroux, 2015), 461–464.
71 Julian Jackson, 'Homosexuality, Collaboration, and Resistance in Occupied France', *Contemporary French Civilisation*, 31 (2007): 58–59; Michael Sibalis, 'Homophobia, Vichy France, and the "Crime of Homosexuality"', *GLQ*, 8.3 (2002): 304.
72 Michael Sibalis, 'La vie homosexuelle en France pendant la Seconde guerre mondiale', in *Homosexuel.le.s en Europe pendant la Seconde Guerre mondiale*, ed. Régis Schlagdenhauffen (Nouveau Monde Editions, 2017), 136, 143–146; Florence Tamagne, 'La deportation des homosexuels durant la Seconde Guerre mondiale', *Revue éthique et de théologie morale* 239, no. 2 (2006): 239check; Hans Georg Stümke, 'The Persecution of Homosexuals in Nazi Germany', in *Nazism*, ed. Neil Gregor (Oxford: Oxford University Press, 2000), 305–307; Wachsmann, *KL*, 127–128; Sibalis, 'Homophobia, Vichy France, and the "Crime of Homosexuality"', 310.
73 Vinen, *The Unfree French*, 104, 171.
74 Eric Jennings, 'Vichy fut-il aussi antinoir?' in *L'Empire colonial sous Vichy*, 222; Broch, 'The Resistance in Colour'.
75 Ginio, *French Colonialism Unmasked*, 101.
76 Thomas, 'The Vichy Government and French Colonial Prisoners of War', 666, 675; Scheck, 'French Colonial Soldiers', 439–440.
77 Thomas, 'The Vichy Government and French Colonial Prisoners of War', 658.
78 Jennings, 'Vichy fut-il aussi antinoir?', 215.
79 Ginio, *French Colonialism Unmasked*, 111.
80 Jennings, 'Vichy fut-il aussi antinoir?', 228.
81 Jennings, 'Vichy fut-il aussi antinoir?', 224–226.
82 Scheck, 'French Colonial Soldiers', 440.
83 Thomas, 'The Vichy Government and French Colonial Prisoners of War', 680, 684, 691–692.
84 Jackson, *The Dark Years*, 360.
85 Marrus and Paxton, *Vichy France and the Jews*, 228, 250–252.
86 Hyman, *The Jews of Modern France*, 173; Marrus and Paxton, *Vichy France and the Jews*, 250–252.
87 Hyman, *The Jews of Modern France*, 172.
88 Jackson, *The Dark Years*, 362.
89 Robert Gildea, *Children of the Revolution: The French, 1799–1914* (Cambridge, MA: Harvard University Press, 2008), 353–354; Zeev Sternhell, *La droite révolutionnaire 1885–1914: Les origines françaises de fascisme* (Paris: Gallimard, 1978), 148–152, 158–169, 182–194; Passmore, *The Right in France from the Third Republic to Vichy* (Oxford: Oxford University Press, 2013), 50.
90 There are many accounts of the Affair. Eric Cahm's *The Dreyfus Affair in French Society and Politics* (New York: Longman, 1996 [originally published 1966]) is a highly readable overview.
91 Gérard Noiriel, *Immigration, antisémitisme et racisme en France (XIXe-XXe siècle). Discours publiques, humiliations privies* (Paris: Hachette, 2007), 210–221, 254–255; Stephen Wilson, 'The Antisemitic Riots of 1898 in France', *The Historical Journal* 16, no. 4 (1973): 789–806.

92 Pierre Quillard, *Le Monument Henry. Listes des souscriptions classes méthodiquement et selon l'ordre alphabétique* (Paris: P.V. Stock, 1899), ix–xii; Richard Griffiths, *The Use of Abuse: The Polemics of the Dreyfus Affair and Its Aftermath* (New York; Oxford: Berg, 1991), 14.
93 Jackson, *The Dark Years*, 79.
94 Vicki Caron, *Uneasy Asylum: France and the Jewish Refugee Crisis, 1933–1942* (Stanford: Stanford University Press, 1999).
95 Marrus and Paxton, *Vichy France and the Jews*, 70–71.
96 Fogg, *The Politics of Everyday Life in Vichy France*, 113.
97 Adler, 'The Jews and Vichy', 1072–1073.
98 Vinen, *The Unfree French*, 144.
99 Marrus and Paxton, *Vichy France and the Jews*, 3; Vinen, *The Unfree French*, 135. See also Michael Mayer, 'The French Jewish Statue of October 3, 1940: A Reevaluation of Continuities and Discontinuities of French Antisemitism', *Holocaust and Genocide Studies* 33, no. 1 (2019): 4–22.
100 'Comment Pétain a annoté la loi sur les juifs en 1940', *L'Express*, 3 October 2010, https://www.lexpress.fr/actualite/societe/comment-petain-a-annote-la-loi-sur-les-juifs-en-1940_924570.html (accessed 21 November 2019)
101 Yves C. Aouté, 'La Place de l'Algérie dans le project antijuif de Vichy (Octobre 1940–Novembre 1942)', *Revue Française d'histoire d'outre mer* 80, no. 301 (1993): 601.
102 Marrus and Paxton, *Vichy France and the Jews*, 4.
103 Hyman, *The Jews of Modern France*, 165.
104 Gildea, *Marianne in Chains*, 234; Marrus and Paxton, *Vichy France and the Jews*, 152–160.
105 Peschanski, '1939–1946, les camps français d'internement', 14–15.
106 Michael Curtis, *Verdict on Vichy: Power and Prejudice in the Vichy France Regime* (London: Phoenix, 2004), 116.
107 Marrus and Paxton, *Vichy France and the Jews*, 84.
108 Guéhenno, *Diary of the Dark Years*, 94.
109 Marrus and Paxton, *Vichy France and the Jews*, 84, 136, 153.
110 Marrus and Paxton, *Vichy France and the Jews*, 181–186; Fogg, *The Politics of Everyday Life in Vichy France*, 139–140.
111 Fogg, *The Politics of Everyday Life in Vichy France*, 143.
112 Marrus and Paxton, *Vichy France and the Jews*, 181–182, 214.
113 Adler, 'The Jews and Vichy', 1073–1075.
114 Renée Poznanski, *Les Juifs en France pendant la Second Guerre mondiale* (Paris: Hachette, 1997), 573–579.
115 Jacques Biélinky, *Un journaliste juif à Paris sous l'Occupation. Journal 1940–1942* (Cerf: Paris, 2011), 62–63.
116 Biélinky, *Un journaliste juif à Paris sous l'Occupation*, 63–64.
117 Hélène Berr, *The Journal of Hélène Berr* (New York: Weinstein Books, 2008), 50.
118 Richard Millman, *La question juive entre les deux guerres. Ligues de droite et antisémitisme en France* (Paris: A. Colin, 1992), 223; Zytnicki, 'La politique antisémite du regime de Vichy', 155.
119 Aouté, 'La Place de l'Algérie dans le project antijuif de Vichy', 602.
120 Aouté, 'La Place de l'Algérie dans le project antijuif de Vichy', 603, 612–613; Cotillon, 'L'Empire français dans la Révolution nationale', 46; Vinen, *The Unfree French*, 138.

121 Aouté, 'La Place de l'Algérie dans le project antijuif de Vichy', 609–610; Cantier, *L'Algérie sous the régime de Vichy*, 235.
122 Zytnicki, 'La politique antisémite du regime de Vichy', 155, 157.
123 Mohammed Kenbib, 'Moroccan Jews and the Vichy Regime, 1940–42', *The Journal of North African Studies* 19, no. 4 (2014): 545–547.
124 Zytnicki, 'La politique antisémite du regime de Vichy', 155.
125 Terrence Peterson, 'The "Jewish Question" and the "Italian Peril": Vichy, Italy, and the Jews of Tunisia, 1940-2', *Journal of Contemporary History* 50, no. 2 (2015): 237–254; Michael R. Marrus and Robert O. Paxton, *Vichy et les Juifs* (Paris: Calmann-Lévy, 2015), 768.
126 Zytnicki, 'La politique antisémite du regime de Vichy', 166.
127 Zytnicki, 'La politique antisémite du regime de Vichy', 172.
128 Ginio, *French Colonialism Unmasked*, 26–27; Ramognino, 'L'Afrique de l'Ouest', 85.
129 Jennings, *Vichy in the Tropics*, 46–47.
130 Jennings, *Vichy in the Tropics*, 144–146.
131 Jennings, *Vichy in the Tropics*, 95–96.
132 Jackson, *The Dark Years*, 217.
133 Burrin, *France under the Germans*, 156.
134 Jacson, *The Dark Years*, 217.
135 Berr, *The Journal of Hélène Berr*, 98–105.
136 Burrin, *France under the Germans*, 157–158.
137 Jackson, *The Dark Years*, 358.
138 Pierre Birnbaum, *La France aux Français. Histoire des haines nationalistes* (Paris: Seuil, 1993), 187–188.
139 Hyman, *The Jews of Modern France*, 174–176.
140 Jackson, *The Dark Years*, 361.
141 Poznanski, *Les Juifs en France pendant la Second guerre mondiale*, 461–462; Panicacci, *L'Occupation Italienne*, 195–196.
142 Marrus and Paxton, *Vichy et les Juifs*, 772.
143 Marrus and Paxton, *Vichy et les Juifs*, 774.
144 Luca Fenoglio, 'Between Protection and Complicity: Guido Lospinoso, Fascist Italy, and the Holocaust in Occupied Southeastern France', *Holocaust and Genocide Studies* 33, no. 1 (2019): 90–111.
145 Poznanski, *Les Juifs en France pendant la Seconde guerre mondiale*, 461–469; Panicacci, *L'Occupation Italienne*, 193–212. Marrus and Paxton, *Vichy et les Juifs*, 778.
146 Burrin, *France under the Germans*, 156–158.
147 Marrus and Paxton, *Vichy France and the Jews*, 346–356.
148 Adler, 'The Jews and Vichy': 1078.
149 Jackson, *The Dark Years*, 362.
150 Hyman, *The Jews of Modern France*, 168–169.
151 Sweets, *Choices in Vichy France*, 132.
152 Jackson, *The Dark Years*, 357, 370; Renée Poznanski, 'Stand Up for the Image of France or Follow French Opinion: The External Resistance and the Persecution of the Jews', *European Review of History: Revue européenne d'histoire* 25, no. 2 (2018): 251–252.
153 Hyman, *The Jews of Modern France*, 177–178.
154 Michael R. Marrus, 'Jewish Leaders and the Holocaust', *French Historical Studies* 15, no. 2 (1987): 318–319, 321, 326, 328.

155 Marrus, 'Jewish Leaders and the Holocaust', 324; Adler, 'The Jews and Vichy', 1076.
156 Marrus, 'Jewish Leaders and the Holocaust', 323.
157 Hyman, *The Jews of Modern France*, 182–184.
158 Poznanski, 'Stand Up for the Image of France or Follow French Opinion', 257, 265–266.
159 Wieviorka, *The French Resistance*, 77.
160 Poznanski, 'Stand Up for the Image of France or Follow French Opinion', 267–269, 273–274.
161 A breakdown by country of the Righteous Among Nations may be found at the Yad Vashem website: https://www.yadvashem.org/righteous/statistics.html (accessed 22 October 2019).
162 Wieviorka and Tebinka, 'Resisters: From Everyday Life to Counter-State', 166.
163 Jacques Semelin, *Persécutions et entraides dans la France occupée. Comment 75% des Juifs en France ont échappé à la mort* (Paris: Seuil-Les Arènes, 2013), 853, 855.
164 Jacques Semelin, *La survie des juifs en France, 1940–1944* (Paris: CNRS Editions, 2018), 20.
165 Jackson, *The Dark Years*, 370.
166 Adler, 'The Jews and Vichy', 1078.
167 Renée Poznanski, *Les Juifs en France pendant la Seconde guerre mondiale* (Paris: CNRS Editions, 2018), 579.
168 Daniel Lee, *Pètain's Jewish Children: French Jewish Youth and the Vichy Regime, 1940–1942* (Oxford: Oxford University Press, 2014).
169 For a comaprative perspective see Marrus and Paxton, *Vichy France and the Jews*, 356–372; Pim Griffioen and Ron Zeller, 'Anti-Jewish Policy and Organization of the Deportations in France and the Netherlands, 1940–1944: A Comparative Study', *Holocaust and Genocide Studies* 20, no. 3 (2006): 438.
170 Raul Hilberg, 'Auschwitz and the "Final Solution"', in *Anatomy of the Auschwitz Death Camp*, ed. Yisrael Gutman and Michael Berenbaum (Bloomington: Indiana University Press, 1998), 89.
171 Poznanski, *Les Juifs en France pendant la Second guerre mondiale*, 580, 609.
172 Wieviorka, *The French Resistance*, 427.
173 Robert O. Paxton, 'Jews: How Vichy Made It Worse', *New York Review of Books*, 6 March 2014, https://www.nybooks.com/articles/2014/03/06/jews-how-vichy-made-it-worse/ (accessed 22 March 2019).
174 Paxton, *Vichy France*, 185; Vinen, *The Unfree French*, 136.
175 Werth, *Deposition*, 227.

Chapter 6

1 Jackson, *The Dark Years*, 561–567. See the speech in French here: https://www.reseau-canope.fr/cnrd/ressource/texte/3948 (accessed 21 November 2019)
2 Keith Lowe, *Savage Continent: Europe in the Aftermath of World War II* (New York: St Martin's Press, 2012), 13.
3 Vinen, *The Unfree French*, 358–359.

4   Koreman, *The Expectation of Justice*, 9; Sandra Ott, *Living with the Enemy: German Occupation, Collaboration and Justice in the Western Pyrenees, 1940–1948* (Cambridge: Cambridge University Press, 2017), 83; Wieviorka, *The French Resistance*, 343–344.
5   Koreman, *The Expectation of Justice*, 26–28.
6   Jackson, *The Dark Years*, 519–520.
7   Gildea, *Marianne in Chains*, 333.
8   Koreman, *The Expectation of Justice*, 26.
9   Wieviorka, *The French Resistance*, 348–350.
10 Vinen, *The Unfree French*, 316.
11 Ginio, *French Colonialism Unmasked*, xv, 175.
12 Cornil, 'La repression de la Résistance en Indochine'; Pollack, 'Résister sous les tropiques', 305–306.
13 Vinen, *The Unfree French*, 323.
14 Jackson, *The Dark Years*, 557; Lowe, *Savage Continent*, 168.
15 Jackson, *The Dark Years*, 544–545; Marie-Louise Roberts, *D-Day through French Eyes: Normandy 1944* (Chicago: University of Chicago Press, 2014), 151–152; Wieviorka, *The French Resistance*, 375.
16 Wieviorka, *The French Resistance*, 376.
17 Jackson, *The Dark Years*, 544–545; 557.
18 Wieviorka, *The French Resistance*, 358.
19 Albertelli and Levasseur, *Atlas de la France Libre*, 66–67; Cobb, *The Resistance*, 176; Wieviorka, *The French Resistance*, 357.
20 Vinen, *The Unfree French*, 318.
21 Jacques Cantier, 'Les horizons de l'après-Vichy. De la "Libération" de l'Empire aux enjeux de mémoire', in *L'Empire colonial sous Vichy*, ed. Jennings and Cantier, 341.
22 Cantier, *L'Algérie sous le regime de Vichy*, 372.
23 Cantier, 'Les horizons de l'après-Vichy', 342–343.
24 Thomas, *The French Empire at War*, 139–148.
25 Jennings, *Vichy in the Tropics*, 39.
26 Pollack, 'Résister sous les tropiques', 306.
27 Jennings, *Vichy in the Tropics*, 124–126.
28 Ginio, *French Colonialism Unmasked*, 26.
29 Cantier, 'Les horizons de l'après-Vichy', 351–352.
30 Jennings, *Free French Africa*, 251; Thomas, *The French Empire at War*, 249–254.
31 Thomas, *The French Empire at War*, 123, 153, 180–185; Cantier, 'Les horizons de l'après-Vichy', 342.
32 Werth, *Deposition*, 279.
33 Guéhenno, *Diary of the Dark Years*, 263.
34 Koreman, *The Expectation of Justice*, 148.
35 Grenard, *La France du marché noir*, 230.
36 Ott, *Living with the Enemy*, 87; Gildea, *Marianne in Chains*, 360.
37 Wieviorka, *The French Resistance*, 381.
38 Koreman, *The Expectation of Justice*, 252–254.
39 Gallup, *The Gallup International Public Opinion Poll*, 44; 55.
40 Grenard, *La France du marché noir*, 280.
41 Koreman, *The Expectation of Justice*, 73–74, 79.

42 Koreman, *The Expectation of Justice*, 80–81; Gildea, *Marianne in Chains*, 365–370.
43 Gildea, *Marianne in Chains*, 336.
44 Henry Rousso, 'Vichy, le grand fossé', *Vingtième Siècle* 5 (1985): 66.
45 Marrus and Paxton, *Vichy France and the Jews*, 329–339.
46 Wieviorka, *The French Resistance*, 327.
47 Knapp and Bardoli, *Forgotten Blitzes*, 3.
48 Werth, *Deposition*, 264.
49 Mark W. Willis, 'Not Liberation, but Destruction: War Damage in Tunisia in the Second World War, 1942–43', *The Journal of North African Studies* 20, no. 2 (2015): 189, 191–194.
50 Knapp and Bardoli, *Forgotten Blitzes*, 233.
51 Matthew Cobb, *Eleven Days in August: The Liberation of Paris in 1944* (London: Simon and Schuster, 2014), 335–337.
52 Knapp and Bardoli, *Forgotten Blitzes*, 240; Roberts, *D-Day through French Eyes*, 75–82.
53 Simon Kitson, 'Criminals or Liberators? French Opinion and Allied Bombing of France, 1940–1945', in *Bombing, States and Peoples in Western Europe 1940–1945*, ed. Claudia Baldoli, Andrew Knapp and Richard Overy (London: Continuum, 2011), 288–290.
54 Roberts, *D-Day through French Eyes*, 69.
55 Knapp and Bardoli, *Forgotten Blitzes*, 239; Roberts, *D-Day through French Eyes*, 69.
56 Raffael Scheck, 'French Colonial Soldiers', 436.
57 Knapp and Bardoli, *Forgotten Blitzes*, 2–3.
58 Roberts, *D-Day through French Eyes*, 101.
59 Vinen, *The Unfree French*, 330–331.
60 Koreman, *The Expectation of Justice*, 43–44.
61 *Welcome to the Riviera-Bienvenue sur la Côte d'Azur: Instruction Book and Guide to the United States Riviera Recreational Area*, Nice, 1945, http://www.americainworldwartwo.amdigital.co.uk/ (accessed 23 October 2019).
62 Gildea, *Marianne in Chains*, 338.
63 Roberts, *What Soldiers Do: Sex and the American GI in World War II France* (Chicago: Chicago University Press, 2013), 61–67.
64 Vinen, *The Unfree French*, 333.
65 *French Conversation Guide Containing Dialogues and Useful Sentences* (Algiers: Imprimerie Burgos, 1941–1945), http://www.americainworldwartwo.amdigital.co.uk/ (accessed 23 October 2019).
66 Roberts, *What Soldiers Do*, 239–247.
67 Capdevila, 'La mobilisation des femmes dans la France combattante', 1–5.
68 Elodie Jeauneau, 'Images et representations des premières soldates francaises (1938–1962)', *Clio. Femmes, Genre, Histoire* 30 (2009): 242; Jeauneau, 'Des femmes dans la France combattante'.
69   Murraciole, *Les Français libres*, 299–301.
70 Driss Maghraoui, 'The *goumiers* in the Second World War: History and Colonial Representation', *The Journal of North African Studies* 19, no. 4 (2014): 577.
71 Deroo and Champeaux, 'Panorama des troupes colonials françaises', 7.

72	Echenberg, '"Morts pour la France": 364; 374; Deroo and Champeaux, 'Panorama des troupes colonials françaises', 8–9.
73	Jennings, *Free French Africa*, 168–169.
74	Cantier, 'Les horizons de l'`après-Vichy', 342.
75	Jennings, *Free French Africa*, 163–164; Murraciole, *Les Français libres*, 61.
76	Broch, 'The Resistance in Colour'.
77	Murraciole, *Les Français Libres*, 277; Thomas, *The French Empire at War*, 253–254.
78	Echenberg, '"Morts pour la France"', 374–375; Thomas, *The French Empire at War*, 253.
79	Peter Novick, *The Resistance versus Vichy: The Purge of Collaborators in Liberated France* (London: Chatto & Windus, 1968), 198.
80	Koreman, *The Expectation of Justice*, 93.
81	Cobb, *Eleven Days in August*, 352.
82	Koreman, *The Expectation of Justice*.
83	Koreman, *The Expectation of Justice*, 100.
84	Vinen, *The Unfree French*, 339; Novick, *The Resistance versus Vichy*, 202–208.
85	Koreman, *The Expectation of Justice*, 92; Vinen, *The Unfree French*, 339; Novick, *The Resistance versus Vichy*, 202–208.
86	Koreman, *The Expectation of Justice*, 50–51.
87	Koreman, *The Expectation of Justice*, 107.
88	Ott, *Living with the Enemy*, 90, 101.
89	Giolitto, *Histoire de la Milice*, 502–506.
90	Koreman, *The Expectation of Justice*, 49–50.
91	Liaigre, *Les FTP*, 88.
92	Vinen, *The Unfree French*, 340.
93	Vinen, *The Unfree French*, 341.
94	Ott, *Living with the Enemy*, 87–88.
95	Vinen, *The Unfree French*, 347.
96	Koreman, *The Expectation of Justice*, 109; Duchen, 'Crime and Punishment in Liberated France', 23–241; Duchen, 'Crime and Punishment in Liberated France', 236.
97	Alain Brossat quoted in Koreman, *The Expectation of Justice*, 100.
98	Fabrice Virgili, *Shorn Women: Gender and Punishment in Liberation France* (Oxford: Berg, 2002), 1.
99	Koreman, *The Expectation of Justice*, 113.
100	Koreman, *The Expectation of Justice*, 114.
101	Koreman, *The Expectation of Justice*, 137.
102	Vinen, *The Unfree French*, 321.
103	Cantier, *L'Algérie sous le régime de Vichy*, 384–385n77; Cantier, 'Les horizons de l'après-Vichy', 343.
104	Cantier, 'Les horizons de l'après-Vichy', 344.
105	Novick, *The Resistance versus Vichy*, 146–147.
106	Novick, *The Resistance versus Vichy*, 146–148.
107	Novick, *The Resistance versus Vichy*, 191–197.
108	Atkin, *Pétain*, 194.
109	Novick, *The Resistance versus Vichy*, 174. Novick gives the figure 81 per cent.

110 Atkin, *Pétain*, 195–196.
111 Cobb, *Eleven Days in August*, 350.
112 Dank, *The French against the French*, 277.
113 Ott, *Living with the Enemy*, 99.
114 Koreman, *The Expectation of Justice*, 97.
115 Henry Rousso, 'Did the Purge Achieve its Goals?' in Richard J. Golsan, ed., *Memory, the Holocaust and French Justice: The Bousquet and Touvier Affairs* (Hanover: University Press of New England, 1996), 102.
116 Koreman, *The Expectation of Justice*, 97.
117 Cobb, *Eleven Days in August*, 350–351.
118 Diamond, *Women and the Second World War in France*, 153.
119 Rousso, 'Vichy, le grand fossé', 65.
120 Cobb, *Eleven Days in August*, 356.
121 Dank, *The French against the French*, 277.
122 Koreman, *The Expectation of Justice*, 96.
123 Ott, *Living with the Enemy*, 98–117.
124 Paxton, *Vichy France*, 340.
125 Koreman, *The Expectation of Justice*, 97.
126 Koreman, *The Expectation of Justice*, 102–103.
127 Guéhenno, *Diary of the Dark Years*, 272.
128 Koreman, *The Expectation of Justice*, 112.
129 Vinen, *The Unfree French*, 354.
130 Koreman, *The Expectation of Justice*, 147.

Chapter 7

1 See, for example, Michael R. Marrus, 'Coming to Terms with Vichy', *Holocaust and Genocide Studies* 9, no. 1 (1995): 23–41; Omer Bartov, 'Review: The Proof of Ignominy: Vichy France's Past and Presence', *Contemporary European History* 7, no. 1 (1998): 107–131.
2 Wieviorka, *The French Resistance*, 459–460.
3 Rousso, *The Vichy Syndrome*.
4 Richard J. Golsan, *Vichy's Afterlife: History and Counterhistory in Postwar France* (Lincoln and London: University of Nebraska Press, 2000).
5 Conan and Rousso, *Vichy*.
6 Rousso, *The Vichy Syndrome*, 219–221. For a recent survey on the presence of the Vichy past in novels, see Manuel Bragança, 'Vichy, un passé qui ne passe pas?', *French Cultural Studies* 25, no. 3/4 (2014): 309–319.
7 Rousso, *The Vichy Syndrome*, 16, 18, 71.
8 Wieviorka, *The French Resistance*, 455–456.
9 On the memory of the 1940 defeat, see Carswell, *The Fall of France in the Second World War*, 259–266. See also, Charles Laubier, 'Les soldats morts pour la France en 1940 méritent une commémoration', https://www.lemonde.fr/idees/article/2015/05/08/les-soldats-morts-pour-la-france-en-1940-meritent-une-commemoration_4629979_3232.html (accessed 21 August 2019).
10 Robert Gildea, *France since 1945* (Oxford: Oxford University Press, 1996), 30–56.

11 Richard F. Kuisel, 'Coca Cola and the Cold War: The French Face Americanization, 1948–1953', *French Historical Studies* 17, no. 1 (1991): 96–116.
12 Richard I. Jobs, 'Tarzan under Attack: Youth, Comics and Cultural Reconstruction in Postwar France', *French Historical Studies* 26, no. 4 (2003): 687–725.
13 Paule René-Bazin, 'Archives de France et Comité d'histoire de la Deuxième Guerre mondial au prisme des archives de la Résistance', in *Faire l'histoire de la Résistance. Actes du colloque international (18–19 mars 2008)*, ed. Laurent Douzou (Rennes: Presses Universitaires de Rennes, 2010), 75; Laurent Douzou, *La Résistant française: une histoire périlleuse. Essai d'historiographie* (Paris: Seuil, 2005), 70–71.
14 Pierre Laborie, 'Acteurs et historiens dans l'écriture de l'histoire de la Résistance', in *Faire l'histoire de la Résistance*, ed. Laurent Douzou, 90.
15 Wieviorka, *The French Resistance*, 4.
16 John Flower, 'A Continuing Preoccupation with the Occupation', *French Cultural Studies* 25, no. 3/4 (2014): 300.
17 Gildea, *Fighters in the Shadows*, 448–449.
18 Jacqueline Sainclivier et Dominique Veillon, 'L'histoire de la Résistance dans le travail du Comité d'histoire de la Deuxième Guerre mondiale: la production éditoriale', in *Faire l'histoire de la Résistance*, ed. Laurent Douzou, 63.
19 Cantier, 'Les horizons de l'après Vichy', 356.
20 Rousso, 'Vichy, le grand fossé': 67, 71.
21 Gallup, *The Gallup International Public Opinion Poll*, 81.
22 Aron, *Histoire de Vichy*, 94.
23 Siegried, 'Le Vichy de Pétain', 748.
24 Siegfired, 'Le Vichy de Pétain': 747.
25 Gildea, *France since 1945*, 43–46.
26 Henri Michel, *Les courants de pensée de la résistance* (Paris: Presses Universitaires de France, 1962), 775.
27 Cantier, 'Les horizons de l'après Vichy', 359–360.
28 Flower, 'A Continuing Preoccupation': 300.
29 Gildea, *Fighters in the Shadows*, 452.
30 Wieviorka, *The French Resistance*, 461.
31 Rousso, *The Vichy Syndrome*, 90.
32 Hoffmann, 'Collaborationism in France during World War II', 375.
33 Yves Florenne, '*La France dans l'Europe d'Hitler*, de E. Jäckel', April 1968 https://www.monde-diplomatique.fr/1968/04/FLORENNE/28335 (accessed 17 April 2019).
34 Jan Sigmann, 'Un point de vue allemande sur la France de 1940 à 1944', *Annales. Histoire, Sciences Sociales* 26, no. 1 (1971): 54–56.
35 Paxton, *Vichy France*, 51.
36 Paxton, *Vichy France*, 147.
37 Paxton, *Vichy France*, 231–233.
38 Paxton, *Vichy France*, 294–295.
39 Paxton, *Vichy France*, 235.
40 Moshik Temkin, '*Avec un certain malaise*: The Paxtonian Trauma in France, 1973–1974', *Journal of Contemporary History* 38, no. 2 (2003): 298–301.

41 Temkin, 'Avec un certain malaise', 292.
42 Temkin, 'Avec un certain malaise', 294n13.
43 Bragança, 'Vichy', 310.
44 Vincent Cassanova, '*Le Chagrin et la pitié* de Marcel Ophüls', https://fresques.ina.fr/jalons/fiche-media/InaEdu04001/le-chagrin-et-la-pitie-de-marcel-ophuls.html (accessed 13 March 2019); Flower, 'A Continuing Preoccupation', 301–302.
45 Roussou, *The Vichy Syndrome*, 229–230.
46 https://fresques.ina.fr/jalons/fiche-media/InaEdu04001/le-chagrin-et-la-pitie-de-marcel-ophuls.html (accessed 13 March 2019); John F. Sweets, 'Hold That Pendulum! Redefining Fascism, Collaborationism and Resistance in France', *French Historical Studies* 15, no. 4 (1988): 747–748.
47 Jackson, *The Dark Years*, 14–15.
48 Marrus and Paxton, *Vichy France and the Jews*, 359.
49 Marrus and Paxton, *Vichy France and the Jews*, 363.
50 Marrus and Paxton, *Vichy France and the Jews*, 182.
51 Laurent Douzou, 'Les résistantes, point de l'historiographie', in *Les femmes dans la résistance en France*, ed. Mechtild Gilzmer, Christine Levisse-Touzé and Stefan Martens (Pairs: Tallandier, 2003), 32–35.
52 Gildea, *Fighters in the Shadows*, 469.
53 See, for example, Ania Francos, *Il était des femmes dans la Résistance* (Paris: Stock, 1978) and Margaret L. Rossiter, *Women in the Resistance* (New York: Praeger, 1986); Gildea, *Fighters in the Sadows*, 469–471.
54 On the trials of the 1990s, see Richard J. Golsan, ed., *Memory, the Holocaust and French Justice: The Bousquet and Touvier Affairs* (Hanover: University Press of New England, 1996) and Simon Kitson, 'Bousquet, Touvier and Papon: Three Vichy Personalities', http://www.port.ac.uk/special/france1815to2003/chapter8/interviews/filetodownload.27676.en.pdf (accessed 17 April 2019).
55 Jackson, *The Dark Years*, 623.
56 Jackson, *The Dark Years*, 614.
57 Jackson, *The Dark Years*, 622–623.
58 http://www.mitterrand.org/A-propos-du-Vel-d-Hiv.html (accessed 21 November 2019)
59 James Shields, 'The Front National: From Systematic Opposition to Systemic Integration?' *Modern & Contemporary France*, 22, no. 4 (2014): 494.
60 Pascale Perrineau, 'Le Front national, 1972–2015', in *Histoire de l'extrême droite en France*, ed. Michel Winock (Paris: Points, 2015), 272–273; Pierre Milza, 'Le Front national crée-t-il une culture politique?' *Vingtième Siècle* 44, no. 1 (1994): 40n1; Michel Winock, *Nationalisme, antisémitisme et fascisme en France*, rev. edn (Paris: Editions du Seuil, 2014), 62; Peter Fysch and Jim Wolfreys, *The Politics of Racism in France* (Basingstoke: Palgrave Macmillan, 2003), 142.
61 Marlise Simons, 'Chirac Affirms France's Guilt in Fate of Jews', *The New York Times*, 17 July 1995, https://www.nytimes.com/1995/07/17/world/chirac-affirms-france-s-guilt-in-fate-of-jews.html (accessed 17 April 2019).
62 'Le discours de Jacques Chirac au Vel d'hiv en 1995', *Le Figaro*, published online 31 March 2014, http://www.lefigaro.fr/politique/le-scan/2014/03/27/25001-20140327ARTFIG00092-le-discours-de-jacques-chirac-au-vel-d-hiv-en-1995.php (accessed 17 April 2019).
63 Sweets, 'Hold That Pendulum!', 744.

64 Jackson, *The Dark Years*, 17.
65 Wieviorka, *The French Resistance*, 463.
66 Atkn, *The French at War*, 10.
67 Lindsey Dodd and David Lees, 'Introduction', in *Vichy France and Everyday Life: Confronting the Challenges of Wartime, 1939–1945*, ed. Lindsey Dodd and David Lees (London: Bloomsbury Academic, 2018), 7–10.
68 Dodd and Lees, 'Introduction', 7.
69 Temkin, '*Avec un certain malaise*': 297; Gildea, *Fighter in the Shadows*, 13–14.
70 Robert O. Paxton, 'The Truth about the Resistance', *The New York Review of Books*, 25 February 2016, https://www.nybooks.com/articles/2016/02/25/truth-about-french-resistance/ (accessed 17 April 2019).
71 The suburbs of around French urban centres, used in particular to describe the impoverished suburbs of Paris.
72 Michael F. O'Riley, 'National Identity and Unrealized Union in Rachid Bouchareb's "Indigènes"', *The French Review* 81, no. 2 (2007): 279.
73 O'Riley, 'National Identity and Unrealized Union': 280.
74 Sylvain Boulouque et Stéphane Courtois, '"L'armée du crime" de Robert Guédiguian, ou la légende au mépris de l'histoire. Un hommage caduc à force de fictions', *Le Monde*, 14 November 2009, https://www.lemonde.fr/idees/article/2009/11/14/l-armee-du-crime-de-robert-guediguian-ou-la-legende-au-mepris-de-l-histoire_1267221_3232.html (accessed 19 April 2019).Chris Millington, 'Celebrating the Resistance: L'armée du crime', *Fiction and Film for Scholars of France: A Cultural Bulletin* 3, no. 6 (2013) https://h-france.net/fffh/maybe-missed/celebrating-the-resistance-larmee-du-crime/ (accessed 17 April 2019).
75 I thank Aaron Cothliff and Chloe Hodges for helping me to understand this topic. I thank them, too, along with Amelia Cothliff and Colin Hodges, for being excellent company. The information in this paragraph comes from: https://callofduty.fandom.com/wiki/Isabelle_DuFontaine; https://callofduty.fandom.com/wiki/Camille_%22Rousseau%22_Denis#cite_note-1; https://www.callofduty.com/wwii/resistance-event; https://metro.co.uk/2018/01/19/call-duty-wwii-best-selling-video-game-2017-america-7242375/; https://www.lefigaro.fr/secteur/high-tech/2018/02/26/32001-20180226ARTFIG00068--fifa-call-of-duty-et-zelda-au-sommet-des-ventes-de-jeux-video-en-france-en-2017.php; https://fr.wikipedia.org/wiki/Box-office_France_2009; https://fr.wikipedia.org/wiki/L%27Arm%C3%A9e_du_crime#Distribution (each site accessed 23 October 2019).
76 Cantier, 'Les horizons de l'après Vichy', 356.
77 See, for example, Daniel Lefeuvre, 'Vichy et la modernisation de l'Algérie. Intention ou réalité ?' *Vingtième Siècle, revue d'histoire* 42, no. 2 (1994): 7–16 and Pascal Blanchard and Gilles Boëtsch, 'La France de Pétain et l'Afrique: Images et propagandes coloniales', *Canadian Journal of African Studies/Revue Canadienne des Études Africaines* 28, no. 1 (1994): 1–31.
78 Eric Jennings and Jacques Cantier, 'Introduction', in *L'Empire colonial sous Vichy*, eds. Jacques Cantier and Eric Jennings, 8.
79 Jennings, *Free French Africa*, 264.
80 Jennings, *Free French Africa*, 2–6, 271.
81 Wieviorka, *The French Resistance*, 5.
82 Gidea, *Fighters in the Shadows*, 15.

83 'Discours d'hommage aux martyrs du Bois de Boulogne, le 16 mai 2007', *Le Monde*, published online 30 April 2008, https://www.lemonde.fr/politique/article/2008/04/30/allocution-de-nicolas-sarkozy-lors-de-la-ceremonie-d-hommage-aux-martyrs-du-bois-de-boulogne-le-16-mai-2007_1040045_823448.html (accessed 17 April 2019); Gildea, *Fighters in the Shadows*, 1–2.

84 Luc Cédelle, 'La lecture de la lettre de Guy Môquet divise les enseignants', *Le Monde*, published online 19 October 2007, https://www.lemonde.fr/societe/article/2007/10/19/la-lecture-de-la-lettre-de-guy-moquet-divise-les-enseignants_968843_3224.html (accessed 17 April 2019); Pierre Schill, 'Pourquoi je ne lirai pas la lettre de Guy Môquet à mes élèves à la rentrée', *Libération*, published online 22 May 2007, https://www.liberation.fr/tribune/2007/05/22/pourquoi-je-ne-lirai-pas-la-lettre-de-guy-moquet-a-mes-eleves-a-la-rentree_93735 (accessed 17 April 2019).

85 Flower, 'A Continuing Preoccupation': 304.

86 Charlotte Coutard, 'La Rafle du Vél d'Hiv: du général de Gaulle à François Hollande, le long parcours de reconnaissance de l'État français', 16 July 2017, https://www.franceinter.fr/histoire/les-presidents-francais-au-vel-d-hiv (accessed 21 November 2019)

87 'Rafle du Vél' d'Hiv: Hollande accuse "la France" et s'attire une salve de critiques', *FranceInter.fr*, published online 16 July 2017, https://www.francetvinfo.fr/france/rafle-du-vel-d-hiv-en-accusant-la-france-hollande-s-attire-une-salve-de-critiques_121721.html (accessed 17 April 2019).

88 'Tsiganes internés sous Vichy: Hollande reconnait la responsabilité de la France', *Libération*, published online 29 October 2016, https://www.liberation.fr/france/2016/10/29/tsiganes-internes-sous-vichy-hollande-reconnait-la-responsabilite-de-la-france_1525102 (accessed 17 April 2019).

89 Katrin Bennhold and Stephen Castle, 'E.U. Calls France's Roma Expulsions a "Disgrace"', *The New York Times*, 14 September 2010, https://www.nytimes.com/2010/09/15/world/europe/15roma.html (accessed 17 April 2019).

90 'Speech by the President of the Republic Emmanuel Macron at the Vel d'Hiv commemoration', published online 16 July 2017, https://www.elysee.fr/emmanuel-macron/2017/07/18/speech-by-the-president-of-the-republic-emmanuel-macron-at-the-vel-dhiv-commemoration.en (accessed 17 April 2019).

91 Henry Rousso, 'Après la déclaration de Marine Le Pen sur le Vel d'Hiv, quelle responsabilité de la France et des Français sous l'Occupation', *Huff Post*, published 11 April 2017, https://www.huffingtonpost.fr/henry-rousso/le-pen-vel-dhiv-vichy_a_22034882/ (accessed 17 April 2019).

92 Julian Jackson, 'La Rafle', *Fiction and Film for Schoalrs of France: A Cultural Bulletin* 1, no. 1 (2010), https://h-france.net/fffh/the-buzz/la-rafle/ (accessed 17 April 2019).

93 Annette Wieviorka, '"La Rafle", drame pédagogique et hymne à la France', *Libération*, published online 15 March 2010, https://next.liberation.fr/cinema/2010/03/15/la-rafle-drame-pedagogique-et-hymne-a-la-france_615139 (accessed 17 April 2019).

94 Alain Michel, *Vichy et la Shoah. Enquête sur le paradoxe français* (Paris: Editions CDL, 2012), 14.

95 Michel, *Vichy et la Shoah*, 25.

96   Michel, *Vichy et la Shoah*, 356; 369.
97   Michel, *Vichy et la Shoah*, 14.
98   Pascal Riché, 'Robert Paxton: L'argument de Zemmour sur Vichy est vide', https://www.nouvelobs.com/rue89/rue89-politique/20141009.RUE6133/robert-paxton-l-argument-de-zemmour-sur-vichy-est-vide.html (accessed 19 August 2019).
99   Eric Zemmour, *Le Suicide francais* (Paris: Albin Michel, 2014); Tony Todd, 'French Best Seller Says Vichy Regime "Tried to Save French Jews"', https://www.france24.com/en/20141012-french-bestseller-vichy-save-jews-zemmour (accessed 19 August 2019).
100 Semelin, *Persécutions et entraides dans la France occupée*, iii. This book was 'abridged, revised and updated' in 2018 (with a preface by Serge Klarsfeld) and published as Semelin, *La survie des juifs en France*.
101 Semelin, *Persécutions et entraides dans la France occupée*, iv; Semelin, *La survie des juifs en France*, 19.
102 Semelin, *Persécutions et entraides dans la France occupée*, 853; 855.
103 Semelin, *Persécutions et entraides dans la France occupée*, 603–604.
104 Poznanski, *Les Juifs en France pendant la Second guerre mondiale*, 606–608.
105 Michael R. Marrus and Robert O. Paxton, *Vichy et les Juifs* (Paris: Calmann-Lévy, 2015), 887.
106 Marrus and Paxton, *Vichy et les Juifs*, 894.
107 Semelin, *La survie des juifs en France*, 19.
108 Semelin, *La survie des juifs en France*, 20–22.

Chapter 8

1   'Up Yours Delors', *The Sun*, 1 November 1990, 1.
2   https://en.wikipedia.org/wiki/Cheese-eating_surrender_monkeys (accessed 21 August 2019).
3   Jackson, *The Dark Years*, vii.
4   Peter Allen, 'REVEALED: France's SECRET Links to the Nazi Holocaust', https://www.express.co.uk/news/world/629873/France-secret-links-Nazi-Holocaust-revealed-Hitler (accessed 21 August 2019).
5   https://thegreatestbooks.org/lists/38 (accessed 21 August 2019).
6   https://en.wikipedia.org/wiki/Inglourious_Basterds#Casting (accessed 21 August 2019).
7   See, for example, 'Nolan's Dunkirk Film Accused of "Rudely" Ignoring France's Crucial Role in Saving British', https://www.thelocal.fr/20170719/dont-forget-the-bravery-of-the-french-at-the-battle-of-dunkirk (accessed 21 August 2019); '"Dunkirk": Quelle est cette Bataille de Dunkerque que Christopher Nolan raconte dans son film', https://www.huffingtonpost.fr/2017/07/19/dunkirk-quelle-est-cette-bataille-de-dunkerque-que-christoph_a_23035932/ (accessed 21 August 2019).
8   Wieviorka, *The French Resistance*, 411; Wieviorka and Tebinka, 'Resisters: From Everyday Life to Counter-State', 153.
9   Thomas, *The French Empire between the Wars*, 5.

ANNOTATED BIBLIOGRAPHY

A note for the reader
Intended for the Anglophone student of France in the Second World War, this annotated bibliography comprises English-language sources only. I have included works to which I refer regularly in teaching and those that I recommend that my students read. In general, the entries pertain to the first edition of each text. The full list of English and French works used for this book may be found in the notes to each chapter.

Arnold, Edward J., ed. *The Development of the Radical Right in France from Boulanger to Le Pen*. Basingstoke: Palgrave, 2000.
The twelve chapters in Edward Arnold's collection concern the history of the radical right from the Boulanger Affair of the 1880s to the turn-of-the-century Front National. There are three chapters relevant to France and the Second Wold War: Philippe Burrin, 'The Ideology of the National Revolution'; Julian Jackson, 'Vichy and Fascism'; and Ariane Chebel d'Appollonia, 'Collaborationist Fascism'. Burrin's essay is a succinct summary of the main themes of Vichy's domestic programme. Jackson addresses the strength of fascism in Vichy France, examining in turn the project for the single party, foreign influences on the regime's policies and the changing nature of the governments of the Etat Français. D'Appollonia's essay concerns the relationship between the Paris collaborationists and fascism. Each contribution serves as a good introduction to their relative topics and a basis from which further research may be conducted.

Atkin, Nicholas. *The French at War, 1934–1944*. Harlow: Longman, 2001.
This short book is an excellent introduction to France in the Second World War. Divided into six chapters ('Interpreting the Vichy Regime'; 'The Third Republic, 1934–1940', 'The Defeat'; 'Vichy'; 'Collaboration'; and 'Resistance'), *The French at War* offers a readable overview of its subject without neglecting nuance and detail. The appendix contains twenty-eight translated documents pertaining to the themes of the book. Atkin addresses neither everyday life under the Occupation nor the colonial history of Vichy; the time at which this book appeared explains these omissions. The book contains a glossary, a 'Who's Who' and a guide to further reading in both French and English.

Baldoli, Claudia, and Andrew Knapp. *Forgotten Blitzes: France and Italy under Allied Air Attack, 1940–1945*. London: Bloomsbury, 2012.
Forgotten Blitzes brings to light a neglected part of the Allied campaign to liberate Europe: the destruction of French and Italian towns and cities by American and British bombs. British readers may be surprised to learn that only Germany was

more heavily bombed than either country and many more bombs fell on citizens of France and Italy than on the British. Claudia Baldoli and Andrew Knapp deploy convincing statistical data to demonstrate the extent of the destruction while their use of testimony brings a human face to the tragedy. The authors also examine bombing in propaganda, the participation of civilians in protecting their cities and the role of aerial attacks in the liberation of Europe. For readers unable to read Knapp's 2014 *Les Français sous les bombes alliées, 1940–1945*, this book offers an alternative.

Baldoli, Claudia, Andrew Knapp and Richard Overy. eds *Bombing, States and Peoples in Western Europe 1940–1945*. London: Continuum, 2011.
This book contains seventeen chapters on various aspects of the everyday experience of bombing in Britain, France, Germany and Italy during the Second World War (several of the chapters take a comparative perspective). Those that concern France are: Lindsey Dodd on state aid and charity to the victims of bombing during 1940–1944; Michael Schmiedel on social responses to Allied bombing; Simon Kitson on French public attitudes to the Allied air war against France; and Olivier Dumoulin on bombing as depicted in British, French, and German newsreels. Richard Overy's introduction is an excellent overview of the state of this subfield of Second World War Studies. The collection is an important addition to the growing literature on the subject under the guidance of its pioneering editors.

Blatt, Joel., ed. *The French Defeat of 1940: Reassessments*. Oxford: Berghahn Books, 1998.
This collection contains thirteen essays on aspects of the defeat of 1940. Notable among the contributions are Nicole Jordan's chapter on the military tactics of the French army, William D. Irvine's contribution on the crisis of French politics and society during the 1930s, Martin S. Alexander's essay on the Franco-British alliance and Stanley Hoffmann's concluding piece on the post-war resonance of the débâcle. The political and military history of the fall of France dominates the contents of the collection; the social and cultural impact of the invasion and the effect on colonial communities are not covered here.

Broch, Ludivine. *Ordinary Workers, Vichy and the Holocaust: French Railwaymen and the Second World War*. Cambridge: Cambridge University Press, 2016.
The subject of Broch's book is the cheminot or railway worker, a figure who after 1944, thanks to heroic tales of the sabotage of the railways, became intimately associated with the French resistance. Broch problematizes this simplified image of the 400,000 wartime cheminots through an examination of the railway workers accommodation of the Occupier, not least in the deportation of the Jews from France by train. The book presents an intimate investigation of the everyday life of the cheminots and their relationship to their engines and their professions. Painting a complex picture of everyday life, *Ordinary Workers* is an important contribution to this burgeoning area of historical investigation.

Burrin, Philippe. *France under the Germans: Collaboration and Compromise*. New York: The New Press, 1996.
Originally published in 1995 as *La France à l'heure allemande*, *France under the Germans* is an important contribution to the historiography of

collaboration from Swiss historian Philippe Burrin. Burrin in fact rejects the term 'collaboration' in favour of 'accommodations' (the title of part two of the book), arguing that the former term is too tarnished with moral judgement to be used objectively. Part one addresses Vichy's policy of collaboration and part three concerns French ideological commitment to Nazism. The book is therefore a history of both high politics and the grass roots, of political leaders and of the average French person struggling to negotiate the complexities of the Occupation.

Cobb, Matthew. *The Resistance*. London: Simon & Schuster, 2009.
Cobb's book is a stimulating and readable account of the development of the Resistance from the defeat of France to the Liberation. The book is written for a public audience and it therefore lacks the self-conscious engagement with the historiography that academic works demand. However, Cobb has included a useful bibliography and glossary as well as a number of short biographies of some of the main characters featured in the text.

Cobb, Matthew. *Eleven Days in August: The Liberation of Paris in 1944*. London: Simon & Schuster, 2014.
Cobb's second book about France and the Second World War is a history of the liberation of Paris, from 15 to 26 August 1944 (the eleven days of the book's title). The length of the book (367 pages) and its relatively narrow focus make it useful as a micro-history of the Liberation. While the book has some of the hallmarks of an academic text, not least an impressive amount of research in French, British and American archives, the writing has the fast pace and style of a book aimed at a public audience.

Dank, Milton. *The French against the French: Collaboration and Resistance*. London: Cassell, 1978.
Dank's book concentrates on collaboration and resistance and includes chapters on, for example, Vichy's policy of collaboration, the LVF and the Milice, and the development and unification of the resistance movements. Yet Dank covers a multitude of topics beyond simply collaboration and resistance. Perhaps the best chapter – 'The Ersatz Life' – is on the daily struggle of the French to survive food and clothing shortages; it is here that Dank's eye for a telling anecdote is in evidence. The book includes a bibliography but it lacks comprehensive notes, a fact that makes it difficult to follow up on the content of the chapters.

Deacon, Valerie. *The Extreme Right in the French Resistance: Members of the Cagoule and the Corvignolles in the Second World War*. Baton Rouge: Louisiana State University Press, 2016.
Deacon explores the resistance of a number of extreme right-wing personalities. These men and women, some of whom worked within the Vichy regime itself, rooted their opposition to Nazism in an extreme nationalism that refused to accept the subjugation of France to a foreign power. Former members of the Cagoule (a fascist-like terrorist cell led by Eugène Deloncle) and the Corvignolles (under Georges Lostaunau-Lacau) fall under the spotlight here. Deacon's book prompts the reader to reconsider the meanings of resistance to contemporaries; democracy and human freedoms did not inspire all opponents of Nazism.

Diamond, Hanna. *Women and the Second World War in France, 1939–1948: Choices and Constraints*. Harlow: Longman, 1999.
Diamond's book offers the perfect introduction to women's experiences during the Second World War and its aftermath in France. Its range of topics is broad: employment, everyday challenges, collaboration, resistance, Liberation and the entry of women into politics after 1944. Diamond includes a mine of data to illustrate each section, from statistics to anecdotes from contemporary women. *Women and the Second World War* is a short, readable work that provides the starting point for deeper engagement with the subject.

Diamond, Hanna. *Fleeing Hitler: France 1940*. Oxford: Oxford University Press, 2007.
This history of the exodus of refugees in 1940 is the most accessible text in English on the subject. Diamond uses a wealth of personal testimonies to bring the experience of the invasion to life. These accounts do more than simply provide colour to the narrative: they expose the divisions of the time and prompt a reconsideration of the historiographical marginality of the civilian experience of 1940. An afterword from Diamond and a guide to English and French language sources provide the basis for further research. A number of testimonies gathered for the book are available to read at fleeinghitler.org.

Dodd, Lindsey, and David Lees, eds. *Vichy France and Everyday Life: Confronting the Challenges of Wartime, 1939–1945*. London: Bloomsbury Academic, 2018.
This collection comprises thirteen essays on a diverse range of subjects: the life of children at home and in school, evacuation and humanitarian aid, colonial prisoners of war, sex and prostitution, cinema and resistance. Lindsey Dodd and David Lees's introduction provides an accessible explanation of the historiography of the everyday life approaches to Vichy France and an argument for its continued importance. The chapters generally employ microhistories to illustrate broader points about the Occupation of France and their stories are stimulating and often moving.

Gildea, Robert. *Marianne in Chains*. London: Macmillan, 2002.
Marianne in Chains is a comprehensive study of the experience of the communities of the Loire Valley during the Second World War. Using oral history interviews and archival sources, Gildea seeks to reconstruct the multifaceted life of the French 'in chains' from daily encounters with the Germans to shortages and rationing. He addresses, too, the orthodox themes of the historiography (resistance, collaboration, anti-Semitism, memory). The introduction gives a fascinating account of Gildea's challenge to the standard interpretation of the Dark Years during a presentation at the Academy of Tours in 1997: 'I was left with the feeling that I had defaced the tablets of stone on which the official history of the Occupation and the Resistance had been written' (1). At nearly 500 pages, students might wish to read certain chapters in isolation.

Gildea, Robert. *Fighters in the Shadows: A New History of the French Resistance*. London: Faber & Faber, 2015.
Gildea's most recent book on France in the Second World War brings the Resistance under the spotlight. A proponent of oral history and the use of

testimony (for which the author makes a case in the introduction of his book), Gildea uses these sources, along with printed documents, to narrate the emergence, development and consolidation of Resistance in France (though the titles of the chapters make it difficult to discern this structure at first glance). The use of interviews allows him both to integrate minority groups into his history and to deploy a telling anecdote. For the student, the introduction provides a good overview of the oral historian's method and practice, and the conclusion is a peerless exploration of the twists and turns of the memory of the war in France since 1945. Like Wieviorka's *The French Resistance*, *Fighters in the Shadows* does not concern resistance beyond France and North Africa.

Gildea, Robert, Olivier Wieviorka and Annette Warring, eds. *Surviving Hitler and Mussolini: Daily Life in Occupied Europe*. Oxford; New York: Berg, 2007.
The six chapters in this collection concern everyday life in Occupied Europe. Authors – among whom one finds historians of France Robert Gildea and Olivier Wieviorka – examine the challenges of finding food, sexual relations with the Occupier, life at school and at work, and the activity of the resistance. Each chapter investigates its theme in a variety of national settings (one of which is, of course, France) and the book thus presents readers with a means to compare and contrast the experiences of ordinary citizens across Europe.

Ginio, Ruth. *French Colonialism Unmasked: The Vichy Years in French West Africa*. Lincoln: University of Nebraska Press, 2006.
Ginio's work is a thorough analysis of the Vichy regime in French West Africa, examining the place of the territory in the regime's broader colonial vision, the attempts to transplant the National Revolution into African society, encounters with indigenous cultures and the long-term effect of Vichy's rule in the context of post-war decolonization. The book is a model for colonial history during the Dark Years for its content, though specific to French West Africa, offer a means to approach the histories of other loyalist colonies (chapter nine in fact makes comparisons with fellow Vichyite territories). Ginio further prompts the reader to reflect upon labels such as resistance and collaboration and to consider their relevance in contexts beyond the French mainland.

Golsan, Richard J. *Vichy's Afterlife: History and Counterhistory in Postwar France*. Lincoln and London: University of Nebraska Press, 2000.
Vichy's Afterlife concerns the troubled memory and history of the regime since 1945. The book broadly examines two themes that have recurred throughout this period: the Occupation as presented in cultural productions (the novels of Patrick Modiano, Louis Malle's *Lacombe Lucien* and Marcel Ophüls's *Hôtel Terminus*) and the trials of various collaborators (Bousquet, Papon, Touvier). It brings into view the influence of other memories and events that have affected French understandings of the wartime past, such as the decolonization of Algeria and the 1990s war in Yugoslavia.

Halls, W. D. *The Youth of Vichy France*. Oxford: The Clarendon Press, 1981.
In this classic book, Halls inspects several aspects of Vichy's policy on youth. The first part concerns the new regime's discourse on youth and the young in the school curriculum and matters of religion. Part two brings into focus Vichy's propaganda

and programme for the renewal of the French nation through its offspring. The
final part concerns youth movements in France, with two excellent chapters on the
Compagnons de France and the Chantiers de la Jeunesse.

Hoffmann, Stanley. 'Collaborationism in France during World War II'. *The Journal of Modern History* 40, no. 3 (1968): 375–395.
Stanley Hoffmann's seminal article addresses what was at the time of writing
a significant gap in the historiography of Vichy France: collaboration. Under
the weight of the Gaullist resistancialist myth, few historians had broached the
darker side of French wartime behaviour. Hoffmann identifies several types of
collaboration (voluntary, involuntary and collaboration for reasons of state) before
examining in detail its ideological variant, collaborationism and its proponents
(journalists, intellectuals, political activists and pacifist left-wingers). He stresses
that there was no absolute division between Vichy's policy of collaboration and
those French committed to a French form of Nazism; points of contact linked them
both.

Horne, Alistair. *To Lose a Battle: France 1940*. London: Macmillan, 1969.
This 700-page examination of the defeat of 1940 is immensely detailed (Horne
devotes 400 pages to the Battle of France itself). According to Julian Jackson, '[a]s
a military narrative of the events of 1940, his book is one of the best ever written'
(Jackson, *The Fall of France*, 192). However, the sheer amount of information may
be daunting for some readers. The value of Horne's *To Lose a Battle* thus lies in its
use as a work of reference.

Jackson, Julian. *France: The Dark Years, 1940–1944*. Oxford: Oxford University Press, 2001.
This is the most comprehensive work in English on the Occupation of France. Over
more than 600 pages, Jackson narrates, analyses and explains a host of topics: the
interwar years and the defeat, Vichy and the National Revolution, collaboration
and resistance, anti-Semitism, the Liberation, and the history and memory of the
period. The level of detail is encyclopaedic yet the writing is succinct and accessible.
While the book can be used as an introduction to certain topics (especially with
regards to the historiography of Vichy, as explored in Jackson's introduction), it
serves best as a source for in-depth research. The clear arrangement of the chapters
makes it easy to use as a reference work, too. Published before the blossoming
of Vichy's colonial history in the early 2000s, the book devotes relatively little
attention to the French Empire.

Jackson, Julian. *The Fall of France: The Nazi Invasion of 1940*. Oxford: Oxford University Press, 2003.
This is the definitive work in English on the French defeat of 1940. Jackson
explores the causes of the collapse and its consequences. The book begins with an
account of the defeat in which the tragedy unfolds like a popular drama. Chapters
two, three and four concern Franco-British relations, French domestic politics,
and the nation at war. The fifth chapter of the book presents a useful summary
of the historiography as well as a counter-factual history in the form of a British
defeat in 1940. The exodus of civilians and the colonial contribution to the battle

for France receive little attention and students should consult Hanna Diamond's *Fleeing Hitler* and Rafael Scheck's *Hitler's African Victims* on these subjects respectively.

Jackson, Julian. 'Homosexuality, Collaboration and Resistance in Occupied France'. *Contemporary French Civilization* 31, no. 2 (2007): 53–81.
Few English-language works focus on homosexuality in Vichy France. Jackson's aim in this article is not to expose Vichy's discrimination against homosexuals (on this topic see also Michael Sibalis, 'Homophobia, Vichy France, and the "Crime of Homosexuality"'. *GLQ* 8, no. 3 (2002): 301–318). Rather, he investigates attitudes to, and the prevalence of, homosexuality in collaborationist and resistance groups. In spite of a paucity of evidence, Jackson draws out the contemporary assumptions that linked homosexuality with collaboration while problematizing the connection between a virile heterosexuality and resistance.

Jennings, Eric. *Vichy in the Tropics: Pétain's National Revolution in Madagascar, Guadeloupe and Indochina*. Stanford: California University Press, 2001.
Taking Madagascar, Guadeloupe and Indochina in turn, Jennings examines Vichy's attempts to plant its vision of the new France in colonial territories. In doing so, he takes account of the aims and visions of colonial administrators and their adaptation of the National Revolution to a foreign setting. The book includes little on resistance in these territories and it is best used as a point of comparison and contrast with works on the National Revolution within France itself (many of which ignore Vichy's global political project).

Jennings, Eric. *Free French Africa in World War II*. Cambridge: Cambridge University Press, 2015.
In this powerful book, Jennings prompts the reader to question the Eurocentric focus of much work on France and the Second World War. He presents a thorough examination of the beginnings of Free French resistance in Africa and the importance of this continent's territories to the success of de Gaulle's campaign. This is not, however, a celebration of Free France, and Jennings reveals the exploitation of Free French Africa's human and material resources with startling clarity. The epilogue on the remembrance (and forgetting) of Africa's contribution to the liberation of France exposes the complicated relationship between post-colonial France and its historical imperial holdings. All students of France and the Second World War should read this book, if possible in conjunction with Jean-François Murraciole's, *Les Français libres. L'autre résistance* (Paris: Tallandier, 2009).

Kedward, H. R. 'France'. In *The Oxford Companion to World War II*, edited by I. C. B Dear and M. R. D Foot, 308–326. Oxford: Oxford University Press, 2001.
Contained within the 1,000 pages of *The Oxford Companion to World War II* is a hidden gem of a chapter by H. R Kedward. Kedward's huge knowledge of the topic is in evidence and the chapter covers the interwar years, the various iterations of the Vichy government, the Empire, civil defence and the armed forces, the intelligence services, the navy, resistance, and culture. There is much detail contained within each section, including very useful statistical data on topics as

diverse as French tank production, German requisitions of French goods and the resistance movements. It is worth exploring the rest of the book for related topics, for example, Alistair Horne's entry on the fall of France (322–326).

Koreman, Megan. *The Expectation of Justice: France, 1944–1946*. Durham, NC: Duke University Press, 1999.
Koreman uses three case studies of French towns – Saint-Flour in the Cantal, Moûtiers in the Savoie and Rambervillers in the Vosges – to explore the delivery of justice in the difficult period following the Liberation of France. She brings under investigation three conceptions of justice (the legal, the social and the honorary) and their implications for the everyday lives of the French. The book is not only useful for its explanation of the motives and practices behind the postwar purge but also for its exposé of the daily challenges faced by the French in the aftermath of the war.

Lee, Daniel. *Pétain's Jewish Children. French Jewish Youth and the Vichy Regime*. Oxford: Oxford University Press, 2011.
This fascinating work explores the 'coexistence of Vichy and French Jewry before the summer of 1942'. Indeed, Lee argues that to understand the experiences of Jews in France during the Dark Years solely from the perspective of victimization ignores the avenues through which this persecuted minority could continue to live semi-normal lives before the radicalization of Vichy's anti-Semitism in 1942. The very pluralism of the regime at Vichy, its inability to implement effectively its policies throughout France and the contradictions at the heart of the National Revolution left some room for manoeuvre, and even engagement, with the Etat Français.

Lemmes, Fabian. 'Collaboration in Wartime France, 1940–1944'. *European Review of History/Revue européenne d'histoire* 15, no. 2 (2008): 157–177.
Lemmes's article introduces the reader to the complexities of classifying behaviour as collaboration. The first part of the article examines definitions of collaboration and the problems of applying the label to behaviour in the past. The second part of the article concerns the collaboration between French business and the German authorities. It sheds light on the Nazi exploitation of French economic and human resources and the profits that French firms – especially those in the construction industry – made from deals with German organization such as the Todt. Lemmes's focus on economics is novel in a literature on collaboration so dominated by political and personal reasons for working with the Occupier.

Marrus, Michael R., and Robert O. Paxton. *Vichy France and the Jews*. New York: Basic Books, 1981.
Marrus and Paxton's *Vichy France and the Jews* changed completely understandings of the role that France played in the persecution of the Jews during the Second World War. It revealed in compelling detail the ways in which the Vichy state facilitated Nazi persecution while enacting its own anti-Semitic agenda that drew on deeply rooted French prejudices. The most damning sections of the book concern the apparent indifference of the French public to the fate of the Jews and a comparative look at the impact of anti-Semitism in France and other semi-independent governments in Hitler's Europe. Readers wishing to consult attempts

to rehabiliate France's wartime record in this area, such as Jacques Semelin's recent works, should read *Vichy France and the Jews* as a priority.

May, Ernest R. *Strange Victory: Hitler's Conquest of France*. London: I.B. Tauris, 2009.
Strange Victory is a detailed account of the fall of France in 1940. At nearly 500 pages in length, it is perhaps too long to serve as an introduction to the topic. However, a number of chapters can be used in isolation, such as those on Daladier, Gamelin and the Dyle-Breda Plan. The conclusion neatly summarizes May's arguments and works effectively as a stand-alone essay on the causes of the French defeat, though the reader can come to their own opinion on May's contention that luck played a determinant role in the German victory. The appendix contains a comprehensive chart of the structure of each army's command and total number of forces available in May 1940.

Mouré, Kenneth. 'Food Rationing and the Black Market in France (1940–1944)'. *French History* 24, no. 2 (2010): 262–282.
For readers unable to consult Dominique Veillon's *Vivre et Survivre en France, 1939–1947* (1995) or Fabrice Grenard's *La France du marché noir (1940–1949)* (2008), the work of Kenneth Mouré offers an excellent English-language alternative. In this article, Mouré surveys Vichy's system of rationing, its inherent problems, and the measure that the state and ordinary French took to solve the problem of shortages. Readers should consult, too, Mouré's 'La Capitale de la Faim: Black Market Restaurants in Paris 1940–1944'. *French Historical Studies* 38, no. 2 (2015): 311–341; 'Black Market Fictions: *Au bon beurre*, *La traversée de Paris* and the Black Market in France'. *French Politics, Culture and Society* 32, no. 1 (2014): 47–67; and '*On vit mal*: Food Shortages and Popular Culture in Occupied France, 1940–1944'. *Food, Politics and Culture* 10, no. 2 (2007): 261–295, co-authored with Paula Schwartz.

Nord, Philip. *France 1940: Defending the Republic*. New Haven, CT: Yale University Press, 2015.
Nord seeks to distinguish his work from others texts on the French defeat through the adoption of a comparative approach. He demonstrates quite convincingly that France was no better or worse prepared to fight in 1940 than Britain, the United States, the Soviet Union and Nazi Germany. The book's argument that the French public, after a brief flirtation with Vichy, turned back towards democratic Republicanism is more contentious for it downplays both opposition to the Republic throughout French society and support in favour of alternatives. Written in a rather informal style, *France 1940* is an enjoyable introduction to the fall of France for the student or general reader. It is best read alongside Jackson's *The Fall of France*.

Ott, Sandra. *Living with the Enemy: German Occupation, Collaboration and Justice in the Western Pyrenees, 1940–1948*. Cambridge: Cambridge University Press, 2017.
Sandra Ott, a specialist in the history of the Basque region, explores the Occupation and Libertaion of the Pyrenean borderlands through a series of microhistories. The stories of a black marketeer, a teenaged informer and a Basque

shopkeeper, among others, present the reader with complex human stories through which to reconsider resistance, collaboration and liberation in France.

Paxton, Robert O. *Vichy France: Old Guard and New Order*. New York: Alfred A. Knopf, 1972.
Robert Paxton's *Vichy France* not only changed the way historians approached the period of the Occupation but also forced the French nation to reconsider its past. Paxton's judicious use of German archives overturned a decades-old orthodoxy according to which Vichy had defended French interests at home while de Gaulle had waited to strike from abroad. He revealed that the Etat Français had sought collaboration with Germany in order to secure for France a prime position in Hitler's New Order. Meanwhile, its National Revolution looked to fundamentally refashion France in a nationalist and authoritarian mould. All students of Vichy France must read this book.

Pollard, Miranda. *Reign of Virtue: Mobilizing Gender in Vichy France*. Chicago: University of Chicago Press, 1998.
Reign of Virtue underscores the centrality of gender to Vichy's National Revolution. Pollard traces the regime's emphasis on family and reproduction to the Third Republic, the regime under which the pronatalist movement emerged. The book proceeds to explore policy and action in the domains of female sexuality and motherhood, fatherhood and conceptions of virility, state intervention and welfare, women's work and Vichy's attempts to curb abortion.

Potter, Charles. *The Resistance, 1940: An Anthology of Writings from the French Underground*. Baton Rouge: Louisiana State University Press, 2016.
This book is a valuable resource for students of Vichy France. Charles Potter has translated four texts authored by resisters – Jean Moulin's *First Fight*, Germaine Tillion's 'First Resistance in the Occupied Zone', Henri Frenay's *National Liberation* and Jean Garcin's *We Were Terrorists*. Moulin's account of his time in Chartres (as Prefect of the Eure-et Loir) during the chaos of June 1940 is particularly striking, from his encounters with civilians to his interrogation and torture. A glossary and timeline complete this useful collection.

Roberts, Marie-Louise. *D-Day through French Eyes: Normandy 1944*. Chicago: University of Chicago Press, 2014.
Mary-Louise Roberts has written an important book on the experience of the inhabitants of Normandy during the Allied campaign in northern France of 1944. *D-Day through French Eyes* is essentially a collection of the excerpted and translated testimonies of civilians and their encounters with the American invader (Roberts wrote the book for an American audience and the American army is therefore her focus). Roberts selected the testimonies for their 'rich sensory detail'; the result is a vivid account of the French experience of invasion and Liberation during summer 1944.

Rousso, Henry. *The Vichy Syndrome: History and Memory in France since 1944*. Cambridge, MA: Harvard University Press, 1991.
In this book (a translation of the 1987 *Le syndrome de Vichy*), Henry Rousso diagnosed France's obsession with its wartime past. He divides the history of

the postwar era into a number of phases ('Unfinished Mourning (1944–1954)'; 'Repressions (1954–1971)'; 'The Broken Mirror (1971–1974)'; 'Obsession (after 1974)'), analysing each in turn for evidence of the continued 'presence of the past' in French politics and society. Part two focuses on certain 'vectors' of memory (commemorations, films and novels, history texts) and the diffusion of the collective memory of the Dark Years. Whether or not one agrees with the Vichy syndrome thesis (see Bertram M. Gordon's 'The "Vichy Syndrome" Problem in History', *French Historical Studies* 19, no. 2 (1995): 495–518 for a critical assessment of Rousso's concept), *The Vichy Syndrome* is essential reading for students of the period.

Scheck, Raffael. *Hitler's African Victims: The German Army Massacres of Black French Soldiers in 1940*. Cambridge: Cambridge University Press, 2006.
This pioneering book sheds light on a subject rarely evoked in histories of the French defeat. Scheck provides a wide-ranging treatment of the subject from roots of European racism in the colonial conquests to the implications of the episode for the French and German militaries. *Hitler's African Victims* is a shocking and important account that speaks not only to the context of France in 1940 but also to the brutalization of twentieth-century warfare more generally.

Schwartz, Paula. '*Partisanes* and Gender Politics in Vichy France'. *French Historical Studies* 16, no. 1 (1989): 126–151.
Schwartz's article on women in the resistance is a classic in the historiography of wartime France. She reassesses women's roles in resistance movements, exposing their activities both behind the scenes in traditionally 'feminine' roles – secretaries, nurses, caregivers – and on the frontline of the fight against Nazism as liaison agents and armed fighters. Schwartz further examines conceptions of gender within resistance groups that saw women adopt masculine codenames and styles of behaviour to gain acceptance from their male colleagues. Despite their importance to the operation of the resistance, by the end of the war women were phased out of the movements as the Free French looked to re-establish a regular army.

Schwartz, Paula. 'The Politics of Food and Gender in Occupied Paris'. *Modern & Contemporary France* 7, no. 1 (1999): 34–45.
This short article is situated at the intersection of the histories of everyday life and gender under Vichy. Schwartz examines the marketplace and the high street during times of shortage in order to highlight the gendered character and conceptions of places that blurred the line between the public and the private. This article should be read in conjunction with Kenneth Mouré's work on rationing and the black market in Vichy France.

Sibalis, Michael. 'Homophobia, Vichy France, and the "Crime of Homosexuality"'. *GLQ* 8, no. 3 (2002): 301–318.
In this article, Michael Sibalis explores Vichy's repression of homosexuality as epitomized in Pétain's amendment to Article 334 of the Penal Code in August 1942. Sibalis, however, gives the lie to the belief that Vichy undertook a virgorous and systematic persecution of gay French men and women. While the regime tapped into long-held homophobic prejudices in French society, it was relatively moderate in its repression. A number of homosexuals were deported, but this decision lay

with the German authorities. Readers of French may also like to consult Michael Sibalis, 'La vie homosexuelle en France pendant la Seconde guerre mondiale', in *Homosexuel.le.s en Europe pendant la Seconde Guerre mondiale*, ed. Régis Schlagdenhauffen (Nouveau Monde Editions, 2017), 131–151 and Florence Tamagne, 'La deportation des homosexuels durant la Seconde Guerre mondiale', *Revue éthique et de théologie morale* 239, no. 2 (2006): 77–104.

Sweets, John. *Choices in Vichy France: The French under Nazi Occupation*. Oxford: Oxford University Press, 1986.
Sweets's book, written in response to the work of both Robert Paxton on Vichy and Marcel Ophüls's *Le chagrin et la pitié*, is an even-handed treatment of collaboration, resistance and everyday life in Clermont-Ferrand. Sweets examines Vichy's attempts to mobilize French children and adults, collaborationism, persecution, the German opinion of the French and the liberation. Perhaps the best section of the book is the sixth chapter on public opinion, a pointed rejoinder to Paxton that forces the reader to contemplate the meaning and suitability of the terms collaboration and resistance when applied to the behaviour of the French under Occupation.

Thomas, Martin. *The French Empire at War, 1939–1945*. Manchester: *Manchester University Press*, 2007.
Thomas investigates the experience of the overseas French territories in Africa, the Middle East, Madagascar and Indochina. He focuses in the main on the realm of military affairs and high politics in these areas. As such, the book functions as an excellent work of reference for the ever-changing wartime state of affairs in the French colonies loyal to Vichy yet it does not cover factors such as resistance or the response of colonial peoples in great depth.

Vinen, Richard. *The Unfree French: Life under the Occupation*. London: Penguin, 2007.
In *The Unfree French*, Richard Vinen aims to provide a social history of the Occupation, that is, from the point of view of the French population. His focus is on the everyday reality of the war for a number of groups: women, prisoners of war, Jews, young people and the French who worked in Germany. As a work of popular history, it is eminently readable but does not include the straightforward structure of academic works that some students may require.

Wieviorka, Olivier. *The French Resistance*. Cambridge, MA: The Belknap Press of Harvard University, 2016.
In terms of its coverage, readability and easy-to-follow structure, Wieviorka's book is ideal for students (though, at over 400 pages, few will probably read it from cover to cover). It traces the history of the resistance from the early days of June 1940 to the Liberation. Wieviorka integrates into this narrative traditionally under-examined topics such as the ethnic diversity of resistance fighters. Written for a broad audience, it is relatively light on the historiography of the subject and the final section on the memory of the resistance is inferior to Gildea's chapter on the same subject in *Fighters in the Shadows* (with which this book could be read in conjunction). The focus of the work is resistance in *France* and opposition to Vichy and the Occupier in France's colonial territories is neglected.

INDEX

33rd SS Charlemagne division 73, 191
Abetz, Otto 57, 59, 66, 69, 70, 72, 118, 183
Albrecht, Berty 95, 164, 183
Algeria 17, 30, 34, 35, 133, 137, 148, 149, 159
  anti-Semitism 117, 121, 135
  contribution to the French war effort 18
  punishment of collaborators 148
  repression 109, 157
  sport 45
  war of independence 159
Alibert, Raphaël 103, 117, 158, 183
Alliance (resistance network) 90–1, 183
Annet, Armand 36, 45, 109, 135, 137, 150, 158, 183
anti-Semitism 129–30, 180 (*see also* Commissariat Général aux Questions Juives)
  anti-Semitic legislation 103, 117
    German anti-Semitic legislation in France 117–18
    North Africa 121–2
  apparent refuge in the Italian Zone 125
  arrests of Jews in France 114, 115, 124, 127
    Vél d'Hiv roundup 115, 123
    and French memory 166, 171
  Aryanization 118, 119, 122, 138–9
  deportation of Jews from France 103, 115, 123, 129
  differentiation between French and foreign Jews 123, 124
    within the Parisian Consistory 120
    within the UGIF 127
  during the 1930s 116
  France and the Final Solution 122–6
  Vichy's knowledge of the fate of the Jews 125–6
  in France before 1940 115–16
  in the French Empire 122
  French pseudo-scientific bodies 123
  in the historiography of Vichy 164
    revisionism 172–3
  internment of Jews 109, 121
    Drancy 109, 123, 125
  interwar France 11
  Jewish responses 120
  Jewish Statutes 38, 114
    June 1941 117
    October 1940 103, 117, 120
      application in overseas territories 122
  North Africa 104, 121–2
  Pétain 117
  public response 119–20, 123–4
  response of the Free French 127–8
  response of resistance groups 127
  suspension of Crémieux decree 117, 135
Arme Féminine de l'Armée de Terre (AFAT) 141–2
Armée Secrète 97, 134, 183
Aron, Robert 32, 144, 158
  'sword and shield' thesis 158
Aubert, Pierre-Emile 30, 36, 44, 136, 183
Aubrac, Lucie 91, 95, 164, 165, 183
Aubrac, Raymond 95, 183
Auxiliary Feminine Corps *see* Corps Auxiliaire Féminin

Barbie, Klaus 165, 183
Barnaud, Jacques 34
Barthélemy, Joseph 23, 183
Baudoin, Paul 4
Berthelot, Jean 34

Bir Hakeim 79, 84, 100, 161
black market 50–2, 87, 88, 138, 146
   (*see also* food)
Bléhaut, Henri 29
Bloch, Marc
   Fall of France 1, 6, 23, 183
Blum, Léon 6, 11, 183–4
Boisson, Pierre 30, 32, 36, 79, 108,
      110, 122, 134, 135, 136, 150,
      184
Bonnard, Abel 35, 184
Bousquet, René 36, 105, 158, 184
   arrest of Jews in France 123
   friendship with François Mitterrand
      166
   post-war indictment 165
Bouthillier, Yves 4, 36, 157, 184
Brasillach, Robert 67, 71
Brazzaville
   conference (1944) 136–7, 157, 159
   Free French base 76, 84, 177
Brévié, Jules 29
Brinon, Fernand de 35, 36, 72, 131,
      184
British Expeditionary Force (BEF) 1, 2,
      13, 14
Brossolette, Pierre 95, 97–8, 184
Bucard, Marcel 67
Bureau Central de Renseignement et
      d'Action (BCRA) 80, 82, 85,
      100, 184

Call of Duty (videogame) 169
Cameroon 30, 76, 83, 84, 85
Carcapinio, Jérôme 34
Cayla, Léon 36, 44, 45, 150, 158,
      184
Caziot, Pierre 36
Ceux de la Libération (CDLL) 93, 98,
      127, 184
Ceux de la Résistance (CDLR) 97, 98,
      184
Chambres Civiques (Civic Chambers)
      144, 150
   summary of sentencing 150
Chantiers de la Jeunesse 29, 38, 43,
      128, 168, 184
   French overseas territories 43–4
Châtel, Yves 121, 135, 184

children 42
   black market 51
   Exodus 212
   with German fathers 65
   love of Pétain 31
   memory of the Occupation 171–2
   persecution of Jewish children 103,
      115, 123, 124
   propaganda 41
   rationing 47, 49
   rescue of Jewish children 126, 127,
      128
Chirac, Jacques 168, 175
   comments on France and the
      Holocaust 166–7
Churchill, Winston 1, 3
   Charles de Gaulle 78, 79
   Fall of France 13, 14
Cold War 156–7
collaboration
   definition 56, 60, 73
   with German security forces 104–5
   historiography 158–9, 160–2, 163
   Holocaust 122–124, 125
   'horizontal collaboration' (sexual
      relations with German
      soldiers) 64–5
   Italy 59, 105
   Japan 59, 105
   Laval 32–3
   meaning in the French Empire 60
   military collaboration 57–8, 107
   motives behind the policy of
      collaboration 36–7, 55, 56,
      73–4
   public responses 32, 63–4, 73–4
   punishment of collaborators
      Algeria 148
      big business 150–1
      Darnand 149
      Darquier de Pellepoix 150
      estimated numbers executed 144
      Flandin 149
      French West Africa 148
      journalists 151
      Laval 139
      legal institutions 144, 148–9
      local purge 144–8
      post-war amnesties 158

242 INDEX

public dissatisfaction with 151
summary of sentencing 152
trial of Marshal Pétain 149
Vallat 150
violent punishment 143–4, 145, 147
women 145–7, 150
resistance attacks on collaborators 92–3
supply of labour to Germany 60–3 (*see also* Relève scheme; Service du Travail Obligatoire)
types of 56, 57, 58–9
collaborationism
collaborationist parties 67–71, 74 (*see also* names of particular parties)
collaborationists at Vichy 35–6
connections with collaboration 67
definition 58
German attitudes 66–7
military collaborationism 71–3
Colonel Passy (André Dewavrin) 80, 101, 186
Combat (resistance movement) 90, 95, 184
Armée Secrète 97
emergence and development of 93
membership 101
Comité d'Histoire de l'Occupation et de la Libération (Historical Committee of the Occupation and the Liberation) *see* Comité Français de la Deuxième Guerre Mondiale
Comité Français de la Deuxième Guerre Mondiale (French Committee for the Second World War) 157
Comité Français de Libération Nationale (CFLN) 76, 86, 87, 98, 132, 135, 140, 148, 184–5
Comités Départementaux de Libération (Departmental Liberation Committees, CDL) *see* Liberation

Commissariat Général aux Questions Juives (CGQJ) 119 (*see also* anti-Semitism)
founding of 118
communists
Cold War 156
Front National (resistance group) 97, 98
interwar France 11
Liberation of France 132
party of the '75,000 martyrs' 156
repression 106, 108, 109
response to the invasion of the Soviet Union 91–2
violent resistance 91–2 (*see also* Francs-Tireurs et Partisans)
Conseil National de la Résistance (CNR) 177, 178, 185
founding 98
Liberation 132–3, 143
plans for post-war France ('Programme of Action for the Resistance') 132–3
Constantini, Pierre 68
Corps Auxiliaire Féminin 81, 144
Corps des Françaises Libres 141
Corps des Volontaires Françaises (CVF) 81–2
Cours de Justice (Courts of Justice) 144, 150
summary of sentencing 150
Croix de Feu 11

Dakar 57, 110, 143
attack (1940) 79, 86, 100, 108
Daladier, Edouard 4, 6, 13, 185, 197 n3
Prime Minister of the Third Republic 11, 17
Dannecker, Theodor 123
Darlan, François 32, 34, 118, 134, 135, 185
collaboration with Germany 57–8
collaboration with Italy 58
deputy Prime Minister at Vichy 34–5
Darnand, Joseph 36, 132, 149, 185
founder of the SOL 32, 106
leader of the Milice 35, 106–7

Darquier de Pellepoix, Louis 123, 150, 190
d'Astier de la Vigerie, Emmanuel 91, 163, 183
Deacon, Valerie 170
Déat, Marcel 36, 132, 185
   attitude to Vichy 67
   career in politics 68
   collaborationism 58–9, 69, 70, 71
   founding of the RNP 59, 68
   and single-party project 58–9
Decoux, Jean 19, 30, 36, 108, 150, 158, 185
   anti-Semitism 122
   Japanese occupation of Indochina 59, 60, 136
   National Revolution 42, 45
Défense de la France 91, 98, 185–6
   membership 93
      female membership of 82, 95
Delestreint, Charles 97
Deloncle, Eugène 67, 71, 186
Dernière Colonne 91, 93
Dewavrin, André *see* Colonel Passy
Dodd, Lindsey 168
Doriot, Jacques 11, 67, 68, 74, 132, 186
   attitude to Vichy 69
   collaborationism 70, 71
   political career 69
   service in the LVF 71–2
Dreyfus Affair 115–16
Dunkirk 1, 3, 13

Empire Defence Council (Conseil de Défense de l'Empire) 76
Estéva, Jean-Pierre 121–2, 186
Exode *see* Exodus
Exodus 2, 20–2
   civilian casualties 22

Fascism
   fascist parties during 1940–1944 70–1
   interwar France 10–11
   National Revolution 39
   Vichy 35
femmes tondues (shorn women) *see* Germany; Liberation; Women
Fighting France *see* Free France

Flandin, Pierre-Etienne 34, 37, 149, 158, 186
Fogg, Shannon L 167
Food
   German export from France 28
   lack 2, 22, 26, 43, 48, 49–50, 52, 84
   Liberation 137, 138
   poor quality in French camps 108, 109, 112
   production 48–9
   rationing 46–7
   système D 47, 49, 51, 88
   Vichy's policy on 41
Forces Aériennes Françaises Libres (FAFL) *see* Free France
Forces des Français libres *see* Free France
Forces Françaises de l'Intérieur (FFI) 131, 132, 142, 143, 186
   attitude of the Allies 134–5
   attitude of the Free French 142
   casualties 134
   contribution to the Liberation of France 134
   origins 134
   supply of weapons 135
Fourcade, Marie-Madeleine (née Méric) 90–1, 187
Franc-Tireur 93, 95, 97, 101
Francs-Tireurs et Partisans (FTP) 92, 134, 202
   foreigners 94, 168
France
   armistice with Germany 4–5
   armistice with Italy 5
   bombing 20, 139–40
   cost of Occupation 28
   Demarcation Line xi, 26–7, 28, 29, 34, 57, 90, 113
   division into zones 26–7, 30–1
   founding of Vichy 25
   governments during 1940–1944 25–6
   invasion 1940 1, 2–4, 9–10, 12–14
   public responses to collaboration with Germany 63–4, 73–4
   state of army in 1940 6–8, 10, 12
   total occupation 35
   trauma of the defeat 155–6
France Combattante *see* Free France

France libre *see* Free France
Free France
  blanchiment (whitening) 143, 182
  casualties 100
  Dakar attack (1940) 79
  feelings of members at the Liberation 142–3
  founding 77–8
  Free French Africa 83–5, 100
  global support 86
  Indochina 85–6
  Jews 128
  membership 77, 81, 86, 177–8
    female membership 81–2
    motivations 82
  military resources 78–9
  post-war plans for the French Empire 136–7
  rallying of colonial territories 84–5
  secret agents 79, 86
  women in 81–2
Freemasonry
  repression 11, 39, 103, 106, 111, 179
Frenay, Henri 90, 93, 95, 97, 98, 99, 167, 187
French Antilles 30, 31, 75, 84, 94, 95, 110, 113, 122, 142, 150 (*see also the names of individual territories*)
French Empire 17 (*see also the names of individual territories*)
  anti-Semitism 122
  colonial subjects in the resistance 94
  colonial troop casualties 17–18
  colonial troops held as POWs 17–19
  colonial troops and the Liberation of France 142–3
  continuity in colonial leadership 36
  contribution to the French war effort during 1914–1918 15
  contribution to the French war effort in 1940 15
  discrimination against non-whites in France 113–14
  extent in 1939 xi–xii, 15
  Fall of France 2
  Free French *see* Free France
  liberation from Vichy/foreign rule 133–4, 135–6
  meaning of collaboration and resistance 60, 89
  memory 170
  racial stereotypes 16
  rebranding as the French Union 157
  repression 109–11, 129, 137
  State Secretariat for the Colonies 29
  Vichy's celebration 29, 40
French Equatorial Africa
  conditions of wartime 52
  Free French territory 83–4, 85
  military contribution to the French war effort 18, 142
  rallying to the Free French 30, 76, 84
French National Liberation Committee *see* Comité Français de Libération Nationale
French West Africa 34, 60, 113, 134, 143, 148, 150
  anti-Semitism 122
  attack on Dakar (1940) 79
  conditions of wartime 47
  contribution to the French war effort in 1940 18
  loyalty to Vichy 30, 32, 36, 84
  racial stereotypes 16, 17
  racism 113
  repression 108, 110–11
  resistance 89, 136
  Tirailleurs Sénégalais (Senegalese Rifles) 16, 17
    in the resistance 94
French Women Volunteers Corp *see* Corps des Volontaires Françaises
Front National (FN, political party) 166, 171, 182 (*see also* Le Pen, Jean-Marie; Le Pen, Marine)
Frontstalags 17, 19, 62, 94, 96

Gabolde, Maurice 107, 158, 187
Gamelin, Maurice 2, 3, 6, 14, 187
  attitude to French soldiery 10
Gannat
  court 108
Gaulle, Charles de xi, 17, 30, 52, 187
  appeal of 18 June 1940 (appel du 18 juin 1940) 75, 77–8

attitudes regarding 82, 86, 91, 95
  resistance leaders 97–8
BBC 80–1
biography 77
blanchiment (whitening) of the Free French 143, 182
CFLN 86, 98
commuting of Pétain's death sentence 149
death 163
founding of the Fifth Republic 159
founding of Free France 78
Free French Africa 76, 82–5, 100, 137
Jews in France 127–8
Liberation of France 131–2, 134, 151–2, 155
'resistancialist myth' 155–61, 162, 174
post-war career 153–4, 162
post-war plans for the French Empire 159 (*see also* Brazzaville)
purge 151
relationship with the Allies 78–9, 87, 98, 134, 135
unification of the resistance movements 97–8
Vichy's 'double game' 32, 159
violent resistance 92
General Commissariat for Jewish Questions *see* Commissariat Général aux Questions Juives
Germany
  anti-Semitism 103, 114–15, 117–19, 122–4, 125, 130, 138
  armistice with France 4–5, 27
  atrocities committed in France 139
  censorship in France 107
  embassy in Paris 29, 58
  exploitation of French resources 28, 49, 60
  French collaboration 35, 36–7, 55, 57–9, 63–4, 104, 105, 177
    attitude to collaborationism 66–7
    Protocols of Paris (1941) 57–8
    supporters of collaborationism 68
  French colonial soldiers 17
  French sexual relations with soldiers 64–6, 145–7
  French soldiers in German army 71–3
  Germanization in north-east France 28
  governance of France 26, 29, 57, 104–5
  gypsies 111–12
  homosexuals 112
  invasion of France 1, 7, 8, 14
  Liberation of France 133–4
  non-whites in France 113
  repression in France 104, 106, 129, 139
  resistance attacks 75–6, 91–2, 101
  total occupation of France 26
  use of French workers for German war effort 28, 60–3, 138
Gestapo 95, 96, 105, 106, 130, 165
Gildea, Robert 168, 170
  definition of resistance 88
  motivation behind resistance 96
Giraud, Henri 14, 90, 148, 187
  Allies' preference to lead France 79, 98, 135
  conflict with de Gaulle 98
Gitton, Marcel 67
Goering, Herman 28
Gouvernement Provisoire de la République Française *see* Provisional Government of the French Republic
Great Britain
  aid to French resisters 135
  attack on Dakar (1940) 79
  blockade of the French Antilles 84
  bombing of France 139–40
  Charles de Gaulle 78–9
  Dunkirk evacuation 13
  Fall of France 1, 4, 7, 12–14
  French aid in Axis war effort against 57, 59
  French forces 78, 79
  invasion of Madagascar 30, 135–6
  myth of the Second World War 175–6
  plans for an Anglo-French Union 13–14
Groupe Rochambeau 142

Guadeloupe 23, 30, 36, 40, 50, 85, 133, 136, 150, 170
Guderian, Heinz 10
Guéhenno, Jean 1, 32, 37–8, 87, 100, 101, 137, 151, 187
gypsies 89, 103, 104, 171
   persecution 111–12, 114, 167, 168, 179

Haute Cour de Justice (High Court of Justice) 144, 149–50, 165
   summary of sentencing 150
Henriot, Philippe 36, 188
Hitler, Adolf 1, 35, 58, 69
   Fall of France xi, 4, 5, 10, 12
   plans for France 25, 37, 55, 73, 161
Hoffmann, Stanley
   types of collaboration 56, 57–8, 160
Hollande, François 171
Homosexuality
   between French and Germans 66
   French discrimination 104, 112, 114
   law of 6 August 1942 112
   Nazi treatment 112
Humbert, Agnès 20, 21, 31, 77, 188
   resistance 90, 95, 108–9
Huntziger, Charles 4, 33, 34, 188

Indigènes (*Days of Glory*) (2006) 168
Indochina 16, 17, 36, 60, 157
   anti-Semitism 122
   conditions of wartime 50
   Japanese invasion 19–20
   Japanese occupation 30, 59, 105, 134, 136, 178
   military contribution to the French war effort in 1940 18
   National Revolution 40, 42, 45
   racial stereotypes 16
   repression 108
   resistance 85–6, 89
Inglourious Basterds (2009) 169, 176
Italy 39
   armistice with France 5
   attitude to Jews 125, 180
   French collaboration 59
   invasion of France 4, 12
   Italianization of Menton xi, 29
   occupation of French territory 5, 27, 28–9, 105
   Protocols of Rome (1941) 59
   repression in France 105
   resistance 89, 92
   Tunisia 121–2

Jäckel, Eberhard 161
Japan
   French collaboration 59, 68
   invasion of Indochina 19–20
   Maison Amicale Interasiatique 68
   occupation of Indochina 30, 59, 60, 86, 105, 136
   repression in Indochina 105, 134, 136
   Société des Amis de Japon 68
Je suis partout 67, 68, 71
Jennings, Eric 30, 84, 85, 113
   on the memory of the colonial contribution to the French war effort 170
Jews
   attitude to Vichy's anti-Semitism
   relations with Vichy 127
   expulsion into France 118
   individual acts of kindness toward 128, 166–7
   Parisian Consistory 117, 120, 127
   rescue organizations 126, 128
   size of community in France 116–17
   survival rate in France 126, 128
      reasons behind 128, 130, 172–3
   Union Générale des Israélites de France (UGIF) 126–7, 191

Kenpeitai 105
Klarsfeld, Serge 164, 172
Kleist, Ewald von 3
Koestler, Arthur 11
Kufra, 84, 100, 170

La rafle (*The Round-up*) (2010) 172
La Réunion 30, 36, 40, 44, 60, 94, 110, 113, 122, 133, 136
La Rocque, François de 11, 67, 116
Labarthète, Henri du Moulin de 157
Laborie, Pierre xi, 167
Lacombe, Lucien (1974) 163

L'armée du crime (*The Army of Crime*) (2009) 168–9
Laval, Pierre 26, 31, 32, 69, 72, 131, 132, 158, 188
　anti-Semitism 103, 123, 124, 125, 172
　'the dark force behind Vichy' 32, 158–9
　deputy Prime Minister at Vichy 32–4
　execution 149
　French labour for Germany 61–2
　National Revolution 37, 46
　policy of collaboration 55, 74
　relations with Pétain 32–3
　resumption of power in April 1942 34–6, 52
　sacking on 13 December 1940 33–4
Le chagrin et la pitié (*The Sorrow and the Pity*) (1971) 163
Le Pen, Jean-Marie 166
　comments on the Holocaust 166
Le Pen, Marine
　comments on Vichy 171–2, 182
Lebrun, Albert 3, 188
Leclerc, Philippe 84, 131, 142, 143, 188
Lee, Daniel 167–8
Lees, David 168
Légion Française des Combattants 31–2, 39, 44, 67, 106, 150, 189
　Légion Française des Combattants de l'Afrique Noire 32
Légion des Volontaires Français contre le Bolchevisme (LVF) 189
　founding of 71–2
　membership 72, 73
Lémery, Henri 23, 29, 189
Lévy, Jean-Pierre 97, 98
Liberation
　civilian experience of 140–1
　Comités Départementaux de Libération (Departmental Liberation Committees, CDL) 132
　contribution of the resistance 134
　French overseas territories 133–6
　French participation 134
　Gaullist 'Commissars of the Republic' 132, 152
　geographical considerations 133–4
　living conditions in France 138

Operation Dragoon 131
Operation Overlord 133, 134
Operation Torch 133
Paris 131
Libération-Nord 97, 98, 189
　origins 93
Libération-Sud 91, 95, 97, 189
　membership 101
　origins 93
Ligue Française d'Épuration, d'Entraide Social et de Collaboration Européenne 68
Loustaunau-Lacau, Georges 90

Macron, Emmanuel 171
Madagascar 23, 36, 125
　anti-Semitism 122
　British invasion 30, 135–6
　conditions of wartime 49, 50, 137
　military contribution to the French war effort in 1940 18
　National Revolution in 40, 44–5
　racial stereotypes 16
　repression 109
Maginot Line 8–9, 14
Mandel, Georges 4, 17, 197n3
Manouchian group 94, 168–9
Manstein, Erich von 9
Maquis, 139
　founding 98–9
　living conditions 99
　reputation 100
Marchandeau law
　repeal 113
Marion, Paul 43, 67, 189
Marrus, Michael
　Vichy's anti-Semitism 119, 164, 173, 180
　challenge to Marrus and Paxton's research 172–3
　Vichy France and the Jews/Vichy et les Juifs (1981) 164, 172
Martinique 30, 32, 95, 133, 136
Maurras, Charles 38, 67
Ménétrel, Bernard 36
Michel, Alain 172
Michel, Henri 68, 157, 162
Milice Française 35, 53, 104, 124, 138, 144, 145, 165, 177, 181, 189

founding 106–7
membership 107
Militärbefehlshaber in Frankreich (MbF) 29, 104
Mitterrand, François 162
   Vichy past 166
Monnet, Jean 13
Montoire
   October 1940 meeting 32, 55, 63, 76
Môquet, Guy 161, 171
Morroco 17, 30, 133, 137
   anti-Semitism 104, 121
   conditions of wartime 47
   military contribution to the French war effort 18
   racial stereotypes 16
Moulin, Jean 17, 22, 87, 165, 167, 177, 189
   interment in the Panthéon 160
   unification of the resistance groups 96–8
Mouvement Social Révolutionnaire (MSR) 67, 71, 190
Mouvements Unis de la Résistance (MUR) 97, 98, 105, 190
   membership 101
Musée de l'Homme 90, 94, 95
Mussolini, Benito 5, 17, 59, 122

National Council of the Resistance *see* Conseil National de la Résistance (CNR)
National Revolution 26, 32, 52, 53, 129, 135, 166
   aims and origins 37–8
   children, families and eugenics 41
   collaborationism 56, 58, 67
   French Empire 26, 42, 44, 46, 53, 109, 122
   gender 40–3, 65
   global dimensions 39–40
   homosexuality 66
   ideological roots 38–9, 46
   repression 103, 106, 112, 179
   sport 45
   youth 43–5
Noguès, Charles 121, 135, 190
Nuit et brouillard (*Night and Fog*) (1956) 163

Oberg, Karl 105, 123
Operation Dynamo *see* Dunkirk
Organisation Civile et Militaire (OCM) 93, 97, 98, 190
Organizzazione per la Vigilanza e la Repressione dell'Antifascismo (OVRA) 105

Papon, Maurice 165, 190
Parti Ouvrier et Paysan Français 67
Parti Populaire Français (PPF) 11, 68, 190
   anti-Semitism 116, 125
   attitude to Vichy 67
   collaborationism 69–70, 71, 74
   membership 69–70
Parti Social Français (PSF) 11, 67, 116
Paxton, Robert 168, 174
   assessment of the scale of resistance 91, 162
   collaboration 162, 167
   definition of resistance 87, 162
   opinion of oral history 168
   Vichy's anti-Semitism 119, 130, 164, 173, 180
      challenge to Marrus and Paxton's research on 172–3
   Vichy France: Old Guard and New Order (1972)/*La France de Vichy* (1973) 161–2
   reception in France 162
   Vichy France and the Jews/Vichy et les Juifs (1981) 164, 173
   impact upon the historiography 164
Pétain, Philippe xi, 1, 39, 47, 68, 138
   anti-Semitism 117, 121, 172
   attitudes to wartime conduct 158–9
   biography 31, 190
   Charles de Gaulle 77, 149
   collaborationism 69, 72
   cult of personality 31–2
   Fall of France 6, 12, 13, 14
   founding of Vichy 25
   French Empire 29, 30, 85
   Laval 32–4
   leader of Vichy 26, 35, 36, 52, 131–2
   National Revolution 37, 41, 43
   policy of collaboration 55, 91, 178

popularity with the French public 31, 88, 138
post-war image 154, 158
post-war trial of 149
    public attitudes to 149
Prime Minister of the Third Republic 4
racist legislation 113
support for an Armistice 4, 23
Peyrouton, Marcel 36, 158, 191
Pineau, Christian 93, 191
Platon, René Charles 29, 32, 33, 36, 122, 125, 150, 191
Pleven, René 13
Popular Front (1936–1938) 6–7, 11
Portes, Hélène de 4
Portugal
    Pétain's admiration 39
Poznanski, Renée 173
Prisons 103, 108–9
    internment camps 109
Prisoners of War (POWs) 5, 30, 39, 57, 61, 66, 89, 96, 138, 151
    French colonial POWs 17, 18, 24, 62, 114, 140, 143, 181–2
Propaganda Abteilung 69, 107
Prouvost, Jean 4
Provisional Government of the French Republic 132, 133, 137, 151, 152
    de Gaulle's resignation from 156
Pucheu, Pierre 34, 67, 70, 190
    execution 148
Purge
    Algeria 148
    big business 150–1
    Darnand 149
    Darquier de Pellepoix 150
    estimated numbers executed 144
    Flandin 149
    French West Africa 148
    journalists 151
    Laval 139
    legal institutions 144, 148–9
    local purge 144–8
    post-war amnesties 158
    public dissatisfaction with 151
    summary of sentencing 152
    trial of Marshal Pétain 149

Vallat 150
violent punishment 143–4, 145, 147
women 145–7, 150
    estimated number of femmes tondues 146

Rebatet, Lucien 67, 71, 106
Relève scheme 61–2
Rassemblement National Populaire (RNP) 59
    founding 68
    membership 69
Rassemblement du Peuple Français (RPF) 156
Resistance (domestic) xii, 100–1 (see also the names of individuals, movements and networks; Conseil National de la Résistance; Maquis)
    attitude to Allied bombing of France 140
    contribution to the Liberation of France 134–5
    definition 87–8, 89
    difference between movements and networks 75
    estimated scale 87, 101
    French Empire 76, 94–5
    Gaullist myth 153–4, 155–61
    individual acts 76
    Italy 89
    Japan 89
    Jews 127
    membership 93–6
        diversity 89, 94, 169–70
    movements 91, 93
    networks 90–1
    plans for post-war France 132–2 (see also Conseil National de la Résistance)
    punishment of collaborators 143–4, 145–8
    repression 104–11
    types 87–8, 90, 94–5
    underground press 91
    unification 76, 96–8
    Vichy 90
    violence 75, 91–2, 96, 143–4, 145–6
    women 82, 87, 95–6

Resistance (external) *see* Free France; Charles de Gaulle
Revue d'histoire de la Deuxième Guerre mondiale 157
Reynaud, Paul 1, 3, 4, 13, 14, 41, 77, 111, 191
Riom
  prison 109
  trial 6
Ripoche, Maurice 93, 127
Robert, Georges 36, 113, 122, 136, 150, 191
Rochambelles *see* Groupe Rochambeau
Rommel, Erwin 3, 79
Ronan, Claire 23
Roosevelt, Franklin 1, 4
  Charles de Gaulle 79, 87
Rousso, Henry 182
  Gaullist resistancialist myth 153
  Vichy Syndrome xi, 154
Royal Air Force (RAF) 2, 13

Salazar, António de Oliveira 39
Samuel, Lucie *see* Aubrac, Lucie
Samuel, Raymond *see* Aubrac, Raymond
Sarkozy, Nicolas 171
Sauckel, Fritz 61–2
Secret Army *see* Armée Secrète
Semelin, Jacques 128
  attack on Marrus and Paxton 173
Service du Travail Obligatoire (STO) 28, 35, 62–3, 69, 94, 98–9, 138, 191
  responses 62
Service d'Ordre Légionnaire (SOL) 32, 106, 191
Shirer, William 1, 4, 20
Sicherheitsdienst (SD) 29, 69, 105
Siegfried, André
  Pétain's 'double game' 159
  'Vichy de Pétain, Vichy de Laval' thesis 32, 158–9
Sigmaringen
  Vichy government-in-exile 36, 131
Sorin, Constant 23, 36, 40, 122, 136, 150, 191

Soviet Union 1, 11, 58, 65, 167
  German invasion 70–1, 73
  consequences in France 75, 91
  supply of labour to Germany 63
Spears, Louis 13
Special Sections 35, 42, 107, 108, 111, 129
Stalin 1, 11, 69
Sweets, John
  definition of resistance 87, 167
Syria 30, 57, 137

Tassigny, Jean de Lattre de 131, 142
terrorism 35, 42, 92, 94, 100, 107, 108, 111, 116, 179
Tillion, Germaine 90, 95
Todt organization 61, 191
Touvier, Paul 165, 191

Union Générale des Israélites de France (UGIF) *see* anti-Semtism; Jews
United States of America 35, 36, 39, 75, 121, 134, 142, 169
  bombing of France 139–40
  Cold War policy in Europe 156
  contacts with Frenay 97, 98
  myth of the Second World War 175
  opposition to de Gaulle 79
  reception of soldiers in France 139–40
  sexual harassment of French women 141
  sexualisation of war aims 141
  supply of weapons to the resistance 135
  support for Darlan in North Africa 135
  support for Giraud 79, 135

Vallat, Xavier 118–19, 123, 150, 191
Viannay, Philippe 91, 191
Vichy Syndrome xi, 180 *see also* Rousso, Henry

Waffen-SS 71, 73
Wannsee Conference 1942 114, 122
Wehrmacht 5, 61, 66
  and French colonial POWs 19

French soldiers 68, 70, 71–3
invasion of France 1, 3, 8, 9–10, 14
Werth, Alexander 10, 13, 22
Werth, Léon 20–1, 30, 32, 137, 139, 191
Charles de Gaulle 78, 82
Weygand, Maxime 3, 33, 58, 121, 191
support for an Armistice 4, 6, 14
Wieviorka, Annette 172
Wieviorka, Olivier 94, 133, 170
definition of resistance 88
estimate of the scale of resistance 101
survival of French Jews 128
women in the resistance 76–7
Women
abortion 42
exclusion from the historiography 154
Exodus 21–2

Free France 76–7, 81–2, 141–2
French army 22–3
historiography of the Dark Years 164–5
'horizontal collaboration' (sexual relations with German soldiers) 64–5, 145–7, 152, 181
estimated number of femmes tondues 146
National Revolution 40–3
prison 108–9
pronatalism 40–1
prostitution 66
repression 42
resistance 95–6, 181
sexual harassment at the Liberation 141

Zemmour, Eric 172

www.ingramcontent.com/pod-product-compliance
Lightning Source LLC
Chambersburg PA
CBHW050347230426
43663CB00010B/2022